∽ Lincoln's Censor ∽

DATE DUE

1 8 2009

☙ Lincoln's Censor ❧

MILO HASCALL AND FREEDOM OF THE PRESS IN CIVIL WAR INDIANA

DAVID W. BULLA

2008
Purdue University Press
West Lafayette, Indiana

Library of Congress Cataloging-in-Publication Data

Bulla, David W., 1959–
    Lincoln's censor : Milo Hascall and freedom of the press in Civil War Indiana / by
David W. Bulla.
        p. cm.
    Includes bibliographical references.
    ISBN-13: 978-1-55753-473-6
    ISBN-10: 1-55753-473-X
    1. United States—History—Civil War, 1861–1865—Press coverage. 2. Indiana—
History—Civil War, 1861–1865—Press coverage. 3. United States—History—Civil
War, 1861–1865—Censorship. 4. Indiana—History—Civil War, 1861–1865—
Censorship. 5. Hascall, Milo Smith, 1829–1904. 6. Democratic Party (Ind.)—
History—19th century. 7.Freedom of the press—United States—History—19th
century. 8. Freedom of the press—Indiana—History—19th century. 9. Press and
politics—United States—History—19th century. 10. Press and politics—Indiana—
History—19th century. I. Title.
    E609.B85 2008
    973.7—dc22   2007042141

To my wife, Kalpana Ramgopal,
and my mother, Rebecca W. Bulla

The Soldiers' and Sailors' Monument in the center of downtown Indianapolis, showing a Civil War soldier. Almost 75 percent of Indiana's military-age men (all men twenty to thirty-five and all unmarried men thirty-five to forty-five) served in the war. *(Photo by David W. Bulla)*

Contents

List of Tables

List of Illustrations

Acknowledgments

I would like to thank several people for pushing me through my graduate and pre-tenure years toward completion of this project, which began when I saw Ken Burns' film "The Civil War" in the early 1990s and picked up speed a few years later with my reading of David Herbert Donald's *Lincoln*. I will start my acknowledgments with Mark L'Esperance, education professor at East Carolina University who encouraged me to chase the goal of pursuing a doctoral degree in 1991 when we served as assistant basketball coaches at James B. Dudley High School in Greensboro, North Carolina. Sometime after that, my cousin Maggie Shimon, a resident of New Orleans, Louisiana, provided a major dose of inspiration, insisting I would succeed in my graduate school endeavors. Another person who encouraged me in my graduate studies was Dr. Kay Phillips of the University of North Carolina at Chapel Hill. I would also like to thank three of my former editors for their contributions to my career: Irwin Smallwood, Wilt Browning, and Allen H. Johnson.

At Indiana University, where I received my master's degree in journalism, I would like to thank David Weaver for turning me in the right direction on this project. Dr. Weaver pointed me toward two writers whose scholarship would prove so valuable to this study, Fredrick Seaton Siebert and Jeffery A. Smith. Also at Indiana, I was fortunate enough to come under the influence of several professors, including Jack Dvorak, Carol Polsgrove, Edward Gubar, Michael Evans, Andy Rojecki (now at the University of Illinois at Chicago), and Cleve Wilhoit. Three scholars whose work originated at IU also have been critical to the development of this study: Jon Paul Dilts, Craig D. Tenney, and Stephen E. Towne. They provided the backbone for my historical analysis and interpretation of press suppression in the Hoosier State during the Civil War. Towne's continued exhaustive research on the press in Civil War Indiana has made my interpretation far less tenuous than it would have been otherwise. I want to also mention the work of John W. Miller, whose 1982 bibliography of Indiana newspapers provided a wealth of details for my study. Emma Lou Thornbrough's cultural study of Indiana from 1850–1880, Gilbert R. Tredway's examination of Democratic opposition to Lincoln in Indiana, and Willard H. Smith's study of Schuyler Colfax were also essential to my study. I would also like to thank journalist Brian Hartz, a fellow graduate student from my Indiana University days who allowed me to sleep on his couch while I was doing research on Hascall long after I graduated from IU. Another Bloomington friend, Andy Graham of the *Herald-Times*, has discussed Indiana and the Civil War with me about a thousand times, usually at Nick's English Hut on Kirkwood.

At the University of Florida, I was very fortunate to have my first class with Leonard Tipton, who stimulated my interest in mass communication theory. I would also like to thank my teaching mentor, Julie E. Dodd, who, along with Dr. Wilhoit at Indiana and Dr. Phillips at UNC-Chapel Hill, helped me sharpen my teaching skills. I would also like to thank Gregory A. Borchard, journalism professor at the University of Nevada at Las Vegas. Dr. Borchard and I served under Dr. Dodd as teaching assistants at UF, and we have shared our thoughts about Civil War journalism history and teaching in many long conversations. His expertise on the mid-nineteenth-century press, especially on the professional career of Horace Greeley, is outstanding. Dr. Borchard has also been a careful reader of my research. Thanks also to Rob Marino for all of his editing, and to Jody Hedge for her support during my three years in Gainesville.

This paper would not be possible without the invaluable assistance of my committee, led by Bernell Tripp, who has helped shape it on every step of its journey toward completion. Dr. Tripp insisted all along that this be a paper that is based on what I was seeing and reading as a researcher, not on preconceived notions from secondary sources. I have been a very lucky novice scholar to be afforded that level of freedom. Dr. Bertram Wyatt-Brown has been a most exacting editor and has constantly reminded me of the war's enormous social, political, and military complexity. The mind and work of Wyatt-Brown is a treasure not only for the University of Florida but also for U.S. historical scholarship. Dr. Meg Lamme has been a sounding board for a wide range of ideas on this topic, especially where this paper fits into nineteenth-century mass communication history, what it ultimately means to the world of communications history scholarship, and what it means to the vein of study for my career. She has constantly challenged me to make connections to the larger body of U.S. journalism history scholarship. Dr. Marilyn Roberts recruited me to the University of Florida, and I am indebted to her for my career at UF. I appreciate all the guidance she has given me. David Sachsman, Kit Rushing, and Dwight Teeter of the Symposium on the 19th Century Press, the Civil War, and Free Expression at the University of Tennessee at Chattanooga have given me a wonderful experience every fall with their first-rate conference. Much of what I have written in the following pages first was bounced off the participants in their symposium. The criticism is always fair, insightful, and helpful. I also have benefited greatly from presenting papers to the American Journalism Historians Association, the Association for Education in Journalism and Mass Communication, and the Great Lakes History Conference, as well as my interaction with history professor Christopher Curtis.

I also want to thank Diana and Clark Hadley of Mooresville, Indiana, for the photography and hospitality; and Dru Frykberg for the outstanding assistance with my research. I also appreciate all the hard work of my research assistants—Joe Owens, Porismita Borah, Rut Rey, Sarah Barrow, and Emily Keats—as well as Matt Neznanski, who looked up a ton of articles for me. I want to thank the Goshen *News* and photographer Jeff Arbogast for their assistance with this project. Steve Charter at the Center for Archival Collections at Bowling Green State University, Susan Sutton at the Indiana Historical Society, and Matt Allison of the Indiana Historical Bureau also provided valuable assistance. I would like to thank Michael Bugeja of the Greenlee School of Journalism and Communication at Iowa State for all his help in seeing the project to completion. Two very important researchers have been inspirations to me—Hazel Dicken-Garcia and Michael Kent Curtis, the former for her studies of the nineteenth-century press and the latter for his examination of freedom of expression in U.S. history. Dr. Calvin L. Hall of Appalachian State University has been an able research colleague and friend throughout the writing of this book, as has my mentor, Eric Abbott.

The best part of this research has been the reading of primary documents. I would like to thank the staffs at the following libraries and archives: Indiana State Library in Indianapolis; Indiana Commission on Public Records, Indiana State Archives in Indianapolis; Parks Library at Iowa State University; Allen County Library in Fort Wayne; Smathers Library at the University of Florida in Gainesville, Florida; Library of Congress; Elkhart County, Indiana, Historical Society; Goshen, Indiana, Public Library; Marshall County, Indiana, Historical Society; Indiana Historical Bureau; Dayton, Ohio, Public

Library; Chicago Historical Society; Indiana University at Bloomington Wells Library, the Lilly Library, and the School of Journalism Library; the Roux Library at Florida Southern College; the Center for Archival Collections at Jerome Library, Bowling Green State University; Main Library, University of Central Florida in Orlando; State Historical Society of Iowa Library and Archives; the Lincoln Museum in Fort Wayne; and the Lincoln Bookstore in Chicago. I also want to thank the staffs of the National Park Service at the following battleground sites: Chancellorsville, Kennasaw Mountain, Stones River, Shiloh, and Fredericksburg.

I want to thank my mother, Rebecca Williams Bulla, for providing me with the love to see this project through to its completion; my sister Catherine Bulla Rachide, for constantly reminding me that I would see this project to the end and become a college professor one day; my friend Joseph D. Pearlman for his editing and helping keep things in perspective; my friend Eric P. Ries for his editing and for visiting the Civil War Correspondents Memorial Arch at South Mountain, Maryland; and my wife, Kalpana Ramgopal, for keeping me on track and focused when I wanted to branch out and study other communication phenomena. Kalpana is a thorough editor, and she constantly has encouraged me to write concisely and to tell her what a journalist today can learn from Civil War press suppression. Becki Corbin, author liaison at Purdue University Press, has been a vital resource and an upbeat presence as I prepared the manuscript for publication, as has editor John Joerschke.

Last but not least, I want to say a word about my two literary heroes. Walker Percy, who never wrote a novel about the Civil War, did discuss it in his non-fiction, and alluded to it in his novels, especially *The Last Gentleman*. Shelby Foote was not the only literary figure to tackle the war, but he was one of the few who made the crossover from literature to history so seamlessly. Digesting his three-volume set is a daunting task, but his prose reads so smoothly that it is the equivalent of hearing him speak—which anybody who watched the Burns film or heard Foote talk with Brian Lamb on C-SPAN knows is sheer pleasure. Although both are now gone, their published words will last a long time.

∽ Lincoln's Censor ∽

꿍 CHAPTER ONE 꿍

Introduction

On May 5, 1863, at five o'clock in the morning, Daniel E. "Ed" VanValkenburgh slept in the backroom of Wheeler's Bank in Plymouth, Indiana, a town
twenty-six miles south of South Bend in the north-central region of the nineteenth state.[1] VanValkenburgh, the editor of the Plymouth *Weekly Democrat*,
was awakened by a soldier who broke down the door to his room. Twelve
more soldiers found their way into the bank, and their lieutenant asked Van-
Valkenburgh to get dressed. The lieutenant then informed VanValkenburgh
that he was being conveyed down the Michigan Road to Indianapolis. There
awaited Milo Smith Hascall, a brigadier general and commander of the District of Indiana, a man who had spent most of his adult life in Goshen, which
is twenty-six miles northeast of Plymouth.[2]

The editor lived in a twenty-nine-year-old town of approximately 1,000
inhabitants that first had a newspaper in 1851. By 1863, Plymouth had two
newspapers, one for each major political party. So political were the town's citizens that newspaper obituaries would include their party affiliation. However,
the affiliation was left out of the paper of the opposition party.[3] On April 30,
VanValkenburgh had written an editorial in the *Weekly Democrat* denouncing
Hascall, who on April 25 had released General Order No. 9. The order stated
that any newspaper or public speaker giving encouragement to those who
would resist the Enrollment Act of 1863 "or any other law of Congress passed
as a war measure, or that endeavor to bring the war policy of the Government

into disrepute" would be treated as a traitor and subject to a military commission.[4] Officially, newspaper editors faced the prospect of suppression if
Hascall deemed content in their papers to be disloyal. In response to the general order, VanValkenburgh wrote: "Brig. Gen. Hascall is a donkey, an unmiti-
gated, unqualified donkey, and his bray is long, loud and harmless—merely
offensive to the ear, merely tends to create a temporary irritation . . . Will Brig.
Gen. Hascall please inform us why the citizens of Illinois and Kentucky, sister
States, are permitted to express their minds freely, and the citizens of Indiana
alone are selected for this abject submission."[5] Hascall, who had served as a
teacher, county court clerk, and district attorney in Goshen, did not take the
name-calling lightly and sent his soldiers to arrest VanValkenburgh as a political prisoner and to suppress the *Weekly Democrat*. The soldiers transported
VanValkenburgh first to Indianapolis and then to Cincinnati, where Major
General Ambrose E. Burnside heard VanValkenburgh's story. Burnside, who
was born in Indiana and who, as commander of the Department of the Ohio,
was Hascall's commanding officer, discharged the editor. Burnside advised the
editor "to be more careful in the future as to the manner in which he criticized
those in authority."[6]

A week later, VanValkenburgh resumed publication, printing a half-
sheet. It included an editorial that stated the *Weekly Democrat* would have
to live with the same rules "imposed upon every journal" in the Department
of the Ohio under Burnside's General Order No. 38.[7] VanValkenburgh did
not mention Hascall's order, which was based on Burnside's General Order
38 of April 13, which considered declaring sympathies with or aiding the enemy in any way as treasonous.[8] Hascall's General Order No. 9 served as a re-
minder to dissident editors in Indiana that he intended to enforce Burnside's
Order No. 38, which applied to Indiana, Ohio, Illinois, Michigan, and most
of Kentucky.[9]

Thus, in the middle of the United States' bloodiest war and in the middle
of the country, while the union and the freedom of the slaves hung in the balance, President Abraham Lincoln and his military subordinates interpreted
the primary constitutional right of freedom of the press as being subject to
extra-legal constraints. The U.S. Constitution does not say that freedom of
the press depends on circumstances, nor does the Indiana Constitution, although the state constitution does include a responsibility-for-abuse clause
in the free press section of its bill of rights. At the time of the Civil War, the
state supreme court had heard no cases that interpreted the vaguely worded
responsibility-for-abuse clause. Based on the policies and actions of Burnside,
Hascall by-passed the First Amendment and suspended newspapers in Indi-

ana by invoking the president's privilege to suspend the writ of habeas corpus during times of extreme political emergency. Under this umbrella, Hascall harassed the Democratic editors of Indiana, including VanValkenburgh, who was jailed. Hascall and Burnside believed that by suspending habeas corpus Lincoln was giving them tacit approval to silence disloyal Democrats in this way. Lincoln never formally gave his generals the power to squelch editors and would only step in to overturn their decisions if he thought what they had done went too far.

Meanwhile, Hoosier Democratic editors argued that civilian authority had supremacy over the military because the war was not taking place in Indiana. The Democrats worried about the degree to which their civil rights were being infringed upon. They even worried that democratic processes would be suspended—a legitimate concern since Burnside would declare martial law in Kentucky in July and only allow "loyal" persons of his choosing to vote while federal soldiers guarded the polls. The pro-Democratic Detroit *Free Press*, which had a strong influence on the Democratic newspapers of Indiana, supported the war and the Union, and its editor, Henry N. Walker, worried that the absence of freedom of the press in Indiana and elsewhere where suppression was taking place made "the ballot-box a farce" and gave the Republicans an unfair advantage in elections.[10] Republican editors countered that maintaining the Union was more important than maintaining civil rights and the war was only a temporary condition. When peace returned, Republican editors maintained, unfettered expression would too. Of course, that would be in a Union that the Republicans controlled politically.

This study focuses on the suppression of Democratic newspapers in Indiana during the spring of 1863. It takes into account legal, political, military, and journalistic factors that resulted in the attempt to silence Democratic editors in the Hoosier State. The major legal issue included the suspension of the writ of habeas corpus, which Lincoln interpreted to be within his power during a rebellion, and

Milo Smith Hascall after the Civil War.

the matter of whether civilian or military authorities had jurisdiction in the Northern states. Suspending the writ of habeas corpus, something done by both Lincoln and Congress by the spring of 1863, opened the door for suppression of the Democratic press in Indiana.

The majority of Northerners silenced by Lincoln and his subordinates were Democrats. In Indiana, there were twelve acts of official suppression during the war, all coming against Democratic newspapers.[11] Hascall was responsible for suppressing eleven Democratic papers, all within six weeks during the spring of 1863. The twelfth act of suppression occurred in 1862 when the Union Army briefly silenced the editor of the prowar Democratic newspaper in New Albany, Indiana, for divulging too much information about troop movements, but it allowed him to return to press after he promised to be more circumspect in the future.[12] Because unfettered free expression is essential in a democracy and because there is no evidence to suggest that Hoosier editors in the mid-nineteenth century thought otherwise, press suppression had the potential of giving the Republicans an advantage in elections at a time when the Democrats were making major gains at the ballot box across the state. What agents of the federal government did to the press in Indiana during the war suggests that the Republicans and their military allies had doubts about the efficacy of some democratic processes—including unlimited freedom of the press—in wartime. The two-party system, often lauded as making the North stronger than the South in this war, was seen as impeding the progress of the war by Lincoln and his military subordinates. Debates about war policy or an alternative to war, tinged with political rhetoric, infuriated both Union officers and soldiers, most of whom were volunteers.

The political press in Indiana severely tested the flexibility of the First Amendment. In Indiana, journalism was a remnant of the party press era of 1800–1830. The editors published four-page newspapers that cost a reader $2 to $3 a year.[13] The content included advertising, fiction, editorials, and news reports, which were interpreted along party lines.[14] These newspapers were not the mass-produced, steam-press penny papers of the nation's mainly Eastern urban areas. These newspapers were produced on hand presses and had circulations of less than 900.[15]

In general, U.S. newspapers were undergoing major changes during the middle decades of the nineteenth century. It was a transitional stage in which the political-personal press was gradually giving way to the penny and professional press. The men and women who produced American newspapers and magazines tended to favor one political cause or party. While some newspapers, led by the New York *Times* nationally and the *Indiana Journal* in the

Hoosier State, were already searching for a different approach to journalism, less biased and personal, and more dispassionate, most reporters and editors fit into partisan political camps and wrote with an agenda. Democratic reporters and editors tended to downplay victories and overstated defeats. Republicans overstated victories and emphasized the importance of loyalty to the federal government. Overall, there was an increased emphasis on reporting because of the nature of war, with its battles and strategy, and the invention of the telegraph, which caused more and more newspapers to report fresh war news because it could be transmitted far faster than before.[16]

At the same time, the newspapers of the Civil War era already were beginning to be dominated by commercial interests. A Civil War newspaper in Indiana, usually four pages in length, contained advertising on all of its pages.[17] Yet the papers of Indiana tended to still be driven more by politics than their counterparts in the East, and the editors of Indiana lived more on the frontier and often had to fend for themselves. It was not unusual for a Hoosier editor to have guns in his newspaper office.[18] While political animosity often was communicated in very personal terms, newspaper owners did not limit themselves to political warfare. They also tried to drive competitors out of business. Indeed, violence against Democratic newspapers was often egged on by Republican editors hoping to bankrupt their rivals. Republican editors often wished openly that harm might come to the editor or building of the Democratic paper in town. The editors of the Republican newspapers in Richmond, Indiana, let it be known that they hoped Richmond *Jeffersonian* editor James Elder would meet harm. Elder, who took out an insurance policy of $2,000 for his personal protection, was subsequently seriously wounded by a railroad worker who hit the editor on the head with a heavy wrench.[19]

Generally, few if any precedents had been established in Indiana for legal restrictions on writing about the military.[20] Statehood came in 1816—after the Alien and Sedition Acts and the War of 1812—and anti-abolitionist legislation in the 1830s, 1840s, and 1850s was not aimed at the nineteenth state. There had been no test of the state's responsibility-for-abuse clause in the press section of its bill of rights. Furthermore, there had been very few court cases involving newspapers, and less than a handful involving libel.

Indiana's press suppression during the Civil War was not an isolated phenomenon. Editors in Maryland or Missouri, proslave states that stayed in the union, faced suppression too, as did editors in New York, Oregon, and California.[21] Most scholarly research, though, focuses on New York editors, who took the greatest liberties to criticize Lincoln's war and his war measures. There are only a few case studies of Midwestern suppression. These include the

The building that housed the Goshen *Democrat* still stands in downtown Goshen on South Main Street. Here Melvin Hascall, Milo's brother, served as editor. It was not suppressed in the Civil War. *(Photos by David W. Bulla)*

incarceration of Dubuque, Iowa, *Herald* editor Dennis A. Mahony, the suppression of Wilbur F. Storey's Chicago *Times*, mob intimidation of the Columbus, Ohio, *Crisis*, and the military commission trial, conviction, and banishment of Democratic maverick Clement L. Vallandigham, a former congressman and newspaper editor who still contributed to the interpretive writing for the Democratic paper in Dayton, Ohio.[22]

The suppression of Democratic newspapers in Indiana by Hascall, commander of the District of Indiana, had a temporary chilling effect on political press of the nineteenth state, and it, combined with other factors, led to the end of partisan journalism in Indiana in the last decades of the nineteenth century. Of the eleven Democratic newspapers that Hascall suppressed during the war, seven survived and remained in business at the end of the war. Three of the Democratic papers changed their names after suppression. The Franklin *Democratic Herald* closed down in 1863 after it was destroyed for the second time during the war by Union troops and never re-opened.[23] Ten of the eleven Democratic newspapers had Republican counterparts in their towns, and all ten of those Republican papers remained in business at the end of the war. Two Republican papers changed their names. (See Table 1.1 below.)

The Hascall incident was part of a broader official attempt to suppress Democratic newspapers in the North during the Civil War, and the depth of that suppression has been underplayed in most histories of Civil War journalism. Unlike Maryland and Missouri, Indiana was not a slave state, and most of its Democratic editors supported the union, though not emancipation.[24]

The fact that Hascall went after editors of newspapers in the northern two-thirds of the state, most of them near his home of Goshen, suggests he felt confident he could intimidate the Democratic editors in places like Plymouth, South Bend, and Warsaw because he was intimate with the Republican political leaders in these towns, men who owned or significantly influenced pro-Union newspapers. The brigadier general ignored the Democratic editors in the area's largest city, Fort Wayne, precisely because he knew the Democrats

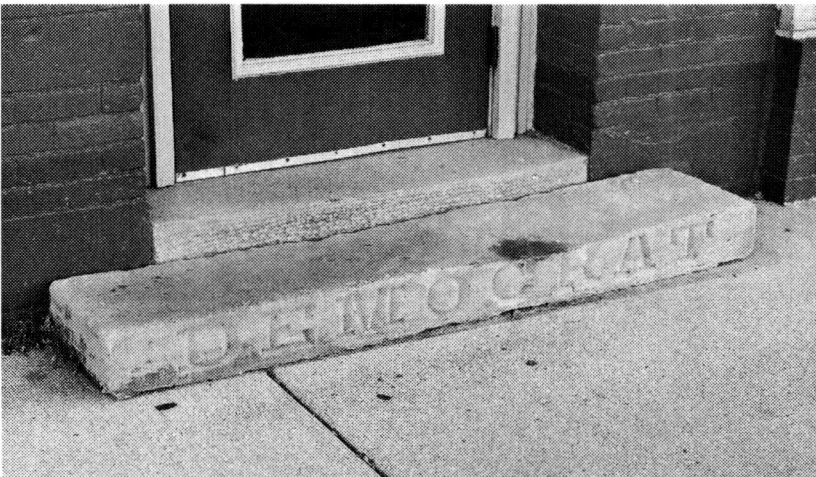

During the Civil War, Daniel E. VanValkenburgh worked the press at the Plymouth *Weekly Democrat* and slept in Wheeler's Bank by night. After the war, he would remain editor of the newspaper until July 1874. *(Photo by David W. Bulla)*

Table 1.1 Status of newspapers in cities where suppression occurred

Democratic newspapers

City	County	Title of Paper	Cond. Apr. 1865	Exist 1875
Bluffton	Wells	*Banner*	Existed	Yes
Columbia City	Whitley	*News*	Name changed to *Post*	Yes, as *Post*
Franklin	Johnson	*Democratic Herald*	Destroyed in 1863	No
Hartford City	Blackford	*Blackford Democrat*	Shut down in 1863	Yes, as *-News*
Huntington	Huntington	*Democrat*	Existed	Yes
Knox	Starke	*Starke County Press*	Existed	No
Plymouth	Marshall	*Democrat*	Existed	Yes
Rushville	Rush	*Jacksonian*	Existed	Yes
South Bend	St. Joseph	*Forum*	Shut down in 1863	Yes, as *Herald*
Warsaw	Kosciusko	*Union*	Existed	Yes, as *Nat. Union*
Winamac	Pulaski	*Pulaski Democrat*	Closed in '63–'64, Re-opened as Repub. paper in 1864	Yes, as *Democrat*
			7/11 = 64 percent	9/11 = 82 percent 8/11 = 73 percent

*-Hartford City *News* had changed its affiliation to Republican in 1873.

Republican newspapers

City	County	Title of Paper	Cond. Apr. 1865	Exist 1875
Bluffton	Wells	*Union*	Existed	Yes, as *Chronicle*
Columbia City	Whitley	*Republican*	Existed	Yes, as *Commercial*
Franklin	Johnson	*Jeffersonian*	Existed	Yes
Hartford City	Blackford	*Union*	Existed	No
Huntington	Huntington	*Indiana Herald*	Existed	Yes
Knox	Starke	No paper in Civil War	—	—
Plymouth	Marshall	*Republican*	Existed	Yes
Rushville	Rush	*Republican*	Existed	Yes
South Bend	St. Joseph	*St. Joe Valley Register*	Existed	Yes
Warsaw	Kosciusko	*Northern Indianian*	Existed	Yes
Winamac	Pulaski	*Republican*	Existed	Yes
			10/10 = 100 percent	9/10 = 90 percent

were stronger there and the press was more sophisticated in Allen County. He also did not threaten editors in Indianapolis, which was split between Republicans, led by Governor Oliver P. Morton, and Democrats, who had the majority in the legislature and a powerful paper in the *Indiana State Sentinel*. Hascall also did not suppress Democratic editors in the southern counties, where he had less intelligence and where pro-South feelings were more prevalent. In essence, the closer a county was to losing its Republican majority in political offices, the less likely occurrence of suppression there.

On the legal side, Civil War suppression would mark the last time in U.S. history when military leaders appointed by the leaders of one political party officially suppressed editors representing another party. In the future, attempts to control the press during wartime would come in other ways. After the Supreme Court ruled against the suspension of habeas corpus in 1866, the executive branch generally left editors alone, although during Reconstruction a newspaper in Mississippi was suppressed by the federal government, resulting in the legal proceeding *Ex Parte McCardle*, and white supremacists in the Democratic Party in North Carolina destroyed an African American newspaper in Wilmington in an act of state-sponsored terrorism that resulted in a violent overthrow of a lawful coalition government in that city.[25] Generally, though, government interference with freedom of the press became more sophisticated, as presidents resorted to controlling the flow of information and the military figured out new ways to exert a level of control over the press in wartime. The press enjoyed a fairly symbiotic and positive relationship with the U.S. Army during the Spanish-American War, but learned a great deal about sophisticated forms of restraints from the Japanese in the Russo-Japanese War of 1904. The Japanese government kept reporters—including those from American newspapers—four miles from the front. They also were placed in pools, with a military information officer giving one news roundup per day, and all dispatches had to go through a Japanese government censor.[26] Major free-expression cases—*Schenck v. U.S.* and *Abrams v. U.S.*—arose after the passing of the Espionage Act of 1917 and the Sedition Act of 1918.[27] Yet freedom of the press received broad protections in the twentieth century, thus making wartime constraints even more problematic. Using the due-process clause of the Fourteenth Amendment, the U.S. Supreme Court held in *Gitlow* (1925) that there would be a universal understanding of free press and free speech, instead of state-by-state interpretation. In effect, *Gitlow* nationalized the First Amendment, and, thus, in the twentieth century and beyond, an interpretation of Indiana's responsibility-for-abuse clause would become moot. The next time the writ of habeas corpus was effectively suspended would be during World War II when Japanese Americans were rounded up and placed in concentration camps. Those Japanese Americans lost all of their civil rights, and when they tried to publish camp newspapers, they were subject to censorship. During World War II, the media in general chose to limit its critique of war policy. Self-censorship was seen as more desirable than government regulation.

Hascall played a major part in increased suppression of the Democratic press in the Civil War, as part of a pattern of intimidation by the military. As Stephen E. Towne noted in his study of press suppression in Indiana during the war, there were "many more instances of violence, coercion, threats, and arrests" against the Democratic press than had been documented in previous studies.[28] In a 1986 study, Jon Paul Dilts had found a total of twenty-nine episodes of "threats or actions" against the Democratic press in Civil War Indiana.[29] Towne's study found sixty-nine incidents of intimidation or suppression against Democratic newspapers and another twenty-two against Republican newspapers.[30] Towne found twenty-three cases of violent intimidation of Democratic newspapers by federal troops or veterans. Clearly, Hascall's edict created an atmosphere in which violence and intimidation against Democratic newspapers in Indiana during the war was an acceptable practice—behavior that runs counter to both the Indiana and U.S. free press tradition but is not unheard of during wartime.

The suppression of Democratic newspapers in Civil War Indiana was simultaneous to the loss of long-held power by the Democratic Party in the state. The Democrats' decline moved the state away from the transitional political-personal press era. This study maintains that the Democratic editors became less partisan after the war because independence made free-press principles easier to assert in times of political turmoil. Indiana's Democratic party was in disarray after the war, so many editors decided to sell. Thomas Tigar of the Fort Wayne *Sentinel* was representative of this group. Tigar had run the *Sentinel* for twenty-three years. Instead of continuing a paper whose party openly opposed emancipation, Tigar retired and took up such civic activities as being a member of the school board, volunteering for the fire department, and working on the board of health.[31]

After the war, independence was not yet the norm in Indiana journalism. Even the few Indiana editors who claimed to be independent usually were not. "It was a time when an editor either sought political office himself or played a major role in deciding who did," observed Harry J. Maihafer.[32] The census of 1860 counted 4,051 periodicals in the U.S., with 186 in Indiana, and the overwhelming majority of newspaper editors claimed political allegiance.[33] After the Civil War, something happened because the partisanship began to wane. Gradually, editors put less emphasis on the political-interpretative function of the press and put more on the informative function, both the news and advertising role. This did not happen instantaneously in April of 1865. It was a gradual process.

Some of the Democratic papers in Indiana went out of business after they were suppressed or intimidated. Other Democratic papers went out of business because the economy in Indiana was fairly sour during the war. Many other Democratic papers stayed in business. Of those, most chose to turn down the volume and be less vituperative against Lincoln and Hascall's General Order No. 9, especially after news that Van-Valkenburgh had been arrested and sent to Cincinnati circulated around the state.

William David Sloan, a journalism historian, has noted the time after the Civil War was a chaotic one for the U.S. press. Sloan says "the successful newspapers *trimmed* [emphasis Sloan's] their political sails, strengthened their financial base through advertising, and changed their news to ride through the swirling, changing times."[34] In general, all of the editors in Indiana became more dependent on advertising, and the emphasis on war news, especially on who died and who won battles, opened eyes to the informative function of the press. Switching from an interpretive to an informative function meant that editors needed to claim political independence. In turn, political independence would make criticism

Ambrose E. Burnside actually was born in Liberty, Indiana, in Union County. He had led the Army of the Potomac for a while and done as Lincoln asked in taking the war to Robert E. Lee, but the Fredericksburg, Virginia, disaster effectively ended his command of the Union's top army. Part of his duties as commander of the Department of the Ohio included keeping the Union Army well manned. His failure at Fredericksburg made it more difficult to convince men to enlist. *(Photo from the Library of Congress)*

Abraham Lincoln did not sign any executive order that allowed censorship, but he did revoke the writ of habeas corpus, which he believed a president has the power to do in times of rebellion; furthermore, Union officers did censor, rarely with much resistance from the president, and soldiers destroyed, ransacked, and intimidated Democratic newspapers. *(Photo from the Indiana Historical Society)*

of the government in times of crisis more acceptable to society because it would not be seen as merely partisan politics.

The Democratic editors learned a lesson: they discovered they could not rely on the editors of the opposition party to defend their First Amendment rights during a time of extreme political crisis. This study does not make the case that these newspaper editors ended the political function, at least not entirely. Rather, over time, the press after the war emphasized the political function less and emphasized other functions more. Consequently, when the next political crisis would come, newspaper editors in Indiana would be in a position to be more united on the principles of the free-press guarantee in the First Amendment and the Indiana Constitution.

Journalists continued to struggle with government controls on the press in the twentieth century during extreme political crises, but journalists would be more united in their commitment to freedom of the press. If censorship were to occur, it often would be self-censorship or censorship brokered behind the scenes. The boom of professionalism in the twentieth century fostered this process, which included the development of professional schools of journalism beginning with the University of Missouri in the early decades of the century. More and more, journalists came to see that they were on the same side in their relationship with government.

Lincoln's Censor: Suppression in Microcosm

This study looks at the Hascall press suppression incident in depth. It places Indiana press suppression in 1863 into its cultural context. It examines legal, political, military, and journalistic factors that led to Hascall's General Order

No. 9 and the brigadier general's recall by Lincoln's Secretary of War, Edwin M. Stanton. It also places Civil War press suppression in its place in U.S. journalism history and looks at it as a phenomenon within the development of the U.S. press. This study offers an interpretation of the state of the First Amendment during the Civil War. It tries to isolate the free-press tradition in the United States up until the time of the war and, therefore, attempts to avoid the present-mindedness that sometimes handicaps studies of freedom of the press. It will show that the free-press tradition survived despite both the itch to suppress by the government and the urge to push the boundaries of reasonable political speech to an extreme by members of a partisan press.

Hascall during the war, in the course of which he rose to the rank of brigadier general. He was related to Gettysburg hero Joshua L. Chamberlain, as Hascall's sister Phoebe Ann was married to Ebenezer Mattoon Chamberlain, whose nephew was Joshua L. Chamberlain. *(Photos from the Bentley Family Papers, Center for Archival Collections, Bowling Green State University)*

Media historians have tended to view suppression of the press as either a necessary evil during times when the stability of government is in jeopardy or as abomination against free-thinking men. What actually occurred in Indiana is somewhere in between these two views of suppression. Because the press suppression under study here occurred during a civil war, drawing all Democratic editors with the same stroke of disloyalty would be inaccurate. Most Democratic editors wanted the Union restored, but they differed in their understanding of how it should be restored. This included some editors who opposed the war and wanted a negotiated peace.

This study also looks at generals Hascall and Burnside and editor Van-Valkenburgh as men trying to do their jobs, as citizens of a democratic republic during the time of its most extreme political crisis, and as men who thought they were doing what the situation dictated. Thus, this study shows that communication and suppression of communication are inseparable in wartime, and that the principals on both sides are very human actors. In war,

Secretary of War Edwin M. Stanton was supremely efficient, and that included suppressing civil liberties of many Northern Democrats. *(Photo from the Indiana Historical Society)*

journalists will always face problems with access and knowing what limits are placed on what they write. It was the case in the Civil War, and it was also the case in the U.S.-Iraq War, which occurred while this study was taking place. Government officials eternally will think they are best at deciding what limitations ought to be placed on the press, while journalists always think they should determine those limits. In some cases, the two groups can come to a compromise, but that is not always the case. In a society with a free-press tradition, principle calls for the press to make the final determination. Even Abraham Lincoln understood this. Yet power tends to make the call more often than not, and that means that the press will get to make the call only if it develops a level of strength. Over time, experience has shown that the strongest press is a united, professional, and economically sound press. Even then, government will do what it naturally does: it will seek access to and control of information and ideas.

Previous studies have attempted to look at press suppression in Indiana in three ways: (1) as part of a broader national picture of the Union Army and the Lincoln administration attempting to control the press during the war under the principle of emergency war powers; (2) as supporting Fredrick Seaton Siebert's hypothesis about the relationship between government and the press during periods of social and political instability; and (3) as an attempt to show that press suppression and intimidation in the state during the war was part of a historical pattern of violence against dissenters in the U.S. The present study explains how the journalism of the period impacted suppression and demonstrates that other studies have tended to underplay the conditions created by the party press. It shows how the party press contributed to Hascall and Burnside's decision to suppress, and it explicates the defense of suppression by Republican editors and the defense of freedom of the press by Democratic editors. In the end, the study finds that it was paradoxical that a minority party's newspaper editors contributed to the expan-

sion of the historical area of press freedom even as it advocated policy that
stalled the freeing of black men.

Significance of Historical Study

None of the existing studies on suppression and intimidation of the press in
Civil War Indiana fully takes into account the partisan and personal nature of
journalism in the state at the time. These inquiries tend to be Developmental
or Consensus studies. They attempt to place suppression in Indiana in terms
of the development of the press in the state or to place suppression in terms of
how it contributed to the Union victory and the destruction of slavery. They
do not focus on the ideological war waged between Indiana's Democratic and
Republican editors, an internal struggle that took place parallel to the larger
conflict between the two sections of the country. The Developmental studies assume that journalism led politics, when the opposite was the case. The
Consensus studies assume that most Hoosier editors wanted a war for union
and freedom for the slaves. That was the case for approximately half of the
editors in the state. The war for the Union was the primary motive for almost
all editors of both parties, but emancipation was a primary objective for only
a minority of Republican editors in the state.

Editors of both parties in Indiana were interpreters of events within two
major political ideologies: those who favored a new America without slavery
and those who favored the pre-war America with its constitutional protection
of slavery in the Southern states. Both types of editors were not primarily
reporters of the news. Rather, they were commentators who manipulated new
information within a specific political agenda.

This study of press suppression in Indiana works within a broader cultural context, namely the fight over how the country's major political institutions would continue and how the two major political ideologies in Indiana
contended to determine the shape of those institutions. This fight, which was
ever evolving, centered on freedom, mainly the freedom of the slaves. Ironically, the Democratic editors, who supported the constitutionally sanctioned
right of Southerners to hold slaves, would have their freedom of expression
hindered by those Republican editors who wanted freedom for the slaves. The
editors of Indiana were political functionaries, and many of them would have
waged political war against their opponents no matter the cause. Their jobs
were to inform and galvanize voters, to serve as party cheerleaders.

This study includes the cultural context of press suppression and tries
to isolate Indiana journalism in the war in terms of its meaning within Hoosier society. The context allows the historian to go beyond the surface story

of press suppression and focus on the foundation on which the events of the spring of 1863 occurred. As historian Gerald J. Baldasty observed in his study of the press in the Jacksonian era, too many nineteenth-century press studies focus on the "great men" of the newspaper world. A contextual study focuses "on the interactions between a variety of social groups."[35] It describes the social structures and political complexities in which suppression took place, as well as how and why the communication phenomenon took place. Hoosier newspapers were mouthpieces of their parties and prophets of gloom, doom, and boom. The people of Indiana read them to be informed, swayed, and entertained, and they read them with the same intensity that today's Americans watch television. Newspapers were an everyday aspect of nineteenth-century Indiana life, as much as churches, trains, and corn.

The understanding of freedom of the press held by the various principals in this study represents a large part of the intellectual context that made up nineteenth-century Indiana. Citizens of the state lived mainly in small towns and on farms, and politics was as familiar a part of the social landscape as the churches in every town. Hascall was a teacher, attorney, and businessman in Goshen before the war. He had practiced law in Elkhart County and served as a prosecuting attorney and county clerk, both elected positions. His brother, Melvin B. Hascall, owned the Goshen *Democrat* in the 1840s and again in the 1870s, and his brother-in-law and law partner, Ebenezer Mattoon Chamberlain, served as a Democratic judge, state senator, member of the Indiana house, and a U.S. congressman. The family had been solidly Democratic before Milo and another brother, Amasa N. Hascall, jumped to the Republican Party in the late 1850s.

Most Hoosier attorneys had read the state constitution, but placed little emphasis on that part of the bill of rights that dealt with freedom of the press. Article 1, Section 9 of the 1816 Indiana Constitution had a responsibility-for-abuse clause that made each citizen accountable for spoken or written words. Similar wording is found in the 1851 Indiana Constitution. Yet neither the 1816 nor 1851 constitution spelled out what abuse meant. That lack of clarity in the state constitution left it to the courts and the legislature to determine what abuse meant and how the state could implement any limitation of the generally broad area of press freedom.[36] Yet there was little if any interpretation of the responsibility-for-abuse clause by courts in the state. Hascall's report on his tenure as commander of the District of Indiana makes no mention of this clause as a defense for General Order No. 9.

Furthermore, this inquiry looks at Civil War press suppression in Indiana from the perspective of the middle party in a complex political contest that involved the new Republican Party, the Northern Democrats, and the Southern Democrats. Positioned in the middle, the Northern Democrats attempted to stay a conservative course while upholding the Union but were facing pressures from the two extremes, the abolitionists in the North and the secessionists in the South. Indiana's Democrats saw union in almost religious terms yet persisted in their Jeffersonian-Jacksonian vision that would uphold slavery in the South. It was a difficult political balancing act. Thus, generally, Indiana's Democrats accepted the temporary sovereignty of the Republican Party and supported the war. That dynamic changed in September of 1862 with announcement of the Emancipation Proclamation. From that point forward, the Democrats became less united about the war and intensified their criticism of Lincoln and the war effort.

Democrats in Indiana were a diverse lot. They were conservatives in the southern counties who had kin in Southern states. They were immigrant Catholics in the state's larger cities. They were small farmers who just wanted a piece of land to cultivate and harvest. They were merchants and manufacturers along the Ohio River who did not want war to interrupt their trade. They were former Whigs who were discontented with the radical Republicans.

Their political arguments were not out of the mainstream as is sometimes portrayed by historians, and their plight continues to have relevance to the study of politics in a democracy, which often relies on coalitions. Previous studies have tended to see Democratic editors as being disloyal and favoring peace. However, most Indiana Democrats were not for separate nations because they were too imbued with unionism. Some wanted a negotiated peace, but they wanted the South to return to the Union, and after Fort Sumter, many wanted it by coercion. Democrats hoped this could be accomplished with as little bloodshed as possible. In the spring of 1861, they were not expecting or supporting a protracted war.

The Republicans needed the Democrats in the Civil War, and Lincoln needed Indiana, especially since he had to worry about the loyalty of its slaveholding neighbor to the south. The early coalition between Republicans and Democrats, never in total harmony, kept Indiana supportive of the war. That would change in September of 1862, not just because of the announcement of the Emancipation Proclamation, but also because of Lincoln's general suspension of the writ of habeas corpus two days later. The Democrats also wanted to regain political power and took advantage of Lincoln's ill-timed edicts to score stunning victories at the poll that fall.

The Democrats' relative position in the political battle occurred in the context of civil war and demonstrated the vulnerabilities that the minority party faces in times of extreme political tension. Thus, official suppression of the Democratic press in Civil War Indiana makes for a case study of how the majority and minority interact in times of extreme political crisis and how this interaction affects freedom of the press.

Methodology

This study is primarily a historical narrative. It is an examination of Hascall and the Civil War Indiana press in its historical context. The narrative of this study offers a structured way of explaining how a member of the federal military attempted to control the expression of newspaper editors in Indiana in 1863. The historical context includes the military and political fighting of the war and the development of the press in the United States in the nineteenth century.

Analyzing and interpreting the content of the Democratic and Republican newspapers of Indiana in the war period make up the bulk of the primary research for this study. Among the papers analyzed were the existing papers that were suppressed. These include the following: Plymouth *Democrat*, South Bend *Forum*, Columbia City *News*, Warsaw *Union*, Winamac *Democrat*, and Stark County *Press*. The study also includes a frame analysis of Democratic and Republican editorials about the Emancipation Proclamation. It analyzes Republican and Democratic newspapers from the following Indiana cities: Indianapolis, Fort Wayne, Richmond, South Bend, Delphi, Logansport, Plymouth, Goshen, and Evansville. These cities have been chosen because they had robust newspaper traditions at the time and because copies of both a Democratic and Republican paper in these towns exist in the Indiana State Library.

Ownership patterns were also examined for this study. Ownership was analyzed for Democratic and Republican papers in the following cities where suppression occurred: Plymouth, Columbia City, Huntington, Rushville, South Bend, Bluffton, Warsaw, Winamac, Hartford City, Franklin, and Knox. To examine the general status of ownership change in the state, papers in these cities were compared to the Democratic and Republican papers in a group of cities that were chosen randomly. An analysis of ownership in the major towns in counties chosen randomly includes these counties: Bartholomew, Cass, Dearborn, Delaware, Fountain, Gibson, Knox, LaPorte, Morgan, Ohio, Pike, Tipton, Wabash, and Wayne. The ownership trend in this group was compared and contrasted to that of the eleven cities where suppression occurred.

The context of Hascall's specific role in press suppression in Indiana in 1863 was developed by examining military communication by Hascall, Burnside, and Lincoln; public letters written by Hascall to Indiana's newspaper editors; Hascall's correspondence with Burnside; the newspaper exchange between Hascall and Democratic Congressman Joseph K. Edgerton of Fort Wayne; and communication by Governor Morton, including the many letters he received from citizens about alleged Democratic disloyalty and secret societies.

This study focuses on the newspapers of northern Indiana, in the towns that are within seventy-five miles of Goshen, where Hascall lived and was an attorney before the war. Commentary by editors from other Democratic and Republican newspapers, especially the Indianapolis *Journal*, Indianapolis *Indiana State Sentinel*, the Fort Wayne *Sentinel*, and the Fort Wayne *Dawson's Daily Times & Union*, further develop the context. Non-Indiana newspapers were also examined, including ones from New York, Chicago, Detroit, Cincinnati, Dayton, and Columbus, on the basis of their understanding and interpretation of key events in the spring of 1863. Papers from these cities were chosen because of the tendency of Indiana editors to borrow heavily from out-of-town papers. Text from papers in these cities frequently appeared in Hoosier newspapers, and editors of the larger city papers often provided political leadership for newspapers in the small towns.

A thorough textual analysis of the framing of the Emancipation Proclamation helps illuminate how rhetoric shaped the political debate between Democrats and Republicans. The majority of the documents examined came from the 1861–1865 period. However, to understand the press background, several newspapers from the 1840s and 1850s were consulted. Hascall's brother briefly owned the Goshen *Democrat* in the late 1840s, and the Fort Wayne *Sentinel* was studied in depth to see how an editor and his paper grew as a town became a city—and a political editor became a professional editor.

This study features an emphasis on the interrelationship between Hascall and the society in which he and the Democratic editors he suppressed lived. The thoughts and actions of Hascall cannot be separated from the political, legal, and military issues of the era in which he lived. The portrait of Hascall developed here shows a highly professional man who wanted to help Burnside efficiently counteract the loss of manpower at a critical moment in the war. It also looks at where he came from, how he was educated, and what mindset he brought to suppression.

In citing both primary and secondary sources, this inquiry grapples with the verifiability of facts, interpretive bias, the limits of time and space, and the difficulties of proving causation. The research built the bibliography in an evolutionary manner, keeping itself open to new studies and not limiting itself to books, scholarly journals, newspapers, manuscripts, diaries, correspondence, and government documents. The focus at all times was on newspaper content, especially in the months of April, May, and June of 1863. This study also remained open to the use of any material that might be relevant to press suppression during the Civil War in general and in Indiana in particular. One piece of documentary evidence so discovered was a photograph of a newspaper building from the period.

Primary documents were evaluated in terms of the internal and external criticism concepts developed by William David Sloan and James D. Startt.[37] For example, Hascall and other principals' hand-written notes were hard to read. Collation was used to determine if in fact a written memo to a subordinate was that of the brigadier general or that of someone else. It was also double checked with certain rhetorical tendencies found in his West Point correspondence and his report of his tenure as commander of the District of Indiana in the Union Army.

Avoiding a sense of present-mindedness was a key component of the study. The objective was to see the political, social, legal, and military landscape as the principals involved saw it. For example, twenty-first-century notions of racial equality prejudice an understanding of the overtly racist attitudes of almost all of the principals in this study. Likewise, there was a conscious attempt to avoid presuming the twenty-first-century understanding of the First Amendment and the relationship between press and government, especially since this study was also conducted during a time of war—but a very different war. The typical libertarian understanding of press freedom that is the mainstream in U.S. journalism today has no place in a study that attempts to accurately understand press suppression in the Indiana of 1863. However, it does provide a guidepost for what lies ahead in the history of the First Amendment.

This study attempts to answer the following questions: (1) What response did Democratic and Republican editors have to official press suppression in Indiana? (2) How did Hascall's suppression of Democratic newspapers affect the suppressed newspapers? (3) Did press freedom in Indiana survive suppression? (4) How effective was Hascall's policy? (5) Did this episode of official press suppression in Indiana confirm or reject Siebert's hypothesis about press-government relations in times when the stability of a government is in jeopardy?

This case study explores press freedom from a cultural perspective. It demonstrates a paradox: political movements that are not progressive sometimes sustain or promote—even advance—press freedom. Conversely, more progressive political movements can hinder press freedom, if only temporarily. By all accounts, Hascall was not a bully or a brutish man. He did not try to shut down the press or establish a censor's office. Later in the war, he would even help spare the life of several deserters by saying that the application of military law was not consistent.[38] Hascall did what Burnside asked him to do in Indiana because he thought the war necessitated extra-legal means to achieve the ultimate goal of victory and defeat of the Confederacy. The arguments used to defend press suppression were no different than those used by John Adams, Andrew Jackson, and James K. Polk.[39] Wartime creates a special situation, and unusual expediencies are used to deter citizens' behavior that potentially aids the enemy. Whether or not there is such a necessity is debatable. What Lincoln achieved in the Civil War is the expansion of the war powers to allow the president to have the prerogative to decide when press suppression and intimidation can take place. For a man who advanced equality and freedom with one bold stroke on September 22, 1862, this precedent creating a tool for press suppression in wartime is an unfortunate and paradoxical legacy for the sixteenth president. The media in twentieth- and twenty-first-century wars have had to live with this legacy. The U.S. government has become more sophisticated in how it contracts the area of press freedom during wartime, and the press constantly seeks ways to contend with this sophistication.

This study also shows that a partisan press model has a major flaw in that newspapers were not united on a principle of freedom of the press. The Civil War press only believed in freedom of the press for the majority—or the victors. That the Republican editors of Indiana cheered on Hascall and Burnside showed that partisanship came before principle. Essentially, this weakens the overall power and importance of the press in a democratic society, and it seems one of the major consequences of the Civil War was that the U.S. press became more united after the war, perhaps in part because of Democratic press attrition but also because journalists learned to make the interpretive function secondary to the informative function as a way to survive economically.

Structure of This Study

This study is a narrative of the events, ideas, and processes that led to official press suppression in Indiana in the spring of 1863. It is designed to give a coherent interpretation of how suppression took place in the nineteenth state. Chapter Two examines Indiana society in the 1860s, and Chapter Three looks at the legal and theoretic context of suppression. It looks at both the federal and state constitutions, and Siebert's hypotheses about the relationship between the government and the press during wartime. Chapter Four illustrates the nature of the party press in Civil War Indiana. Chapter Five examines press suppression in the North. Chapter Six looks at the concepts of unionism and emancipation, key issues that united and divided the state. Chapter Seven follows the career of Hascall and narrates his suppression of the state's Democratic newspapers in the spring of 1863. Chapter Eight touches on the immediate consequences of press suppression, particularly the response of both Republican and Democratic editors. Chapter Nine looks at the aftermath of official press suppression in Indiana and assesses Hascall's spring in Indiana in terms of the broader history of federal suppression of the press in the Civil War. Chapter Ten, the conclusion, deliberates on the broader picture of press suppression and discusses unresolved issues, as well as the direction of future research of press suppression by journalists caught in the middle of strong political or social forces.

Implications

The suppression of Democratic newspapers in Indiana had a temporary chilling effect on Democratic editors in the state. It occurred before the demise of the party press in the state in the last few decades of the nineteenth century. The inference is that Indiana's Democratic editors learned a lesson about the relationship between a partisan political press and the area of press freedom during wartime. Yet it is unclear if Democratic editors learned such a lesson. The vast majority of the Democratic newspapers that Hascall suppressed in Indiana survived after the war. Partisanship did not die out immediately after the war, and some Hoosier newspapers stayed closely associated to political parties well into the twentieth century. Yet most of the editors of the suppressed papers got out of journalism, and Democratic editors in general moved on. Thomas Tigar's highly successful Fort Wayne *Sentinel*, which he had owned for more than two decades, is the epitome of Democratic newspaper demise. Tigar, who supported Democrats for decades, nonetheless supported the war. He generally espoused a more moderate view than his brethren. If any Democratic editor should have survived the war, it was Tigar. Yet he closed up shop in 1865.

This study also suggests that what happened with the Democratic editors in Civil War Indiana was part of a larger phenomenon involving the relationship between the executive branch of the federal government and the press. The expansion of presidential powers during the Civil War had specific effects on the area of press freedom, though enforcement of federal power was dependent upon the interpretations and motivations of federal officers like

Hascall and Burnside. Contraction continued during the twentieth century and into the twenty-first century. In some cases, such as World War II, the press tended to go along with the decrease in the area of press freedom during wartime. In other cases, such as Vietnam, it did not.

A question that remains is this: What is the validity of Lincoln's elasticity argument? That is, what about wartime requires a temporary suspension of some civil rights? The president claimed the war powers were temporary and that the press would regain its area of freedom after the war. Moreover, what effect if any exists in peacetime on having temporary suspension during wartime? The proper relationship between government and the press as well as the increased area of press freedom is presumed to resume after conflict ends. Another critical question is this: In a democracy, do the citizens really want a weakened press during wartime? What are the benefits? The responses to this question from government and media tend to be self-serving. Government says suppression is desirable for reasons of security. The press says unfettered communication is desirable because elections have not been suspended and voters need the best information they can get about all aspects of society. What, though, is best for a democratic nation? It is a question that is still unanswered.

Finally, Siebert's hypothesis is supported by this study. As the war news for the Union moved in a negative direction, dissent increased, and as dissent increased, the government contracted the area of press freedom in Indiana. Because Governor Morton had effectively neutralized the majority-Democratic legislature, the Republicans remained in control of the state government in the Hoosier state. Thus, Hascall had the necessary condition for suppression, a chorus of Republican editors who supported his attempts to squelch the Democratic press. Furthermore, many of the most Democratic counties in the state had the highest percentage of men fighting the war, and thus these men were not at home to support the rights and opinions of the Democratic editors. By contrast, the Democratic editors in New York, who were far more vituperative than their Hoosier counterparts, were allowed to write more freely because Democrats controlled the state and city governments there.

CHAPTER TWO

Milo Hascall's World:
Indiana in the Civil War Era

Milo Smith Hascall was not a martial monster who wanted to end freedom of the press in his state. He was a Yankee immigrant to the northern part of the state who had tried several professions before he came to Goshen, Indiana, in September of 1847.[1] Milo Hascall was West Point educated and a self-taught lawyer. He also was a businessman and a leading citizen of Goshen. Nothing in his past suggested that he would trample on journalists' right to print as they pleased. Indeed, one of his brothers had been an editor and would be again after the war.

Hascall was born in Le Roy, New York, on August 5, 1829, and raised there for the first eighteen years of his life. (For the highlights of Hascall's life, see Table 2.1 below.) His father, Amasa Hascall, was born in Thompson, Connecticut, on July 28, 1787, and his mother, Phoebe Diana Smith Hascall, was born December 31, 1792, in Benson, Vermont.[2] Milo Hascall was their ninth and last child. Two of the Hascall children, Hiram and Ella, died young.[3] His other siblings included Chauncey S., Phobe Ann, Amasa N., Avaline, Melvin B., and Henriette. Amasa Hascall, a farmer in Le Roy, had served in the War of 1812 and was active in Genesee County Whig politics, becoming a constable and collector. He toured his jurisdiction on horseback, reining in the desperados of western New York. Amasa also played the violin and was

24

paid for his performances.[4] Phoebe Smith Hascall died in 1852, and Amasa Hascall married his first wife's cousin, Vesta G. Alderman, who had two sons by a previous marriage.

Although Milo grew up on a farm, he attended school throughout boyhood and at sixteen began to study at Ingham Academy.[5] Le Roy, between Rochester and Buffalo, struggled economically in the 1830s and 1840s, and the family migrated west to Elkhart County in Indiana. When Milo arrived in Goshen, he worked for his brother Chauncey S. Hascall, who was the first Hascall to come to Elkhart County, in 1837, and owned a general store.

Using his family's connections, Milo Hascall earned a nomination by Indiana Democratic Congressman Charles W. Cathcart to the U.S. Military Academy at West Point, New York. He attended USMA from 1848 until 1852, graduating fourteenth in a class of forty-three. His studies there included algebra, geometry, trigonometry, French, geography, English grammar, ethics, and rhetoric.[6] His class read Hugh Blair's *Lectures on Rhetoric and Belles Lettres*.[7] The Goshen resident was in fairly heady company while at West Point. Among the men who attended the U.S. Army training school at the same time as Hascall were Phillip Sheridan, who would serve as a Union general a decade later; Jerome Napoleon Bonaparte Jr., great nephew of Emperor Napoleon Bonaparte; Marshall Tate Polk, nephew and adoptive son of President James K. Polk; Thornton A. Washington, a descendant of George Washington; and William R. Calhoun, grandson of John C. Calhoun, who like Thornton Washington served in the Confederate Army.[8] Of these, only Bonaparte finished higher than Hascall in the class of 1852.[9]

After West Point, Hascall performed garrison duty and served as a brevet second lieutenant in the Second Artillery at Fort Adams, Rhode Island. Yet this was a century before the military-industrial complex and a civilian career was more exciting and more lucrative than being a member of a peacetime, insubstantial army. With little chance for promotion in the peacetime Army, Hascall resigned his military commission at Fortress Monroe, Virginia, on September 30, 1853, did some traveling, and returned to Goshen.[10] He worked at the Hascall store but did not like the work, so he became a teacher for a brief time. Milo Hascall was one of several members of his family who served as teachers in Goshen, including Chauncey S. Hascall's wife, Emma Brown Hascall, as well as brothers Melvin B. and Amasa N. Hascall. His brother-in-law and future law partner, Ebenezer Mattoon Chamberlain, also had been an educator, opening a school in Goshen when he first came to Elkhart County in 1832.[11] Chamberlain said Goshen was a more diverse town

Table 2.1 Key dates in the life of Milo S. Hascall

- Born August 5, 1829, in Le Roy, New York
- Attended the U.S. Military Academy at West Point, New York, 1848–52 and graduated fourteenth in a class of forty-three
- Performed one year of garrison duty and artillery service (Second Artillery) in Fort Adams, Rhode Island
- Not much chance for promotion in peacetime Army, so Hascall resigned his military commission
- Returned to Goshen and worked as teacher, attorney, railroad contractor, district attorney, and county clerk of courts; his brother, Melvin B. Hascall, owned the Goshen *Democrat* in the late 1840s
- Became a Republican in the 1850s; as a Republican, ran for Elkhart County Clerk, a public office, and won; he followed in the footsteps of Elbridge G. Chamberlain, his brother-in-law, who had been Elkhart's clerk in the 1840s
- Married Julia Swift of Elkhart, November 27, 1855; their only child died in 1857
- At the start of the Civil War, volunteered for the Union Army from Indiana
- Helped establish Seventeenth Indiana Volunteers (infantry); all men in the regiment were from Elkhart County
- Worked as a captain under General Thomas A. Morris
- Served at Philippi, West Virginia, a small skirmish
- Commissioned as a colonel, given command of the Seventeenth Indiana Volunteer Infantry Regiment
- Established Camp Hascall at Parkersburg, West Virginia, in August of 1862
- Took part in action at Greenbrier, West Virginia, in October of 1861; then Elkwater, Huttonville, and Cheat Mountain
- Moved Seventeenth to Louisville, Kentucky
- In December of 1861, Hascall was given brigade responsibility, Fifteenth Brigade, Army of the Ohio
- Fought at battle of Shiloh, Tennessee, April 7, 1862; received flag of truce from CSA Gen. Pierre G.T. Beauregard
- Worked under Don Carlos Buell at the battle of Corinth, Mississippi
- On April 25, 1862, Hascall was promoted to brigadier general
- Took part in Stones River, Tennessee, battle December 31, 1862, to January 2, 1863
- Fought in "Red Forest" under General Thomas J. Wood; became a division commander there
- Hired to track down deserters as the head of the District of Indiana in the spring of 1863—started that post in March and was promoted to commander of the district in April
- Attempted to suppress eleven newspapers in northern two-thirds of Indiana in May-June 1863

- Relieved of command in Indiana on June 8, 1863
- Briefly led Indiana soldiers in pursuit of CSA guerilla John Morgan in mid-July 1863
- Served in Twenty-Third Corps of Army of the Ohio in July and August 1863; stationed in Lexington, Kentucky
- Traveled to Knoxville, Tennessee, in the fall of 1863; took part in the Union occupation of Knoxville
- Commanded a division as part of the U.S. Army's Twenty-Third Corps in the siege of Atlanta under General John M. Schofield's Army of the Ohio; served in various battles leading up to Atlanta campaign, including Kennesaw Mountain
- Schofield recommended Hascall for a promotion to major general (second star)
- Hascall did not receive that promotion; it is not known why (political?)
- Resigned from the Union Army on October 27, 1864
- Returned to Goshen, became co-owner of Salem Bank and a lumber business, worked in veterans affairs; brother Melvin B. Hascall regains ownership of Goshen *Democrat* in 1873
- Built Hotel Hascall in Goshen in 1881
- Julia Swift Hascall died September 11, 1883
- Married Rose J. Miller, a Canton, Ohio, socialite, in 1886
- Moved to Chicago and worked in real estate in the 1890s, building Lexington Hotel
- Died August 30, 1904, in Oak Park, Illinois
- Buried at Forest Home Cemetery in Forest Park, Illinois
- Hascall family regains ownership of Goshen *Democrat* in the twentieth century; paper is renamed the Goshen *Times* and was published by Frank L. Hascall for more than three decades

than the communities in the southern parts of Indiana. Residents migrated to Elkhart County from New England, New York, Pennsylvania, Ohio, Michigan, Kentucky, Illinois, Germany, and England.[12]

GOSHEN ATTORNEY

In the fall of 1853, Milo Smith Hascall returned to Goshen and became a railroad contractor for the Michigan Southern and Northern Indiana Railroad but soon read law under Chamberlain, his brother-in-law who had read for the bar in Bangor, Maine.[13] No evidence exists of what Hascall read, but at that time law students who attended Indiana University studied international, constitutional, and common law as well as equity and would read the following: Story's "Commentaries on the Constitution," "Equity," and "Equity Pleading"; Chitty on contracts, bills, and pleading; Stephen on pleading; and

Milo S. Hascall's grave at Forest Home Cemetery in Forest Park, Illinois.
(Photo by David W. Bulla)

Kent's "Commentaries."[14] After he read for the law, Hascall began a career as an attorney, including a stint in the late 1850s as prosecuting attorney for the Court of Common Pleas and clerk of the Elkhart Circuit Court, both elected positions. Typically, Chamberlain and Hascall dealt with squabbles over land, and much of their practice centered on foreclosures.[15]

In the early years in Goshen, the family was Democratic politically, and one of Milo S. Hascall's brothers had been a co-owner of a Democratic newspaper in Goshen during the late 1840s. The first mention of Melvin B. Hascall owning the Goshen *Democrat* occurred in that paper in November of 1846. The *Democrat* announced that brothers Erastus W. H. and William R. Ellis

Gravestone with Milo Hascall's dates at Forest Home Cemetery.
(Photo by David W. Bulla)

were terminating their co-ownership of the paper by "mutual consent."[16] The names of Melvin B. Hascall and Erastus Ellis appeared on the masthead that week.[17] The announcement said that Erastus Ellis would handle the editorial responsibilities and that the paper would remain "a faithful chronicler of the events of the day, and a true and steadfast exponent of Democratic Principles, as we understand them."[18] Melvin B. Hascall stayed on as co-owner until 1848 and would own the paper again after the Civil War. The newspaper, under a different title, would be in the Hascall family again in the twentieth century in the hands of publisher Frank L. Hascall.[19]

Advertising for Hascall & Earle's general store appeared while Melvin B. Hascall shared the helm of the *Democrat* with Erastus Ellis.[20] The store advertised saddles, harnesses, ladies' clothing, and "Fall and Winter Goods." The owners also solicited farmers to sell them wheat, corn, oats, barley, rye, flax seed, beeswax, Timothy seed, ginseng, tallow, hides, and staves. Advertising for the store was a mainstay in both the Goshen *Democrat* and the Republican Goshen *Times* for the next several decades. One Hascall advertisement would claim that "if 'O'd Hascall' has got the things you want, it's no use to spend time to look any where else."[21]

The relationship between the Hascalls and E. W. H. Ellis continued after Ellis and Melvin Hascall split as co-owners of the *Democrat*. In 1852, Ellis and Chauncey S. Hascall became partners in a dry goods, grocery, and hardware store.[22] By 1858, the store would be owned by Chauncey Hascall, Martin Brown, and Charles B. Alderman.[23] It was called Hascall, Alderman & Brown's Dry Goods and Groceries. Charles Alderman's mother was Vesta Alderman, who had married Amasa Hascall after Phoebe Hascall died October 17, 1852. Charles Alderman was a lifelong Democrat who would serve as Goshen's mayor from 1875 until 1882.[24]

Milo Hascall married Julia Swift of Elkhart on November 27, 1855, and they had only one child, who died in 1857.[25] Julia Swift Hascall would spend plenty of time at the front with her husband. Both she and Melvin Hascall's wife served as nurses. Milo Hascall's first wife died on September 11, 1883. Like his father, Milo would re-marry, exchanging vows with Rose Schwarz Miller of Canton, Ohio, on June 22, 1886.[26] Rose Hascall also had been married before and was a Canton socialite.

In the 1850s, the Hascall brothers became split politically. While Milo would follow E. W. H. Ellis to the Republican Party on the basis of anti-Nebraska sentiment, both Chauncey and Melvin remained active in the Democratic Party beyond the Civil War. Both held various appointed and elected positions, and Melvin proved to be a War Democrat who served as a colonel

AMASA HASCALL   MRS. AMASA HASCALL

Milo Hascall's father, Amasa Hascall, and his wife Phoebe Diana Smith.
The father had a farm in Le Roy, New York, before the family moved west.
*(Photo from the Bentley Family Papers, Center for Archival Collections,
Bowling Green State University)*

in the Civil War. In 1858, a Goshen newspaper printed a song written by Milo
Hascall about the good fortunes that awaited the Republicans in the fall election, a song he sang at the party Basket Dinner Meeting in Jefferson Township.[27] In the summer of 1858, he was considered for county treasurer but
came in second to friend and future banking partner John W. Irwin.[28] At this
time, Milo Hascall was both an attorney and a real estate agent.

In the summer of 1859, Republicans chose Hascall to stand for county
clerk on the same ticket with Erastus Ellis, who ran for county auditor, and
future partner Irwin, who ran for treasurer. The Goshen *Times* made the case
for Hascall's election, saying that the attorney "is a zealous, active, and earnest
Republican—battles for the cause valiantly, through good and through evil
report. He is capable, honest, and deserving."[29] On October 11, 1859, Hascall won the clerk's race, and Ellis and Irwin also won. Republicans swept
the county-wide slate of offices.[30] Hascall would serve on the Central Committee of the Elkhart County Republican Party the following spring when it
decided its candidates for the 1860 fall elections. The Elkhart Republicans

The Hascall family farm in New York State before the clan moved to northern Indiana. *(Photo from the Bentley Family Papers, Center for Archival Collections, Bowling Green State University)*

backed Abraham Lincoln for president. On June 22, 1860, Republicans of the Tenth Congressional District met at Kendalville. That day Hascall introduced a resolution allowing members of the minority of county or district conventions to vote independently of the majority, and "the resolution was finally laid upon the table."[31] That is, it did not pass.

The tide in Elkhart County shifted from the Democrats to the Republicans in the election of 1854. The Republican majority continued to expand in 1856, and Milo Hascall rode with that rising tide. The Goshen *Democrat* blamed the Democracy's setbacks on Methodists. "They are made up for the most part of uneducated and selfish men, as little acquainted with the laws which govern them as they are faithful to the religion they profess to teach."[32] The Democrats' attack on Methodism was due in large part to temperance, which Hoosier Republicans accepted in forming a coalition with Free Soilers, Know Nothings, moderate Whigs, and anti-Nebraska Democrats.

The Hascalls' prominence in Goshen was both political and social. They were so prominent that the building where they worked was called "Hascall's Building," and it was located on "Hascall's lot."[33] Later, there would be a Hascall Hall and a Hascall Hotel. A typical advertisement for Milo Hascall's law and real estate practice would request potential clients to call on him at Hascall's Building, "first door to the left up stairs."[34]

Indiana Society at Mid-Century

The state that Milo Smith Hascall lived in was a relatively young one. Indiana had become a state in 1816, and at mid-century it still in many ways resembled a frontier society. Because farming was the rule and most people lived in rural areas, life was fairly stark—planting and harvesting, followed by long winters and unpredictable springs. Hoosiers tended to be Jeffersonian-Jacksonian in political sentiment, believing in small farms, small towns, and small government. The emphasis was on democracy, republicanism, equality, limited government, and laissez-faire capitalism. For a while, Hoosiers were willing to make improvements by using credit and going into debt. The state of Indiana made an internal improvements law in 1836, and the economy was bustling. Yet it did not last. In 1837, a recession rocked the state's economy and the state government went broke. After that, Hoosiers became frugal and spent little money on government. The governor received no salary, and streets in cities were unpaved and unlit. Garbage was not collected, and rarely did towns build sewage systems. Lawlessness was not uncommon, and public services were scant. Private security forces performed the role of the police, and vigilantism occurred frequently. Newspaper editors, who sometimes doubled as postmasters and shopkeepers, kept shotguns in their offices in case of a surprise attack by disgruntled readers or members of the opposition party.[35] It was this violent and frontier society in which press suppression took place in 1863. Indeed, throughout the Civil War years in Indiana, violence and threatened violence against the press were routine. Indeed, thirty percent of Democratic newspapers in the state experienced acts of violence against them during the Civil War.[36]

Yet significant change was taking place. Most of the pioneers had already moved farther west to the Great Plains and Rocky Mountains, and they left "cleared fields and peaceful communities" in Indiana by mid-century.[37] Civilization in the form of churches, schools, newspapers, theaters, railroads, and the telegraph tempered the "bleakness of western life" and began to erode the sense of Indiana being the frontier.[38] Similarly, railroad construction in the 1850s was extensive. In 1850, the Hoosier State had 228 miles of completed track. By 1860, the number of miles jumped to 2,135—the single greatest increase in railroad mileage in any decade in the state's history.[39] The rail business was very profitable during the war.[40]

Meanwhile, the population, although it was still overwhelmingly rural, was gradually becoming more urban. In 1850, 95.5 percent of the population was rural, and, by 1860, the figure was 91.4 percent.[41] Indiana had 988,416 people in 1850 and 1,350,428 in 1860.[42] Only Ohio and Illinois had greater populations among the Midwest states in 1860.

Another significant change was immigration. The immigrant population of the Hoosier State doubled from 1850 to 1860.[43] Most of those immigrants were Germans and Irish. In 1860, fifty-six percent of the foreign-born residents of Indiana were from Germany, and most of them were artisans and laborers.[44] The Irish comprised twenty percent of the foreign-born population in 1860, most were extremely poor.[45] Many Irish came to Indiana escaping the potato famine back home. Illiteracy was high among the Irish, who played a major role in building the canals and railways in the Hoosier

The Haskell Coat of Arms

The Haskell coat of arms (Haskell is an alternative spelling of Hascall). *(Photo from the Bentley Family Papers, Center for Archival Collections, Bowling Green State University)*

State. The majority of the Germans and Irish were Catholics, though some of the Germans were Lutheran, German Evangelical, or Reformed.[46]

Another major change was the rapid ascent of the Republican Party in a state that had been dominated by the Democrats for most of its history. In some ways, Indiana had the hallmarks of a developing nation. Democracy, though fully in place, was full of corruption. Immigrants could vote before obtaining citizenship. Both Democrats and Republicans used illegal voters in the election of 1856, and some Democrats voted more than once. Newspaper editors were often political operatives in the state, many of them major players. Editors produced highly partisan sheets—most of them weeklies—that were long on interpretation and short on informative reporting. Editors played crucial roles in helping develop government policies and reader attitudes. Politicians either bought their own newspapers or gave patronage to them in order to gain favorable public opinion in the press. It was as natural for politicians in nineteenth-century Indiana to own or heavily influence newspapers as it is for today's politicians to hire press secretaries and marketing experts to create advertising strategies.

Socially, Indiana tended to be modest and conservative. Hoosiers wanted a quiet, secure lifestyle. They did not have to be overly successful in

*Facsimile of appointment of General Hascall
to West Point Academy*

Milo Hascall's West Point appointment letter. Hascall did well there, but there
was little to do in the Army in the 1850s, so he returned to Goshen to find work.
*(Photo from the Bentley Family Papers, Center for Archival Collections, Bowling
Green State University)*

terms of material gain, but they wanted to have enough to sustain themselves
and make a decent living. Their democratic and republican institutions "are
diffusing over their citizens the benign influences of domestic quiet, whole-
some laws, and the preservation of their civil and religious rights and privileges."[47] They subscribed wholly to the Bill of Rights, although the state constitution was written with a built-in sense of responsibility for not abusing the
rights and privileges of natural law.

One of the reasons for this conservative bent was the fact that the majority of the folks who settled the Hoosier State had come from the South. In
1860, "Indiana still had more Southerners than any other state north of the
Ohio," and, at that time, fifty-seven percent of Indiana's population was born
in Indiana.[48] Hoosiers had brought with them many of the agriculturally-
based attitudes of the Jeffersonian-Jacksonian majority in the South. Farming,
family, and putting food on the table were constants. Although the majority

of Hoosiers had some connection to the South, they wanted little to do with slavery—either the aristocracy of the planter class or the competition and migration of blacks. After the publication of *Uncle Tom's Cabin*, most Hoosiers were sympathetic to slaves. Yet colonization remained the preferred solution once abolition had been implemented. Fear of racial mixing in society was the rule in Indiana, though some Quakers in the eastern counties of the state believed in assimilation.

Yet the trend was away from Southern-influenced Hoosiers. By 1850, the majority of people who migrated to Indiana from free states eclipsed those who had migrated there from slave states.[49] Most Hoosiers came from Ohio, followed by Kentucky, Pennsylvania, Virginia, North Carolina, and New York, respectively.[50] Emigration from Indiana was significant but did not outpace immigration to the state. However, the rate of exodus did increase during the 1860s and 1870s.[51] Despite Know Nothingism and not having a major urban area, Indiana's foreign-born population grew from approximately six percent of the population as a whole to nine percent by 1870.[52] The counties with the highest percentage of foreign-born residents were Vanderburgh, Allen, Marion, Dearborn, and La Porte.[53] By 1870, in Evansville, approximately thirty percent of the population was born in other countries, and the figure was twenty-eight percent in Fort Wayne.[54] Blacks, mainly from the South, did move to Indiana in this period, and the black population of the state was between one and two percent in the 1850s and 1860s.[55]

"ONE COUNTRY, ONE CONSTITUTION, ONE DESTINY"

A conservative spirit existed in the Midwest, and this form of conservativism carried with it an anti-secession attitude. "One country, one constitution, one destiny" was an often-heard rallying cry in Indiana.[56] Historian Kenneth M. Stampp declared that Hoosiers "professed a blatant nationalism and an unwavering faith in the grand future in store for the American nation. 'Manifest destiny' was an article of faith and not an empty phrase to be exploited by the demagogic politician."[57]

In general, Hoosiers were thrifty, hard working, skeptical of too much government, placed a great deal of importance on integrity, and believed in free—as opposed to slave—labor. Hoosiers were strongly nationalistic, and they felt the union of states was nearly sacred. Their belief in limited government would be tested in the Civil War. The Democrats would come to believe that much of Lincoln's approach to the war effort eroded Jeffersonian democracy. During the war, Democratic mass meetings frequently re-endorsed the Virginia and Kentucky resolutions of 1798. Indiana's Democrats were also

Milo Hascall's brother Amasa N. Hascall, who was sent from the homestead in Le Roy, New York, by his father, Amasa Hascall, to find a larger plot of land to farm in Indiana. Amasa N. Hascall ran a dry goods store in Goshen and was said to have literary talent. *(Photo from the Bentley Family Papers, Center for Archival Collections, Bowling Green State University)*

anxious about the growing power of the military.[58] They feared that the overall centralization effort of Lincoln and the Republicans was a revolution that went back to Alexander Hamilton and John Adams, the great Federalists. The U.S. Constitution and national destiny superseded regional interests. "Devotion to the Union was strong in Indiana, and as the growing sectional bitterness between North and South created increasing tensions, Indiana leaders and newspapers repeatedly reaffirmed this devotion" to the union, a historian noted.[59] With unionism so strong, other principles tended to be subordinated.

Indiana accepted the Compromise of 1850, as long as it kept the Union together. Hoosiers tended to stay moderate on the issue of the expansion of slavery. Richard W. Thompson, a Whig from Terre Haute, said: "Both Northern and Southern ultra groups went too far. The ultra feelings of neither of these parties have yet—to any great extent—reached the West."[60] Suspicion and resentment toward the Northeast was universal, although Democrats tended to be more willing to express this sentiment. Many of Indiana's citizens felt the needs and wants of the Northeast superseded those of the other major regions of the country, and that the Midwest states were under-represented in national policy-making decisions.

Indiana society of the 1850s and 1860s was also diverse. This was due in large part to "the tug of divergent economic forces"—bankers, factory owners, merchants, railroad, timber owners, farmers, farm hands, mechanics—who did not have one overwhelming interest that kept them together, except of course survival. While almost sixty percent of the society was native born, thirty-seven percent were people who had migrated from other states and ten percent of Indiana's population was foreign born.

In addition to corn, flour, and hogs, Hoosiers also harvested timber. The lumber and furniture industries flourished, with walnut being the wood of choice. The building of the railroads in the 1850s was another major source of industry, and mining was developed in Brazil and Terre Haute. Coal production jumped from nearly 60,000 tons in 1850 to 320,000 tons in 1865.[61] With the railroads came the development of the limestone industry, especially in Bedford and Bloomington. In the southern part of the state, the building of steamboats was a major industry. Centered in Jeffersonville and New Albany, the industry shifted its production to government contracts during the war. Flour grist mills, meatpacking, and the manufacture of farm equipment were also prevalent in the state. Industrial companies in general were rather small enterprises with an average of only 3.5 employees per operation.[62]

Milo Hascall's brother Melvin Hascall ran Goshen's Democratic newspaper, and the building in which it is housed remains on North Main Street at Clinton in downtown Goshen. (Photo from the Bentley Family Papers, Center for Archival Collections, Bowling Green State University)

The wartime economy featured increasing investment. Capital investment grew from $7.75 million in 1850 to $52.05 million in 1870.[63] There was a panic in 1857, but the war, while straining the monetary system, produced no bank failures in Indiana. Congress introduced greenbacks and placed a tax on state bank notes to try to remove them from circulation. Predictably, Democrats objected to the centralization of the banking industry.

Wages generally rose during the war, by about a dollar for most types of labor. Most Hoosiers worked on farms. Manufacturing occupations were fourth behind farming, professional/personal services, and trade/transportation. The economy generally grew during the war, though southern Indiana suffered recession because of the decreased commerce on the Ohio River. Southern-county Hoosiers ignored a law by the governor during the war that made it illegal to send goods to Louisville or farther down the Ohio.

Pro-Union vigilantes inspected boats, rail cars, and warehouses.[64] A severe economic downturn for the entire state would not come until eight years after the war ended.

SLAVERY AND TEMPERANCE

The biggest social issues in these two decades were slavery and temperance. One legacy of migration from the South was the complex history of race in Indiana, and this is a key to understanding the mindset of most Democratic newspaper editors in Indiana during the Civil War. Before it became a state, Indiana had slavery, even though it was not supposed to exist under the by-laws of the Northwest Ordinance. Yet antislavery forces won the day in the first state constitutional convention in 1816. Slavery was prohibited by the first constitution, which included a provision making it impossible to ever introduce slavery into the state, but no such provision was made for segregationist measures.[65]

Indiana would develop antiblack laws at later constitutional conventions. Historian Emma Lou Thornbrough, who has written extensively about race in Indiana, observes: "There were few persons who wanted to see slavery introduced into the state, but there was widespread and intense race prejudice and fear of the competition of Negro labor—due in part to the fact that a large part of the population of Indiana came from the nonslaveholding class of southern whites."[66] Like most Midwesterners, Hoosiers wanted little to do with blacks. They wanted a sanctuary from what they considered the messy conditions in the South. Hoosiers felt the slave-owning planters were immoral and indecent for forcing others to do their work for no pay, but they also felt that blacks were an inferior race. Negrophobia was not just commonplace. It was the mindset of almost all Hoosiers. "The result was a proscriptive code designed to keep the small Negro population in an inferior position and to prevent the settlement of Negroes from the slave states," Thornbrough wrote.[67]

Blacks represented only one percent of the population, and antiblack codes of the mid-century were severe. A Negro was defined as anyone with one-eighth or more of "black blood." Hoosier laws stated that only white men could vote, and blacks could not testify in court if a white man was a party in the case. Intermarriage was forbidden. Blacks had to post bond if they entered the state, which was forfeited if one was charged with a crime. Blacks were not allowed to enter the state to settle. Those blacks already in the state were encouraged to colonize elsewhere.[68] Not until after the war were black children able to attend public schools. They were not allowed in public schools even if they paid their own tuition.

One group consistently protested against these race-based
laws, the Quakers in eastern Indiana. Many of the Quakers migrated
to Indiana from North Carolina,
where their antislavery views were
not tolerated in public, including
in newspapers. So sympathetic
to the black condition were the
Quakers that they took part in the
underground networks that helped
runaway slaves move to sanctuary
in the North and Canada. Fugitive
slaves frequented Quaker towns,
and the Underground Railroad
went through Richmond. Indiana Quakers saved freed blacks
from being returned to the South
and provided education for black
children.[69]

Franklin A. Hascall, who helped Milo
Hascall and John W. Irwin run the Salem
Bank in downtown Goshen. (Photo from
the Bentley Family Papers, Center for
Archival Collections, Bowling Green State
University)

Many Christians found it
hard to reconcile black inferiority
with Christian dogma. Yet few Hoosiers advocated abolition and assimilation. They believed the fact that the United States was a white nation, and
that blacks faced few prospects for success in the country. Since blacks could
never attain equality in the state, assimilation would establish a permanent
underclass. Thus, even the most open-minded Hoosiers preferred the colonization solution. The Indiana Colonization Society was formed in 1829. It
hoped to colonize freed blacks in Africa, where they would sow the seeds of
Christianity.[70]

Indiana's race policy could be summed up succinctly: Prevent blacks
from moving in and move out blacks living in the state. Many Quakers
thought expatriation was unrighteous and opposed it. Almost everybody else
thought it was the best solution. "Almost every session of the Indiana legislature passed a resolution in favor of colonization. In his message to the General
Assembly in 1850 Governor Joseph A. Wright pointed out that both southern
and northern states were adopting increasingly harsh measures toward free
Negroes and urged that Indiana take her stand 'in this great struggle for the
separation of the black man from the white,' as the only means of ameliorating
the condition of the unfortunate Negro, Thornbrough wrote."[71] The Indiana

legislature started a colonization fund in 1852. From 1852 until 1865, a law remained on the books in Indiana that provided for this fund. The state legislature also petitioned Congress to use federal funds to colonize blacks.

Some Hoosiers saw through the sham of colonization and began to move toward an abolitionist point of view. The militant antislavery movement developed slowly in Indiana, probably because racism was too deep-seated in large part because of the feeling of separateness that whites coming mainly from the South had adopted earlier in the nineteenth century. The movement remained small even through the war.

The slavery issue caused a schism in one denomination. The Old School and New School Presbyterians split in 1837. The New School Presbyterians "bombarded every General Assembly of the church with memorials on the subject of slavery."[72] Henry Ward Beecher of Lawrenceburg saw that colonization and abolition were polar opposites on a moral scale. The Methodist newspaper *The True Wesleyan* withdrew from the church because the Methodist Church in Indiana would not exclude slaveholders from membership.[73]

The recently formed Disciples of Christ tended to stay away from the race issue. Alexander Campbell, the founder of the Indianapolis-based church, wanted to let abolitionists and anti-abolitionists grapple with slavery among themselves. Meanwhile, Ovid Butler, founder of what would become Butler University, believed in universal brotherhood. He preached against enforcement of the Fugitive Slave Law. Another schism developed among Quakers, this one over abolition and who owned the issue. The Indiana Yearly Meeting of Friends closed its churches to antislavery lectures. The Indiana Quaker church wanted the drive against slavery to come from within. The Quaker church in the state did not want its members taking part in other antislavery associations. Eventually, Quakers who remained active in other antislavery societies split with the main church in the state and formed the Indiana Yearly Meeting of Anti-Slavery Friends.[74] This group opposed both slavery and colonization. It represented about eight percent of the Quakers in Indiana. Some Quakers thought that agitating against slavery should not be done in public ways or through political action, but that it should remain a spiritual matter.

RELIGIOUS LIFE IN THE 1850S AND 1860S

Although the Quakers were influential, they were relatively small in numbers and confined mainly to the eastern part of Indiana. Methodists and Baptists were the most numerous denominations in the state, followed by the Presbyterians and the Disciples of Christ. Catholic numbers were rising in the northern part of the state, especially in Fort Wayne, which had considerable immigration of Irish and Germans. There were only two Congregational churches in the state, according to the 1850 census. The Bible and God were referred to frequently, and biblical authority was often invoked in public speeches and writing. A reference to God was included in the 1851 preamble to the Indiana Constitution, which emphasized democracy and a gracious and providential God: "We the people of the State of Indiana, grateful to Almighty God for the free exercise of the right to choose our own form of government."[75] For the powerful Methodists, conscience was the key to life. They believed in keeping their lives and faith simple. Earnest prayer was critical to salvation. Religion was an important component of the social order of mid-century Indiana. Sunday was a day of rest and worship.

Although religion was a mainstay in Indiana society in the 1850s, ministers did not make much money. Typically, ministers made approximately $100 per year. That increased to approximately $600 by 1863. Salary was not always paid in cash. Food, clothing, and furniture were also used as payment.[76] The use of itinerants was not uncommon, especially among Baptists, the state's second largest denomination. Baptist itinerants received about half the pay of Methodist ministers.

Revivals, conversions, the teaching of morals, and imparting information from the Bible were key elements of Hoosier religion. Sunday school was a major part of the process, though their numbers declined during the war.[77] Churches prohibited the playing of games on Sunday, including the new sport of baseball, because they diminished the importance of spiritual matters.[78] The sale of alcohol was banned on Sundays. Things loosened up during the war. The expansion of the rail system also had an impact on the piety of Hoosiers. Germans were blamed for turning the Sabbath into a day of pleasure.[79] The need to raise troops to fight the war would cause a decline in attendance. Yet some congregations experienced revivals during the war because of the strong emotions raised by the political questions and the deaths of so many thousands of soldiers. Prayers became more oriented toward victory and survival and less toward spiritual matters. Ministers served as chaplains, and some Methodist preachers recruited troops or enlisted themselves.[80]

Churches played a key role in education because Sunday schools nurtured reading. However, Indiana was behind the other Northern states in public education. At the time of the Indiana Constitutional Convention in 1851, it had the lowest literacy rate of any Northern state because it "had never levied a tax or paid out money for an educational purpose."[81] Caleb Mills, a classics professor at Wabash College, castigated the state for not doing something about

the education of its young. Mills felt spending for education would outweigh
the consequences of not educating Hoosier children.[82] Part of the problem was
that Hoosiers believed public schools mainly benefited the poor and therefore
were of relatively insignificant value for taxpayers. Furthermore, Hoosiers felt
education was solely a local priority and that the state government should stay
out of the schooling business.

The 1851 state constitutional convention began to turn the tide in favor
of public education by providing for common schools with free tuition and
open admissions.[83] Accordingly, the constitution provided for a state superintendent of public instruction, a paid position. The common (public) schools
were supported by state taxes, and local authorities administered the schools.
Indiana schoolhouses were small and generally inadequate, but by 1859 nearly
700 had been built and 7,500 by 1865.[84] Teaching was not a full-time occupation, and teachers received approximately $50 to $60 a year in pay. In part,
the salary was low because of an Indiana Supreme Court ruling that made it
illegal for local townships to supplement or pay for teachers' salaries.[85]

During the war, education went backwards. Schools were closed for
several years at a time, especially in southern Indiana. Bills were proposed in
the General Assembly to make it legal for localities to raise taxes for education, but they languished and were never passed. One fruit of the war was that
Governor Oliver P. Morton extended common schools admissions to blacks
in 1865. Church-sponsored education tended to be rare and was found mainly
in places where there was a lack of common schools. Catholics built the most
extensive education program of the church schools. Approximately twenty-
five percent of the parishes in Indiana had parochial schools by 1850.[86]

INDIANA'S POLITICS IN THE 1850S AND 1860S

Politically, slavery also was a complex issue. The antislavery Liberty Party
came to Indiana in 1841. Liberty Party leader Stephen S. Harding of Ripley
County thought the U.S. Constitution was antislavery and that the founding fathers "had not expected it to be perpetuated."[87] The major result of the
Mexican-American War from 1846 to 1848 was that the United States had
to decide the nature of new territories—whether they would be free or slave.
Generally, at the start of the 1850s, both Democrats and Whigs supported the
principles of the Wilmot Proviso, which meant that they opposed the spread
of slavery in the territories. David Wilmot, a first-term Democratic congressman from Pennsylvania, added an amendment to an appropriations bill that
said that there would be no slavery in any territory coming from the Republic
of Mexico after the Mexican-American War.

The Wilmot Proviso became the seeds of sectional conflict for the next fifteen years. It came out of Northern Democrats getting weary of Southern dominance of the party, and it was payback for Southern Democrats sabotaging the Van Buren campaign in 1844. Wilmot was not problack and did not want to see blacks diffuse throughout the continent. He knew most Western settlers wanted no blacks in the territories—free or slave. Unlike many Quakers and others who sympathized with the plight of Africans in North America, Wilmot was not a humanist. He was a Jacksonian Democrat who abhorred all concentrations of power, whether it was from New England mercantile or Southern slave interests. For men like Wilmot, outlawing slavery in the territories was primarily politics, one that went with a land reform agenda in the West.[88]

Gideon Welles, a Connecticut Democrat who would later serve as Abraham Lincoln's Secretary of the Navy, voiced the thoughts most Hoosiers were thinking about the slavery-in-the-territories question: "We are not going to extend the institution of slavery as a result of this war."[89] Meanwhile, in response to the James K. Polk administration's conquering of the vast Mexican territories, the Free Soil Party was established in 1848, and both Hoosier Whigs and Democrats began to adopt Free Soil policies. George W. Julian, a Free Soil Party member, was elected to Congress from eastern Indiana. The progressive Julian, who benefited from Democratic support, not only opposed slavery but also believed in a woman's right to vote. Paris C. Dunning, the Democratic Governor of Indiana in the late 1840s and early 1850s, said in 1849 that the slave states had the right to own slaves, but that Congress had the power to prohibit slavery in newly conquered territories. Dunning termed slavery "a baleful influence."[90]

Southerners worried about the balance of power as the West was settled. Then came the Compromise of 1850, which was a catalyst for political diversity in the North, including Indiana. Because of the gold rush, California came into the United States in September of 1850 with no pair. Oregon, which became a state in February of 1859, would also come in without a paired slave state in the southwestern territories. California was very conservative. Indeed, its first two senators were Democrats. Yet it was a free state. The chief architects of the Compromise of 1850 were two nearby senators, Whig Henry Clay of Kentucky and Democrat Stephen A. Douglas of Illinois. In carving up the Mexican territories won by Polk and in response to the policies of the Zachary Taylor administration, Congress decided to admit California as a free state, though its political makeup was favorable to the Democrats and the South. Meanwhile, Utah and New Mexico would be allowed to have popular sovereignty. They would choose whether they would be slave or free. Slavery was adopted in both Utah and New Mexico before the Civil War, although neither was officially a state yet.[91] However, both states had few black slaves, and neither came into the Union until well after the Civil War. The Compromise also abolished the slave trade in Washington, D.C. Furthermore, the Fugitive Slave Law was made more stringent. The Compromise of 1850 passed narrowly and mirrored the fragile regional divisions in the country.

INDIANA'S DEMOCRATS PREFER TO COMPROMISE WITH THE SOUTH

In the 1850s, the pro-Democrat *Indiana State Sentinel* editor Jacob P. Chapman opposed slavery in general and its extension in the territories in particular. Indiana Democratic Congressman Graham N. Fitch chastised Southern Democrats who talked about secession over admitting California as a free state. Wright, Indiana's governor from 1849 until 1857, supported the Compromise of 1850. In general, though, Hoosiers believed in compromising with the Southerners to prevent disunion, and they wanted to take advantage of the anti-Taylor sentiment created by the president's policy of making new free states out of the territories conquered in the Mexican War.

Taylor, a Southern Whig who owned slaves, pushed for California and New Mexico coming in as free-labor states. This actually worked in the Democrats' favor. Southern Democrats felt betrayed, and the Whigs lost their appeal nationwide. Whigs in Indiana remained in a compromise position—no extension of slavery in the territories and no right to interfere with slavery in the state where it already existed. Hoosier Democrats, though, were alarmed by the Compromise. They wanted to avoid irritating their Southern brethren. Union was more important than limiting the expansion of slavery. Most Hoosier Democrats figured that a good chunk of the territories would not be hospitable for a slave system because of the climate and topography. Thus, slavery in the territories was more about a large political argument than a reality for human beings, so they took an attitude of compromise with the South.

As the 1850s began, the Democrats began to distance themselves from the Free Soil principles that they had adopted in 1849. A sort of weariness over slavery began to emerge in Indiana. Hoosier Democrats focused on what they termed the "finality" of the Compromise. It was the final solution to the slavery problem, and Democrats in the state wanted no more agitation from either extreme. In order to preserve the peace and save the union, Democrats wanted it to be as far as either side would go. The entire Hoosier delegation to the U.S. House of Representatives voted for a resolution that stated that the

Compromise of 1850 was the final law on slavery and that further agitation against slavery was unwarranted. The Indiana Democratic state convention endorsed the same resolution in 1852. Perhaps in large part because this was the sentiment of most Hoosiers, Democrats dominated the election results in the state in 1852.

Democrats dominated politics in early Indiana. Only in 1836 and 1840 had Indiana voted for a Whig. Democrats had a stranglehold on Indiana from 1842 until the Civil War. In 1850, Democrats controlled the legislature, all state officers were Democrats, both U.S. Senators were Democrats, and eight of the ten congressmen from Indiana were Democrats. Approximately two-thirds of the representatives to the 1850 Indiana Constitutional Convention were Democrats. The Democrats placed the emphasis on a strict interpretation of the Constitution, limited government, low tariffs, and opposition to monopolies.

Most Hoosier Democrats opposed slavery. Yet some Democratic editors who opposed slavery nonetheless worried about what would happen with its abolition. Mainly, they were concerned about the flow of blacks to the North if slavery ended. They worried blacks would increase the competition for jobs. These Democratic editors wanted a program in place to deal with the dramatic change in U.S. society if abolition should come to pass.

Meanwhile, the Indiana Whigs were smaller in numbers than Democrats and generally lacked cohesion. What kept them together was their dislike for Democrats. Whigs were also held together in part because most admired Henry Clay of Kentucky. Hoosier Whigs tended to be bankers, attorneys, businessmen, or newspapermen. John D. Defrees, owner of the Indianapolis *Journal* who had migrated to Indiana from Tennessee, was one of the leading Whigs in the state. Schuyler Colfax, editor of the South Bend *Register*, was another prominent Whig. Born in Virginia, Richard W. Thompson of Terre Haute supported government aid to the railroads, but Thompson was no friend of the abolitionists. The Whigs would disappear in the 1850s but were resurrected as the Republicans and would become one of the most significant political entities in U.S. history. Indiana Whigs opposed the extension of slavery in the territories, but they refused to advocate interference in states that already had slavery.

Hoosiers in general felt more comfortable with a conservative policy of accepting the constitutional status quo—a basically free-labor North and a slave-labor South. Racial equality was an abstraction to most Hoosiers, and the few Quakers and Free Soilers who might be for it were too much in the minority. This was part of a larger national pattern: "During the 1850s, the Free Soilers and Republicans tried to enact black suffrage in a few other Northern states, but failed. . . . So pervasive was racism in many parts of the North that no party could win if it endorsed full racial equality, noted James McPherson."[92] Both Hoosier Democrats and Whigs (Republicans) did not see ending slavery in the South as a winning political issue.

Another key social issue in Indiana was temperance. In 1847, Indiana legislature passed a law that allowed townships to have referendum that would determine if liquor licenses would be issued in those localities.[93] German and Irish immigrants, a fast-growing segment of the population, opposed restrictions on alcohol. Furthermore, distillery owners in the state, many of whom were German, opposed restrictions on the sale of alcohol. Many ordinary citizens thought the campaign to make all drinkers of spirits into devils went too far.[94] Some Democrats opposed temperance laws because the laws would lead to the seizure and destruction of private property, which they deemed as unconstitutional as taking Southern planter's slaves. These factors made Hoosier politicians a little hesitant on temperance. Indiana had several temperance publications, including John W. Osborn's *Temperance Advocate*.

Other issues did not quite take off the way slavery and temperance did. The right to vote for women had little popular support in Indiana. Still, in 1859, Dr. Mary F. Thomas of Richmond presented a petition with more than one thousand signatures on it to the state legislature asking for equal political rights for women. Thomas spoke before the legislature, the first time in Indiana history that a woman had done so. Peace activism also made only a small ripple in the political currents. Thornbrough noted: "Some of the same persons who were interested in the antislavery and temperance movements were interested in the peace movement. A convention of delegates from various parts of the state met in Indianapolis in June of 1851, to pass resolutions approving the objects of the World Peace Convention which was to meet at Frankfurt-am-Main in 1851. Jeremiah Sullivan was president of the convention."[95] Generally, though, pacifism met with little interest in the state, in part because Quakers were focused on antislavery.

Partisanship was hallmark of Indiana politics as the Civil War approached. Politics was a non-stop activity in Indiana in the 1850s and 1860s. Article I of the 1816 Indiana State Constitution states: "We declare, That all men are born equally free and independent, and have certain natural, inherent, and unalienable rights; among which are the enjoying and defending life and liberty, and of acquiring, possessing, and protecting property, and pursuing and obtaining happiness and safety."[96]

In 1852, Democrats put up Franklin Pierce on a states' right, pro-Compromise-of-1850 platform. Meanwhile, Winfield Scott won the nomination of the Whigs, who said they would acquiesce to the Compromise of 1850. The Free Soilers chose John P. Hale on a platform that opposed the Compromise of 1850. Pierce won, and the Whigs and Free Soilers were dead.

Nationally, the rise of the Republicans came directly from the January 4, 1854, bill by Committee on the Territories chairman Stephen A. Douglas that called for popular sovereignty in the territories. It was a bill that would organize the land west and northwest of Missouri. The Nebraska Territory included Nebraska, most of the Dakotas, Montana, Wyoming, part of Idaho, and part of Colorado. Missouri did not want to be surrounded on three sides by free states, and the Kansas-Nebraska Act in effect repealed the Missouri Compromise. It opened the way to a new free-for-all to determine which new states coming out of territories would be slave and which free. Douglas maintained that the Compromise of 1850 itself had repealed the Missouri Compromise because it made popular sovereignty the law of the land above 36-30. Douglas felt that the climate would prevent slavery from taking in much of the Nebraska Territory. The bill was a victory for Southern Democrats, but it also woke up the North as abolitionists now had their issue.

Protest meetings took place all over the North in the spring and summer of 1854. There was a fusion of Whigs, disaffected Democrats, Free Soilers, and Know Nothings. McPherson added: "The Republicans took over the Free Soil commitment to the principle of the Wilmot Proviso as their central tenet: no slavery in the territories, no more slave states."[97] The Kansas-Nebraska Act continued the process of diversifying Hoosier politics. Kansas-Nebraska splintered the Democrats into two groups, those who opposed the repeal of the Missouri Compromise of 1820 and those who went along with President Pierce, including Jesse D. Bright, Indiana's three-term U.S. senator. The former saw the Missouri Compromise as a solemn pledge.[98] What the Missouri Compromise had established was a political algebra as Americans colonized the continent. Missouri came in as a slave state, while Maine came in as a free state. From that point forward, for every slave state admitted, a free state would be admitted. The supporters of Kansas-Nebraska took their cue from the *Indiana State Sentinel*, which branded its opponents as abolitionists.[99] Another Democratic paper in Indianapolis countered that most Democratic newspaper editors in the state did not favor Kansas-Nebraska.[100]

In the long run, the majority of the Hoosier congressional delegation caved and supported the act. Only two Democrats and one Whig from Indiana voted against Kansas-Nebraska as it made its way through the U.S.

House, and both Hoosier senators voted for it.[101] Yet this made for chaos. In
district meetings, many Hoosier Democrats expressed disapproval of Kansas-
Nebraska, and they were "read out of the party."[102] These men began to talk of
forming a new political party that opposed popular sovereignty.

Many of those Hoosier Democrats who opposed Kansas-Nebraska also
were for temperance. Indiana Democrats had opposed the extension of slavery in 1848 and 1849. Now, with Douglas's popular sovereignty, they were allowing territorial citizens to decide the question. This was a reversal of policy.
Democrats claimed that in neither Kansas nor Nebraska was there a majority
for slavery within the state.

Immigration was another major social and political issue. In 1850, there
were 55,000 aliens in the state. By 1860, that number had reached 110,000.[103]
Indiana required only one year of residence for aliens to acquire the right
to vote, as long as they stated their intention to become citizens. This was
a Democratic measure, and most German and Irish immigrants were pro-
Democratic because of it. Some Whigs became attracted to the Know Nothing movement, which was anti-immigrant in character. Whigs wanted to see
the elimination of the right to vote for aliens who had not become citizens yet.
The Know Nothing movement, also known as the American Party, diffused
rapidly in Indiana, replacing the Whigs. The Know Nothings in Indiana were
anti-Catholic and anti-immigrant.[104] Their main goal was to see that only U.S.
natives voted and were elected to political office.

The People's Party was a fusion of old Whigs, anti-Nebraska Democrats,
some Know Nothings, and Free Soilers, who had renamed themselves Free
Democrats.[105] Anti-Nebraska and pro-prohibition, the People's Party would
become the Republican Party. Their main goals were the restoration of the
principles of the Missouri Compromise and preventing the extension of slavery into the territories.

Hoosier Democrats, who had a stranglehold on Indiana politics since
1840, now found themselves vulnerable. Although they had opposed the extension of slavery in 1848 and 1850, the Democrats now supported Douglas
and popular sovereignty. To many, this made the Democrats look like they
were proslavery. The *Indiana State Sentinel* said that no Hoosier Democrat if
he were living in Kansas or Nebraska would vote for slavery. The newspaper
added that self-determination and states' rights were valuable principles in a
democratic society.[106]

So the People's Party focused on antislavery. The Democrats countered
with charges of anti-immigrant bias because the Fusionists included the Know
Nothings. To broaden their base, the Fusionists included pro-temperance

men.[107] That was perhaps the decisive fact as the People's Party swept the elections of 1854, when prohibition became the law in Indiana.[108] However, prohibition was short-lived. Judge Samuel Perkins of the Indiana Supreme Court ruled the prohibition law was unconstitutional in 1855. Perkins, who also was editor of the Richmond *Jeffersonian*, was commenting on the arrest of a German-born citizen who had been arrested for breaking the prohibition law. Judge Perkins, a Democrat, feared a Hoosier revolution if prohibition remained the law of the state. "News of the decision was telegraphed throughout the state, and the saloons were back in business," Thornbrough noted.[109] The People's Party would have a temperance plank in 1856, but it was not a major issue in that election.[110]

Just as temperance became a liability for the emerging Republican Party, the Democrats were beginning to find that favoring Kansas-Nebraska was a losing proposition for them. In Kansas, where men from other states were agitating for slavery, popular sovereignty was a sham. Meanwhile, Hoosiers began to move to Kansas in 1856, and they had a close-up view of what was happening in a territory that would achieve statehood on January 29, 1861. With these migrating Hoosiers writing relatives, friends, and business associates back home, Indiana was more interested in the popular sovereignty issue than most Northerners.

ATTITUDES TOWARD SLAVERY

Issues involving slavery were also becoming more important to Hoosiers. The Fugitive Slave Law provision of the Compromise of 1850 frustrated many Hoosier politicians, but they supported it in order to avoid disunion. While Democratic editors tended to uphold the law, Republican editors abhorred it but gave in because it was the law of the land and that lawlessness was unacceptable. Overall, the Fugitive Slave Law strengthened antislavery sentiment in Indiana. Hoosiers viewed runaway slaves sympathetically, and the publication of *Uncle Tom's Cabin* in 1852 opened the eyes of an even higher percentage of Hoosiers. Sympathy for freed slaves increased and focused attention on an Indianapolis resident named John Freeman. A black, Freeman had lived in Indianapolis for a decade before a man from Missouri tried to arrest him and return him to his owner in the slave state that was farthest north and west. Although Freeman was jailed for more than two months, he was freed because there was no proof that he was the escaped slave for whom the Missouri man was looking.[111] The case further turned public opinion in the state against the Compromise and Kansas-Nebraska.

Between 1840 and 1860, two Democrats dominated Indiana politics, Wright and Bright, who was Indiana's U.S. senator from 1845 to 1862. Wright and Bright were rivals. Bright, who lived in Madison, had moved to Indiana from New York. He owned land in Kentucky that was worked by slaves. Because he served three terms, Bright built considerable power in the U.S. Senate. He was mentioned as a presidential candidate in 1857. Wright, a Methodist, had come to Indiana from Pennsylvania as a boy. He had grown up on a poor farm. Wright was for colonization, temperance, and agriculture.

In 1856, Indiana's Democrats endorsed popular sovereignty, supported Bright for president, and condemned the anti-immigrant mindset of the Know Nothings. Other than Bright, Ashbel P. Willard became the top man in the Democratic Party in the state. Willard, the lieutenant governor under Wright, was nominated for the governor's post in 1856. Bright wanted to be president, but he failed to earn enough national support to make his candidacy feasible. He disdained Douglas of Illinois and settled on James Buchanan, who would become the Democratic candidate to face Republican John C. Fremont.

The Indiana Republicans were a fragile group. A few Hoosier Whigs switched to the Democracy because they thought the People's Party was too sectional in nature.[112] Some Free Soil men were upset with Indiana Republicans for not being more antislavery. The People's Party platform called for the immediate admission of Kansas as a free state and a five-year requirement for naturalization. The party opposed any extension of slavery in the territories and declared that immigrants could not vote before they became citizens of the state. In 1856, the People's Party chose as its gubernatorial candidate Oliver P. Morton, who would become the state's most powerful politician during the Civil War. Morton, a former Democrat, moved away from the Democrats because he opposed the Wilmot Proviso and wanted to stay out of the slavery issue. Morton was also uneasy with popular sovereignty.

In the late 1850s, both Democrats and Republicans in Indiana considered themselves to be conservatives. Republicans in Indiana wanted to conserve the integrity of the Missouri Compromise, with one new free-labor state for every new slave state admitted. The Democrats thought they were conserving the limited-government principles of the Founding Fathers. The Whig faction of the Republicans said they were conservatives because they had been around so long. The Whigs continued to praise the legacy of Henry Clay. They claimed that if Clay were alive in 1856, he would have been a Republican. These Hoosier Whigs denounced radical Republicans as abolitionists who would cause disunion. The Whig Republicans wanted no part of such disharmony. Democrats, meanwhile, wanted to conserve the social order in Indiana and began to appeal more and more to Hoosiers' Negrophobia.

In the October 1856 elections, Willard defeated Morton by less than 6,000 votes.[113] Among the key issues in the campaign was South Carolina Congressman Preston Brooks' cane attack on Massachusetts Senator Charles Sumner and the political turmoil in Kansas. Sumner delivered a speech titled "The Crime Against Kansas," and Brooks caned Sumner for what he called libel against his cousin, South Carolina Senator Andrew Butler. Brooks was praised profusely in the South, but Hoosiers were outraged.

Hoosier Democrats openly used the race card and charged Republicans with being amalgamationists who would give blacks full equality, with that leading to intermarriage.[114] Appeals to save white girls from black husbands abounded.

Overall, Democrats sustained power in Indiana. In November of 1856, Buchanan defeated Fremont by approximately 24,000 votes in Indiana.[115] Democrats maintained both U.S. Senate seats and six seats in the U.S. House—compared to five for the Republicans. One new trend found some German-born Hoosiers switching to the Republicans. By 1860, only one of eight German-language newspapers in the state supported Douglas. In 1856, Republicans swept Ohio, Michigan, and Wisconsin while making major inroads in Illinois. The Democrats maintained a majority in the Indiana House, but the Republicans, with two Know Nothings joining an alliance, held a one-vote edge in the Indiana State Senate. Thus, the Republican influence in the Hoosier State was growing quickly.

During the 1856 campaign, Republicans and Democrats seemed civilized enough. They often rode together as they made speeches across the state. On the day of the election, voting irregularities were common in Indiana. For example, in the southern border counties, citizens of Kentucky crossed the Ohio River and voted in Indiana. Thornbrough noted that state law "required the voter to vote in the township or precinct in which he resided, and inspectors were required to swear that they would 'not knowingly' permit an unqualified person to vote, but there was no provision for voter registration and no guarantee that election boards would be bipartisan."[116] Furthermore, Democrats opposed any residency requirement for voting.[117]

Some voters were paid to vote. Candidates provided the ballots, and the state provided locked ballot boxes. "Candidates tried to have their ballots printed on a distinctive type and color of paper—a practice which made it easy to determine whether or not voters voted that they were paid to do," Thornbrough noted."[118] Governor Wright, who left office in 1857, feared election corruption would lead to rule by an "unlicensed mob."[119] Republicans said that Democrats, mostly Irish immigrants, voted more than once. Democrats countered that Republicans in some counties brought in voters from other counties to vote for Republicans in local elections.[120]

Because the Republicans had a majority in the Indiana Senate, the state was left in gridlock until 1861. In 1857, the two houses were in such a stalemate that they failed to act on budget issues before the session was over. Accordingly, Indiana failed to raise revenue and appropriate money to state operations in 1857. Because of this financial crisis, the Indiana institute for the blind and the state hospital for the insane had to be closed for a few months.[121]

Events in Kansas began to shape Democratic national politics, and there was fallout in Indiana. In 1857, President Buchanan and Senator Douglas of Illinois battled over Kansas. The territorial government, favoring slavery, held a constitutional convention at Lecompton, Kansas. The Lecompton constitution made it impossible to abolish slavery in Kansas. Because he wanted the Kansas question to be settled, Buchanan accepted Lecompton. Douglas, though, was convinced that the majority of the people in Kansas wanted it to be free. Indiana's senators and its eight Democratic congressmen voted for Lecompton, but the people of Indiana seemed more on Douglas' side. Thirty Democratic newspapers in the state condemned Lecompton, and three-fourths of the Democratic press in the state opposed Lecompton.[122]

Under the leadership of Morton, Republicans improved to seven seats from Indiana for the U.S. House of Representatives in 1858, a gain of two seats, and, as the 1850s ended, the Republican Party was growing in the northern part of the state where Goshen's Milo Smith Hascall would come down on the Democrats the hardest in 1863. Hascall knew Indiana. He knew there would be less opposition to General Order No. 9 in the northern part of the state, and he believed Republican editors would actively endorse his no-dissent policy.

THE ELECTION OF 1860

Hoosier Republicans put success over principle in 1860. They wanted a winner for president. The major goal: Republicans wanted to win a majority in the Indiana legislature. This would be so they could elect a Republican to the U.S. Senate and could re-district the state to suit their desires. Yet Republicans were not united on their view on slavery. "Except for a handful of old Free Soil-Liberty men Republicans were inclined to be cautious and to try to do nothing which might alienate the most conservative old-line Whigs in southern Indiana."[123] The pragmatic Morton believed it was best to put slavery on the back burner.

Hoosier Republicans, though, did oppose the extension of slavery into the territories. Indiana's Republicans supported Abraham Lincoln for president in 1860. A former Whig and a Midwesterner, Lincoln was seen as a moderate, as less likely to support the abolitionist agenda the way William H. Seward would. Lincoln also would appeal to Republican conservatives and be more attractive to German voters than Edward Bates, the Missourian who had been a Know Nothing supporter in 1856.[124] Hoosier Republicans opposed Seward because he was too radical and wanted a candidate who could win Indiana and nationally. Thus, Lincoln was their man. Both Morton and Henry S. Lane, a banker, lawyer, and former congressman from Crawfordsville, held that nominating Seward would lead to Republican defeat in Indiana. Lane was nominated for governor and Morton for lieutenant governor. But Lane would be made senator if Republicans won the Indiana legislature, and Morton would move into the governor's seat.

Democrats in Indiana supported Douglas. Because of this, Bright lost his power in the state. Popular sovereignty remained the key plank for Democrats, who also endorsed the Dred Scott decision by the U.S. Supreme Court. For governor, Democrats nominated Thomas A. Hendricks. Indiana Democrats stuck with Douglas through the Charleston and Baltimore conventions. Indiana Democrats were infuriated with Southern Democrats for splitting up the party, privately believing "that the Democratic split insured a Republican victory."[125]

Meanwhile, Bright supported Breckenridge and worked to wrestle control of the Democrats back. He constructed a newspaper in Indianapolis called the *Old Line Guard* to promote his views and policies. Lane, who had fought in the Mexican War, said Republicans could live with the compromises in the Constitution over slavery. Lane also supported the Fugitive Slave Act. Morton said slavery should be prohibited in the territories and opposed the Dred Scott decision. Scott was a Missouri slave of an Army surgeon who had lived in Illinois and Wisconsin. Illinois was a free state, and Wisconsin had been a free territory at the time Scott lived there. The owner died in 1846, and Scott sued his heirs for freedom. The case made it all the way to the U.S. Supreme Court, which ruled Scott was still a slave, not a citizen, and his sojourn in free states or territories did not free him. Indiana Republicans condemned the decision.

Democrats pushed the image of Republicans seeing blacks as being equal, especially when it came to suffrage. Some Democrats warned that Republican policies would lead to black migration to Indiana. This would put blacks in competition for white-held jobs. Democrats also claimed that Republicans favored blacks more than poor white immigrants—a theme that would continue through the Civil War. Morton began to claim that slavery in the territories would inhibit white emigration to the West. Indirectly, this meant that slavery was actually beneficial to Indiana because it would keep whites in the state from moving westward. However, Morton was not about to make this argument.

In 1860, Indiana Republicans requested that Seward avoid the state during the campaign. In October, Lane won the U.S. Senate seat and Morton won the gubernatorial race, and Republicans gained a seven-to-five edge in the Hoosier delegation to the U.S. House of Representatives. Republicans now held both the state house and senate. Then, in November, Lincoln won Indiana and the national vote.

With a Republican in the White House, the Democratic editors of Indiana worried that the Southern states would secede. When South Carolina seceded, the Hoosier union sentiment stayed firm. Both Republicans and Democrats in Indiana called for compromise and avoiding the use of force to stop secession. The pro-Republican Indianapolis *Journal* wrote that the Southern states did not have the right to secede, but it also said that war was horrible. The *Journal* argued for the return of the Missouri Compromise line and the abolition of personal liberty laws, which forbade Indiana officers from aiding in the arrest of fugitive slaves or using their jails for holding runaway slaves. Union meetings were called throughout the state. Hoosiers held tenaciously to the concept of one nation. The hope was that the seceding states would see their folly and eventually return to the fold. Both Republicans and Democrats in the state thought the secession crisis was temporary, and the union would be restored by summer, if not sooner. Lincoln had a similar view.

One man in Indiana began to clamor for putting the rebellion down with force, and that was the governor elect. Morton claimed in November of 1860 that coercion was merely enforcement of the law: "If it was worth a bloody struggle to establish this nation, it is worth one to preserve it."[126] Public opinion began to shift after Morton's speech, but still the majority in Indiana favored compromise and peace. Democrats in particular began to think Morton was agitating for war.

The economic situation was a major issue. A business slump occurred at the end of 1860 and beginning of 1861. The southern part of Indiana had closer ties to the South because the Ohio River was a major transportation outlet to the rest of the world. Southern-county Hoosiers did not want to be on the boundary between hostile nations. They feared what would happen if they could not sell their goods down the river and onward to the Mississippi River and New Orleans. Stagnation was the rule in the counties along the Ohio River. The legislature passed the Felonies Act, which made it illegal to correspond with or sell commerce to the Confederates, and Morton tried to prevent Hoosiers in the southern part of the state from sending goods down the river to sell in Louisville or New Orleans.[127] As a consequence, southern-county Hoosiers asked for relief from the state government. However, legislators from the northern part of the state had little interest in relief, and the two sides did not reach a compromise.

Morton sent a Hoosier delegation to a peace conference in Virginia in February 1861, but Morton thought war was inevitable. The governor was impatient with Lincoln's seeming inactivity and went to Washington, D.C., in March to express his support of a tough policy on the South. Morton also told the president that Indiana would supply troops for the military force that would be needed to quell the rebellion. Some Democratic editors thought Indiana should side with the South for economic reasons. They believed that Indiana had more in common with the Southern states than with New England. They also felt that choosing Lincoln would mean choosing rail as the main way to transport goods, as opposed to choosing the river routes to the South.

Then the Confederate occupation of Fort Sumter occurred on April 13, 1861. Democratic newspaper editors in Indiana blamed what they considered to be an abolition administration in Washington. This was due in large part to the presence of Seward in Lincoln's cabinet. Soon, though, most of the newspapers in the state supported the necessity of putting down the rebellion. The pro-Democratic *Indiana State Sentinel* said it supported Lincoln and union, but that it had the right to criticize the policies of the Republicans. Even Democratic newspapers that did not want to fight secession believed a large federal force should be raised to protect the federal capital.

Patriotism replaced partisanship in the spring of 1861. Union became the rallying cry for almost all Hoosiers. Morton began to see himself as a war governor. On April 24, 1861, he proclaimed: "We have passed from the field of argument to the solemn fact of war."[128] A resolution of the legislature announced that Indiana was firmly behind the defense of the U.S. government, and that Indiana would provide men and money for war. Thornbrough observed: "Although the war which was beginning ultimately resulted in a vast expansion of Federal powers and a diminution in the role of the states, much or the war effort, particularly in the early stages, was borne directly by the states. The role of the war governors was of crucial importance, and no governor played his role more valiantly or effectively than did Morton."[129]

HASCALL: A MORTON MAN

Governor Morton's role was to raise troops. In Goshen, Hascall, a staunch Republican, was a Morton man. The attorney helped lead the enlistment campaign in Elkhart County, where prowar sentiment was high. The war was not unpopular in Indiana, which raised more troops than the federal quota required. Morton also had to purchase the arms for Indiana soldiers to fight the war. In building a capable militia, the governor was building up his own power base. Not only was he the political leader of the state, he was also Indiana's military leader, though he never dressed in uniform. Morton was so prowar that he took little time in raising troops. He wanted aggressive action taken against the Confederates. Morton had purchased arms and supplies for Indiana troops, who received blankets, underclothes, and utensils from citizen donations.[130] However, Morton and the federals generally did not get along. He thought Indiana was being neglected and constantly let the Lincoln administration know his views on the war.

Morton was very concerned about his neighbor to the south. Lincoln had a go-slow policy on Kentucky. The president did not want to lose the slave state. He thought it was of strategic value. He believed a tough policy would push public opinion in favor of joining the Lower South. Morton wanted none of that. He thought rebel forces in Kentucky needed to be dealt with severely. Morton wanted Indiana troops in West Virginia—where Hascall served early on—to be relocated in Kentucky.

Thornbrough observed that the counties in southern Indian feared Kentucky would secede and "thus bring the boundary of the Confederacy to the Ohio River." She noted that Lincoln listened to Kentucky politicians who told him to wait for the Confederates to strike first. Impatient with this line of reasoning, Morton urged Lincoln to occupy strategic places in the Commonwealth.[131] Yet Lincoln would not budge. Morton had his critics, too, including Michael C. Garber, editor of the Madison *Courier*. Garber wrote that Morton kept the troops in the center of the state and failed to protect the southern border of Indiana from potential marauders from Kentucky. Garber also complained that Morton was awarding state contracts to out-of-state bidders rather than Hoosier businessmen.[132]

Morton and the federal authorities clashed over recruitment policies and the care of Indiana's troops. Morton was anxious that Indiana's soldiers would be treated as second-class citizens. The governor was providing thousands of men to fight the war. He was asking them to die for their state and country, and he wanted them to receive the recognition and compensation that he felt they deserved.

While Hoosiers were eager to fight in 1861, they did not have a general agreement on why they were fighting. In 1861, the legislature passed resolutions stating Indiana should not support a war of aggression against slavery or any other constitutional rights belonging to any state. Most Hoosiers supported Kentuckian John J. Crittenden's resolution, which would revert back to the east-west line of the Missouri Compromise.[133] The rallying cry for Crittenden was the "Constitution as it is, the government as it was."[134] Democrats were critical of both abolition and secession. Democrats were middle men. The *Indiana State Sentinel* said that the union must be preserved, and that it could not be preserved by abolition. Most Hoosier Republicans were cautious about the slave issue. They worried that antislavery talk might turn voters against the Republicans. They also worried about losing the slave states that had stayed in the Union. Pro-abolition Republicans believed that since slavery had been the reason for the war, abolition was its logical objective. In the long term, peace could be maintained only through universal emancipation.

Schuyler Colfax, the St. Joseph Valley *Register* editor and congressman from South Bend, wanted to confiscate slaves in the South because they gave the Confederates strength at home. Colfax argued that slaves were doing the behind-the-scenes work that kept the Rebel army marching. Liberate the slaves, Colfax held, and the South's military machine would fall apart. It was addition by subtraction, and, for Republicans like Colfax, abolition became a military measure.[135] By 1863, this would be a policy that would divide Indiana along party lines, with Republicans accepting emancipation as a war measure and Democrats viewing it as a social goal that would wreck havoc on the state after the war.

Meanwhile, the militia of the state had to be organized. In the spring of 1861, Morton had little difficulty getting volunteers. Hoosiers were eager to serve. In fact, no matter how it is computed, Indiana ranked second in the percentage of her population that served in the Union military. The problem was there were more volunteers than there were arms and provisions. After Fort Sumter, Lincoln initially called for only 4,000 men from Indiana, but more than 12,000 volunteered from the Hoosier State in less than a week and Morton offered 10,000 to the U.S. Army on April 15, 1861.[136] Hascall, for instance, raised a large contingent of volunteers from Elkhart County, but it was late in getting to Camp Morton in Indianapolis and had to be sent back home.[137] Individuals who were not picked in their hometown units also wandered into camp. Some men volunteered in the spirit of unionism. Others looked forward to adventure. Still others needed the money, and others "saw through the field of active military service the road to future success."[138]

Two major problems that Morton faced were the fact that there had been no regular militia in twenty-five years and a dearth of officers in the state. Only a handful of West Point graduates lived in Indiana, including

Goshen attorney Hascall. Other West Point alumni included Thomas A. Morris and Joseph J. Reynolds. Several Hoosiers had fought in the Mexican War, including Lew Wallace, whom Governor Morton appointed to the office of Adjutant General after Sumter.

Regimental commands were offered to men who performed recruiting duties in their hometowns. Morton also went after prominent Republicans around the state, many of whom, like Hascall and Wallace, had been Democrats only a decade before. Early in the war, in the spirit of unity that ruled in Indiana, Morton also rewarded Democrats with commands.[139] Commissions and advancement in the Indiana militia depended largely on Morton's approval. Yet, as time passed, companies began to elect their own officers.[140]

In the summer of 1861, Morton signed the Six Regiments Act. It established six regiments to form a brigade that would serve for three months. Hascall served as a captain and aide-de-camp under Brigadier General Thomas A. Morris. Some of those regiments had been organized and drilling on their own before the war began.[141] Most of the men in the original six regiments reenlisted for three years when their three months were up later in 1861. Overall, Indiana would organize fifty-three infantry regiments, three cavalry regiments, and twelve batteries of artillery in the first year of the war. Most regiments came from the same county, but some were based on nationality, such as the all-German Thirty-Second and the all-Irish Thirty-Fifth.[142]

Enlistments would begin to lag during the following winter. The war went on longer than expected, and the coldness of winter dampened the war spirit. The war news was marginally better in the spring of 1862, especially with victories on the western front. Sensing the end might be near and that it had enough troops to finish the job, the federal War Department stopped recruiting volunteers. Morton, of course, was so prowar that he just acted as if Washington had not stopped the recruiting process.[143] When the Lincoln administration realized the war was not going to end in the summer of 1861 as the military tide turned in favor of the Confederacy, Morton discovered a new state of affairs in Indiana: men did not want to enlist. Mostly, these were farmers who did not want to fight while it was time to plant, manage, and harvest their crops. The governor urged Lincoln to adopt a conscription policy.[144] Congress authorized Lincoln to start a preliminary draft on July 17, 1862, and the second most controversial government policy of the war was borne. Only emancipation would cause more controversy in Indiana. The development and maintenance of the draft would severely test civil liberties—and civil authority—in Indiana.

CHAPTER THREE

Legal, Theoretic Context of Freedom of the Press in Civil War Indiana

Milo Hascall's precise understanding of freedom of the press is not known for certain because he did not write anything down about either the First Amendment or the press clause in the Indiana Constitution. It can be inferred that he thought editors ought to act responsibly during the war. He did write a letter in the Goshen Republican newspaper attacking the "disloyal" course that the Goshen Democratic paper was taking early in the war.[1] Of course, that was the same Democratic paper his brother had owned in the 1840s and would again in the 1870s.

Clearly, though, Hascall's General Order No. 9 was in opposition to the general spirit of press freedom in both the state and federal constitutions. Yet it is also true that conceptualizations of freedom of the press had little development in the nineteenth century, especially in state and federal courts. That would come in the twentieth century with such cases as *Gitlow v. New York*, *Near v. Minnesota*, and *New York Times v. Sullivan*.[2] Still, even in a frontier state like Indiana, journalists generally understood freedom of the press in the libertarian sense, but neither the federal nor state constitutions offered guidance about constraints on press behavior in wartime.

Social, political, and economic conditions have a role to play in the relative degree of freedom of the press. For example, wartime conditions have generally meant a contraction of the area of freedom for the press, while peacetime has generally meant an expansion. Likewise, the interpretation of the courts, both state and federal, has had an effect on press freedom, as have political events. Because each state has its own press clause, there has never been one unchangeable and universal concept of press freedom in the United States.

Societal needs also have had a role in interpreting the degree of freedom of expression. A typical reading found an expansion of press freedom for the party in power and a reduction for the party out of power. This was particularly the case during the party press era of the nineteenth century, the period this study examines. Yet it was also the case during the Revolutionary War period. A level of hypocrisy existed in that Americans espoused civil rights such as freedom of speech and freedom of the press, but they opposed free expression by those loyal to the colonial governments.

This freedom of the press for majority-party journalists was a view held by journalists. Meanwhile, legal and historical perspectives about First Amendment rights are different. Constitutional scholars and journalism historians have not developed a consensus about what the framers understood about free expression, especially during a time of extreme political crisis such as a civil war. In large part, this is because the framers did not write down their views on the application of the principles in the First Amendment; no records exist of the debates on the amendment.[3] Ultimately, the adopted First Amendment is very concise and somewhat ambiguous, and its current understanding has developed through historical, social, political, and professional challenges to the understanding that posits a broad area of freedom of expression.

Still, it is true that freedom of the press in the United States comes out of tradition that feared a strong central government, and the general principle—the rule, not the exception—in the nation's history has been that newspaper printers, publishers, and editors have printed with minimal government restraints.[4] In large part, this protectivist stance originated because the United States was founded in an independence movement with a firm basis in freedom of thought, conscience, and expression, including the freedom of the press. That the leadership of the thirteen original colonies attacked the British monarchy with words, as well as arms, had no small role in the adoption of a strong free-press tradition in the nation's history. This led to the adoption of the Virginia Declaration of Rights free press clause when the Bill of Rights was added to the Constitution. From there, though, the First Amendment has undergone a voyage that has not always stayed the course of the revolutionary era.[5]

Instead, as the nation has developed and faced different political, social, and economic situations, freedom of the press has been interpreted in more than one fixed way. Moreover, the free-expression tradition of today includes a right for the people to be informed. Yet nowhere in Madison's early or final draft of the First Amendment does he mention this right. This quasi-right has evolved over time as a natural outgrowth of the freedom of religion, speech, press, assembly, and the right to utter public criticism. The free-press clause of the First Amendment may imply the public's right to be informed, but it is not stated explicitly. The right to know goes back to John Milton in the *Areopagitica*.[6]

BORROWING FROM THE BRITISH

The U.S. principle of freedom of the press derives from the British tradition of the common law, in which Sir William Blackstone held that the government could not exercise prior restraint but could punish after publication through seditious libel laws. The U.S. tradition of free expression, then, comes as a response to 300 years of press restrictions that included those seditious libel laws, as well as licensing and printer bonds.[7] One view of the First Amendment is that it repudiates the English common law and allows for greater freedom of expression than British citizens had in the eighteenth century.[8] In *The Federalist Papers*, Alexander Hamilton was skeptical about any definition of freedom of the press that did not "leave the utmost latitude for evasion." For Hamilton, freedom of the press was desirable, but any successful description in a constitution was impractical. He said it was dependent on public opinion, the spirit of the times, and the sentiment of the government.[9]

The American free press tradition started with the trial of the *New-York Weekly Journal* printer John Peter Zenger in 1735. This case, which resulted in jury nullification because the jury ignored the narrow instructions of the judge, helped establish a precedent that juries could return not guilty verdicts in seditious libel cases and that truth could be a defense, as opposed to the defense trying to distance itself from the actual publishing of offending words.[10] Legally, it did nothing to change seditious libel.[11] What it did, though, was change public opinion. Gradually, Americans came to view truthful public criticism of government, based on skepticism, as legitimate expression. Thus, a resistance to government prosecutions of seditious libel developed in pre-revolutionary English North America, and prior restraint became less widely accepted.[12] Americans came to believe, in the words of historian Leonard W. Levy, "intemperance in governing justified intemperance in expression" and that criticism of an arbitrary administrator, if true, is not criminal.[13]

The British colonial government did not stop trying to silence its critics. Contempt of the colonial legislative assembly replaced seditious libel as
the manner in which the government tried to silence wayward printers. First
Amendment scholar Don R. Pember wrote that American printers were incarcerated and fined "for publications previously considered seditious."[14] Yet
newspaper printers began to write what they pleased, setting the tone for
the next 270-odd years of American journalism. Overall, the area of press
freedom expanded, as did the diversity of ideas and thoughts on a variety of
subjects—from politics to religion to science. The American Revolution continued the pattern of expansive press freedom, and the failure of the Articles
of Confederation and the original Constitution to contain a list of civil rights,
including freedom of the press, was highly controversial and led directly to
the adoption of the Bill of Rights.

The reasons for free expression, including the freedom of the press, include the discovery of truth through sampling a multiplicity of ideas. Moreover, participation in democracy is enhanced by a free exchange of ideas and
the advancement of knowledge, while an open forum provides for a check on
abuse of power by government officials. The free flow of information allows
society to better diagnose, understand, and solve its problems, and, under
natural law, human beings tend to desire to express themselves without inhi-
bitions because it leads to self-fulfillment.[15]

James Madison, the Virginia statesman, was a primary architect of
the First Amendment. Madison, a firm believer in freedom of religion and a
states' rights advocate who wanted a limited central government, was skeptical about a national bill of rights because he thought the state constitutions
had sovereignty and because he feared that changing the instrument would
become too easy and too routine.[16] Other framers said many natural or inherent rights existed and that it would be inconsistent to list some and not
others.[17] Yet Madison changed his mind for political reasons and wanted to
see the inclusion of the amendments to the Constitution.[18] He wanted to see
an enumeration of acknowledged principles because he feared that a powerful
legislature might enact laws that would tightly control the press.[19]

Madison's 1789 work on a select committee in the United States House of
Representatives centered on the careful inspection of free-expression clauses
in the various state constitutions. Madison, who emphasized freedom of conscience and the free practice of religion, pushed through an amendment that
would become the federal free-expression standard. The first draft stated: "No
state should infringe the right of trial by jury in criminal cases, nor the right
of conscience, nor the freedom of speech or of the press."[20] Madison felt this

amendment was the most important one, though at the time it was actually the fourteenth, not the first. However, the Senate rejected it because it gave the states the power to prohibit or not prohibit. The language was rewritten, resulting in the existing First Amendment, and a total of twelve amendments were sent to President George Washington in September of 1789. Ten of those were ratified on December 15, 1791.

THE SEDITION ACT

The first major challenge to the First Amendment came less than a decade later in the form of the Sedition Act. In 1798, President John Adams, a Federalist, pushed this law through Congress. The Sedition Act, which came out of a partisan debate, made it illegal to print false, scandalous, and malicious words about the president, Congress, or the federal government, exempting only the office of the vice president, which was held by Republican Thomas Jefferson.

Under the Sedition Act, the federal government convicted fourteen editors, all Republicans, and three Republican newspapers faced suspension.[21] Jefferson wrote: "The object of that [act] is the suppression of the Whig [Republican] press."[22] The Federalists thought the Constitution gave Congress the power to pass seditious libel laws and insisted on the Blackstonian interpretation of freedom of the press.[23] Scholar Jeffery A. Smith noted that the government arrested journalists for public statements of opinion, which are impossible to prove as being either true or false. One journalist received a fine and nine-month jail sentence for a pro-Jeffersonian election pamphlet that "accused the president of being a 'professional aristocrat' and 'hoary headed incendiary' who wanted to embroil the country in a war with France. Realizing that it would not be used against them, Federalist journalists had called for the statute and urged its use against the 'Gallic' competitors."[24] The lone Federalist skeptic in the Sedition Act debate was John Marshall, who thought it was intended to "create, unnecessarily, discontents and jealousies."[25] Much the same partisan arguing would take place in Indiana in 1863, with Republicans supporting suppression and Democrats invoking a libertarian view of freedom of the press.

Jefferson won the presidency in 1800, and he released all jailed under the Sedition Act and let the bill die during his term.[26] Madison and Jefferson vigorously denounced the Sedition Act, claiming that the First Amendment protects freedom of expression by congressional restraint and denies the federal government from being able to try individuals for sedition. Under the Virginia Report of 1799–1800, the Virginia General Assembly adopted

Madison's interpretations, and Jefferson's opinions were published in the Kentucky Resolutions of 1798.[27] Jefferson centered his arguments on the rule of reason, the sovereignty of the people over the government, and the right of the people to unrestricted discussion in a democracy.[28]

Jefferson and Madison leaned toward a libertarian view of freedom of expression. Libertarians see freedom of expression in terms of principle. They are not concerned with pragmatism or compromise but see the right to expression as a natural inclination and that no other human being or group of human beings should prevent that person from thinking, saying, or writing what he pleases. The libertarian is an absolutist. That is, in his view, there are no limits on free expression.

In examining the issue in the colonial and revolutionary periods, Levy came to the conclusion that there was no purely libertarian view of freedom of expression during the constitution-framing years and reasoned that the Sedition Act was the turning point in the history of the First Amendment. Levy was of the opinion that seditious libel under the common law did not disappear with the American Revolution and Constitution. He also held that the framers formed no consensus about the nature of expression. However, the Republican response to the Sedition Act was libertarian in nature, and while it was a partisan view, it "launched the rapid emergence of the new libertarianism in America."[29] Levy showed that legal and journalistic interpretations of freedom of the press have developed over time. With the exception of Madison, every other major figure in the early stages of the nation's history was inconsistent in his understanding of free expression.[30] Madison made libertarian defenses of freedom of the press from the time of his work on the select committee until he was president.

FREEDOM OF THE PRESS IN THE NINETEENTH CENTURY

Generally, there was little legal action on the First Amendment front during the nineteenth century. When the Civil War came, the First Amendment had faced challenges during the War of 1812 and Mexican War, and on the state level with the anti-abolitionist laws of Southern states. Yet it had rarely been interpreted in the courts, especially on the federal level.[31] Between 1791 and 1889, the U.S. Supreme Court heard only twelve cases involving the First Amendment. Legal scholar Michael Gibson wrote: "The relative silence of the court regarding freedom of expression during the first three-quarters of the nineteenth century reflects that the federal government was not attempting to limit the rights of its citizens."[32]

The major pre-Civil War incidents in which the press clause of the First Amendment was tested came during the War of 1812 and the Mexican War. Both cases involved military officers suppressing civilian newspapers.

At least four Federalist papers were attacked during the War of 1812. General Andrew Jackson declared martial law in New Orleans and censored a Federalist paper in that city. The paper's editor published a letter critical of Jackson for not lifting martial law once the Treaty of Ghent had been signed. Judge Dominick Hall tried to free the editor with a writ of habeas corpus, but Jackson had Hall banished from New Orleans. Once formal word of the treaty reached Jackson, the judge returned to New Orleans and promptly fined the general $1,000 for contempt of court. Madison, by then the president, asked Jackson to report on the matter. Jackson claimed military necessity required him to act against the press. The president did not punish his military officer, but he did say that Jackson acted unconstitutionally and would have to answer to the Constitution.[33]

It was not clear if the Articles of War applied to civilians, nor was it clear who had the authority to impose martial law. Jackson said he had to submit to the law and paid the fine. Congress would later refund Jackson, but it never cleared his name in the event. Jackson showed an indifference to civil rights when they got in the way of military objectives. He defended himself by saying that unfettered free speech was incompatible with military discipline, and that freedom of the press "is more dangerous when it is made the vehicle of conveying intelligence to the Enemy or exciting to mutiny among the soldiery."[34] In Jackson's view, rights could be suspended in the short term to ensure "the permanent preservation of constitutional Rights, & that there could be no question whether it was better to depart, for a moment from the exercise of our dearest privileges, or have them wrested from us forever."[35]

Madison said no words in the Constitution vindicated Jackson's actions. Although Madison was not moved by Jackson's interpretation of things, later presidents would be. In many ways, this temporary suspension of rights for their long-term preservation became the basis for the Lincoln-Republican-Union Army defense of what happened in Indiana in the spring of 1863. It was the basis for Lincoln's argument in the Corning Letter that responded to New York Democrats who opposed the Vallandigham conviction. It is also ironic in that it came from one of the ideological giants of the Democrats, Jackson, who was in many ways the grandfather of American pragmatism and was one of the two gods of Hoosier Democrats at mid-century.

Jackson's heavy-handedness did not end with the War of 1812. He would later try to enact a law that would stop the mailing of antislavery publications to the South. Congress did not buy it. Individual Southern states then passed their own laws. Some Southern postal carriers decided not to deliver abolitionist mail on their own to avoid mob action. This created a tension because Washington was telling the postmasters to deliver the mail since its delivery conformed to the law of the land.

Jackson's tendency to control the press contrasted with Madison's hands-off approach. For his part, Madison did not claim an executive prerogative to silence dissident journalists during the War of 1812, one of the few times in U.S. history when the country has been invaded. Madison resisted the urge to suppress, and this was a sign that at least one of the founding fathers preferred libertarian principles to security-first rationales for martial law and suppression of the press.

It is not clear if martial law is constitutional—nor is it clear that the United States can declare it in invaded countries. War is rather murky on constitutional issues. Smith observed: "The publications that survived became semiofficial voices of the military, printing general orders and poetry submitted by soldiers."[36] However, attacks by Whig editors back in the United States were not suppressed. Yet, Smith continued, the use of the military in a summary fashion against journalists in remote parts of the country was relative safe policy. "However, inasmuch as military justice exists to retain military discipline and martial law is not authorized by any specific provision of the Constitution, commanders did not have definite authority for their actions against civilians, even if they thought criticism was treasonous," Smith observed.[37]

POLK AND THE PRESS

During the Mexican-American War, President James K. Polk, a Democrat, supported the suppression of both American and Mexican newspapers in the war zone. According to historian James McPherson, Manifest Destiny tended to be more attractive to Democrats because they wanted space and wanted it quickly. Republicans wanted to be patient and were willing to take more time. Historians tend to agree that Polk and the Democrats viewed expansionism partly as a way to increase the number of slave states. Polk wanted to expand U.S. territory, and he countered criticism of his war and war policy by saying his critics were aiding and abetting the enemy. In war zones, U.S. military officers used martial law to suspend civil liberties, including freedom of the press. Ten newspapers, five American and five Mexican, were suppressed by officers in the field.[38] Polk's party organ in Washington, D.C., the *Union*, said newspapers in the war zone critical of the administration were treasonous.[39] The leading Whig paper said leadership ought to respect freedom of the press and be able to withstand intensive public criticism.[40]

Newspapers printed critical correspondence from soldiers. General Zachary Taylor, a Whig, criticized the war in a personal letter that was leaked to the press, and Polk complained publication of the letter gave aid to the enemy because it contained sensitive information.[41] Taylor replied that the letter was not meant for publication, and it contained nothing of value for the enemy—other than the appearance that a key general opposed the degree of war. He added that other soldiers and politicians had also expressed misgivings about the war. Secretary of War William Marcy brought up Paragraph Sixty-Five of Army regulations: No letter by servicemen should appear in public for at least a month after the termination of a campaign. The Whig congressmen pointed out that uncritical correspondence from soldiers routinely appeared in newspapers like the *Union*, and the thirty-day rule had been ignored in those pro-war or neutral cases.

A pattern developed in which critical newspapers were shut down, censored, or faced economic pressure or the threat of violence, while the surviving papers became the semiofficial voices of the military.[42] General Ambrose E. Burnside, who would play prominently in the press suppression of Democratic newspapers in the Midwest in 1863, similarly targeted "disloyal" papers while having a pro-Union paper established when he conquered eastern North Carolina in 1862. The use of military action against the opposition party's press far from Washington and New York was much more palatable than jailing the editors of the nation's most prominent and highest circulated newspapers.

Now two precedents existed for the use of martial law to silence the wayward press during wartime. Madison inveighed against Jackson, but did not punish him. Later, the Democrats and Whigs avoided a direct look at civil rights violations in the Mexican War because the president was of one party and the key generals who instituted martial law were of the other party. Polk's single-minded pursuit of the expansionist war precluded criticism from the Whig editors.

Another test was the antiabolitionist laws in the South from roughly 1830 to 1850. More than thirty abolitionist newspapers were started in the North during this twenty-year span. Lawmakers in the South responded to abolitionist diatribes by enacting laws making it illegal to criticize slavery—because, they claimed, abolitionist sentiment would incite slave riots.[43]

These state laws criminalized the publishing and possession of abolitionist newspapers. The most severe penalty was death, on second offense. Southern states attempted to get extradition of wayward editors from Northern states. They also attempted to suppress the mail. The former never worked, and the latter worked only occasionally. As president, Jackson himself denounced the mailing of incendiary antiabolitionist publications to the South.[44]

Wartime continued to be the time when restraints on the press would be a major issue. During the Civil War, President Lincoln, his administration, and the military would undertake a concerted, albeit a fragmented, campaign to control the press, especially Democratic newspapers. Lincoln also took control of the telegraph wires, which were owned by a private company, and his administration stopped the delivery via the mails of certain anti-war, anti-Republican publications.[45]

After the Civil War, the frequency of suppression decreased. However, two cases merit attention. The first involved Vicksburg, Mississippi, *Times* editor William H. McCardle, who was arrested and incarcerated in 1867 for criticizing federal officials and telling citizens to abstain from voting. Maintaining his arrest violated his right to freedom of the press, the Mississippi editor fought his case, which advanced to a habeas corpus hearing by the U.S. Supreme Court. However, Congress forced the Court to dismiss the case on jurisdictional grounds. In 1868, Congress actually repealed the Habeas Corpus Act of 1867, the very law that McCardle's attorney had cited to make a claim for a Supreme Court hearing. This repealed act denied the Court jurisdiction retroactively, even though the justices had already heard the facts in the case.[46]

Thirty years later, in Wilmington, North Carolina, a mob of white citizens razed the black-owned *Daily Record* newspaper, in part because editor Alexander Manly wrote a commentary that said not all interracial sex is rape. Manly was responding to a speech in support of lynching. The destruction of the *Daily Record* was part of a state-sponsored terrorist campaign—whose leadership included the editor of the state's most powerful paper, the Raleigh *News & Observer*—to limit the political and economic power of African American citizens and usher in an era of segregation. Blacks were so intimidated by mob rule that they sat out the election in November of 1898, sending a fusion party of Republicans and Populists packing and returning Democrats to power in eastern North Carolina.[47]

In the twentieth century, the government tried various approaches to control the press in wartime. In World War I, Congress passed and President Woodrow Wilson signed sedition and espionage acts. The former gave the president the power to create a censorship board and the Committee on Public Information, a propaganda organization. The latter gave the postmaster general the authority to exclude seditious materials from the mails. During World War II, President Franklin Delano Roosevelt created an office of censorship and another propaganda department. After graphic coverage of the war in Vietnam—in which nightly television broadcasts from the front lines displayed the savage nature of war—the executive branch decided to be less open, and access to the military and the theaters of operation diminished in the Gulf War and the current war in Iraq. This trend shows that even without a party press, the federal government still has the regulatory itch in times of war, but it also shows that the government had to develop more sophisticated ways to impose press constraints in a highly developed democratic society. This state of affairs contrasted to the relative ease with which Hascall implemented rather Draconian constraints in 1863 Indiana.

Indeed, the nature of the press changed dramatically after the Civil War. During the next 140-odd years, U.S. newspapers became less partisan-interpretive and more commercial-informative. The newspapermen of the Civil War era were working within a party format, especially away from the major Eastern urban areas. In Indiana, almost every newspaper had a political affiliation, and with the single exception of the Indianapolis *Journal*, none had a sophisticated commercial orientation yet.

THE CONSTITUTION AND THE PRESS

Legally, the means for interpreting the legitimacy of suppressing the press in the North—including Indiana—came from three specific sections of the U.S. Constitution. First, the First Amendment states that Congress "shall make no law respecting an establishment of religion" and guarantees the freedom of religion, speech, press, peaceable assembly, and the right "to petition the Government for a redress of grievances." These words of the amendment, written by Madison and based in part on ideas about civil liberties he shared with Jefferson, are bolstered by centuries of libertarian thought. The values that free expression advance include attaining self-fulfillment, practicing self-government, pursuing freedom of thought, checking the misuse of power, and resolving conflict.[48] However, there is nothing in the First Amendment about executive control of expression. Although Congress could make no law, the president might be free to fashion press constraints if conditions warranted such action. Yet Indiana Congressman Daniel W. Voorhees argued frequently that the Constitution gave the president no power over the press. Voorhees declared: "If the Congress of the United States cannot, under the Constitution,

pass any law interfering with the freedom of speech [or the press], can anybody else do it? No."[49]

The limits imposed on free expression by Lincoln, his administration,
and his military officers during the war came from Article I, Section 9 and
Article III, Section 3 of the Constitution. Invoking these two sections of the
Constitution directly challenged the free expression tradition not only on the
federal but also on the state level. For example, the constitution of Pennsylvania states: "The printing presses shall be free to every person who undertakes
to examine proceedings of the legislature or any branch of government, and
no law shall ever be made to restrain the right thereof."[50] The free expression
tradition represented in this state constitution makes no mention of a suspension of free expression at times of war. Meanwhile, Article I, Section 9 touches
on the privileges of those charged with federal crimes: "The Privilege of the
Writ of Habeas Corpus shall not be suspended, unless in Cases of Rebellion
or Invasion the public safety may require it."

Lincoln believed this section gave him the power to imprison citizens
of the nation without having to tell them why they were being arrested. The
president did not seem to think he needed approval from Congress to arrest
and confine thousands of dissenters.[51] Congress did pass its own Habeas Corpus Act on March 3, 1863, but it did not say whether previous suspensions by
the president were legal.[52] During the spring of 1863, Burnside and Hascall
used this justification for suspending the writ to bolster their ploy to suppress
free expression in the Midwest.

This interpretation of executive war powers would receive two major
legal challenges. Former Ohio Congressman Clement Laird Vallandigham,
arrested by Burnside on May 5, 1863, mounted one of the challenges and the
other came from a Hoosier named Lambdin P. Milligan. In the Vallandigham
case, the Supreme Court would rule in favor of the Lincoln government, upholding the legality of military commissions in the Northern states during
the war. In 1864, the court rebuffed the plea of Vallandigham's attorney that
a civilian court should have tried the Democrat. According to legal scholar
James G. Randall, Vallandigham's attorney argued: "The charge on which the
prisoner was tried was unknown to the law ... and the sentence was in excess
of jurisdiction."[53] A lower court judge had ruled that the military commissions that tried citizens such as Vallandigham were necessitated by the war
situation.[54] The Supreme Court did not say exactly the same thing. In fact, it
seemed to duck the whole issue by refusing to review the military commission that tried and convicted Vallandigham. The Supreme Court said it did

not have jurisdiction over a military court, and, thus, the decision seemed to justify the lower court judge's view that the military commissions in the Civil War were legal.[55] That Congress was not allowed to review, debate, and vote on such a concept seems to have been missed by not only the Lincoln administration and the wartime Congress, but also by Civil War legal scholars.

Two years later, in *Ex Parte Milligan*, the Supreme Court reversed itself on this issue. A member of two pro-South secret societies, Milligan helped Confederate prisoners gain their release and marched with them into Kentucky and Missouri to return to fighting the Union.[56] A resident of Huntington, Indiana, Milligan had been convicted of treason by a military commission and received a capital sentence. A military commission sentenced Milligan to be hanged on May 19, 1865, which would come after the end of the war. Milligan appealed to the Supreme Court for a writ of habeas corpus and won. The court announced, "If there was a law to justify this military trial, it is not our province to interfere; if there was not it is our duty to declare the nullity of the whole proceedings."[57] The decision added that the Constitution does not legitimize martial law for the threat of invasion. Rather, there has to be an actual invasion. At the time of Milligan, the South had not invaded Indiana, although John Morgan had invaded Indiana and Ohio in the summer of 1863. In effect, the court ruled that the war did not suspend the Constitution and the Bill of Rights. Justice David Davis wrote, "The Constitution of the United States is a law for rulers and people, equally in war and peace, at all times, and under all circumstances."[58]

Randall concluded that Lincoln's war powers were extensive and if overused, they offered the "opportunity for dictatorship."[59] However, Randall did not think Lincoln went too far. Congress appeared to check some of Lincoln's power by requiring prisoners to be indicted in civilian courts, but this was impractical and universally ignored. Randall maintained that the improper use of military commissions in areas not under invasion was exceptional, and that Lincoln was not as disposed as military officers like Burnside to overuse constraints on the press. Randall wrote that in most cases all that occurred was detention, and he called that chapter in U.S. legal history "unfortunate."[60] Randall concluded that Lincoln and his underlings modestly suppressed the Democrats and their editors.

Mark E. Neely, whose Pulitzer Prize-winning *The Fate of Liberty* confirmed Randall's study, maintained Lincoln too broadly defined dangerous speech. Yet Neely said Lincoln and his generals really did not chill the press to an unacceptable degree.[61] Historian Paul Finkelman, while agreeing with both

Randall and Neely that most civil liberties arrests were trivial, remarked that "political arrests occurred, and their significance may be greater than Neely acknowledges, especially when it comes to the press."[62] Finkelman conceded that most arrests were for security reasons, but some were political and a few were intended to "eliminate the political opposition."[63]

Measuring the degree of civil liberties suppression is difficult. F. C. Ainsworth did an exhaustive study of the National Archives that revealed 13,535 arrests for political reasons from February 1862 until April 1865. Neely believes this number has to be exaggerated, or the definition of a political prisoner was broad. Therefore, Neely maintained, the high number of Northern political prisoners was not unreasonable.[64] That is, in Neely's view, Lincoln and his military officers were right to arrest dissidents. However, it is not clear why the number might have been exaggerated or how the term political prisoner was misconstrued. Rather, the question is what degree of squelching dissent in a democracy is reasonable. Neely pointed to Lincoln's use of the Andrew Jackson precedent to justify his suspension of habeas corpus. Lincoln said Jackson's declaration of martial law in New Orleans and defiance of habeas corpus in 1815 did not mean "the permanent right of the people to public discussion, the liberty of free speech and the press" were abridged.[65]

Another legal issue that arose was the tendency of criticism to disaffect the citizens of the Northern states. Republican papers like the Cincinnati *Commercial* felt criticism of the Lincoln government had a paralyzing effect on the public. The *Commercial* editor said: "All denunciation of the President, his measures and his motives, in so far as it has any effect at all, being to destroy public confidence in the Government and to disaffect the people, is to that extent, ... fatal in its tendencies."[66]

Criticism of the government is, to a certain extent, destabilizing. Such is the contentious nature of democracy. Yet the Republican papers did have a point—civil war is an exceptional case. Furthermore, another key political question is whether the existence of the government has primacy over the form of government. Do traditions, habits, and rights matter more than the stability of the government? Vallandigham, for example, thought that he was being loyal to the principles of self-government, and he thought that was more important than being loyal to the principals of government.

The third relevant section of the Constitution concerns the definition of treason. Article III, Section 3 states: "Treason against the United States, shall consist in levying War against them, or in adhering to their Enemies, giving them Aid and Comfort."[67] This portion is particularly important because Lincoln and his military leaders decided to interpret political speech and political commentary in newspapers that did not support the war effort as being tanta-mount to giving aid and comfort to the enemy. Furthermore, Burnside would use the two witnesses' clause to ensnare Vallandigham.

Harold Nelson, a First Amendment scholar, observed that the nature of the relationship between the government and those who were most concerned about free expression reached a major pass during the Civil War—that by the end of the war the press had learned that total war meant compromising on some democratic forms, including freedom of the press. Meanwhile, the government came to realize "that a people tutored in access to news needed information when war came if its maximum support was to be elicited."[68] The political leaders of the party in power had to balance the expectation for a nearly unlimited flow of information with the need for security. Support for a war effort is a two-way street; the government needs the support of its citi-zens, but citizens need an understanding of events, administration, and poli-cies to make informed democratic choices.

THE HYPOTHESES OF SIEBERT AND STEVENS

Fredrick Seaton Siebert, in his study of civil war and free expression in the English Civil War, developed the hypothesis that "the area of freedom con-tracts and the enforcement of restraints increases as the stresses on the sta-bility of the government and of the structure of society increases." Similarly, Siebert held that "the extent of government control of the press depends on the nature of the relationship of the government to those subject to the gov-ernment."[69]

Another theoretical framework to consider is that of John D. Stevens, who maintained that the more heterogeneous a population the greater the freedom of expression it will tolerate, even in a time of war.[70] Because Indiana was more homogenous in its population than, say, New York, Pennsylvania, or Massachusetts, it was easier to suppress dissenters such as the Hoosier State's Democratic editors. It is worth noting that Lincoln's administration did far less in trying to check the fulminations of newspapers in New York, by far the North's most heterogeneously populated city, than it did in the more homog-enously populated Midwest. Yet politically, like the nation, Indiana was frag-mented, and radical changes had been taking place since the Mexican War. Socially, although immigration was taking place, especially from Germans and Irish, emigration from the state was happening too. The state was essen-tially divided into southern, central, and northern thirds. Southern Hoosiers were descendants of men and women who had traveled from North Carolina, Virginia, Tennessee, and Kentucky. Hoosiers in the central part of the state had settled from the southern part of the state, while the northern third was inhabited by settlers from New York, Pennsylvania, and Ohio, as well as the German and Irish immigrants.

Newspapers themselves mirrored the heterogeneity of the state. There were Republican, Democratic, People's Party, Whig, Free Soil, and Union papers. Most newspapers were written in English, but a number were written in German. Denominational papers existed too, with Quaker and Methodist papers being the most conspicuous. Thus, Indiana was relatively heterogeneous, and this explains, in part, why Hascall's period of suppression was short—and why Morton did not choose to come down hard on the Democratic press before or after Hascall's six weeks in office in Indianapolis. Of course, Morton did not have to further agitate the Democrats with official state action because soldiers and veterans did the work for him.

In the election of 1860, Republicans won because they had majorities in most of the counties in the northern two-thirds of the state. Support for the Democrats was stronger in the southern third of the state.[71] Editors in counties where Southern descendants were more numerous, mainly in the southern third of the state, saw less suppression and intimidation than the counties where the descendants were from New England, New York, and Pennsylvania. Democratic editors had greater immunity from Hascall where Southern descendants with pro-Democratic sentiments were present.

Indiana did have a heterogeneous press. Every town had at least two newspapers, and most had more than two. Few publishers and editors were in the business to make lots of money. Because politics mattered most to them, their unfettered expression of those ideas was a central principle—and one in keeping with the federal free-press clause. Still, the state abuse clause left a gray area that enabled Hascall to engender support from the Republican newspaper editors who, emboldened by the support of both the state and federal executive branches, strongly upheld the silencing of Democratic editors. But Indiana's press was not varied in the sense that it was overwhelmingly political. This, along with the relatively frontier nature of much of its society, provided fertile ground for intimidation of the minority press.

From the legal perspective, Hascall's intimidation of the Hoosier Democratic editors would mark one of the last times in U.S. history when editors representing one political party in a single state would be officially suppressed by military leaders. In the future, the control over the press during wartime would come in other ways. After the Supreme Court ruled against the suspension of habeas corpus in 1866, the executive branch would learn to leave editors alone and put more emphasis on controlling the flow of information and framing wars for mass audiences using propaganda techniques. Major free expression cases—*Schenck v. U.S.* and *Abrams v. U.S.*—emerged just after World War I after the passing of the Espionage Act of 1917 and the Sedition Act of 1918, but none involved press suppression.[72] There was no real press suppression in World War II as the overwhelming majority of newspapers in the U.S. were supportive of the war effort, in large part because President Franklin D. Roosevelt generally supported freedom of the press and called the free flow of information "the very bloodstream of our nation."[73]

While Hascall was trying to coerce the Democratic editors of Indiana to watch their language, Burnside had Vallandigham tried by the military commission. Burnside charged Vallandigham with publicly expressing sympathies for the rebellion, "declaring disloyal sentiments and opinions, with the object and purpose of weakening the power of the Government in its effort to suppress an unlawful rebellion."[74] Although no copy of the speech is extant, Vallandigham allegedly said Lincoln had a plan to end the war the day before Fredericksburg. Vallandigham, who supposedly spat on a copy of General Order No. 38, also said that Lincoln was about to set up district governments all over the country.[75] At the trial, the verbose Burnside introduced a letter from Richmond proposing that Southern senators return to Congress. The two plainclothesmen then testified against him. Congressman S. S. Cox of Ohio was the only witness that the Vallandigham team called. After three hours of deliberations, the commission found the ex-congressman guilty. Vallandigham applied for a writ of habeas corpus, but Judge Humphrey H. Leavitt, a Democrat, denied it.[76] The commission sentenced Vallandigham to a prison in Boston for the duration of the war, but Lincoln commuted it to exile to the South. Vallandigham was released in Murfreesboro, Tennessee, eventually boarded a blockade runner to Bermuda, and went on to Canada. He would run for governor of Ohio in the fall of 1863 and lose in a landslide to Republican newspaper editor John Brough. Vallandigham would also show up at the 1864 Democratic Convention in Chicago.

INDIANA'S RESPONSIBILITY-FOR-ABUSE CLAUSE

On the state level, freedom of the press is guaranteed, but the Indiana Constitution, like several other state constitutions, includes a responsibility clause: "That the printing presses shall be free to every person who undertakes to examine the proceedings of the Legislature, or any branch of Government; and no law shall ever be made to restrain the right thereof. The free communication of thoughts, and opinions, is one of the invaluable rights of man; and every Citizen may freely speak, write, and print on any subject, being responsible for the abuse of that liberty."[77]

Indiana, therefore, was one of several states that did not have an absolutist-libertarian construction of freedom of expression. The Hoosier Constitution did not specify what the "responsibility for the abuse of that liberty" meant. It is a verbatim borrowing of the wording in the New York Constitution.[78] Thus, an interpretation of what the responsibility clause implied would be subject to interpretation.

However, the Indiana courts did not interpret the responsibility clause in the nineteenth century. Of course, it is no surprise such abstract arguments were not made during the Civil War, when the Union's survival was at stake and the resources of the state were directed toward fighting the war and defending the state. As Margaret A. Blanchard observed, the responsibility-for-abuse clause in several states showed that more and more state governments had come to the conclusion that freedom of the press and freedom of speech "had to be limited by requiring the responsible exercise of the rights promised."[79] It is important to remember that Hascall came from New York, and the New York Constitution's press clause well could have been his understanding of freedom of the press, and that what happened in Indiana in the spring of 1863, in the brigadier general's judgment, represented the misuse of freedom of the press by some Democratic editors in the state. Clearly, though, the federal constitution's guarantee that Congress cannot abridge the freedom of the press would have to be interpreted within these state constitutions that called for responsibility of the right. That would not occur until World War I, so Lincoln, Burnside, and Hascall had no guidance on the subject.

During the press crisis in Indiana in the spring of 1863, no Republican editors made direct reference to the "responsibility-for-abuse" clause in the Indiana State Constitution as they defended Hascall and attacked the Democratic editors. This was a situation where abuse could be debated, but perhaps the Republican editors felt this was a federal issue, and therefore the First Amendment superseded Article I, Section 9 of the Indiana Constitution. For the Republican editors of Indiana, loyalty was more the issue than abuse of liberty.

Thus, a paradox exists in the U.S. version of freedom of the press. The vaguely worded U.S. Constitution offers no limits on free expression. It says that Congress—though not the president or the courts—cannot abridge the five freedoms guaranteed by the First Amendment. Yet some state constitutions, including the one adopted by Indiana, stated there is a limit to free expression, and that limit is being responsible for the abuse of expression, though no branch of the state government could make laws restraining expression. The suggestion is that a citizen must self-censor himself, must know when they should speak publicly and when they should be silent. Yet the Indiana Constitution does not specify what abuse really means and does not establish how an individual can self-enforce this responsibility.

Alexander Meiklejohn, in his twentieth-century exegesis of freedom of expression, came to the conclusion that U.S. citizens do have responsibilities, and those include freely participating in self-government—which the government cannot regulate. Meiklejohn also said that government can regulate freedom of expression in that it can determine how citizens peaceably communicate in an assembly, or it can determine what community standards it will allow to be proscribed. However, Meiklejohn said one type of speech cannot be restrained: communication that is related to the democratic process—meaning any spoken or written words that ultimately have an effect on elections, including words that question the nature of the Constitution or government policy during a war. In his estimation, the government serves the interests of the citizens, and political speech is an expression of the will of those citizens. Thus, political speech is inviolate.[80] In his view, Burnside and Hascall, working for the federal government, would have had the right to make sure that all voices that wanted a public could be heard and that no voice could drown out another. Yet they had no given power to silence any political speech, even those that could be construed as antiwar or pro-Confederacy. In Meiklejohn's view, Indiana's Democratic editors had the right to express themselves on the actions and policies of the Lincoln administration, on judicial interpretations, and on any laws made by Congress.[81] Thus, Meiklejohn condemns arbitrary use of power over the press by any branch of government. He is saying the First Amendment has an absolutist construction that prevents conditional abridgement as occurred in Civil War Indiana.

SIEBERT ON GOVERNMENT-PRESS RELATIONS DURING WAR

Siebert, a scholar at the University of Illinois in the twentieth century, undertook an exhaustive study of press freedom in England from the time the first book was published there until the time of the American Revolution. Siebert's observation was that government control over the press declined over time. The University of Illinois scholar examined three primary facets of government control: (1) the nature of control, (2) the degree of enforcement, and (3) the degree of compliance. Siebert concluded that while government control declined as England developed, that control waxed and waned, depending on political conditions. Furthermore, the scholar showed that it is the nature of government to exercise a certain level of control—to promote order and stability—over the press, in much the same way that the government seeks a level of control over other elements of society.[82] Likewise, government attempts to regulate any publication that undermines "the basic structure of society."[83] Siebert holds a consensus develops in society—by the majority in a democracy—that a certain level of control is desirable, and that no control of expression would lead to chaos. The question is what form and what degree of control, and then how well does the government enforce the limits and to what extent does a citizen comply with them.

Siebert posited two hypotheses about the nature of government control over the press: (1) the extent of control depends on the relationship between the government and the governed; and (2) the area of freedom decreases, and enforcement of restraints expands as the stresses on the structure of society and the stability of government increase.[84] A more secure government has less need to develop restraints on the press. Conversely, an insecure government is more likely to develop restraints. Likewise, the "more direct the accountability of the governors to the masses, the greater the freedom of the press."[85] The area of freedom of the press tends to expand in democratic societies, but even a democratic government will contract that freedom during times of extreme political crises, especially during wartime.

During the Civil War in Indiana, there was only one occasion in which official contraction of press freedom took place, and that was in the spring of 1863 under Milo Smith Hascall's General Order No. 9.[86] Hascall's order was a case of official suppression. In announcing General Order No. 9 to the public on April 25, 1863, Hascall noted that extreme measures were necessary because he claimed he had evidence of agitation by covert societies in Indiana.[87] The brigadier general believed that Indiana society was in grave political danger and feared an uprising in the state. Yet there was little evidence that pro-Democratic secret societies had the wherewithal to start a rebellion. Indiana was virtually a dictatorship by the spring of 1863, under Governor Oliver P. Morton. Press freedom in the Hoosier State would have been expected to contract under Siebert's hypothesis. It did for the six weeks that Hascall, an officer of the federal government, was in power as the military commander of the state. However, it did not contract because Morton shut down the majority-Democratic legislature when it tried to pass propeace resolutions.

Although he wanted aggressive action against dissent, Morton never thought Hascall had jurisdiction. So the governor did not openly support what the Goshen attorney was doing. Yet he did not stand in the way either, though he clearly wanted Hascall removed from office.[88] Morton wanted to keep the Democrats under control, but he wanted to do it himself, in his own way, with his men. He wanted no part of Burnside and Hascall's meddling in his state.

There is no way to know if and how Morton would have come down on the Democratic editors, though he often complained about their treasonous words. Once Hascall stirred up the hornets' nest, no discreet political leader would go the suppression route again. Yet Morton demanded loyalty of Democrats all over the state. He looked to the Kentucky and Maryland paradigms, where "military force was systematically employed to suppress legitimate political opposition and to insure the election of supporters of the administration."[89] General Jerry T. Boyle dispersed a Democratic convention in Frankfurt, Kentucky, on February 18, 1863. In effect, Hascall would do the same thing at a Democratic mass meeting in Indianapolis in May of 1863, at the height of his bitter war with the opposition press in the state.

There was a legal case that occurred just before Hascall took office in Indiana that had a bearing on press suppression in the Hoosier State. Pennsylvania Supreme Court Chief Justice Walter Hoge Lowrie made a strong and lasting case for freedom of the press in wartime when he had ruled in February 1863 that a district attorney and marshal who seized the West Chester *Jeffersonian* acted illegally. Lowrie absolved President Lincoln of any role in a conspiracy to squelch the Democratic newspaper in August of 1862, a key claim of editor John Hodgson. Still, Lowrie called the district attorney and the marshal "mere trespassers" and upheld freedom of the press for Hodgson, who was every bit as antiadministration as the Democratic editors in Indiana.[90]

FREEDOM OF THE PRESS IN A DEMOCRACY

Another aspect of the contraction of the area of freedom during times when the government feels insecure is the nature of the government. That is, in a democracy, freedom of the press comes to mean unfettered freedom for the majority and restraints for the minority. This tends to get ratcheted up during war, and that is what happened in Indiana as Republican editors screamed to Hascall that they knew of Democratic editors who were "endeavoring to bring the war policy of the government into disrepute." These Republican editors praised Hascall and wanted to see him do more to "treasonous" and "disloyal" Democratic editors. Suppression was not only legal but a necessary war measure to keep Democrats from appealing to covert elements that wanted to drive a wedge between the Northeast and Midwest.

The Republican editors were not concerned with the First Amendment rights of their Democratic brethren. Historian G. R. Tredway, who has written extensively about the Democrats of Civil War Indiana, reasoned that the Republican editors were concerned only with partisan politics: "To Republicans any manifestation of discontent with their conduct of state and national affairs could only be treason."[91] Of course, as Tredway noted, Democrats "protested mightily against the abridgement of a free press" and connected it to the Lincoln administration's overall suppression of civil rights. Democratic editors told their readers to retaliate, but few if any Republican papers faced violence from Democrats.[92] Most incidents of intimidation of Republican editors in Indiana came from Union soldiers. This lack of retaliation by Democrats suggests that there was a chilling effect in Civil War Indiana, and that Hascall's policy was effective, even if he did not last more than six weeks in office as commander of the military district. After Burnside removed Hascall following Morton's repeated requests for his head, intimidation replaced suppression as the main way to tone down recalcitrant Democratic editors. "Countenanced by partisan officials," mob action became the method of restraint of Democratic editors, and the primary members of the mob were Union soldiers.[93] Tredway claimed that Democrats were concerned about "the possibility that the administration would interfere with the free elective process in the North in order to keep itself in power" and that this "would mean the end of political democracy and the inauguration of a one party state, the embryo of which seemed already discernible in arbitrary arrests, military trials, and the covert sanctioning of partisan violence directed against opponents of the administration."[94] In the parlance of the twentieth century, Morton and the Republicans seemed to be wielding power in a banana republic. Hascall was trying to chase down deserters and Confederate sympathizers, to keep enrollments above the quota level, but, in the long run, his official suppression of the press helped to develop an atmosphere of increased restraint.

Perhaps one reason the aggressive Morton did not act against the Democratic press of Indiana was the fact that his power was limited. Jon Dilts, a media law scholar, suggested that Morton did not act against the press because the state government was too unstable to counter Democratic press criticism of the Lincoln war effort.[95] Thus, the federal government, in the form of the military, had to step in. On one level, this was the case. Yet Morton was far too egotistical to let the federal government have all the credit if suppression worked. Rather, Morton did not stand in the way of Hascall and soldier-led mobs as they attacked the Democratic press, precisely because intimidation of Democratic journalists helped neutralize the political opposition in the state, an opposition that was on the rise in the spring of 1863. It was a delicate balancing act because too much heavy-handedness would unduly upset the Democrats. Thus, Morton had Hascall called off, and the governor was able to finesse the promotion of a more circumspect district commander in Orlando B. Willcox to replace Hascall. The hiring of Willcox to replace Hascall did not mean Morton wanted to let up on the Democratic editors. Indeed, in the weeks after Hascall's removal, Democrats in Indiana were feistier than ever, some even resorting to violence against draft officers.

Meanwhile, the Democrats really had little choice in accepting this temporary chilling effect on their right to press freedom, even if they were not really choosing themselves to act responsibly. Tredway remarked: "It should have been plain ... that self-interest dictated to Indiana Democrats that they confine themselves to the field of legitimate politics. In view of the election results the preceding autumn, ordinary political activity would be much more likely to bring them success than an armed revolt."[96] Furthermore, the military was far better armed and equipped to fight than the Democrats who opposed the war or the war policies. The best way for the Democrats to fight was in the legislature and at the ballot box. The work of Hascall, with the tacit approval of Burnside, Morton, and the Lincoln administration, worked to counteract those legitimate political objectives of the Hoosier Democrats and their representatives in the press.

CHAPTER FOUR

Journalism in Civil War Indiana

Just as the period of 1861–65 was a transitional era in the history of Indiana politics and society, so too was it a transitional phase for journalism. The party press of the early decades of the nineteenth century was gradually being replaced by a new type of journalism that was still partisan but was becoming more personal and increasingly less dependent on the parties for financial support. Although Indiana's newspapers supported political parties, the rapid growth of newspapers in the state meant a lower percentage of papers were receiving patronage. Thus, a type of journalism was emerging that was equal parts political and personal. The editor's personality was a central feature of the paper, and he interpreted the news in terms of his own political beliefs. Editors tended to be leaders in their towns, and ownership often helped them advance their personal objectives, including attaining economic success. Thus, the journalism of mid-century Indiana can be described as a transitional political-personal press with a movement toward economic and political independence—that is, it was moving in the direction of both a profession and an industry. Yet politics remained the essential feature of most Hoosier newspapers in the 1860s, and editors often were major political players, some even winning local, state, or federal offices. Political journalism, too, meant subjective, unbalanced, and distorted views of the world. Journalists of the mid-nineteenth century had not yet adopted standards of objectivity, accuracy, and fairness that would come in the twentieth century.

Meanwhile, technology was changing how journalists told their stories. Telegraph was becoming ubiquitous, allowing reporters in the field to transmit information back to the home office over long distances and editors at home to share information with newspapers from around the country.[1] Reporters made use of the relatively new technology, providing instant updates on battles and other war news. This led to the creation of extras, secondary editions printed when significant telegraphic news was sent back to the home office.[2] In some cases, extras had to be printed when Democratic newspapers were suspended or destroyed. When James Elder's Democratic newspaper in Richmond, Indiana, was destroyed by rioters, he printed a one-sheet "Extra" the following week to explain why his subscribers were not receiving their paper that week. He also told his side of the story, speculating that the words of the three Republican papers in town had prompted the riot, which resulted in the destruction of his $2,000 printing facility.[3] On the other hand, editors, who had long exchanged papers with friends and foes, now could exchange more quickly using the telegraph. Some editors began to participate in associations, early wire services.

Furthermore, the nation's most ambitious and profitable newspapers—namely the New York *Herald* and its rival the *Tribune*—utilized the enormous expansion of the railroads to circulate throughout the country and reach mass audiences never dreamed of in the party press days.[4] The urban papers also benefited from an 1852 federal law that allowed newspapers to reduce postal rates by fifty percent if they paid in advance. The *Tribune* and *Herald*, which had circulations near or above 100,000, could afford to pay in advance.[5] Most papers in Indiana could not, and some editors feared the giant New York papers were becoming too influential, replacing the leading Washington, D.C., political papers of the pre-Penny Press era—and that New York journalism was not representative of the political views of Hoosiers.

The telegraph lines in Indiana were built along the ever-growing railroad tracks in the state. As the railroad mileage expanded quickly in the 1850s, so too did the telegraph lines in the state. When the Civil War came, some editors of Indiana dailies began printing so-called "telegraph" editions that updated military information overnight. This was part of an expansion movement in Indiana journalism in which newspaper owners were increasing productivity by expanding from weeklies to dailies to extra editions. One such paper was the Logansport *Democratic Pharos*, which came out with a single-sheet *Daily Telegraphic Pharos* in 1861 as the war intensified.[6]

The enormous amount of information the telegraph could deliver led in part to the invention of the inverted-pyramid form of news writing, whereby a reporter writes an information-filled first paragraph that summarizes the main topic immediately. Stories were also much shorter because the telegraph company charged for transmission by the word. It was cheaper to write less flowery prose and focus on the key information that a reporter wanted to impart to his readers.[7] Likewise, for the first time in the history of mainstream U.S. journalism, the emphasis on speed caused reporters to become stars because by-lines were used to tell the public who had written the story, although most reporters used pseudonyms to avoid detection by the military authorities who attempted to control their access to vital information.[8]

Another technology that had an impact on Civil War journalism was photography, which was in its infancy. Photography was beginning to boom as a small business in several towns in the state. Photographic rooms opened to exhibit and promote photography.[9] Hoosier soldiers routinely visited photographers to have their pictures taken. Although photographs of the Civil War appeared in exhibitions, the visual record of the conflict captured the graphic horrors of war in a way that had never been seen before. Indeed, visually oriented journalism blossomed during the war. Two magazines rose to prominence during the war, *Frank Leslie's Illustrated Newspaper* and *Harper's Weekly*, because of their use of artwork. *Frank Leslie's* started in 1855 and *Harper's Weekly* in 1857, and both took advantage of advances in printing to publish more graphic information than newspapers did. Both sent sketch artists to the combat zones to cover the war.[10] Portraits of prominent players in the war, as well as drawings of battles and maps, became staples of these two magazines. Hoosiers subscribed to these national weeklies, although they were more likely to subscribe to James Gordon Bennett's weekly New York *Herald* or Horace Greeley's weekly New York *Tribune*, but most Hoosiers saw little of the war on a day-to-day basis through this new technology. Those who did get to view photographs were more likely to see works of traveling art, such as Goodwin and Wilder's "Polyorama of the War."[11]

Most newspapers in Indiana were four-page weeklies. The front page usually had advertising and news on it, and sometimes fiction or poetry. The second was the featured page, and it consisted of national and international news and editorials as well as more advertising. The rest of the paper was usually a combination of local news and classified advertising. Indeed, local news was slowly becoming a key component of Indiana journalism. For example, Frank Gregory emphasized local news in his pro-Republican *Aurora Rising Sun Visitor*.[12] Most editors did not make huge profits from their journalistic endeavors, usually only a few hundred dollars per year. In fact, many were able to run their papers only with help from political parties or wealthy patrons or partners. Abraham Lincoln himself was a silent partner in a German-language newspaper in Illinois.[13] Schuyler Colfax, an Indiana congressman who would become speaker of the U.S. House of Representatives, owned the Republican paper in South Bend. Colfax's paper wielded immense power in his district, and his editor, Alfred Wheeler, canvassed in much the same way Greeley did in New York.

In 1850, there were approximately 100 newspapers in Indiana. By 1860, there were approximately 180 newspapers in the state, and, by 1880, there were nearly 500 newspapers in Indiana.[14] Almost all were weeklies in the small towns of the state. The best guess by historians is that the majority of Indiana newspapers in that period lasted only a year.[15] Four hundred dollars was a typical year's income—$1,600 for advertising and subscriptions, as opposed to $1,200 for expenses, most of which was expended on printing paper. A paper cost from a penny to five cents per edition. *Harper's* and *Frank Leslie's*, the two national weeklies, were eight cents for each edition. Subscriptions were highly encouraged, and they averaged, for a year's worth of a newspaper, from $1 to $3. Discounts were given for payment at the start of the subscription. Editors encouraged readers to spread the word about a newspaper, and friends of the editors often helped expand the circulation rolls. "More Subscribers Wanted" notices appeared frequently.[16]

Advertising was growing in popularity among Indiana's editors as a way to increase revenue, and column-inches devoted to advertising continued to increase. Most editors required advertisers to pay before publication. Five lines or less typically would cost 50 cents for the first publication. After that, it cost twenty-five cents if no changes were made in the advertisement. Public service announcements for charities cost twenty-five cents for five lines or less.[17] A half a column would cost $25 and a whole column $40.[18] A wide variety of goods were pushed on the pages of these four-sheeters. These included: government bonds, insurance, bank services, physicians' services, hotels, tobacco products, furniture, clothing, shoes, food, drugs, fake remedies, liquor, tools, sewing machines, musical instruments, ice, books, stationery, land, gold, artwork, jobs, paint, house decorations, and dramatic presentations. Several ads pushed "bitters," a cure-all for many of the disabilities that soldiers faced from combat and sickness. The ads claimed that consumption of bitters would save "hundreds of lives."[19] Some advertising was disguised as news items. For example, a Fort Wayne paper on one occasion interspersed the following sentence throughout its page-two columns: "Remember the sale of building lots in 'North Side Addition,' tomorrow at 1 o'clock."[20]

In an 1850 Indiana newspaper, most news was national, exchanged by telegraph or correspondence, but newspapers also devoted a great deal of space to political speeches, government proclamations, and new laws. By the

Civil War, more papers were including local news. For example, a Fort Wayne Republican newspaper commented on the elections of 1864 as follows: "The election passed off quietly in this city yesterday. Scarcely any one was refused a vote, indeed a large aggregate vote was needed to allow a large copperhead majority. The only effort of the opposition was to get men to vote, the consequence was that the largest vote ever polled in Fort Wayne was received. The copperhead majority in the township is, we learn, less than sixteen hundred. We can scarcely imagine why they confined themselves to that number, and we feel thankful they not make it more."[21] Other local news in a typical Civil War Indiana newspaper concerned crime, the courts, churches, agriculture, and business. Prices of goods from a grocer were included, as were train schedules. Newspapers also included notices about when doctors and dentists would be in their offices. Birth, marriage, and death notices appeared too. An example of a death notice read: "John Lamb, who was committed to the county jail last week for assault and battery on his wife, died of delirium tremens last evening."[22] No further commentary was provided. Witnessing the success that Bennett had in printing the sensational in New York, Indiana papers also included stories about unusual happenings. For example, a story in the Indianapolis *Journal* speaks of a Fort Wayne native who was only twenty-eight inches in height at age twenty-two.[23]

Agricultural news was often central to the mission of many Indiana newspapers. A Fort Wayne paper routinely carried reports on crop conditions from around the state. After giving an assessment on how the crops were doing in Allen County, it quoted other newspapers from around the state on crop conditions in those locales. For example: "The St. Joseph Register says of that section: As far as we can learn, the late cool nights have not in the least damaged the fruit, and the prospects of a very heavy fruit crop this season are very flattering."[24] Another type of local news was political announcements. Men announcing their candidacy for office would ask the editors of the party's papers to write a few lines, such as the following in a Fort Wayne paper: "C.A. Reker offers himself as a candidate for County Register, subject to the decision of the Democratic Convention."[25]

Some news items were simply statements of facts from government documents or the census. The following sentence appeared in a South Bend paper: "The Quakers of Indiana have paid two hundred and fifty thousand dollars to the U.S. Treasury for exemption from military duty."[26] No commentary accompanied the statement. However, since the paper, the *Forum*, was Democratic, it went without saying that the paper was inveighing against what it thought was Quaker hypocrisy—being for abolition, but not being willing to fight for it.

Another way newspapers generated copy was from the traditional exchange of information from other newspapers, especially by newspapers of the same political party. This practice had begun in the early days of the state when federal law allowed for the free exchange of newspapers by printers. For example, the Richmond *Jeffersonian* printed a Cincinnati *Enquirer* account of a mob destroying a Democratic newspaper in Ohio. The Cincinnati paper noted that the Democratic leaders of Greenville, Ohio, issued an ultimatum that unless Republican leaders brought the rioters to justice, the Republican paper would suffer a similar fate. "The [Republican] leaders agreed to fulfill the demands made upon them . . . No arrests had been made up to yesterday morning," the *Enquirer* reported.[27] Another law allowed for the free circulation of newspapers in the county of origin.[28] Small towns and the state's biggest cities alike often had multiple papers, and editors read and commented on the words of both political allies and enemies.

Another source of content was transcripts of official government documents from out-of-state newspapers and official federal government reports. Unlike New York and other large-city operations, Indiana newspapers could not afford to cover the war from the front, much less other significant national news. Thus, Indiana editors leaned on local, state, and federal officials for "official" news and information. Long, bombastic speeches from Congress, the president, state houses, and governors often appeared, as did historical documents, especially letters or papers from the founding fathers to validate a particular political idea. The orders of military officers were routinely run during the war. Similarly, when news of the war against native Americans reached Hoosier eyes, it usually came in the form of federal government reports. When Indians attacked an outpost in Minnesota, newspapers in Indiana ran a report by Brigadier General H. B. Sibley, who was the commander of U.S. forces in that state. Sibley's report, which had appeared in the St. Paul *Press*, made no attempt to do its own reporting and ran Sibley's report as is. One Indiana newspaper stated Sibley's narrative was "a correct account of the affair."[29] The editor offered no evidence why the narrative of events in Minnesota was "correct."

THE IDEOLOGY OF THE TRANSITIONAL PARTY-PERSONAL PRESS IN INDIANA

Political ideology played a large role in the transitional party-personal press in Civil War Indiana. The subject that dominated that press was the war, and the issue that precipitated the war was slavery. With a press that was still partisan in orientation, vituperative in nature, and widely accessible to the nation's citizens, mid-century journalism played a significant role, aiding the firestorm that would become civil war. Lorman Ratner and Dwight Teeter have observed that journalists of this period did not have a sense of social responsibility. Instead, editors were power players, and they were part of factions that had very different ideas about how to handle the most important issue of the day—that is, slavery. Radical Republican editors pushed an abolitionist agenda; Southern Democrats and their conservative allies in the North trumpeted secession; and moderates on both sides of the aisles held to unionism at any cost, including compromise that reverted back to previously held positions. Once compromise failed, the editorial dynamic was fluid. Most Northern Democrats, even those who would become peace advocates, supported Lincoln's war, however tepidly. Indiana's Democrats were no different.

Yet, as the war's unpredictable meanderings droned on, Democrats in the state worried about the expansion of federal powers, particularly those of the president. Democratic editors believed they represented the middle ground between what they saw as two radical groups: the secessionists in the South, who had no desire for reunion; and the radical abolitionists in the Northeast, who wanted to destroy slavery at any cost. While some Hoosier Democrats believed "the war was a mistake and that there was no way that it could be won," as newspaper historian George Douglas observed, most Democrats in the state supported the war but upheld their right to criticize the prosecution of the war.[30] Many interpreted every Southern victory as a sign that peace talks should commence.

While slavery was the central issue of the war, race was a corresponding issue for Indiana's Democratic editors, who lived in a free state but were suspicious of blacks, free or slave. Like other Midwest states, Indiana had antiblack laws on its books. For instance, Indiana had a law that required black men to pay a bond of $500 to enter the state. This racist law resulted from the perception of citizens in Indiana that blacks were prone to violence and crime.[31] Furthermore, the state wanted to discourage blacks from entering the borders and taking existing jobs for lower wages, and a number of Indiana's Democratic editors intended to promote local growth by being pro-immigration—which meant attracting and maintaining white European immigrants to their communities, especially Irish and Germans.[32] Democratic editors argued that the mass migration of freed slaves into these towns would disrupt this process. Likewise, blacks were not allowed to vote in Indiana, which had been founded by Southern nonslaveholding whites. During the Civil War, Indiana was a state in which blacks represented less than one percent of its population, and most Hoosier Democrats wanted to maintain a racially homogenous population.[33] Countering the Democrats and their adherence to the state's antiblack laws were several Quaker communities in the states, as well as radical Republicans who maintained stops on the underground railroad.

Hoosier Democrats were generally disciples of Thomas Jefferson and his diffused agrarian, anticentral government vision of America. These latter-day Jeffersonians—farmers, laborers, and mechanics—found urbanity unattractive, and they not only believed in small, limited government, but also in small towns and direct democracy. In their eyes, a concentration of a mass of people brought only social hardship and political sham, namely overcrowding, poverty, crime, and a reliance on a republican form of government. Therefore, they had little interest in industrialism, which they saw as being driven by the greed of factory owners. What they wanted was a government conducive to agriculture without debt and a government that kept the domestic peace. Indiana's Democrats believed in an honest job that earned an honest wage. Suspicious of paper wealth and speculation, Jeffersonian Democrats thought both brought corruption.[34] They thought democracy was the best government for achieving this. The greater the participation by all male citizens—except black men—the greater the social harmony. They were skeptical that the greed of industrialization would throw society out of balance.

These Jeffersonians wanted to preserve the Constitution as they believed it had been conceived by the founders, to protect the liberties it guaranteed from any form of tyranny and to protect property rights. In this sense, they were conservatives. Similarly, Jefferson believed in a free press that would serve as a watchdog over the government, thus giving individual citizens more free time to spend on their own interests. Jefferson believed that citizens had to watch their government officials closely to hold them accountable. "The plea of necessity is no excuse for a violation of politicians' oath of office," Jefferson said. "Recollect the price of Liberty is eternal vigilance."[35]

Jefferson believed the press would help inform the public and make the government respect citizens more. Yet the press sometimes tried Jefferson's patience. When he was president, Jefferson was stung by the criticisms of Federalist newspaper editors. Yet he refused to give into the itch to censor, though he did uphold the necessity of libel law against false accusations. He wrote, "I admit … that restraining the press to truth, as the present laws do, is the only way of making it useful."[36] He said the press was "impotent when it abandons itself to falsehood," but that it was a "noble institution" when concerned with truth and was "equally the friend of science and civil liberty."[37] The Hoosier Democratic editors, though not always truthful in their political attacks on Lincoln, nonetheless thought freedom of the press a noble institution and alluded to Jefferson's thoughts on civil rights.[38]

Jefferson did not trust government. He felt it intruded upon personal liberty. However, this trust in personal liberty did not extend to nonwhite men—or women for that matter—although Jefferson believed slaves would one day be free, and that Southerners would come to understand that slavery's demise was inevitable and part of the same spirit of liberty the colonists felt in the American Revolution.[39] Since the colonists did not move to emancipation, he knew one day the paradox would have to be dealt with by the country.

Thus, a strict interpretation of the U.S. Constitution was central to the political ideology of Indiana's Democrats, who read the founding document much more literally than their Republican counterparts, especially the sections that dealt with the powers enumerated to the states. For the Democrats, the Constitution gave shape to the American Revolution. It was prescriptive, and its core was passed down from previous generations. Indiana's Democrats believed the Constitution protected them from martial law during the war. "The military power is and must remain subordinate to the civil power," stated the signers of a resolution passed by "Twenty Thousand Loyal Citizens of Illinois" in response to Ambrose Burnside's suppression of Storey's Chicago *Times*.[40] The signers proclaimed that when the military overstepped its boundaries, its orders and proclamations became void.

As strict constructionists of the Constitution, Democrats construed the Bill of Rights literally and ignored the "responsibility-for-abuse" clause of the Indiana Bill of Rights. John Dawson's Fort Wayne newspaper published key civil liberties passages from the constitutions of the original thirteen states. Dawson was fond of the following sentence that appears in several constitutions from New England states: "The liberty of the press is essential to the security of freedom in a State."[41] Democratic editors in Indiana conveniently did not refer to the press responsibility clause in their own state's constitution. In response to Clement L. Vallandigham's conviction and exile, as well as Hascall's conflict with the Democratic editors, Congressman Daniel W. Voorhees claimed the Constitution was just as valid in wartime as in peace and said nothing in the document made civil rights conditional. He said the Constitution guaranteed that Congress would make no law abridging freedom of expression, and the executive branch would not ignore the rights of citizens to freely speak, write, or assemble.[42] Voorhees said that a public discussion of issues of the day was an "undeniable right."[43] He added, "The Constitution made our Union; without it the Union would have never have had an existence."[44] Indiana's Democrats rejoiced when Supreme Court Justice Roger B. Taney, a Catholic Democrat, issued a writ of habeas corpus as a circuit judge in Maryland for John Merryman, who had been placed in the jail in Baltimore, Maryland, for an indefinite period. Taney wrote in *Ex Parte Merryman* that only Congress had the power to suspend the writ of habeas corpus.[45]

Another major influence on the thinking of Indiana's Democratic editors was the political philosophy of Andrew Jackson, who created a powerful political machine that relied extensively on the press to communicate its agenda. Jackson relied on rural editors to plant his political messages. When he came to power as president, he rewarded those editors with spoils—as many as fifty-seven according to the *National Intelligencer*.[46] The slaveholding Jackson's political ascendancy "increased political participation to a level previously unknown in America," noted historian Reed Smith.[47] For example, Ohio editor Samuel Medary received printing contracts from the government after Jackson was elected.[48]

The essence of Jacksonianism was representative government for citizens who were equal before the law—in this case, white men. This meant none of those equals could be subject to the arbitrary rule of anyone. Minority rights would also be protected. For Jacksonians, there was an ever-present struggle between power and liberty, and that liberty must resist power's tendency to expand. This required the individual to put aside his selfish desires and to put society first. This civic virtue was critical to the success of society. If it were corrupted, then society would change. Thus, Jacksonians looked at change with suspicion, seeing it as a sign of corruption. What made this Jacksonian philosophy unique is that civic virtue was available to all free white men, including the poor. The ideology was widely popular in the United States, and it was largely responsible for the Democratic Party's strength for much of the first half of the nineteenth century. In Indiana, Jacksonianism extended to the way society saw the legal profession. Hoosiers opposed having a professional class of lawyers who attended law schools, precisely because professionalization would create class conflict.[49]

The problem was that Jacksonian ideology was available only to white men. Black men—as well as women and children—did not fit into this universe as equals. Jacksonianism held to a theory of black inferiority, which came from the German concept of *herrenvolk*, which held that Africans were created separately from whites and were not part of the human family.[50] Stephen Douglas, Lincoln's Illinois archrival, would use this concept to extrapolate that Jefferson's "all men are created equal" did not apply to blacks. The *herrenvolk* hypothesis was also used to justify slavery and white superiority. In the spring of 1863, the Democratic paper in Dayton, Ohio, quoted Jackson's "Prophecy" of the war: "The Abolition party is a disloyal organization. Its pretended love of freedom means nothing more nor less than a dissolution of the Union."[51]

Jacksonian ideology was also proagrarian, pro-Union, and anticentralization. Jacksonianism held that small farms, business, and government were better than large farms, business, and government. This philosophy, central to the Democrats' understanding of their country, was called "republicanism."[52] As editor Medary put it, many Democrats were "unawed by the influence of the rich, the great, or the noble."[53] They tended to live on small family farms, and they had little or modest education with low literacy.[54] The Midwest Democrats were losing economic and political power as the North, under the leadership of the Republicans, turned to a more capitalist and industrialist economic system. Accordingly, they opposed tariffs, which caused farm prices to decrease and consumer goods to increase.[55] Many of Indiana's Democratic editors framed their opposition to the war along these lines: the agrarian, antitariff Midwest against the industrial, protariff Northeast. Hoosier Democrats also admired Jackson for seeing the Union as sacred, something that had caused him to split with Calhoun and the other states' rights advocates.[56]

HOME RULE AND RACE

Many Democratic newspapers echoed Jacksonian-Jeffersonian philosophy in their often working-class mission statements. The *Indiana Jacksonian* said its pages would serve as "the Farmer's, Mechanic's and Working Man's Advocate."[57] As the only newspaper in Rush County, Indiana, the *Jacksonian* said it would try to focus less on politics and more on "home interests and home improvement," and that it would "throw open our columns for the discussion of all matters which affect the public weal, and the free expression of the opinions of all parties upon all subjects of general interests."[58] The focus was on issues important to farmers, mechanics, and laborers; small producers that tended to be suspicious of both the top and bottom of society.[59] That is, they were suspicious of both slave owners and industrial owners. They were also suspicious of slaves, who worked for free and were dependent on their owners. These Hoosier workers did not want to be seen as dependent.

The Democrats of Indiana were often wage earners who saw their place in society as a middle state that led to economic independence—small farming or self-employed craft labor.[60] Democrats not only did not want the competition from freed slaves, they also wanted a sort of utopia in the frontier free from constant reminders of dependent labor. They were free, and slaves were not. Furthermore, most free blacks in the Midwest had little political or social freedom, a state of affairs reinforced after 1857 by the Dred Scott case. The Democrats saw themselves as free white labor.[61] This was a critical distinction from the not free black labor in the South, and because of the racial ideology of white superiority that permeated both the North and the South, the Democrats believed there was little chance that labor unity inclusive of blacks and whites would be established in the United States.

Many Hoosier Democrats viewed both slave owner and slave as emasculated, and neither was ruggedly individualistic, as the dominant ideology of the frontier required of men. Slaves were dependent of the paternalism of the masters. The slave owners were dependent on the slaves to do their manual labor. The Indiana Democrats thought they should do their own work, and dependence was a sign of weakness.

A literary work that had an effect on the Democratic editors of Indiana was *Uncle Tom's Cabin*, the proabolition novel written by Harriett Beecher Stowe. *Uncle Tom's Cabin* served as a lightning rod for abolitionism. The antiabolitionist Democrats had to take note of it, even if they intensely disagreed with its message. Because the novel was so successful at changing public opinion, it was a force with which the conservatives had to reckon.

The reaction of Democratic newspapers to *Uncle Tom's Cabin* was predictable. The Putnam County, Indiana, *Sentinel* observed the novel's popularity in England: "Anything calculated to misrepresent American institutions to their injury would not fail to be received with open arms by the British public; more especially when it pandered to their anti-slavery prejudices, as does Uncle Tom."[62] The Putnam County editor praised the novel for being "ingeniously contrived, and skillfully woven for effect. But we think we have a number of popular novels, wherein slavery is introduced, which in point of art, and incident, and most certainly in point of purity, chastity and vigor of style and a high-toned, manly and independent American spirit, are vastly superior." The editor did not name these novels. The editor of the Democratic paper in Indianapolis, reacting with denial, said "we do not admit that the state of the negro-slave is anything like what is pictured in Uncle Tom's Cabin. . . . There may be solitary cases approaching its abomination."[63]

The Democratic editors also read magazines to help form their ideas about politics. One of these magazines was the New York-based *The Old Guard*, which the Lincoln administration suspended in 1862 for opposing the war. Editor C. Chauncey Burr resumed publication in 1863, claiming his mission was to verbally fight against despotism and "mongrelization."[64] Originally an abolitionist, Burr changed his mind on that issue after a tour of the South. He came to conclude that African Americans were inferior. Burr thought there

were multiple acts of creation and several species within the genus *Homo*. He
thought mental aptitude and abilities differentiated these *Homo* species. The
editor held that blacks were dependent on whites and freedom would lead
to blacks' extinction.[65] He tried to frame slavery as progressive, maintaining
it was beneficial to both blacks and whites. Whites were needed to organize
black labor, and blacks provided the required manual labor and did it much
better than their white counterparts. This compact made for a more efficient
society. He also claimed that most blacks who came to North America had
been slaves in Africa.[66]

The New York magazine editor believed society naturally had a hierarchical order, and free will simply allowed men to foolishly try to work against
that order. He saw history as a struggle between order and disorder, and he
thought Lincoln and the Republicans were hell-bent on creating social disorder in North America. He also saw history as deterministic, holding that societies naturally formed ruling and subservient classes. On the political front,
Burr felt that states' rights were essential because the will of the people was
better represented at the state level. Thus, state governments were sovereign
over the federal government. Burr feared that as the country grew, one section
or group of people would use the federal government to force its political desires on the other sections or groups. He thought decentralization would keep
this from happening and that permanent national gridlock was desirable.
He echoed Madison's idea that the diversity created as the country expanded
westward checked centralization.[67]

A supporter of New York governor Horatio Seymour, Burr railed at Lincoln for subverting the Constitution. He said Lincoln had no constitutional
authority to coerce the Southern states back into the Union. Likewise, the
president had no constitutional authority to suppress Northern dissent or suspend the writ of habeas corpus.[68] Like Vallandigham, Burr did not advocate
violent resistance to the Lincoln administration. He told his readers to use the
ballot box and the judicial system to fight what he saw as Lincoln's tyranny.
After the war ended, he continued to frame Republicans as dictators, pointing
to the military occupation of the South as evidence.[69]

POLITICAL PATRONAGE AND THE PARTY-PERSONAL PRESS IN INDIANA

Hoosier editors benefited from their political connections with patronage in
the form of government contracts for printing or postmaster positions when
the party they supported was in power. For example, James H. McNeely, owner
of the Evansville *Journal*, became postmaster after he supported Lincoln in

the 1860 election.[70] Dr. Hubbard M. Smith, owner of the pro-Republican Vincennes *Gazette*, became postmaster in his town in March of 1861.[71]

Editors also benefited from increased readership due to the state's increasing population. The rise in population in the towns and cities led to the first dailies in 1850. Leading this trend was the Indianapolis *Indiana Journal*, which went daily as it covered the Indiana Constitutional Convention of 1850–1851.[72] By 1860, a dozen dailies operated in the Hoosier State. The dailies all continued to publish weeklies, while some would add telegraphic editions during the war. One such paper was the Samuel A. *Hall's Daily Telegraphic Pharos* in Logansport. The trend toward dailies continued after the war. By 1880, Indiana editors produced forty-five daily newspapers throughout the state.[73] Some papers printed a Sunday issue that was more like a magazine, including features and fiction.

Another major development in Hoosier journalism was the rise of press associations, cooperatives that made it less expensive to cover the war but also centralized the flow of information and potentially reduced journalistic competition. This was a way for newspapers to pool information at a time of reporter shortages because so many reporters had to serve in the military. The Associated Press came to the state in 1856 when the Indianapolis *Indiana Journal* and Indianapolis *Indiana State Sentinel* began subscribing to the combine, but most papers in the state could not afford the service and many editors feared it would overemphasize an urban and East Coast view of the world since the AP was owned by seven New York newspapers.[74] However, most editors selectively used wire service news to reinforce previously held political opinions. Nationally, the AP had agents who reported on interesting news items, thus nationalizing the news.[75]

A press association gathered news for most papers in the South and in part this explains why Confederate newspapers seemed to have one set of predictable frames in which to cast the news. Whereas the Associated Press had started before the war and continued to expand during the war, the Confederate Press Association was created to help Southern newspapers deal with a dearth of reporters during the war. P. A. superintendent John S. Thrasher implemented a series of standards and practices, including a call for clear and concise writing. Thrasher also advised reporters to develop sources within the Confederate Army, but not to reveal CSA military secrets.[76] In both the North and South, the press fed an ever-growing news orientation of newspaper audiences, and both the Northern and Southern associations helped develop a common set of standards and practices for the profession.

The Indianapolis *Indiana Journal* foreshadowed the complex corporate conglomerate of the late twentieth and early twenty-first centuries. The *Journal* also owned a book binding concern and had a post office. All three operations were housed in the Indiana State Journal Buildings in downtown Indianapolis. An opponent of Jacksonianism in the first decade of the state's history, the newspaper came of age as a pro-Whig organ. Owner John D. Defrees, who had previously owned a paper in South Bend, sold the *Journal* in 1854 to a group headed by Ovid Butler, who hired Berry R. Sulgrove as editor.[77] Butler and the other owners let Sulgrove run the paper without interference. In the 1850s Sulgrove rang the alarm of Democratic capitulation to the Southern slave power, and in the 1860s Sulgrove used fear to persuade his readers. In Sulgrove's view, if the Democrats got their way, the war would come to every town and village in Indiana.

While the overwhelming majority of newspapers in Indiana were in English, a growing number were written in German. The first was the *Indiana Volksblatt Und Telegraph*, a pro-Democratic paper that began publication in Indianapolis in 1848.[78] The *Volksblatt* printed daily, weekly, and Sunday editions. It would last until 1918, when anti-German sentiment made it unpopular. A Free Soil paper, the *Freie Presse Von Indiana*, began in 1853, also in Indianapolis.[79] The *Freie Presse* was pro-Democratic, but opposed slavery.[80] Successful German-language papers were also launched in Evansville and Fort Wayne.[81] Evansville had both Republican and Democratic German-language papers during the war. Fort Wayne, a bastion of the Democratic Party, had only a pro-Democratic German newspaper during the war, although a Republican paper, the *Indiana Volksfreund*, would start in 1871.[82]

During the war, the editors of Indiana's newspapers continued to print largely political interpretations of the news with highly personal styles that often featured ad hominem attacks on their opponents, especially the editors of other parties.

Nationally, the Civil War era remained largely a period of the party press. Eighty percent of the nation's paper claimed to be political in 1860, according to the federal census.[83] Henry J. Raymond, owner of the New York *Times*, advised President Abraham Lincoln in the election of 1864. South Bend's Schuyler Colfax, Speaker of the House during the war, would be vice president after the war. He was an associate of Greeley and close to the Lincoln administration. Yet changes were on the way toward a more commercial and professional press, especially in the urban areas of the North, including Indianapolis and Fort Wayne. In New York, Raymond moved to make the reporting in his paper more neutral, concise, and accurate. Several papers in Indiana began to follow suit, at least in terms of conciseness and accuracy.[84] In smaller towns, though, most of the newspapers were closely associated with either the Republicans or Democrats, and this led to hotly contested free expression debates in the North. For example, when General Ambrose E. Burnside published on April 13, 1863, General Order No. 38 to squelch free expression in the Midwest states, Republican editors cheered him, citing the war necessity, but Democratic editors cursed him, citing the Constitution as guaranteeing their right to publish as they pleased. Democratic newspaper editors were intimidated and officially suppressed. Sometimes the mails carrying Democratic papers were not delivered, and the commercial telegraph lines were brought under control of the War Department. General Winfield Scott, head of the U.S. Army early in the war, had ordered transmissions be self-censored on July 8, 1861. Then, during the first battle of Bull Run, Scott ordered the telegraphs to be silent.[85] The following winter, Lincoln gave Secretary of War Edwin M. Stanton the authority to censor telegraphic transmissions.[86]

Reporters in the Civil War were not embedded with the military in any systematic fashion. Rather, it was up to the generals in the field to decide if a journalist could witness the action. General William T. Sherman abhorred journalists and tried to have one New York reporter executed for treason.[87] Grant was friendlier to the press and made one reporter, Sylvanus Cadwallader, a spy, an aide-de-camp, and later a political adviser.[88] Overall, though, reporters were relatively free to cover the war from the front. The reporters of the New York and other large-city papers had much more access to the war than most twentieth-century reporters, especially those pooled in the Gulf War and those embedded in the Iraq War. Indeed, only reporters in the Spanish-American War had greater access to the front.[89] Indiana editors in the Civil War used the reporting of the urban reporters to transmit information about the war to their readers. The information from the war zone was transmitted to Indiana by telegraph and paper exchange.

While the military handling of reporters at the front depended on the attitudes of the commanders, the attempt to control the chorus of criticism directed at the president from urban editors was fairly tepid. Rather, Lincoln worked with a few editors to counter the criticisms that came from New York's vociferous Democratic editors, who represented the majority of the city's editors, and Bennett, who was more independent than his peers. Only Raymond and Horace Greeley stood behind Lincoln for the majority of the war, and Greeley proved to be erratic, even calling for a peace conference during the middle of the war, as well as entertaining his own presidential ambitions. Greeley, though, did consistently push for a war of emancipation. Debates are

intense about how much influence he had over Lincoln on this matter, but it
is clear that the president listened to the New York *Tribune* editor closely on
many issues. Because the weekly edition of the *Tribune* circulated widely in
Indiana and both Republican and Democratic newspapers often quoted it,
Greeley's opinions were well known in the Hoosier State.

Serving in the Union Army, many Indiana journalists had an intimate
view of the war. For example, a short list shows that editors of the Blackford
County *Democrat*, Columbia City *News*, Crown Point *Register*, Franklin *Jeffersonian*, Goshen *Democrat*, Greene County *Times*, Liberty *Herald*, Logansport
Journal, Madison *Courier*, Petersburg *Reporter*, Princeton *Clarion*, Steuben
Republican, and Tipton *Republican* all served in the army.[90] Not all editors
serving in Indiana's regiments were Republicans. William Kurtz of the pro-
Democratic Princeton *Clarion* spent so much time recruiting and organizing
the local militia that he did not have enough time to continue with the day-
to-day operations of the paper. Thus, he sold the paper to A. J. Calkins, who
changed the title and the political affiliation of the paper.[91] Indeed, many Hoosier editors were too busy fighting to do much journalism, though some wrote
letters back home that were published. More significantly, their absence had
an effect on the quality of journalism in Indiana. The fact that there were fewer
trained journalists to do the work meant that Hoosier editors had to rely on
inexperienced helpers who came and went—or do all the work themselves.

Indiana's journalists did not make a name for themselves as reporters
during the Civil War. Most papers received their information from other newspapers and telegraphic exchanges. There was little original reporting from the
front. J. Cutler Andrews' *The North Reports the Civil War* does not list a single
Hoosier reporter in his 813-page study. Dispatches from New York and Cincinnati newspaper reporters were the most likely to find their way into Indiana
papers, and the work of Chicago reporters also made it into Indiana papers.
The *Indiana Journal* published a report with a Cincinnati dateline on November 9, 1864, that provided detailed information about General Sherman's troop
strength and strategic intentions. The result was that Washington countered
with planted stories that were designed to mislead the Confederates.[92]

The press, North and South, built a need for news in the public. The
war stories were dramatic, and the political, social, and economic fate of the
nation hung in the balance. Editors of North and South had a profound effect
on the political crisis that caused the war, and then they debated endlessly on
how to either wage, win, or stop the war.

For the most part, the now well-established Penny Press, with its sensationalism and emphasis on the reporting of crime, corruption, and domestic disturbances, would come to Indiana after the war, though it was already visible in papers in the largest cities in the state. Most of the newspapers in Indiana in the 1860s still were in a frontier, booster mode. This environment was more characteristic of the partisan press because party papers performed advocacy journalism. By 1861, most papers in the state were aligned with either the Republicans or the Democrats, although a few Free Soil, People's Party, independent, religious, and one-issue papers existed too. Almost every town had a least one Republican and one Democratic newspaper. Many had more than one for each party. Although ownership was not that stable, the number of newspapers in each city and town was far greater than in the next two centuries.

Another way for the political parties to build an identity was the inclusion of artwork on the editorial page. Most papers in Indiana carried some sort of logo under the masthead. Many Republican papers had the U.S. flag under the masthead on the second page.[93] The Marshall County *Republican* had an eagle landing on a flagpole with the Stars and Stripes wrapped around the pole.[94] Most Democratic papers had no such artwork, though the *Indiana State Sentinel* in Indianapolis included an embossing of a watch.[95] The Plymouth *Democrat* had a graphic in which an eagle rested on a flagpole with the word D-E-M-O-C-R-A-C-Y written on the stripes of the flag.[96] The Fort Wayne *Sentinel*, which flip-flopped between being a Democratic and Republican paper, had a logo in which two hands are shaking over the U.S. Constitution.[97]

Hoosiers were intent on maintaining politics as usual during the war. According to Indiana historian Gilbert R. Tredway, this was because each party refused "to put the country's interests above party advantage. The 1860s featured political vituperation and personal journalism to a degree astonishing to the twentieth century mind."[98] Editors were often major players in the political process, and propaganda filled their columns. Schuyler Colfax, perhaps the preeminent Hoosier politician of the war, continued to guide his South Bend *St. Joseph Valley Register* from Washington, D.C. He fired off letters to his editor, Alfred Wheeler, indicating what he expected in the paper. Meanwhile, Wheeler functioned as Schuyler's eyes and ears back in his home district. Early in the campaign of 1860, Wheeler saw Lincoln emerging as the most attractive Republican candidate, though he feared that no Southern state would vote for him, but Colfax supported Edward Bates.[99]

Meanwhile, Sulgrove, the editor of the Indianapolis *Journal*, was closely aligned with Indiana's war governor, Oliver P. Morton. During the war, the *Journal* was sold to Morton's private secretary, William R. Holloway.[100] John W. Dawson owned the Fort Wayne *Times*, which switched names to *Dawson's*

Daily Times & Union. After the war, Dawson became governor of the Utah territories.[101] Samuel E. Perkins, the chief justice of the Indiana Supreme Court, had been the editor of the Richmond *Jeffersonian*, a paper that was subject to mob attack in March of 1863.[102] Joseph Bingham, editor of the *Indiana State Sentinel*, was the chairman of the Democratic Party in Indiana.[103]

Townspeople knew the identity of the editors, as well as the editorials they wrote. This was before the time of anonymous, team-oriented editorial writing, though commentary did not carry a by-line. Party discipline was the rule, and editors regularly carried the tickets of their party in upcoming election. Announcements about and coverage of local, state, and national mass meetings of the party were routinely included on the editorial page.

What the editors wrote was largely interpretive, and news and commentary often appeared on the same page. The United States had operated in a free-expression environment that had fostered a diversity of political opinion since Thomas Jefferson failed to renew the Alien and Sedition acts when he became president in the first decade of the nineteenth century. James Madison, who abhorred many of the distortions he saw in the political press, thought any solution to the problem of bias to be worse than the problem itself. Madison said forcing editors to print both sides of an issue would be "ideal," but impractical because parties will evolve and change over time. Papers would have to decide which parties to be the most relevant and would constantly have to make new arrangements with the newer ones to include their views.[104]

Journalists operated as leading political operatives, and, until the war, spouted their beliefs and their political venom without threat of official censorship. Their newspapers were aimed at audiences who shared their political point of view. These editors did not merely set the public agenda; they also framed what they wanted their readers to think—and urged them to vote a particular way. For the most part, the editors reinforced previously held positions. Rarely were editors trying to change the opinions of independent voters. Mostly, they countered the political spin of the opposition press. For example, James Elder, the editor of the Democratic paper in Richmond, Indiana, had to defend himself from charges of being a member of the clandestine Knights of the Golden Circle.[105] His defensive editorial appeared just three days before a mob destroyed his printing office. Elder made the point that Republican editors had a vested economic—as well as political—interest in seeing the suspension or destruction of Democratic newspapers. He argued, "The Abolitionist editors reason, 'if we suppress all the other papers, we shall make more money.'"[106]

Throughout the war, Democratic papers faced the constant wrath of soldiers and Union League operatives. Union soldiers ransacked the *People's Friend* in Covington after editor John H. Spence supported the South's right to secede and condemned Lincoln's war. Spence responded by placing a six-pound cannon in the *People's Friend* office.[107]

Because mid-century U.S. political history was dynamic, both Republicans and Democrats would undergo dramatic changes in the 1850s and 1860s. The Democrats would be divided by the election of 1860. The Southern Democrats would lead the move to secede, while the Northern Democrats themselves divided into prowar and propeace factions. In the first two years of the war, most Northern Democratic newspapers supported the war and only after two bloody years did a peace movement begin to take root in Indiana.

A dramatic power struggle was at hand in the Hoosier State during the spring after the Emancipation Proclamation took effect on January 1, 1863. Even the Republicans were not totally united. Governor Oliver P. Morton disagreed with Lincoln administration decisions about military personnel who served in the state's shadow federal government. Indeed, Morton supported states' rights when it came to the sovereignty of his government in Indianapolis. As governor of the state, he thought he was in control of all things Hoosier. He grew exasperated when the Lincoln administration ignored or barely acted on any of his communications to Washington. He was especially frustrated with Lincoln's handling of Kentucky. The president wanted to be careful with that border state, but Morton wanted the Commonwealth run with an iron Republican fist. He did not want any chance of an invasion of Indiana by Confederates through Kentucky. He feared the political ramifications if he could not adequately protect Hoosiers from Southern marauders.

In the spring of 1863, Morton faced several opportunities to tighten the reins in Indiana. Riots broke out in Fort Wayne and Indianapolis during mass political rallies. The former was a mass meeting of proabolitionists in heavily Democratic Allen County on May 2. Afterwards, mobs on both sides attacked and counterattacked. The ruckus lasted approximately ten minutes without fatalities. Eventually, the mayor and marshal restored order.[108] The latter, called the Battle of Pogues Run, occurred on May 20, 1863, during a Democratic mass meeting near the state house. Hascall was at the center of the government's attempt to maintain security. The general had troops and cannons on the street to remind the Democrats who was in charge. Late in the afternoon, Union soldiers stopped a speech by Senator Thomas A. Hendricks. The cavalry moved in, and the masses began a stampede to leave the area. A Republican assumed the podium and began a pro-Lincoln speech. As

Democrats boarded their trains for home, they shot off pistols. Soon Union troops boarded the trains to confiscate weapons, but many of the Democrats threw their weapons out the windows, many of the arms landing in nearby Pogues Creek—and hence the name of the incident.[109]

These episodes were part of a pattern of internal violence in the state. In March, a group of Union soldiers riding through Richmond, Indiana, on a transport train disembarked and destroyed Elder's newspaper.[110] During the entire war, sixty-nine cases of suppression and intimidation of Democratic editors occurred in the Hoosier State, although only twelve of those were official federally sponsored suppression.[111] Since Hascall was responsible for eleven of those in only six weeks during the spring of 1863, Morton lost patience with the Union officer whom he thought was unnecessarily upsetting Democrats, a large voting bloc at the time. Morton eventually petitioned Secretary of War Edwin M. Stanton for Hascall's removal because the governor was afraid the Union military officer was overagitating the Democrats in the Hoosier State.[112] Indeed, Morton had never been thrilled with Hascall as federal military leader of the state. Even though Hascall was a volunteer from Goshen in the northern part of the state, Morton had seen a personal friend, Henry B. Carrington, supplanted by Hascall in April. The governor covertly worked to remove Hascall, whom he considered less organized and effective than Carrington.[113]

The level of suppression of the Democratic press reached its apex during 1863. Those eleven cases of press suppression and intimidation in Indiana during 1863 represented the highest single-year total of the war.[114] Those cases came while Hascall was in office and Democrats were rallying against what they now considered to be an abolitionist war. When Morton effectively closed down the general assembly to prevent its planned entreaties to the South for a peace conference and raised money privately to run the state government, the role of the federal military shadow government increased dramatically. Indiana was a state in turmoil, and Hascall, working as Department of the Ohio Commander Ambrose E. Burnside's proxy, worked to stifle the Democrats as the war news took a turn for the worse.

Starting with Shiloh in the spring of 1862, Hoosier Democrats had begun to see the war in more negative terms. Approximately one-tenth of the 13,047 Union casualties at Shiloh were Hoosiers. After Antietam in September of 1862, Burnside would replace George McClellan as commander of the Army of the Potomac. Burnside, a native of Liberty, Indiana, would oversee the disastrous Union loss at Fredericksburg, Virginia, in December of 1862, and he was reassigned to the post in Cincinnati, overseeing the federal shadow governments in the Midwestern states. When Hascall took office in Indianapolis in the spring of 1863, the Union's top army, now under the direction of Joseph Hooker, was about to suffer another loss, this time at Chancellorsville, Virginia. The Democratic editors, already weary of the carnage, as well as the draft, income tax, and emancipation, became even more critical of Lincoln, the military, and the Republicans and their editors, who argued for suppression of disloyal editors.

The whole political situation was a communications mess, but more importantly it was a contest for power, and framing supplied the way to power. Words like "loyalty" and "disloyalty" indicated how entrenched political positions were, but because the war itself was so lengthy and so dynamic, the molding and maintenance of public opinion was not insignificant. Every military event had a political consequence. A long-standing professional army did not exist in the North or the South. While most Northern soldiers, for example, certainly favored the war effort, many of their brethren back home had somewhat different views of the war. The interpersonal communication between father and son, brother and brother, and friend and friend had major political significance. While the soldiers' views tended to be affected most heavily by their personal experience, the views of the men back home were affected by the editorials and news in their hometown papers. What the editors wrote and how they wrote their words molded public opinion. The very existence of the United States as a one-nation entity hung in the balance, and the editors played a central role in the opinion-making dynamic of the period.

⊂⊃ CHAPTER FIVE ⊂⊃

Journalistic Context of Press Suppression

Newspapers in the Civil War were not suppressed in Indiana alone. They were suppressed throughout the North, especially in the first two years of the war. Suppression of disloyal Democratic papers occurred in Baltimore, Philadelphia, Chicago, New York, and St. Louis, as well as in many small towns. One scholar estimated that at least 135 Democratic papers faced suppression and another as many as 300, although both numbers are likely below the actual level of suppression given that the total for the war in Indiana alone was sixty-nine.[1] As early as August of 1861, Bennett's New York *Herald* printed a list of seven Democratic papers destroyed by mob action, two suppressed by civil authority, two that closed, four that were denied circulation in the mails, and three that had changed to the Republicans. The *Herald* listed seventy-four pro-Southern newspapers still in existence in the North.[2]

Editors faced various forms of suppression and intimidation. Soldiers tarred and feathered Ambrose Kimball, the editor of the Essex County *Democrat* in Haverhill, Massachusetts.[3] Union soldiers arrested Philadelphia *Evening Journal* editor Albert D. Boileau on January 28, 1863, and took him to Fort McHenry in Baltimore. The government suspended Boileau's newspaper because he unfavorably compared Lincoln's intellectual capacities to those of Jefferson Davis. Democrats back in Pennsylvania asked the governor to intercede. Under pressure from Major General Robert C. Schenck, Boileau wrote a letter expressing his regret for criticizing the Lincoln administration. Schenck then released Boileau.[4] The Baltimore *Sun*, which had reported Lincoln's coming through that city in disguise in 1861, chose not to criticize the Lincoln administration rather than to face suppression and tended to ignore Lincoln as much as possible. When Richmond finally fell, the *Sun* offered only a single, matter-of-fact paragraph.[5] Burnside attempted to silence Wilbur F. Storey by suppressing his pro-Democratic Chicago *Times* at the end of Hascall's tenure in Indiana before Lincoln rescinded the suppression order, and John C. Fremont's activities against the press in Missouri rivaled those of Burnside and Hascall. Fremont, who at the time was commander of the Department of the West, declared martial law in 1861 and suppressed the *War Bulletin* and the *Missourian*. Both papers had printed information about military movements.[6] A third paper, the St. Louis *Christian Advocate*, was warned it was about to be suppressed and told to "be a religious paper, as it professes to be, and it will never come under the discipline" of the military.[7] The military closed down the St. Louis *Morning Herald*, while the *Missouri Republican* and St. Louis *Democrat* began printing loyal editorials.[8] Fremont also barred five New York newspapers and the Louisville *Courier* from the mails.[9] Newspapers from Key West, Florida, to Bangor, Maine, to La Crosse, Wisconsin, to Albany, Oregon, were suppressed.[10] At the same time, many Democratic papers were intimidated by the threat of violence or were damaged partially by mob action. Of course, in towns where Democrats had the majority, Republican papers faced similar intimidation.

In Indiana, the leader of the Democratic press was the *Indiana State Sentinel* in Indianapolis. It had started in 1841 during the heyday of the Democratic stranglehold on the state. The *Sentinel* was actually a daily when the legislature was in session from 1841 until 1844. The rest of the time, it was either a twice- or thrice-weekly until it became a daily in 1851. For a while, the paper was housed in the old Capitol in downtown Indianapolis.[11] It was incorporated in 1857, becoming known as the Sentinel Company.[12] Joseph J. Bingham and John Doughty owned the paper at the start of the Civil War, and the *Sentinel* supported Stephen A. Douglas in the election of 1860. Before he enlisted in July of 1861, Doughty sold his share to John R. Elder and John Harkness, who owned the *Indiana State Guard*. The two papers were merged.

Bingham led the charge in early years of the war, maintaining that Democrats would remain an opposition party with the right to criticize and disagree with Lincoln and the Republicans. Bingham believed that if the South turned the war into a quagmire, it would help Democrats regain power in the

North.[13] Bingham would lead the chorus against the unnecessary slaughter, high taxes, and economic deprivation. He believed rational human beings would not pay such a high price for a political stalemate. "Let us reason together. Let humanity, intelligence and common sense settle the controversy," Bingham wrote.[14] On August 31, 1861, soldiers and citizens forced Bingham to take a loyalty oath administered by the mayor of Indianapolis.[15]

Thomas Tigar of the Fort Wayne *Sentinel* was another important Democratic editor in Indiana. The industrious Tigar made the *Sentinel* a daily on January 1, 1861, and his paper was strong on local news.[16] Politically, Tigar tried to stay neutral as much as possible, and that position earned him respect from members of both parties. Ransom Hastings, owner of the Lafayette *Argus*, opposed the Civil War and was ostracized by both Republicans and Democrats. A recruiting officer assaulted Hastings on September 1, 1861.[17]

Before Burnside hired Hascall to shepherd the Hoosier State, there had already been several incidents of press intimidation in Indiana. On August 8, 1862, the War Department issued an order establishing military commissions to deal with those citizens who discouraged voluntary enlistment in speech or writing. This order increased the frequency of press intimidation throughout the North. Iowa, a state that was proud of its support of the war, would be the setting for a case that would have major implications for the spring of 1863.

THE IOWA PRECEDENT

No incident under this order was more alarming to Northern Democrats than the arrest of Dennis A. Mahony, the editor of the Dubuque, Iowa, *Herald*.[18] Mahony, who had been state printer in 1854, the owner of Iowa's first daily, and a state legislator from 1859 to 1861, was held in a Washington, D.C., prison for three months, starting on August 14, 1862.[19]

Mahony, a native of Ireland and conservative Democrat, bought the Dubuque *Herald* on May 8, 1860. He opposed secession, but before Lincoln took office he was against the quelling of the rebellion. However, when the Civil War began in the spring of 1861, Mahony supported the war. In early 1862, he was still behind the war, even though in his opinion it had bogged down into a stalemate both on its eastern and western fronts. Still, the Dubuque Democrat was enthusiastic enough to offer to Iowa's governor, the man in charge of enlisting volunteers to fill the state's quota of Union soldiers, the development of an Irish regiment. However, Governor Samuel J. Kirkwood turned down the offer. In the spring of 1862, Mahony's *Herald* gained the printing contract for city and county government after Democrats swept the local elections. This was critical to the survival of the newspaper since Dubuque merchants, most of whom were Republicans, stayed away from advertising in the *Herald*.[20]

On August 14, the pro-Republican *Iowa Daily State Register* in Des Moines announced the "Arrest of A Traitor," detailing Mahony's detention at four o'clock in the morning the previous day by a group of fifty soldiers led by U.S. Marshal Herbert Melville Hoxie, the former publisher of the *Register*.[21] Mahony awoke, came to the bedroom window, and saw a gathering of men outside. The *Herald* editor assumed that a mob wanted to harm him. Mahony, who had been a teacher, postmaster, and lawyer before buying the *Herald*, apparently tried to "alarm" neighbors, but P. H. Conger, deputy U.S. Marshal, informed the editor who he was and that the situation was impossible because of the size of the force arrayed against him.[22] Then Hoxie, Conger, and the soldiers entered the house and made the arrest.

Allegedly, Mahony yelled, "Here I am, a martyr to Liberty!"[23] Mahony asked on whose authority the arrest was made. Hoxie had received a directive from Secretary of War Edwin M. Stanton on July 26, 1862, authorizing the marshal to arrest and imprison any person who "shall do any act or make any declaration or publication to discourage or prevent enlistment of volunteers to suppress the rebellion."[24] As far back as February 14, 1862, Stanton had said he would go after persons "deemed incompatible with the public safety."[25] At the time he made that order, Stanton thought the war was actually coming to an end—and, of course, he was mistaken. Thus, Hoxie replied to Mahony that the arrest was made by order of Secretary of War Stanton. Mahony asked for the order, but Hoxie did not present it. At that point, Mahony accepted his fate and went quietly.[26] Republican newspapers in Iowa cited Stanton as the issuer of the warrant.

Hoxie told Mahony that he would arrange a meeting with Kirkwood, a Republican. Mahony jotted a note to the governor requesting a meeting, but it never occurred.[27] Kirkwood did respond in writing, but it offered no encouragement. The *Herald* editor and long-time political leader was bitterly disappointed and felt deceived by "one whom I regarded as a friend."[28] Mahony said he had no intention of embarrassing the federal government, but that he had a right to criticize it if "it was committing errors, and surely it is not a crime to say that if one believes it earnestly."[29]

The arrest was reported in the next day's *Herald*, which claimed that Mahony would not retract any of his published words.[30] Furthermore, there is no evidence that Mahony ever actually printed any words that told the citizens of Dubuque not to enlist.[31] In the winter and spring of 1862, Mahony organized Democratic neighborhood meetings in Dubuque and did make resolutions that denounced two areas of so-called "abolition treason": (1) the suspension of the writ of habeas corpus and (2) wartime financial policy, including the personal income tax.[32] In fact, the *Herald* supported the draft, as long as it was conducted in a fair way.[33] Mahony also encouraged Republicans to enlist speedily. The editor did write that if the president or Congress subverted the Constitution, "the people have the right to resist such subversion."[34] Yet there were no specific words that counseled resistance to the draft or voluntarily enlisting.

The *Iowa Daily State Register's* editorial gloated that Mahony would soon be joining Confederate prisoners captured at Fort Donelson "to keep the other Seecesh prisoners" company.[35] The editorial claimed that Iowa had ten thousand members of the pro-South Knights of the Golden Circle. Some KGC members had intimated trouble would follow if any more of its leaders were harmed by state or federal authorities. "Their Chief Priest has felt the strong hand of the Law! Let his disciples attempt his rescue if they dare!"[36]

The pro-Republican Fairfield *Weekly Ledger* claimed that one reason Mahony deserved incarceration was because he and the Democrats had failed to censure former U.S. Senator George Washington Jones at a recent state convention. The *Weekly Ledger* said that Jones, a Dubuque resident, and Mahony were "avowed sympathizers with the rebellion" and that the failure to criticize Jones' pre-war letter to Jefferson Davis was causing "scores and hundreds" of "true patriotic and loyal members of the party" to leave it.[37] Hoxie had arrested Jones the previous Christmas for being a Southern sympathizer.[38] Jones was imprisoned at Fort Lafayette, New York, until February 22, 1862. Jones' position was hurt by the fact that two of his sons joined the Confederate Army.[39]

After Mahony's arrest, Fairfield's Republican newspaper urged loyal prowar Democrats to turn on the party's leadership: "We call upon honest and patriotic Democrats everywhere, and especially in our own State, to scan closely the designs of those corrupt men who are bringing disgrace upon their party. Repudiate them as your brave sons and friends in the army are repudiating them."[40] The Burlington *Hawkeye* claimed that in townships where Mahony's allies held majorities enlistments were minimal. "The principle of Mahonyism just as certainly discourages enlistments as it gives aid and comfort to the rebels."[41] Still, there was no reference to a direct statement or editorial by Mahony discouraging enlistments.

Two days later, Hoxie arrested David Sheward, the editor of the pro-Democratic Fairfield *Union and Constitution*.[42] Again, Hoxie said he was acting on a warrant from Stanton. Sheward's wife, Lora, took over the editor's duties at the *Union and Constitution* and asked his friends "to give me their aid in this emergency."[43] Hoxie took both Mahony and Sheward to Burlington, where Iowa Senator James W. Grimes visited Mahony in his hotel room. Grimes assured Mahony that he would petition Stanton to make the trial a speedy one. On August 18, Hoxie boarded a train, taking both Mahony and Sheward to Washington, D.C.

Before the transit to Washington, Mahony dashed off a letter to the Dubuque *Herald* in which he uttered the mantra of many Northern Democrats, asking his fellow party members to preserve "the Constitution as it is, and the Union as it was."[44] Mahony claimed he was being imprisoned precisely because he had been faithful to the Constitution.[45] Both Mahony and Sheward said they were ignorant of their crimes against the federal government. Each asked for a writ of habeas corpus, and neither received it. Stilson Hutchins, Mahony's assistant at the Dubuque *Herald*, defended Mahony as being loyal to the Constitution and being "an active, influential, trusted citizen of Iowa" for two decades.[46] Hutchins, who was educated at Harvard and had run the Democratic paper in Des Moines before coming to Dubuque, called the arrest "an act of arbitrary power."[47]

The *Register*, meanwhile, chastised both Mahony and Sheward for failing to use their power as editors to adequately support the Lincoln administration and the war effort: "Instead of proffering that aid, they have thrown every possible obstacle in the way of the Union cause, palliating if not defending the great crime of the revolted States."[48]

Charles Mason, who had been Iowa's first Supreme Court Chief Justice before moving to Washington before the war, worked to have Mahony released. Mason found out that Mahony had been turned over to the judge advocate of the volunteers and that Stanton wanted political prisoners like the Dubuque newspaper editor to be tried by military commissions. Mason, who sent journalistic dispatches back to the *Herald* under several pseudonyms, believed that arrests of the Iowans were entirely for political reasons and were intended "to act upon the approaching election in our State."[49] Mason indicated that Mahony, who was not allowed to receive outside news, would be a candidate for Congress and predicted—correctly—the incarcerations would end soon after the election. Mason also wrote that he thought Stanton would not approve of the political arrests of Iowans.[50] The Davenport *Democrat* chastised the state's Republicans for conspiring to imprison Mahony to keep him from successfully running for Congress. The *Democrat* said the *Herald* editor would stand out against any Republican opponent and would overwhelm him in debate.[51]

Six days after Mahony's arrest, a Democratic convention in Fayette County nominated the *Herald* chief to stand as its candidate for the Third Congressional District, something that had been expected before his arrest.[52] The vote was close, with Mahony defeating G.W. Gray of Allamakee County by a single vote.[53] The *Iowa Daily State Register* called the nomination "bold, to say the least" and thought it was wrong for the Democrats to run a man who was in jail.[54] The *Register* also said that some convention delegates opposed Mahony's nomination, and the affair ended in a "row."[55] The *Register* predicted William B. Allison, the Republican nominee and one of Hoxie's friends, would defeat Mahony by three to five thousand votes.[56] The pro-Republican Fairfield *Ledger* said the Democrats "cannot expect any considerable portion of the people of that District to treat such a nomination with anything but scorn, contempt and loathing. And yet his traitorous political satellites will no doubt have the brazenfacedness to go before the people and ask them to cast their votes for him as the purest of patriots."[57] The Chicago *Tribune* said that any man who voted for Mahony also ought to see time in a military prison.[58] Even Wilbur F. Storey's pro-Democratic Chicago *Times* wondered if Mahony's choice was appropriate, stating that it was hypocritical for a law-and-order man like the *Herald* editor to stand for office while he was in prison. Storey, whose paper would be suspended the following June, made the case for the rule of law: "Let Democrats remember that there is but one safe way out of the terrible troubles which rebellion against the law, North and South, has brought upon us. This is, by standing up for the SUPREMACY OF THE LAW at all times, in all places and under all circumstances. If Mr. Mahony has been wrongfully arrested, and if he be innocent, the law will vindicate him, and nothing else can."[59]

Hutchins printed Mahony's views on the topics of the day just before the October election. They included no direct statements that Mahony discouraged enlistments. Instead, Mahony balanced his views by, on the one hand, saying secession was unconstitutional, but on the other saying that the Lincoln administration was "in rebellion to the Constitution."[60]

Allison, who was a colonel in the Union Army, defeated Mahony in October of 1862 in the Third District race to give the Republicans total control of the state's congressional delegation—six congressmen and two senators—as well as the governor's mansion and both houses of the state legislature.[61] The tally in the Third District was 12,112 for Allison, compared to 8,452 for Mahony.[62] The Burlington *Hawkeye* said the citizens of the Third District gave Mahony "a most withering rebuke" that stood as a "warning to Northern 'Butternuts.' "[63] Allison won in part because of redistricting. Democrats garnered forty-three percent of the vote in the state's six congressional districts, but they lost all six seats. The lines had been redrawn since 1860 when Iowa had only two seats in the U.S. House of Representatives, and they had been reestablished in such a way to guarantee Republican victory in each district.[64] Allison also dominated the soldiers' vote by an eighteen-to-one ratio—an amazing fact considering that the majority of the soldiers in the district were Democrats. The *Herald* charged voting irregularities occurred in the military, thus depressing Mahony's vote total.[65]

On November 11, 1862, Stanton released Mahony and Sheward from the Old Capitol prison in Washington and allowed them to return home to Iowa.[66] This occurred only after the two Iowans had signed an oath of allegiance. They also agreed not to sue Hoxie, Stanton, or any other officers of the federal or state government in the future.[67] The 42-year-old Mahony, who was ill, came home to Dubuque to a "huge concourse of citizens," bonfires on the levee, a marching band, speeches by Ben M. Samuels and Judge James Wilson, and a parade through the streets of Dubuque to Mahony's home.[68]

Several months in prison had a temporary chilling effect on Mahony and Sheward since they were unable to write for their newspapers during that time, and Hutchins temporarily softened the rhetoric in the *Herald*. Yet if Mahony's eighty-nine-day imprisonment was supposed to shut him up, it seemed to have the opposite effect. At first, when he returned to Dubuque, Mahony rested, but eventually he would write more vituperatively than before his arrest. However, he added a second medium to his arsenal. While Mahony was in prison, he began writing what would become his seminal work, *The Prisoner of State*, a book about his arrest and incarceration, a scathing attack on arbitrary arrests by despotic government. During the winter of 1862–1863, Mahony worked to have it published and also worked on a pamphlet titled "Four Acts of Despotism." Both were published in New York, the latter in a paper called *The Caucasian*, which had an antiwar editorial bias.[69] Mahony harped on a class theme, saying the draft's substitution clause left the poor men unable to pay $300 for proxies "in the hands of the administration."[70] The pro-Republican Dubuque *Times* claimed that because Mahony published the "Four Acts of Despotism" in New York, he was partially responsible for the draft riots that occurred there in July of 1863.[71]

At the same time that Mahony was in jail, an editor in Ohio was arrested just before the election. In October, a county provost marshal arrested Archibald McGregor, editor of Canton's *Stark County Democrat*, and conveyed him by rail to Camp Mansfield. His wife, Martha McGregor, said that the marshal gave no reason for the arrest. "I know that he has violated no law, and has been ever faithful to the Constitution as it is, and the Union as it was. Perhaps, however, that is his offending.["72] McGregor, whose paper had been attacked in 1861 by a mob that included the son of Canton's mayor, was released by the military three weeks later.[73]

<h2 style="text-align:center">VIOLENCE AGAINST HOOSIER EDITORS</h2>

In Indiana, the Terre Haute *Journal* had supported Stephen A. Douglas in the 1860 presidential election. On October 21, 1861, the *Journal* was destroyed by members of the Forty-Third Indiana Regiment, men who were not enamored of editor Grafton F. Cookerly's antiwar, anti-Republican stance.[74] Supportive of both former Ohio Congressman Clement L. Vallandigham and Indiana Democratic Congressman Daniel W. Vorhees, the *Journal* did not resume publication until December 12.[75] Cookerly sold the paper in 1862 to John S. Jordan and J. B. Edmunds, who had owned it earlier.[76]

Also in the fall of 1861, a Union recruiting officer beat up Lafayette *Argus* editor Ransom Hastings, who approved of Southern secession. Hastings opposed the war and was disliked by both Republicans and Democrats.[77] The recruiting officer who pummeled the editor was provoked by Hastings' criticism of enlistments in the military.[78] Like many of the Democratic editors of the period, Hastings eventually found the endeavor to be too much, ending publication of his daily paper on September 15, 1864.[79]

In the fall of 1862, New Albany *Ledger* editor Luciene G. Matthews was arrested under the Fifty-Seventh Article of War of 1806 for publishing information about where Indiana soldiers had been assigned.[80] Matthews reported to General Horatio G. Wright in Cincinnati.[81] Wright released the editor, who claimed he copied the story from another paper. Because the *Ledger* was "a Democratic paper supporting the war probably served as a mitigating circumstance in the case," journalism historian Robert S. Harper observed.[82]

There were other forms of suppression. For example, the military often drove reporters from the field, saying that their reports were aiding the enemy. Similarly, the telegraph was taken over by the military on July 8, 1861.[83] This made it difficult for reporters to transmit their dispatches to their editors. Sometimes transmission was cut when a paper was trying to send a report to a wire service. The Chicago *Times* reported a dispatch about troop movements to the Associated Press was censored "without any notice of such suppression being given to the agent."[84] Another mode of suppressing newspapers was via the mails. In Memphis, Major General S. A. Hurlbut, who was from Illinois, banned the circulation and mailing of the Chicago *Times* early in 1863 for publishing "false and calumnious articles against the President of the United States, and giving aid and comfort to the public enemy."[85]

OWNERSHIP PATTERNS: AN EFFECT OF SUPPRESSION

Hascall's attempt to suppress Democratic newspapers in Indiana from April 25 to June 6, 1863, had a temporary chilling effect on the Democratic press of Indiana because it destabilized the ownership of those papers and even put several papers out of business. For purposes of this study, relative stability of a newspaper was determined by the number of owners a paper had in a given period of time—in this case, from April of 1861 to April of 1865. An inverse relationship was established. That is, the more owners for a given newspaper over those four years, the less stability it had. In other words, a higher rate of ownership transfer by a newspaper represented less stability, and a lower rate meant greater stability.

A comparison of the ownership patterns of the Democratic and Republican newspapers in the eleven Indiana cities where suppression took place in 1863 shows that Republican ownership was more stable than Democratic. On average, just a little less than two owners (single owners or ownership groups) published Republican papers in the suppression cities from 1861 to 1865. By contrast, Democratic papers in those cities were owned by almost three owners per paper. (See Table 5.1, Part 1 below.) Of the eleven counties examined, the Rush County *Jeffersonian* in Rushville had the greatest ownership turnover during the war with six different owners. Rush County saw frequent violence between the parties during the war, and two draft officials were murdered there in 1863.[86] Four of the eleven counties had at least three owners for their Democratic papers, and two of the eleven counties had three owners for their Republican papers. Five of the eleven counties had a single Republican owner during the paper, compared to two with a single Democratic owner.

Another group of newspapers was chosen randomly from cities in Indiana in which suppression of Democratic newspapers did not occur during the Civil War. In this comparison, ownership change for Democratic papers was, on average, almost doubled (2.9 to 1.6, or 1.8 to 1) in towns where suppression occurred from those where it did not occur. (See Table 5.1, Part 2 below.) Ownership change for Republican papers was, on average, slightly lower (1.7 to 2.0, or 0.8 to 1) in towns where suppression occurred from those where it did not occur. Thus, suppression had a temporary negative effect on the stability of Democratic newspapers. Suppression had little or no positive effect on Republican papers. Republican papers gained little themselves from

Table 5.1   Newspaper ownership patterns, 1851 to 1855, 1861 to 1865, and 1871–1875

1851–1855

Part 1. Counties with suspended Democratic papers in the Civil War

Counties analyzed: Blackford, Huntington, Johnson, Kosciusko, Marshall, Pulaski, Rush, St. Joseph, Starke, Wells, Whitley

Number of counties with Democratic papers = 8

Number of counties with Republican papers = 6

Total number of Democratic owners from 1851 to 1855 = 10

Average Democratic ownership = 1.3

Total number of Republican owners from 1851 to 1855 = 16

Average Republican ownership = 2.7

*-Part 2. Counties without suspended Democratic papers

Counties analyzed: Cass, Dearborn, Delaware, Fountain, Gibson, Knox, LaPorte, Morgan, Ohio, Pike, Tipton, Wabash, Wayne

Number of counties with Democratic papers = 10

Number of counties with Republican papers = 11

Total number of Democratic owners from 1851 to 1855 = 16

Average Democratic ownership = 1.6

Total number of Republican owners from 1851 to 1855 = 18

Average Republican ownership = 1.6

1861–1865

Part 1. Counties with suspended Democratic papers

Counties analyzed: Blackford, Huntington, Johnson, Kosciusko, Marshall, Pulaski, Rush, St. Joseph, Starke, Wells, Whitley

Number of counties with Democratic papers = 10

Number of counties with Republican papers = 10

Total number of Democratic owners from 1861 to 1865 = 29

Average Democratic ownership = 2.9

Total number of Republican owners from 1861 to 1865 = 17

Average Republican ownership = 1.7

*-Part 2. Counties without suspended Democratic papers

Counties analyzed: Cass, Dearborn, Delaware, Fountain, Gibson, Knox, LaPorte, Morgan, Ohio, Pike, Tipton, Wabash, Wayne

Number of counties with Democratic papers = 9

Number of counties with Republican papers = 13

Total number of Democratic owners from 1861 to 1865 = 14

Average Democratic ownership = 1.6

Total number of Republican owners from 1861 to 1865 = 24

Average Republican ownership = 2.0

1871–1875

Part 1. Counties with suspended Democratic papers

Counties analyzed: Blackford, Huntington, Johnson, Kosciusko, Marshall, Pulaski, Rush, St. Joseph, Starke, Wells, Whitley

Number of counties with Democratic papers = 11

Number of counties with Republican papers = 11

Total number of Democratic owners from 1871 to 1875 = 17

Average Democratic ownership = 1.5

Total number of Republican owners from 1871 to 1875 = 14

Average Republican ownership = 1.3

*-Part 2. Counties without suspended Democratic papers

Counties analyzed: Cass, Dearborn, Delaware, Fountain, Gibson, Knox, LaPorte, Morgan, Ohio, Pike, Tipton, Wabash, Wayne

Number of counties with Democratic papers = 12

Number of counties with Republican papers = 11

Total number of Democratic owners from 1871 to 1875 = 23

Average Democratic ownership = 1.9

Total number of Republican owners from 1871 to 1875 = 19

Average Republican ownership = 1.7

	Comparison of Ownership Stability					
	Suppressed Counties			*Nonsuppressed Counties*		
Years	Papers in Counties by Party	Owners by Party	Average Ownership Change	Papers in Counties by Party	Owners by Party	Average Ownership Change
1851–1855	D=8	10	1.3	D=10	D=16	1.6
	R=6	16	2.7	R=11	R=18	1.6
1861–1865	D=10	29	2.9	D=9	14	1.6
	R=10	17	1.7	R=13	24	2.0
1871–1875	D=11	17	1.5	D=12	23	1.9
	R=11	14	1.3	R=11	19	1.7

*-Using John W. Miller's *Indiana Newspaper Bibliography*, the author randomly chose other counties to study for changes in newspaper ownership. An initial number was selected by picking a number by closing the author's eyes and simply opening up Miller's book to a random page. That page number was 19. It was made the starting point of the study—that is, the first page in Miller to analyze would be page 19. A second number was chosen by taking the square of 19, taking its cosine, and then adding the last two digits (7 +7) to come up with 14. Thus, every 14 pages after 19 were examined. If both Democratic and Republicans papers did not exist for a particular city, then it was skipped and the author advanced 14 pages for his next selection. In all, 13 counties were selected for this part of the analysis.

suppression, although they benefited from the negative effects on Democratic ownership, especially when Democratic papers shut down permanently, changed their names, or were destroyed. This left the Republican newspapers with no or weakened Democratic competitors.

Newspaper ownership was also analyzed for two other four-year periods, 1851 to 1855 and 1871 to 1875, to determine if ownership patterns in the Civil War were more or less stable. Democratic ownership in the counties where suppression would occur was more stable in the 1851–1855 period than it was in 1861–1865, with an average of 1.3 versus an average of 2.9 owners. That's more than two times as many owners per paper during the war. However, the number of owners was the same for both periods of time for the thirteen counties where suppression did not occur. On the other hand, Republican ownership stability was slightly lower in nonsuppression counties in 1851–1855 (1.6 compared to 2.0), but it was less stable in the suppressed counties in 1851–1855 than in 1861–1855 (2.7 to 1.7). These numbers suggest that Republican newspapers were more stable when their party was in power at the federal level. Similarly, Democratic newspapers were more stable when their party was in power nationally. Moreover, the 1851–1855 numbers confirm that Democratic papers were less stable in the counties where suppression occurred. Continuing the analysis in the decade after the war, it was found that Democratic ownership was less stable than Republican in 1871–1875. However, the difference was small. Indeed, ownership pattern in the suppression counties was relatively stable, indicating a robust newspaper environment, especially since all eleven counties had both Democratic and Republican papers in that period.

The conclusion can be made that suppression contributed to the temporary instability of Democratic newspapers. Of course, politics played a factor in the conditions of the day. The fact that the Republican Party was in power during the Civil War contributed to the financial stability of the Republican newspapers since patronage was still the rule in these latter days of the partisan press era. Indeed, in the group of thirteen counties randomly chosen for analysis, twelve had Republican newspapers and only nine had Democratic newspapers. In other words, conditions for Republican newspapers were more favorable than for those of the Democrats.

That the Republican papers were more stable during the war may also be attributable to the tendency of the party to attract the business class, whose acumen for making a profit may have been a bit more acute than that of their Democratic counterpart. Moreover, that the Democratic Party suffered perhaps the greatest collapse of party power in the nation's history certainly had an effect. Public opinion generally was against the Democrats for much of the war, except in counties where the Democrats had traditionally held a significant advantage over first the Whigs and then the Republicans.

Journalism in the Midwestern states during the 1860s had not progressed as much as it had in the East. In Indiana, journalism was a remnant of the party press era of 1800–1833. The editors published four-page newspapers that cost a reader $2.50 a year. The content included advertising, editorials, and news reports, which were interpreted along party lines. Little artwork accompanied the articles. This was a text-heavy era.

These newspapers were not the mass-produced, steam-press penny papers of the nation's urban areas. They were produced on hand presses for circulations of only a few thousand at the most. In general, U.S. newspapers were undergoing major changes during the middle decades of the nineteenth century. It was a transitional stage in which the political and personal press was giving way to first the penny and then the professional, commercial press of the twentieth century. The men and women who produced American newspapers and magazines tended to favor one political cause or party.

At the same time, the newspapers of the Civil War era already were beginning to be dominated by commercial interests. A typical Civil War newspaper contained plenty of advertising on its front page, with news and commentary starting on the second page. Despite the presence of these classified-like ads on the front page, Midwestern newspapers still tended to be driven more by politics than their counterparts in the East. The page-two analysis and commentary section was the heart of the newspaper, the place where the editor's voice reached full volume.

Hascall's official suppression of the Democratic editors in Indiana, though it lasted only six weeks, came at a time when the Democrats had gained the advantage in the state general assembly and in the congressional delegation. Major General John C. Fremont did harass editors in Missouri, but it was a border and slave state. Indiana was neither. Suppression was also widespread in Maryland, another slave state. Newspapers were suppressed in California and Oregon, but this was far from the war's main conflict. Most of Indiana's Democrats supported the Union, though not conscription or emancipation.[87]

SUPPRESSION MORE LIKELY IN NORTHERN INDIANA

The fact that Hascall went after editors primarily in the northern part of the state, all near his home of Goshen, suggests he felt confident he could intimidate the Democratic editors of Plymouth, South Bend, Warsaw, Bluffton,

Columbia City, Winamac, Huntington, Rushville, Hartford City, Franklin, and Knox because he was intimate with the Republican political leaders in these towns. Furthermore, the brigadier general bypassed the Democratic editors in the area's largest city, Fort Wayne, precisely because he knew the Democrats were stronger there and the press was more sophisticated in Allen County. He also did not threaten editors in Indianapolis, which was split between Republicans, who had the executive branch, and Democrats, who had the majority in the legislature. This reconfirms John Stevens' hypothesis that constraints work better in homogeneous societies. Since Fort Wayne and Indianapolis had more Democratic support, it would require greater governmental power to support constraints. With the federal military government and state governor out of phase, suppression in Allen and Marion counties was a more difficult proposition.

From 1861 to the late summer of 1862, the war tended to unify the press in Indiana. After Lincoln announced the Emancipation Proclamation on September 22, 1862, the unity disappeared. Democrats began to become more and more critical of the war, while Republicans dug in and began to see the political battle in terms of loyalty and disloyalty. The generally muddy war news of the first two years of the conflict intensified the divide, as did Democratic concerns about conscription and their economic future in a nation of freed slaves and dispossessed slave owners. In a sense, both Democratic and Republican editors began to dabble in the politics of fear. First Burnside's edict and then Hascall's added fuel to the fire. Governor Morton remained quiet, seemed to tacitly approve of the measures, and yet worked behind the scenes to get rid of Hascall and return a closer ally to the head of the federal shadow government in Indiana. Republican editors cheered Hascall. Democrats cursed him, then desisted while swearing loyalty.

Those eleven newspapers that Hascall suppressed generally faced tough times in the first decade after suppression. Seven still existed after the war, three shut down after suppression, and one was destroyed that same year in another incident. Two of the seven that still existed in 1865 changed their titles, and the Pulaski County *Democrat* actually did not print a paper for more than a year after Hascall's suppression before coming back as a Republican paper, the *Weekly Herald*.

Thus, only five of eleven remained pro-Democratic papers with the same title they had the day before Hascall suppressed them. Thus, Hascall's attempt to suppress was successful, though by no means absolute. Four papers out of eleven went out of business, and only five remained intact by the end of the war. Meanwhile, in April of 1865, Republican papers existed in ten of the eleven counties where Democratic papers were suppressed. Only one county, Starke, did not have a Republican paper during the war, and the Pulaski County *Republican* only came into existence in April of 1865.

In the long run, papers connected to both parties survived. By 1875, nine of the eleven Democratic newspapers were operating again, although five under new names. Only one of the nine papers changed allegiance from the Democrats to the Republicans. Of the Republican papers in the cities where suppression occurred, nine of the ten remained in existence in 1875, all Republican.

DEMOCRATIC EDITORS' PHILOSOPHY

In conclusion, an observation can be made about the relationship between the editorial tendencies of the minority and majority newspapers. In a two-party press system in a democracy at times of grave political crisis, the press of the majority party tends to provide the arguments for and information supportive of constraints on expression. The press of the minority party tends to provide the arguments for and information supportive of unlimited expression. The leaders of the majority tend to call on the intellectual resources that support limited expression, while the leaders of the minority called on the intellectual resources that support unlimited expression.

Indiana's Democratic editors during the Civil War tended to espouse the ideas that would support their advocacy of states' right, unlimited civil liberties, limited government, and racial superiority. The tone of their discourse was reactionary and defensive. Many of them felt the abolitionists had painted the Southerners into a corner. Lincoln, who was unable to win the war quickly, became a revolutionary in their mind, especially when he created the conscription laws and the Emancipation Proclamation.

The Democrats' political ideology ultimately served to help develop the history of freedom of the press in the United States. Paradoxically, though, it continued the long tradition of hampering the civil rights of blacks. It continued the same paradox that Jefferson, the slave owner and champion of liberty, failed to resolve in the founding moments of the nation's history. The contradictions would not be worked out completely by the Civil War verdict, and Democratic editors in counties with Democratic majorities continued to spout their vituperation unchecked throughout the war and beyond.

CHAPTER SIX

Unionism and Emancipation in Civil War Indiana

This chapter analyzes Republican and Democratic newspapers in a few select Hoosier cities in September and October of 1862 and in January of 1863. It will isolate and interpret frameworks in the text. Newspapers from the following Indiana cities were analyzed: Indianapolis, Fort Wayne, Richmond, South Bend, Delphi, Logansport, Plymouth, Goshen, and Evansville. These cities were chosen because they had robust newspaper traditions at the time and because copies of both a Democratic and Republican paper in these towns exist in the Indiana State Library. This analysis focuses more on how the content producers utilized framing than it does on what effect the content frames had on audiences, although clearly something happened to the white male voters of Indiana after Lincoln announced the Proclamation in September of 1862. Republicans saw a major reversal in fortune after the fall elections of that year—so much so that the Lincoln administration used desperate and unconstitutional measures to hold the North together politically in the remaining years of the war—especially universalizing the suspension of the writ of habeas corpus.

The study also examines a period of time that was crucial in the development of journalism in the Hoosier State. In the spring of 1863, Hoosier newspaper editors would live under two unique government orders that directly impacted the practice of journalism. First, Major General Burnside, the commander of the Department of the Ohio, promulgated General Order 38 in April of 1863. It stated that anyone encouraging men not to enlist or making oral or written critical or derogatory comments about the war effort of the Lincoln administration would be subject to arrest and a military commission (trial) without benefit of a writ of habeas corpus. A few weeks later, Brigadier General Hascall, the commander of the District of Indiana and Burnside's subordinate, sent out General Order No. 9, which stated he intended to enforce No. 38, especially for those recalcitrant newspaper editors who were carping at the President.

Both Democrats and Republicans in Civil War Indiana had no desire for a divided nation. Even most Peace Democrats in the state wanted reunion, although not with abolition.[1] They wanted a return to the antebellum status quo and wanted it through a negotiated settlement sooner rather than later. Once the war began in April of 1861, Democratic editors used their concept of unionism to maintain a sense of political loyalty when Republican editors were charging many Democrats with being disloyal. For Hoosier Democrats, the concept of unionism was a political weapon designed to keep hard-line Republican Governor Oliver P. Morton from painting the opposition party as abettors of the rebels in the South. The trumpeting of unionism was every bit as much the framing process—rhetorical strategy—as the Republican editors calling the Democrats "Copperheads," "Butternuts," and "traitors." Yet unionism also was a genuine political principle to which almost all Hoosiers subscribed before, during, and after the war. Indiana, as a middle state in the middle of the country, saw the union as being in its best interest.

As a territory of the early West, Indiana had desired statehood, and Hoosiers wanted to see the country grow—not so that slavery could expand, but primarily so that people could always migrate to locate better land to farm and to find greater economic, political, and cultural freedom. When the war came, few if any Hoosiers saw disunion as being in their vested interest. Indeed, Hoosiers did not want to be an interior nation with no ready access to the oceans or subject to taxes imposed by the Confederacy on trade down the Ohio and Mississippi rivers.[2]

Democratic notions of unionism shared some traits with Republican notions of unionism. Both parties wanted to sustain the federal government because both wanted a strong national identity to make the United States a viable entity in the world of nations. Each recognized that the nation was young. Fragmentation of a nation less than a century old would hurt its standing in the world, especially in the eyes of Europe. Both parties wanted to continue the great experiment of a constitutional republican democracy North

American style. Similarly, both parties wanted to avoid being as divided as Europe, and both parties ultimately favored manifest destiny, though at different paces and for different reasons.

Yet the differences between the two forms of unionism were significant and provided the critical rhetorical framing that went on during the war. Both parties' editors used the frames to paint pictures of how the United States should be united. Democrats—and some moderate Republicans—subscribed to a picture or frame of unionism that was largely conservative. Indiana's Democrats harbored no hatred toward the South. Indeed, they tended to believe that Northern abolitionists had backed Southern Democrats into a corner, and secession was an inevitable response to such badgering. Hoosier Democrats, who tended to have Southern roots, saw their brothers in the South as erring, but capable of repentance. The 1860s would be a time to flush out the extremists on both sides, the abolitionists in the North and the firebrands in the South. The Civil War was an indication that extremism had won the day, and democracy could not survive such a state of affairs. In the eyes of the Democratic editors, extremism must be defeated, so both Northern abolitionism and Southern secessionism must be buried. That the country had gotten to the point of war embarrassed many Hoosier Democrats.[3]

Indiana's Democrats believed the solution would come politically, at the ballot box. They saw themselves as the loyal opposition, and their political objective was to regain power and then change would occur. Their goal was for Northern Democrats to regain the presidency and Congress in 1864. At that point, Southern Democrats would end their rebellion and rejoin the union, although few thought about what would happen if the South decided not to return. Voting Lincoln out of office became the chief political objective of Democrats in the Nineteenth State. Accordingly, criticism of Lincoln spiked, particularly as the military progress of the war was limited at best with the narrow win at Antietam, the disaster at Fredericksburg, and the political machinations involving leadership of the Army of the Potomac.

PROWAR SENTIMENT

The majority of Indiana's Democrats were prowar until September of 1862, but all along they refused to support a war of "conquest" or "subjugation." They wanted no interference with slavery in the South, though most opposed its extension in the territories. Their rallying cry from Representative Daniel W. Voorhees, who borrowed it from Clement L. Vallandigham, was "the Constitution as it is, and the Union as it was," a refrain that could be found in almost every Democratic paper in the state.[4] Keeping the rule of law was paramount for Democrats, and the Constitution was the law of the land. If it could be ignored, then rule by the people was in jeopardy. Of course, keeping the Constitution intact meant sustaining slavery in the South and in the border states, making constitutional discipline more important than universal freedom. Democrats in Indiana believed that the Constitution must not be allowed to become a meaningless piece of paper. If slavery were to be outlawed, it must be done legally, by an amendment to the Constitution. When Lincoln announced the Emancipation Proclamation, ostensibly as a war measure, many Hoosier Democrats saw it as a desperate and unconstitutional action by the chief executive. For them, permanent abolition could not be achieved by

Oliver P. Morton, governor of Indiana during the Civil War, was not close to Hascall. Ambrose E. Burnside, commander of the Department of the Ohio, had fired the governor's own pick for commander of the District of Indiana, Henry B. Carrington. *(Photo from the Indiana Historical Society)*

presidential edict. On that September day in 1862, Indiana's Democrats believed that Lincoln turned his back on moderation.

While Republicans focused on winning the war as quickly as possible, Democrats took the broader view and worried about the aftermath of war. Hoosier Democratic newspaper editors speculated on the nature of reconstruction, and radical reconstruction was their great fear. Radical reconstruction meant no clemency and a realignment of the socioeconomic order in the South. Meanwhile, in the Democrats' alternative vision of reconstruction, this would be a time when Northern and Southern Democrats would reunite and control the nation's politics. The South would have slavery, and the North would have free labor. White men's property and freedom would face no threats in either section of the country. The control of property would not be transformed by social and political revolution. In their view, conservatives and moderates would save the day.

Hoosier unionism also meant supporting Union soldiers. Again, this was strategic. The Democrats did not want to be seen as impeding the war effort. Thus, editors like Joseph J. Bingham of the influential *Indiana State Sentinel* in Indianapolis led the way in encouraging draft enlistments. Indeed, Bingham personally recruited soldiers, and other Democratic editors in the state took his lead and did likewise.[5] In part, this was personal. Bingham did not want Berry Sulgrove, editor of the pro-Republican *Indiana Journal*, to do anything better than he did. Therefore, Bingham, who by May of 1861 said the government in Washington "must be sustained," made sure the *Indiana State Sentinel* was a recruiting leader, but the editor's stance on the war was also pragmatic politics.[6] Bingham did not want to give Sulgrove and the other Republican editors in the state any ammunition that Hoosier Democrats were being disloyal. Bingham knew that disloyalty would erode Democratic power. Furthermore, the Republicans had been democratically elected. Resistance to the laws the majority party made was tantamount to anarchy. If anarchy ruled, then the Constitution and freedom would die. Indiana's Democrats had the French Revolution in mind, and they did not want a repeat of the bloodbath that occurred at the end of the eighteenth century. Hoosier Democrats were not enamored of conscription, but most editors told their readers to cooperate with the development of lists of potential draftees—which, for the most part, is what the Civil War draft turned out to be in Indiana, a pool of names that was rarely tapped.

Furthermore, the Democracy, as the party was then known, had plenty to lose. The Democrats had been the dominant party in Indiana for most of the state's existence. Their philosophy had dominated the drafting of the state constitution. Throughout the sectional crisis of the 1840s and 1850s, Hoosier Democrats had remained staunch unionists. They had remained moderate, playing the strategic game of not alienating any political group too much. Joseph A. Wright, the Democratic governor of the state from 1849 until 1857, cast his lot with a national destiny, not Northern or Southern destiny. He had the following inscribed on a block of Indiana limestone in the Washington Monument at the federal capital: "Indiana knows no North, no South, nothing but the Union."[7] In 1850, Wright said Indiana "plants herself on the basis of the Constitution; and takes her stand in the ranks of American destiny."[8] When the war came, Hoosier Democrats were not about to back down from their long-held devotion to union. If anything, the secession movement in the South served to strengthen Hoosier Democrats' unionism because they did not want to lose the political advantage gained by portraying Republicans, especially proabolition Republicans, as extremists whose political views were harmful to the republic.

During the election of 1860, Hoosier Democratic editors warned their readers repeatedly that black equality as pushed by the Republicans would lead to Southern secession. The Democrats had been reading Democratic newspapers in the South, and they blamed Lincoln and the Republicans for pushing the South toward withdrawal from the Union. Hoosier Democratic editors claimed Republicans who agitated for the end of slavery were treasonous because they were forcing the country into civil war.[9] In essence, Republican attitudes and policy were the cause of nullification.

In early 1861, Democratic editors frequently called for union meetings that urged the president elect to be conciliatory and willing to compromise. The Democratic editors urged all political leaders to abandon any policies that would lead inexorably to conflict. They wrote that states had the right to control their domestic institutions and urged all not to violate the Constitution and those laws passed by state and federal legislatures. Democrats began to take on the tone of the law-abiding party. It was a frame by which they tried to force Republicans to take stances that did not go against the Constitution, which upheld slavery. It was a persuasive way to shape the debate, and even the pro-Republican *Journal* in Indianapolis tended to agree with the Democrats, primarily because Sulgrove feared coercion would mean economic ruin for Indiana because of its proximity to vulnerable Kentucky.[10] Sulgrove wrote: "Of what value will an union be that needs links of bayonets and bullets to hold it together?"[11] William Steele Holman, a veteran Democratic congressman from the Fourth District in the southeastern part of the state, said Indiana would "concede and concede and concede, and compromise and compromise and compromise" to preserve the Union.[12]

Another constitutional freedom that rallied Democrats was the right to bear arms. Governor Morton, using federal funds, provided weapons to Republicans and other loyalists as a deterrent against Democrats with anti-war or anti-Lincoln sentiments. Morton wanted to make sure opponents of the federal administration would not get any ideas about covert resistance.[13] State and local officials made it difficult for Democrats to purchase guns during the war, and Democratic editors countered that this violated their Second Amendment rights. After all, Indiana was still in the Union. Although Democrats were able to get arms on what amounted to a black market, editors complained bitterly that antiarms policy aggravated relations between Republicans and Democrats. Democratic resentment of Republicans increased, in response to the implication that non-Republicans who wanted guns were disloyal. To help quell Republican suspicions that Democrats were forming well-armed secret societies that might rebel against the federal government, Bingham denounced both disloyal and loyal secret societies.[14]

EMANCIPATION PROCLAIMS END OF UNITY IN INDIANA

President Lincoln sent his first emancipation message to the country on March 6, 1862, when he put forth a resolution calling for freeing the slaves and compensating their owners. Representative Voorhees, a giant of the Indiana Democracy, would have none of this. The congressman did not want the citizens of his district to have to pay for somebody else's problem. For Voorhees, abolition of this form was a practical problem. It was too expensive—Voorhees figured it would cost hundreds of millions to compensate the slaveholders—and that would be added to a federal debt of $2.5 billion.[15]

The March 6 resolution began to turn many Indiana Democrats against the war. Their war resolve weakened further on September 22, 1862, when Lincoln announced his abolition plan. The Emancipation Proclamation, which would take effect on January 1, 1863, ended slavery in the unconquered lands in the South, as well as the barrier islands off South Carolina. Although it had no effect on slavery in the loyal slave states, Delaware, Maryland, West Virginia, Kentucky, and Missouri, it set the stage for the Thirteenth Amendment, which after the war outlawed the institution permanently throughout the country. It set into motion the integration of the Union Army, for more than 189,000 African Americans would serve in Lincoln's military.[16] This enlistment of black men helped give the North a manpower advantage in the last two years of the war, something that went a long way toward guaranteeing eventual Union victory.

Viewed from the distance of the twenty-first century, the Emancipation Proclamation seems like a just, benign, and righteous edict. Lincoln took the high moral road, and he also added another 190,000 men to his military machine. However, it was not a popular decision when Lincoln made it public, and for the Democratic editors of Indiana, it was the beginning of the end of their enthusiastic support for the war. Governor Morton wrote Secretary of War Edwin M. Stanton, saying: "Every Democratic paper in Indiana is teeming with abuse of New England. They alleged that New England has brought upon us the War by a fanatical crusade against Slavery."[17] Yet it was not the only cause of Democratic dissatisfaction. The quagmire at the front, poor leadership of the military, and the erosion of wartime civil rights also contributed to sagging Democratic keenness for the war. Nonetheless, it was the Emancipation Proclamation that galvanized all of the criticisms of the president's war.

The president's new policy offered little for white men North and South, who wanted no part of the social, economic, and cultural implications of black equality. The edict so upset Northern Democrats and some moderate Republicans that the Democrats staged significant off-year election victories in the months after the bloody battle at Antietam. The greatest gains came in Indiana, Ohio, and Illinois. A Republican majority of sixty-four seats in the U.S. House of Representatives from the Thirty-Seventh Congress would narrow to only twenty-three seats in the Thirty-Eighth Congress.[18] Indiana went from having a Republican majority in its congressional delegation to an overwhelming Democratic majority.

Meanwhile, the major cities of the North, responding to both conscription and emancipation, erupted into violence that would not be equaled again until the 1960s. In July, as the battle at Gettysburg came to a dramatic and decisive close, the streets of New York had their own civil war, as mainly Irish immigrants took out their displeasure with both emancipation and the draft on the city's free blacks. Similar riots occurred in Chicago and Detroit. Even smaller cities like Indianapolis and Fort Wayne, Indiana, had civil unrest. The newly arrived Irish feared that the freed blacks would take their low paying jobs, as had already happened along the docks of the Ohio River in Cincinnati.[19] Freed men used to getting no pay would accept very low pay from employers and would force out those men who were used to slightly higher wages. Why the immigrants took out their frustrations on the newly freed slaves and not the owners speaks volumes about the nature of racism in the United States, and race was a central issue of the war.

The newspaper editors of the North played a major role in the politics of the war, which were inextricably linked to its military facets. The journalism of the day was based more on party than commercial interest. Most newspapers were small and had circulations of less than a thousand. Editors who subscribed to the philosophies of Edmund Burke, Thomas Jefferson, and Andrew Jackson sided with the Democrats. Editors who were fond of the defunct Whigs, free soil, free labor, and unlimited capitalism favored the Republicans. It was still a frontier country, and agriculture was in its twilight years as the nation's primary industry. The spoils of political victory went to the newspaper editors who supported the winning party. State and federal printing contracts helped underwrite the cost of printing and distributing daily and weekly newspapers, as well as one-page daily telegraphic sheets. Advertising was primitive, and except for in major cities, the commercial press that would become the hallmark of twentieth-century journalism had not yet matured.

Morton's statue in front of the capitol in downtown Indianapolis. The Republican governor held the state together through grave financial times and, after the elections of 1862, with the Democrats in control of the legislature.
(Photo by Clark Hadley)

Although Lincoln clearly did not have public opinion on his side when he announced the proclamation, he needed as many newspaper editors on his side as he could muster. He needed to sell all of his war policies to the voting public, and no policy—not even the new income tax or conscription—was less popular than emancipation. Republican editors generally were loyal to Lincoln and tended to support the edict. Democratic editors, who faced suppression and intimidation at the hands of the administration, military, and Republican activists at a time when the interpretation of the First Amendment was not as libertarian as it would become in the twentieth century, screamed that the emancipation was unconstitutional. Democrats said the Constitution allowed Southerners to hold men and women in bondage while counting each slave as three-fifths human for the purpose of determining proportional congressional representation. They thought ending slavery had to be changed by a constitutional amendment, and, of course, they knew Republicans did not have the votes in enough of the states to make that happen. Many War Democrats and some moderate Republicans also opposed emancipation. The majority in the North felt the war was only about saving the Union and nothing more. Even Indiana's Union Party, a coalition of the Republicans and War Democrats, opposed a war for the abolition of slavery, when they met in the summer of 1862 to gear up for the fall elections.[20] Lincoln's decision to add the freeing of blacks as a major *casus belli* came dangerously close to alienating not only key swing voting groups in the Hoosier State, but nearly all of the eligible voters.[21] There were just too few abolitionists in the state.

The continued stranglehold that the party press maintained on journalism meant that a significant amount of text in Indiana newspapers was written with a particular political bent, and that events and issues framing emancipation were written with this bias in mind. Indeed, the party press editors were often major players in the political process, and their editorial content amounted to propaganda. For example, Congressman Schuyler Colfax had owned and remained close to the St. Joseph County *Register*, Supreme Court Judge Samuel E. Perkins edited papers in Richmond and Indianapolis, and John W. Dawson, who helped found the Republican Party in Indiana and would serve as governor of the Utah Territory, owned *Dawson's Daily Times & Union* in Fort Wayne.[22]

Mid-century U.S. political history was dynamic, and both Republicans and Democrats would undergo dramatic changes in the 1850s and 1860s. The Democrats would be divided in half by the election of 1860. The Southern Democrats would lead the move to secede, while the Northern Democrats themselves divided into prowar and propeace factions, though the prowar faction was the larger of the two.

Indiana serves as a case study because it was one of the states where the balance of power between Republicans and Democrats was very close and the situation dynamic. A dramatic power struggle was at hand in the Hoosier State during the spring after the Emancipation Proclamation took effect. Even the Republicans were not totally united. Although Governor Morton wanted to squelch internal dissent, he did not agree with Lincoln administration decisions about military personnel who served in the state's shadow federal government. Riots broke out in Fort Wayne and Indianapolis during mass political rallies in the spring of 1863. The newly formed draft was so unpopular that violence was visited upon the enlistment office of Blackford County in October of 1862 and threats of violence were directed at the draft commission of Fountain County in the winter of 1862–1863.[23] In March, a group of Union soldiers riding through Richmond, Indiana, on a transport train disembarked and destroyed the local Democratic newspaper, an event that was cheered on by the Republican paper and the city's mayor.[24] The same troops attempted to do the same thing in Indianapolis to the *Indiana State Sentinel* later in the day.[25]

Still, the news would get worse. After Antietam, Burnside replaced George McClellan as commander of the Army of the Potomac because McClellan had failed to chase Robert E. Lee and decisively defeat the Confederates. Burnside, a native of Liberty, Indiana, would oversee the disastrous Union loss at Fredericksburg, Virginia, in December of 1862. The editor of the

Cannelton *Reporter* observed: "Burnside's first battle, we fear, will prove one of the saddest of the war. . . . We hope the removal of Buell will not prove to be as great a blunder as the removal of McClellan."[26] In January of 1863, Burnside was reassigned to a post in Cincinnati overseeing the federal shadow governments in the Midwest states. Also in January, the battle of Stones River, Tennessee, ended indecisively. Hascall participated in the battle, commanding the Union First Brigade, First Division of the Fourteenth Corps of the Army of the Cumberland on the left flank.[27] The Union suffered 12,906 casualties in the battle, approximately 1,200 more than the Confederates.[28]

At the same time, negative attitudes toward conscription abounded in the Hoosier State. One reason was that there had been plenty of volunteers when the war started, but many regiments, including Hascall's Seventeenth from Elkhart County, had been sent home because Washington said it had too many soldiers. Now, two years later, when recruiters could find few able-bodied men to sign up, few Hoosiers had a strong sentiment for the draft. Nonetheless, on July 17, 1862, Congress passed a law that authorized states to use conscription if they could not maintain their quotas. A commissioner was appointed in each county to make a list of all male citizens ages eighteen to forty-five. The lists, with exemptions, were forwarded to Indianapolis, and the state commissioner for the draft determined which counties had met their quotas. Those counties that had not were instructed to draw names from their list and send the draftees to Indianapolis. Under the "Commutation Clause," a substitute could be hired for $300.[29] When Lincoln asked for 300,000 more men from the nation on August 4, 1862, Indiana assumed it failed to meet its state quota. Indiana, whose adjutant general described recruiting as being in a "very languid state" at this time, conscripted 3,003 men, though later it would be discovered that the state had actually exceeded its quota and actually should not have forced anybody on the draft rolls to serve.[30]

Democrats, who saw themselves as the common people, felt that being forced to fight for principles they opposed made them like European serfs coerced to fight "under a military despotism."[31] Class warfare also reared its ugly head. A growing sentiment against the war included a sense that wealthy Republicans who favored it were staying at home leaving poor Democrats to do combat. Congressman Holman of Aurora attacked the Commutation Clause and tried to have it removed by amendment to the Conscription Act but lost by twenty votes.[32] Furthermore, the draft included the substitution fee that the wealthy could afford, and many Democrats felt this clause in the law made the war one for the rich, fought by the poor. In addition to the draft resistance that occurred in Blackford and Fountain counties in October of 1862, violence over conscription would occur in Boone, Fulton, Johnson, Putnam, Rush, Sullivan, Greene, and Monroe counties in the spring of 1863.[33] Threats were made against draft commissioners in Randolph and Knox counties.[34] It must be presumed there were threats elsewhere, but they were not reported in the press. The worst of it came in Rushville, where an enrollment officer was murdered.[35]

The unpopularity of the draft, combined with the Emancipation Proclamation and the indecisive war news, gave Democrats the grist they needed for the 1862 fall elections. Even the prowar New Albany *Ledger*, which had been a Democratic paper before the war, stopped supporting Morton and the Union Party and returned to the Democratic fold. Joseph J. Bingham's *Indiana State Sentinel* led the drum beat against emancipation, asking prowar Democrats if they would "sit down to the abolition feast."[36] Morton pleaded for no parties during the war, although the Union Party over which he presided held its state convention in the summer of 1862 to prepare for the fall elections.[37] Morton also made the argument that the maintenance of slave labor in the South enabled the CSA to have the (white) men available to fight the war. He said: "If the rebels do not desire the Government of the United States to interfere with their slaves, let them cease to employ them in the prosecution of the war. . . . Deprive them of slave labor, and three-fourths of the men composing their armies would be compelled to return home to raise food upon which to subsist themselves and families."[38] Democratic leaders like Congressman Voorhees and U.S. Senator Thomas A. Hendricks supported conscription because it was the law of the land, and the Democrats wanted to be seen as the rule-of-law party.[39] They counseled repeal of the law by voting a Democratic majority to Congress.

In the spring of 1863 when Hascall took office in Indianapolis, the Army of the Potomac, now under the direction of Joseph Hooker, was about to suffer another loss, this time at Chancellorsville, Virginia. The Democratic editors, already tired of the overall carnage of the war, as well as the draft, income tax, emancipation, and the organization of black troops, became even more critical of Lincoln, the military, and Republican editors, who argued for suppression of disloyal editors.[40] The whole situation was a communications clutter, but more importantly, it was, like the war, a contest for power, and framing supplied the way to power. Words like "loyalty" and "disloyalty" indicated how entrenched political positions were, but because the war itself was so lengthy and so dynamic, the molding of public opinion was not insignificant. Every military event had a political consequence. A long-standing professional army did not exist North or South.

While most Northern soldiers, for example, certainly favored the war effort, fathers, brothers, and friends back home often had different views of the war. The interpersonal communication between father and son, brother and brother, and friend and friend had major political significance. While the soldiers' views tended to be affected most heavily by their personal experiences, the views of the men back home were affected by the editorials and news in their hometown papers and the talk around town. One man in Monroe County pleaded with his son to quit fighting after emancipation: "I am sorry that I have a son in the servis [sic] to help uphold the old traitor's Emansapation Proclamation Bill . . . lay down your arms and come home if you can."[41] What the editors wrote and how they wrote their words molded public opinion. The very existence of the United States as a one-nation entity hung in the balance, and the editors played a central role in the opinion-making dynamic of the period.

A frame analysis of Indiana's newspapers of 1862 and 1863 showed competing representations of emancipation, the key political issue of the day.[42] A textual analysis attempted to describe the structural and rhetorical elements related to emancipation, with an emphasis on the relationship between freedom and power.[43] Republican and Democratic editors developed frames that arose in the aftermath of the Emancipation Proclamation's announcement in late September and early October of 1862 and its taking effect in January of 1863. Editors emphasized certain traits of emancipation. They also excluded some information and elaborated upon other information in their editorials on emancipation. Other components of framing include headlines, type of article, and placement on the page.

FRAMING EMANCIPATION

Media scholar Robert M. Entman defines framing as selecting attributes of an issue or individual and making them "more salient in a communicating text."[44] The goals of framing include (a) defining or describing a problem, (b) providing a causal interpretation, (c) evaluating a problem, and (d) providing a treatment or solution.[45] In essence, as Entman noted, "Frames call attention to some aspects of reality while obscuring other elements, which might lead audiences to have different reactions."[46] Republican editors tended to frame emancipation in terms of how it would help the Union gain military victory while avoiding the agitation of Democrats with appeals to the morality of abolition or the immorality of slavery. On the other hand, Democratic editors emphasized legal ramifications of emancipation. Another way to look at framing is through vocabulary, content choice, and sentence complexity. The buzzwords and phrases the editors employed cued readers, and the level of sentence complexity corresponded to how the two sides framed their arguments, Republicans focusing on loyalty and the Democrats on constitutionality.

Framing ultimately is about editorial selection and prominence, or salience. As scholar Charlotte Ryan has noted, media framing is "a central political activity," essential to the development of party positions on the issues of the day.[47] In the journalism of the Civil War, frames were developed by editors who were central members of political parties wrestling for control of the country in the hour of its deepest crisis. The framing contest was undiluted, and the gatekeepers were party hacks, not neutral editors. In a sense, there was no traditional framing dialogue because editors were preaching to the choir. Still, the Democratic and Republican editors performed a key role in ordering information about emancipation, and they shaped their readers' view of this significant presidential order when the political order of the country—and, in particular, Indiana—underwent unremitting change.

The Emancipation Proclamation was a key political action taken at a critical juncture in the war. Lincoln had seen what he thought would be a three-month war involving only 75,000 men become a two-year-old conflict involving hundreds of thousands of men that tested the political will of the states that had remained in the Union. His generals proved ineffective, and the South, needing only to defend itself against Northern "invasion," was holding its own on the battlefield. Among Northern resource advantages were superior manpower, industrial capacity, and communication and transportation lines. However, the less-than-expeditious prosecution of the war left many in the North ambivalent about fighting it any longer. Peace advocacy grew in the fall of 1862 and the first half of 1863.

DISAFFECTION FOR THE WAR

In Indiana, the growing disaffection for the war was largely due to its length. It was also due to the fact that many in the state had Southern and Jeffersonian roots, and the majority of Hoosiers were not interested in fighting a war of abolition. The pragmatic Lincoln, who was never a friend of slavery, though he was not an avowed abolitionist either, was having problems increasing enrollments of soldiers. Thus, he hit on a policy that would help increase enlistments while ameliorating some of the political heat from the vociferous abolitionist wing of the Republican Party centered in New England. He decided to free the slaves in the Confederate states, though not in the slave states that remained in the Union. His hope was that the slaves would leave the plantations and join the Union Army. He knew it was a gambit, but he was nearing

desperation after the Union suffered almost twice as many casualties as the
Confederacy in the Second Battle of Manassas in late August 1862.[48]

The Proclamation, though, alarmed many Northerners, especially
Democrats in the Midwest and Irish and German Catholic immigrants in major Northern cities, both of whom were sizable political groups. The Midwest
Democrats wanted reunion, but they had little use for abolition because they
feared that freed blacks would compete for jobs at a time of economic recession. The Peace Democrats, as they came to be called, wanted to go back to
the status quo ante. The immigrants, who distrusted the many anti-immigrant
Know Nothings who joined the Republican Party in large numbers in the
late 1850s, also feared free blacks would take their low-level manual labor
jobs. For example, Irish and German immigrants rioted in Cincinnati in 1863
after they were laid off from their jobs on the docks of the Ohio River only
to be replaced by freed blacks who received lower wages.[49] These two groups
of Northerners believed Lincoln was changing the objective of the war from
reunion to abolition.

The journalism of the Civil War era was almost entirely of a partisan
nature. Very few newspapers in the North were neutral or independent. A
few in the larger cities had been moving in that direction just before the war,
but the conflict so divided the country that staying on the sidelines wasn't an
option. The party press meant that a significant amount of text in newspapers
of the Midwest was written with a particular political bent; events and issues
were written from a specific point of view. The party press editors were often
major players in the political process, and their editorial content amounted to
propaganda. What the editors wrote was largely analytical and interpretive,
and their editorial content did not exist in an era of objective, neutral, independent, and unbiased reporting. Instead, journalists operated as leading political operatives, and their newspapers were aimed at audiences who shared
their political point of view. These editors did not merely set the agenda; they
also framed what they wanted their readers to think. Indeed, framing was a
central activity of these party journalists. Placement, positioning, word order, and word choice were as important as issue choice. Ultimately, framing is
about inclusion and exclusion, and whatever frames the editors on both sides
chose to use had as much to do with including the arguments that would reinforce their opinions as excluding the arguments that would reinforce their
opponents' arguments.

Burnside would make the most famous arrest of the war, nabbing Vallandigham, who was tried, convicted, and exiled to the South for calling

Lincoln a dictator in a speech. Hascall would suspend eleven newspapers in Indiana before Govenor Morton and Secretary of War Stanton decided Hascall was doing more political harm than good and relieved him of command in Indianapolis in June of 1863. Then Burnside suspended a Democratic newspaper in Chicago. Editor Wilbur F. Storey raised a ruckus, and the Democratic-majority Illinois legislature censured Burnside. Lincoln waffled and eventually had Burnside rescind the suspension order.

Meanwhile, Democratic editors attacked Lincoln and the military, claiming violations of their rights under the First Amendment. They also continued their attack on emancipation, saying it made the Fugitive Slave Law moribund, as well as complementary issues like the new federal income tax and the draft, which they claimed was illegal because it was not in the Constitution.[50] Ultimately, the war of words would focus on the reason for the war: union or emancipation. Whether or not the war could have two causes was a central part of the framing. The Democrats tended to avoid such complexity, while the Republican editors championed it.

Headlines helped frame the discussion. Typical Democratic headlines included "Lincoln's Infamous Proclamation," "The Present Crisis," and "Lincoln's Proclamation"; typical Republican headlines included "The President's Proclamation," "The President's Emancipation Proclamation," "The Proclamation," and "The Emancipation Proclamation." Democratic editors either were negative or personal, while Republican editors tended to be more neutral, formal, or deferential.

Almost all of the articles occurred on the second page of either daily or weekly newspapers that were usually four pages in length. The second page was generally reserved for editorial comment with news and commercial advertising often appearing on the front page. There were two types of editorials dealing with emancipation: (1) those that dealt with the issue entirely and (2) those that dealt with the issue in passing. The majority of the cases were single-issue editorials. In terms of placement, editorials on emancipation tended to come at the top half of the page—above the fold. Ten of fifteen Republican editorials were above the fold; ten of thirteen Democratic editorials were above the fold. This suggests that the editors felt this subject was a high priority for readers.

Both Republican and Democratic papers printed the proclamation in its entirety after September 22 when Lincoln first made it public. In a few cases, both Republican and Democratic editors chose to print only key excerpts of the document. The proclamation was generally printed on either page one or page two, usually near the top of the page. Complementary commentary was provided, in all cases on page two. When the proclamation took effect, most of the newspapers reprinted Lincoln's edict.

Several major themes emerged in examining the words about emancipation from both Republican and Democratic editors in Indiana. These included power, constitutionality, loyalty, freedom, race, and revolution. Here the frames worked along dichotomous lines. For example, the theme of disloyalty from Republican editors was countered by the theme of loyalty from the Democratic editors. Republican editors hammered away at how Democrats were being essentially disloyal in not supporting the President's war measures. On the other hand, Democratic editors claimed that Democrats had loyally fought for the war and reserved the right to criticize its prosecution and policies, and even the right to offer another way through the conflict—namely, diplomacy.

Another major frame dealt with the legality of the edict. Democrats questioned its constitutionality, while Republicans defended its constitutionality. Democrats claimed that slavery directly dealt with in the Constitution and assumed its prohibition would require constitutional measures like an amendment—which history affirmed with the passing of the Thirteenth Amendment after the war. However, an amendment was difficult to achieve, and the nation had been too divided to get anywhere close to the three-fourths hurdle necessary to make a change to the Constitution. On the other hand, the Republicans claimed that an act of rebellion was unconstitutional and any measure designed to end it was appropriate.

Imagery also helped frame the debate over emancipation. For example, Republican editors sometimes referred to the rebellion as a monster that had to be tamed. One editor referred to slavery as the cornerstone of Confederacy. Tear down slavery, the editor implored, and you destroy the Confederacy. A Democratic editor called the proclamation "harmless thunder" because he thought it was more verbal than practical.[51]

FRAMING POWER AND FREEDOM

What stands out in analyzing the commentary of the partisan editors in these nine cities is how both sides tended to use power and its relationship to freedom as the organizing principle of emancipation. The contrast comes when the editors developed their frames for each. Republican editors saw power as a necessary and inevitable tool in ensuring the freedom of the Union from rebellion and the ultimate freedom of the slaves. The Democratic editors saw emancipation as going against the grain of the Constitution and the nation's history. In forcing emancipation down the throats of the Southerners, the Lincoln administration was quite literally destroying the economic liberty of Southern white male slaveholders. In the opinion of the Democratic newspaper editors, this opposed everything that the American Revolution stood for. Likewise, the Democrats saw emancipation of the black man in terms of a new, unwanted revolution. What's interesting is that none of the Democratic editors claimed the secession movement itself was legitimate. They hesitated to use the eighteenth-century independence movement as an analog because they did not want to see the country divided. They believed a diplomatic solution could be reached, and Northern radical abolitionists were as dangerous to the nation as fire-breathing Southern slaveholders.

George D. Copeland, editor of the Republican newspaper in Goshen, saw the proclamation in terms of military power. To Copeland, it was merely a war measure "which we believe calculated to weaken and finally compel a surrender of the enemy."[52] He said the Constitution gave Lincoln the power to "use every means known to civilized warfare in the suppression of the rebellion," including killing rebels, freeing their slaves, and/or destroying their property.[53] Copeland also said the Confederates had forfeited their constitutional rights when they started the rebellion. He added that the Rebels could avoid emancipation by laying down their arms.[54] Strictly speaking, this was true, for Lincoln did give the Southerners 100 days to end the rebellion without loss of their slaves. Copeland also hit on the disloyalty theme. He warned that no Northerners should interfere in behalf of the Confederacy, directing this warning at the Copperheads. "Let all good citizens rally to the support of the President in his efforts to crush out this monster insurrection and cease finding so much fault and all will be well," Copeland wrote.[55]

Ignatius Mattingly and John D. Devor, the editors of the Republican newspaper in Plymouth, framed the debate this way: "If we have a right to take the rebels horses and mules, and guns and powder, why not their slaves."[56] Mattingly and Devor saw it as a matter of presidential prerogative, and they had no doubt Lincoln had the right to free the Southerners' slaves. They also focused on the religious and moral dimensions of the issue. They wrote that opponents of the proclamation would "provoke the wrath of God upon the nation for our injustice and oppression of the colored race. . . . No man who has any justice or mercy in his heart can justify American slavery."[57] Hence, opposing abolition was tantamount to supporting injustice.

Alfred Wheeler, the editor of the Republican paper in South Bend, saw the proclamation in terms of Northern good fortune. Writing in the first week of January 1863, Wheeler correlated emancipation's taking effect with a Union

victory at Murfreesboro, Tennessee, and small victories elsewhere in the Volunteer State, in Kentucky, and an attack on Vicksburg. Wheeler wrote: "We
have no rebel successes in any quarter to report to offset any of the above."[58]
Northern victories and stalemates put the Union ahead, in Wheeler's mind.
The proclamation would continue that momentum. Wheeler failed to mention the Democratic gains at the polls in the fall of 1862, but that was another
matter.

Appealing to a sense of history in their readers, Republican editors
Thomas H. Bringhurst and Joseph Dague in Logansport alluded to past American documents. This was central to developing a sense of patriotism and loyalty. They wrote that the Emancipation Proclamation was similar in stature
to the Declaration of Independence because it divorced the nation from an
awful institution, slavery. The Cass County editors, whose paper had favored
the Whigs in the 1850s, called slavery the cornerstone of the Confederacy.
When it "is removed, the whole fabric will crumble."[59] Bringhurst and Dague also wrote that neither Lincoln nor the North could be held responsible
for the death of slavery. Rather, the responsibility belonged to the Southern
slaveholders who forced the war on the nation with secession and Fort Sumter. If the Southerners had not forced the issue, emancipation "would never
have been necessitated."[60] Furthermore, "Constitutional Liberty" could only
be saved through emancipation.[61] They observed that emancipation promised
"the dawn of a glorious morning, which promises to reunite and establish our
national institutions upon a firmer basis than ever."[62] The moment for a new
reunited nation was at hand, and Democrats better support it or keep quiet
and allow it to happen.

Meanwhile, the Indianapolis *Journal* was perhaps the most modern
Republican newspaper in the state. The paper was owned by the Journal
Company, which included Ovid Butler, Joseph M. Tilford, James M. Matthews, and Rawson Vaile.[63] They hired a veteran journalist, Berry R. Sulgrove,
to edit the paper. The Journal Company, closely associated with Governor
Morton, provided the money for the enterprise, and Sulgrove handled the
editorial responsibilities.[64] On January 3, 1863, Sulgrove chose not to provide
commentary about the new law but simply report what the Emancipation
Proclamation said. It was placed between a paragraph on the inauguration
of New York Governor Horatio Seymour, a Democrat, and a report about
the exclusion of the pro-Democratic Chicago *Times* from Chicago Board of
Trade reading room.

Sulgrove provided commentary two days later. It was more matter-of-
fact than most of the editorials written about the Emancipation Proclamation.

It claimed that Lincoln had the right to free the slaves under the war powers of the executive branch. The *Journal* editor affirmed the right a president has to suppress a rebellion and to use whatever means necessary to end the rebellion. Then Sulgrove's piece put the edict in perspective by pointing to the heroic situation Lincoln found himself in. He said, "An act of graver responsibility it has rarely fallen to the last of man to perform."[65] He ended in a religious tone, hoping the Emancipation Proclamation would have "the gracious favor of Almighty God."[66]

The Goshen *Times'* Copeland also saw Lincoln in heroic terms, as the savior of the country, and the proclamation was the instrument of salvation. Copeland wrote in a January 1863 editorial that the president would be best remembered for freeing the slaves precisely because the proclamation was a "great declaration of Freedom."[67] Again invoking the Declaration of Independence, a Republican editor emphasized freedom.

Delphi *Journal* editor James Scott chose not to print his own commentary about the proclamation in his Republican newspaper. Instead, he ran what Governor Morton had to say about emancipation. Morton, always loyal to Lincoln, favored the edict, saying it was "a stratagem of war."[68] The governor went against the opinions of Senator Joseph A. Wright and Lincoln cabinet member Caleb Smith, who were among the state's most formidable politicians.[69] Smith believed emancipation would hurt morale and enlistments because Hoosiers would resent serving in the army with black men.[70] In the party press era, it was not unusual for the editor of a party organ to defer to the words of a congressman, senator, governor, or another party leader. Likewise, John H. Scott, the editor of the Democratic newspaper in Evansville, chose not to print his own views after the initial September announcement. Instead, he ran a series of views from newspapers in Philadelphia and New York. This, too, was a frequent practice in mid-century journalism. Scott attempted to have balance with some of the papers supporting emancipation and some against it. Perhaps the most revealing of those editorials was from the New York *Journal of Commerce*. Its editor observed that the Emancipation Proclamation would distinctly draw the lines between supporters and opponents of the Lincoln administration.[71]

Democratic editors viewed the proclamation with antipathy. They saw the proclamation as a constitutional issue, believed that the chief executive did not possess the authority to end an economic practice that was allowed by the Constitution. Doing so amounted to the type of usurpation reserved for a dictator or monarch, and they added that this went along with the general tenor of trampling civil liberties that began with the suspension of habeas corpus.[72]

Daniel E. VanValkenburgh, editor of the Plymouth *Democrat*, had similar concerns about Lincoln's abuse of power. He observed, "It may be that our liberties are 'clean gone forever.' "[73] VanValkenburgh, who would see his paper suspended by Hascall in May of 1863, felt Lincoln had gone too far in dealing with the so-called "fire in the rear," the dissent of Democrats in the North. The Plymouth *Democrat* editor thought that the loyal people of Indiana deserved better than martial law. Hoosiers had been loyal to Lincoln and fought for the war. VanValkenburgh believed that Democrats who had come to favor a negotiated settlement of the conflict were being treated with the heavy hand of the federal government.

The editor was also skeptical about how emancipation would aid the North in winning the war. VanValkenburgh feared abolitionists were misleading Lincoln. The Plymouth editor referred to comments Lincoln made to the so-called Chicago Committee before he announced the Emancipation Proclamation. Lincoln had told the proabolition group in August that he had his own misgiving about emancipation. "Is there a single Court or magistrate or individual that would be influenced by it there [in the South]. . . . And suppose they could be induced by a proclamation of freedom from me, to throw themselves upon us, what should we do with them [blacks]," he asked rhetorically.[74] VanValkenburgh asked: "Could the President himself successfully answer his own objections to the emancipation policy?"[75] VanValkenburgh thought he could not.

Goshen *Democrat* editor William H. Norton was equally skeptical. Norton, whose paper was owned by Hascall's brother Melvin B. Hascall in the 1840s and 1870s, asked rhetorically: "What good is to be accomplished by this, we are unable to say."[76] Norton also observed that abolitionists had howled for this edict since the day the war began. He wondered aloud why Lincoln worried about how to feed and clothe the freed slaves, but decided to go ahead with the order. "Why so sudden a change," Norton asked.[77] The editor thought the president was not being forthright, that he had planned to free the slaves all along.

Lincoln had told the Chicago group in August that he even feared some blacks would give their guns to Confederate soldiers and that border state soldiers would go over to the South, but Norton had no illusions. Here Norton interjected race into the argument. He thought the Emancipation Proclamation changed the war objective from that of reunion to "the extermination of the white population in the South."[78] VanValkenburgh also said emancipation was based on a "hateful dogma of political equality of the races."[79] The

Plymouth wordsmith supplied no explanation as to how a party that favored the common man could be against political equality.

"Harmless Thunder"

Thomas Tigar, the editor of the Fort Wayne *Sentinel* in heavily Democratic Allen County, ran an editorial by Wilbur F. Storey of the Chicago *Times*. Storey focused his September 1862 editorial on the constitutional issue. Storey said Lincoln could not derive from the Constitution any power that allowed him to free the slaves. He added that military necessity served the Constitution, not the other way around. Storey called the proclamation *"brutum fulmen,"* harmless thunder, since it was practically unenforceable.[80] Sarcastically, Storey took aim at abolitionists who claimed emancipation would end the war within thirty days of its taking effect. Storey wrote: "We are anxious to behold the stupendous and magnificent results which were to flow, like a mighty stream, from the proclamation."[81] Many Democratic editors in Indiana read Storey closely and framed the issue similarly.

Samuel A. Hall, editor of the Logansport *Democratic Pharos*, continued the power theme. He fretted that emancipation would be a powerful tool for the Confederacy, not the Union. Hall thought Lincoln's order would backfire. "Its only effect is to place in the hands of the rebel leaders a most effective argument to rally the entire strength of the South against the government, as indicating a determination to adopt abolition measures so far as it lies in the power of the Administration to do so," Hall said.[82] Calling the order unwise, impolitic, and unjust, Hall also observed that there had been a few public demonstrations in Logansport in support of the Emancipation Proclamation, but that they were small. He wrote: "The demonstrations were decidedly unpopular among all Democrats, and also a large portion of the Republicans who are for the Government but not for crazy abolitionism—are for the Union but do not believe a negro is as good as a white man."[83] Hall, like so many of the Democratic wordsmiths, could not avoid bringing race into his emancipation framework. Indeed, they assumed their audience preferred such framing.

Earlier, Hall had run a pro-Republican *Newburyport Herald* editorial that labeled causing a revolution among the slaves uncivilized and improper for a Christian nation. The Newburyport editor worried that a slave uprising would be primarily directed against white women and children since the men were off fighting the war. Hall worried about atrocities committed against females. He also returned to the constitutional frame, saying that breaking its spirit would make the Union no better than the Confederacy. By any means necessary "is the doctrine of revolutionists."[84] Alluding to the French Revolution, Hall reasoned, "No man's life would be safe and all property [would be] worthless."[85] This mention of the brutal horror of the French Revolution was common among Democratic editors. Hall also said that the abolitionists had somehow tricked the President. He said, "This proclamation was issued against the will and better judgment of the President."[86] Hall was suggesting that Lincoln was too weak to stand up to the radicals in his own party. Ultimately, Hall concluded that emancipation made secession just and necessary as a self-defense measure by the Southerners because it put the freedom of black men ahead of union as the primary reason for the war.

Milton R. Graham, editor of the Delphi *Weekly Times*, also used the power frame. Echoing the arguments of the *Indiana State Sentinel* in Indianapolis, Graham questioned whether Lincoln had the constitutional power to free the slaves. In fact, Graham did a little homework. He had a copy of the daily minutes of the U.S. House of Representatives from February 11, 1861. In it he found that the House adopted a resolution stating that neither the federal government nor the people of the nonslaveholding states had the constitutional right to interfere with slavery in any states of the Union.[87] Of course, Graham failed to tell his readers that this resolution was made by the Democratic-majority Thirty-Sixth House before Lincoln took office in March of 1861, although it is true that before he took office the president did agree with its sentiment. Lincoln also thought in those days that the majority of Southerners would oppose secession and thought the war chatter was a bluff.

Graham, who also wondered why the president caved in to the abolitionists, saved his strongest attack for Lincoln's proposal to financially compensate Southern slaveholders who gave into emancipation. The Delphi *Democrat* editor said: "Do the people of Indiana feel inclined to be taxed to pay for the slaves of even the loyal men of the South?"[88] Hall also said any colonization plan of the freed slaves was "visionary and impracticable."[89] Eventually, Lincoln agreed with this assessment.

Political power was also centermost in the thoughts of John R. Elder and John Harkness, owners of the *Indiana State Sentinel*, whose paper was intimidated twice by the Union military during the war. The *Sentinel* wondered about what effect emancipation would have on the fall elections in 1862, and their concerns would prove prophetic since Democrats scored a major victory in the nineteenth state in the October election. The *Sentinel* also framed the matter in terms of manliness, claiming that freeing the slaves to get them to fight against their masters was embarrassing to North white men. The paper noted: "It is a confession of weakness—an acknowledgement that twenty millions of white people, with every advantage on their side, can not conquer six millions of whites, shut out from the world, and entirely reliant upon their own resources to carry out the war."[90] The *Sentinel* worried about what the proclamation would do to those in the Union military who did not want to fight for abolition.

One newspaper published outside Indiana had an effect on Hoosiers' thinking about the issue, and that was James Gordon Bennett's New York *Weekly Herald*, which had a strong mail circulation in the Midwest. Bennett thought the proclamation could not be enforced, calling it "practically a dead letter" because it had no effect in districts "beyond his [Lincoln's] reach." Bennett also feared that the emancipation edict would make masters treat their slaves more rigidly and would greatly increase the number of contrabands with an insufficient number of soldiers to handle their growing number. Bennett thought emancipation should not occur until the South was defeated, and the *Herald* editor thought a more effective president could achieve victory in sixty days.[91]

The Democratic editors framed emancipation in terms of constitutional power. Based on their interpretation of constitutional law, they believed Lincoln was misusing his power, especially after he suspended the writ of habeas corpus. They were outraged and thought the once-moderate president was turning into a revolutionary. This new attitude of the president flew in the face of the Democrats' Burkean mindset. On the other hand, Republican editors saw emancipation primarily as a war measure, and one that took the high moral road. The Republican editors wanted good news from the war front, and the freeing of black men to help fight it was a pragmatic stratagem to them.

The editors of Civil War Indiana did not try to hide or imbed frames in inverted pyramid news stories. Their persuasive pieces accomplished that work directly. Reporting was limited for these small journalistic operations that usually had circulations of less than 1,000 readers. Information came from the telegraph, other newspapers, and gossip, and the editors shaped the content of their papers. Since they needed patronage, the editors were often dependent on political parties to maintain solvency. The majority of their readers already held strong political positions.

Yet it was a time of major political change in U.S. history. After all, the Republican Party had been around for only a decade and had only taken control on the national level only because of the bolting of the Southern Democrats in 1860. The framing contest was particularly important in 1863 as Democrats gained more and more at the polls. Because each party was divided, swaying blocs was critical to the success of the governing alliance. Without the pro-war Democrats, Lincoln would not have successfully prosecuted the war.

The Republicans showed that negative terms could isolate the opposition and diminish their political arguments. Republican editors referred to the Democrats as Copperheads, the venomous snakes, and repeated the mantra that supporting the Democrats was hazardous and would ruin the nation. This negative framing reinforced the idea that disloyalty harmed the Union and, at the same time, reinforced nationalism. Like politics itself, political discourse had limitations in time of war, the Republicans held. They would also defend the military's suppression and intimidation of Democratic editors in the Hoosier State in May and June of 1863 precisely because they wanted to limit the two-party system as much as possible during the war. The words of the Republican editors would contribute to an atmosphere that allowed pro-Union mobs to destroy several Democratic newspapers in the state, and Hascall's General Order No. 9 would create a chilly atmosphere for political words that were not perceived to be loyal to Lincoln and the military.

Framing emancipation would prove crucial because of the more favorable war news that would come in the summer of 1863. The military victories caused Democratic criticisms of the policy to lose much of their sting, and the more positive Republican frames ultimately won the day as the overwhelming majority of Hoosiers would come to accept black freedom and black participation in the Union military.

When General George McClellan lost the presidential election to Lincoln in 1864, his failed candidacy showed how quickly public opinion could change. Known as a soldier-friendly general, McClellan polled only twenty-two percent of the military vote and only twenty-nine percent of the vote among soldiers in the Army of the Potomac.[92] Lincoln had benefited from victories at Gettysburg, Vicksburg, and Chattanooga. Yet the war bogged down again in 1864, and Lincoln himself felt he was ripe for an upset. However, Union soldiers and sailors had learned to accept emancipation, and enough Democrat civilians who wanted to restore the Union had come to tolerate Lincoln's new cause for fighting.

Thus, the war-measure frame won the contest of public opinion. This chapter in U.S. journalism history shows just how dependent frames can be on outside factors such as military events and the failure to get either England or France to recognize the South. The Republican editors succeeded at defining and evaluating the Union's problem in the second year of the war as being one of insufficient manpower to fight a war of attrition with the South. The Republican editors avoided making it a war about racial or economic reality. Rather, they made it about freedom and equality and alluded to the Declaration of Independence. Instead, it became a war for reunion with newly freed men making the difference. Their newfound freedom would make them highly motivated fighters. Freeing black men and having them fight in the war was the solution Lincoln and the North needed to gain the upper hand. The Democratic editors countered with frames that painted Lincoln as a dictator and a monster. They settled on constitutionality as their main frame. The Chicago *Times*' Storey was particularly brilliant at this tactic. He and his allies also thought emancipation would rally Democrats North and South. It did, but in the long run the Democratic frames were not enough to unite the party nationally, and Lincoln prevailed in the fall of 1864. He made the war a revolution for freedom. African Americans' service in the Union military proved decisive, and they became a pivotal voting bloc for the Republicans during Reconstruction. There is no greater symbol of this transformation in U.S. politics than the fact that CSA President Jefferson Davis' seat in the U.S. Senate before the war went to a black Republican from Mississippi after the war.

The Democrats' constitutional frame may have had greater legal merit, but the Republicans' pragmatic war-measure frame became a sort of national philosophy. If it works, it must be right. Emancipation worked. It won the war, and it gave a new meaning to Thomas Jefferson's words about all men being created equal from the Declaration of Independence. Ironically, Robert E. Lee proposed emancipation for the heavily Democratic Confederacy in the waning days of the war.[93] It was too late. Lincoln's ploy had already made the difference in the war's outcome and the future of the United States.

Only World War I equaled the Civil War for intrusions on press freedom in the history of the United States, and perhaps no state's editors faced more official limitations on its freedom to print words than the Democratic editors of Indiana. The bitter political and military conflict was much more important than the civil rights of newspaper editors. As twentieth-century press critic William J. Small has noted about wartime journalism, "a troubled electorate at such times is willing to look the other way."[94] Retrospectively, the Republicans' frames had the advantage of the changing military fortunes. The conflict hung in the balance, and the words of both the Republican and Democratic editors were powerful instruments in helping to determine the outcome.

Those words were framed in four major ways: in terms of power, freedom, legality, and loyalty. Free labor was the way in the North, even if the Yankees, except the abolitionists, were not open to black social freedom. The freedom to fight for the Union was the ultimate expression of black power at a time when almost all African Americans were powerless. The Republican editors, taking their cue from their president, tapped into that expression with their war-measure frame. Blacks' fighting for Union and their own freedom was one of several decisive factors in the war, though ultimately manpower, gun power, and technological power proved the difference. Lincoln's emancipation was a gambit, but it worked in the long run—and proved to be a seminal presidential edict in the nation's history. Manpower was the North's biggest advantage, at the Union had at least a two-to-one advantage over the Confederacy.

Editors on both sides ultimately realized that frames made complex political, social, and military issues easier to grasp. The frames selected what information needed to be made more prominent to readers. Republican editors defined emancipation in terms of manpower for the Union military to achieve its goals, while Democratic editors defined it as an erosion of political and economic liberty because of presidential abuse of power. Editors of both parties interpreted the issue in terms of power, with freedom as a complementary issue, and each offered a solution that would save the country within a context, in a way that was consistent with their view of the nation and the ideology that served as its theoretical basis.

The editors included some aspects of the issue while avoiding others. For example, the Republicans focused on the manpower issue and avoided the legal issue of whether the president had the authority to free the slaves. Democrats focused on the erosion of freedom caused by a president who was overstepping his constitutional power and avoided the immorality of slavery. Editors on both sides did this because they were seeking specific reactions from their audiences. The framing phenomenon limited the public debate to a shouting contest between the ideas that each side wanted to feature and avoided sober deliberations about the major issues in the war. Journalists served as ideological cheerleaders more than watchdogs of press liberty, and the information-gathering function of the press suffered—as did the democratic process.

∞ CHAPTER SEVEN ∞

Hascall and His War Against Indiana's Democratic Press

At the start of the Civil War, Milo S. Hascall was ready for action. Because he was one of the few Hoosiers who had gone to West Point, he immediately set about rallying to arms the men of Elkhart County. As soon as President Lincoln called for 75,000 volunteers to put down the secession of the Southern states Hascall and his brother, Melvin B. Hascall, volunteered for the Indiana Militia. Indiana's quota was initially set at six regiments, or 4,683 men.[1] On April 14, 1861, Hascall enrolled as a private.[2] He helped establish an infantry regiment. The recruits in the company lived in Elkhart County. Hascall was unanimously chosen captain, and Edmund R. Kerstetter was chosen as his first lieutenant. [3] Kerstetter would remain an officer on Hascall's staff for the next three years. The company was not one of the original six regiments that served from Indiana, and it was not initially accepted by Republican Governor Morton.[4] However, the governor heard that Hascall was a West Point man, so on April 27, 1861, he made the Goshen attorney a captain and aide-de-camp to Brigadier General Thomas A. Morris, stationed at Camp Morton in Indianapolis.[5]

On the day that the Goshen *Times* printed Lincoln's call for volunteers, a letter by Milo S. Hascall was printed in the paper stating his belief that the Goshen *Democrat* was taking a "traitorous course" by printing telegraphic news that would give aid and comfort to the Rebels. Hascall did not give

147

specifics about what the newspaper had printed that might help the South, nor did he explain how Southerners would read the Goshen *Democrat* in a timely fashion that might actually have helped the Confederate Army, which was just being formed. Yet the letter helps establish the sentiment of the time and Hascall's outlook during the war. He also made the either-or argument he would make two years later when he established General Order No. 9. Hascall wrote in 1861: "There is only half a dozen [Democrats in Goshen] to my knowledge that sympathize with it [The *Democrat*] now, and they will very soon ascertain that matters have come to pass now that makes it evident that those that are not for their country are against it."[6] Hascall said those people expressing any sympathy with the Rebels after Fort Sumter "have no rights which freemen can or ought to respect."[7]

This argument essentially would be the one he would use in a public debate on press suppression with Fort Wayne Congressman Joseph Ketchum Edgerton two years later as Edgerton tried to ascertain the specifics of what Hascall was proscribing in terms of public speaking and in the press in Indiana. It is also worth noting that Hascall would not suppress the Goshen *Democrat* in the spring of 1863 when he harassed Democratic editors in surrounding counties. Perhaps his forbearance was due to the fact that his brother Melvin B. Hascall had owned the paper and still was close to some of its supporters. As a consideration to his brother's former ties to the paper, any intimidation Milo Hascall attempted against the Goshen *Democrat* was done quietly through back channels. Perhaps more likely, the *Democrat* was given a wider berth because generally it was a strong supporter of Hascall during his military career, including his brief tenure as commander of the District of Indiana. Moreover, editors William H. Norton and John D. Osborn supported the political career of Hascall's brother, Chauncey S. Hascall, who was chairman of the Elkhart County Democratic Party during the war.[8]

HASCALL IN THE CIVIL WAR

In 1861, Hascall worked as a captain under General Thomas A. Morris and served at Philippi, West Virginia, a small skirmish. Hascall was commissioned as a colonel and given command of the Seventeenth Indiana Volunteer Infantry Regiment. The unit took part in successful action at Greenbrier, West Virginia, in October 1861, after which Hascall moved the Seventeenth to Louisville, Kentucky. In December 1861, Hascall was given command of the Fifteenth Brigade, Army of the Ohio. By January 1862, he had risen to the rank of colonel.[9] He was allowed a trip home to rest during the winter of 1862, after which he took command of a brigade under General Don Carlos Buell.

Before he left, the Goshen *Times* called for the army to make him a brigadier general.[10] First, though, the army raised his rank to lieutenant colonel.[11]

From Cairo, Illinois, he wrote a letter to C.W. Stevens that appeared in the Goshen *Times*. Surveying the scene, Hascall commented: "I have had so much to see to, and have had so little sleep that I am in no condition to write. Bands are playing, regiments are marching, and the whole atmosphere smells of war. Everybody you meet is a soldier, and I begin to realize that we have work on our hands."[12] A week later, the Seventeenth Regiment Indiana Volunteers was in New Haven, Kentucky. At this point in the conflict, Indiana had supplied fifty-two regiments to the war effort—forty-six more than the original April 1861 call-up.

By April of 1862, Hascall had attained the rank of brigadier general, and he and his brigade arrived on April 7 at Shiloh, Tennessee. A report by Hascall from Shiloh was printed in the Goshen *Times* a week after the battle. Hascall, now working under Buell, wrote from the field in Corinth, Mississippi, approximately twenty miles south of Shiloh. He was in charge of both the Seventeenth Regiment Indiana Volunteers and part of the Fifteenth Brigade under Brigadier General Thomas J. Wood, who was in charge of the Sixth Division of Buell's Army of the Ohio. Hascall said he and his men arrived at Pittsburg Landing "at 12 o'clock on the night of April 7, and early [the] next morning I had my whole Brigade in the present position in the advance, ready to fight the enemy should he again attack, or for any other duty that might be assigned it."[13] Buell's army played a key role in the second day of the battle.

Hascall's men had missed much of the battle thanks in large part to rainy weather and engaging the Confederate cavalry near Lawrenceburgh, Tennessee, a distance of some sixty-five miles.[14] Hascall was proud of his men for arriving at Shiloh in time to support the Union cause despite the long and muddy march through southern Tennessee. Hascall reported strong Union sentiment in that part of Tennessee, but he proceeded cautiously to make sure that as his soldiers passed each house the occupants would not go warn the Confederate cavalry.

In June, a report appeared in the Goshen *Times* that a soldier named Joseph Guthridge was slandering Hascall's reputation. Guthridge, who had deserted from his regiment, allegedly called Hascall a coward. Colonel John T. Wilder's letter to the *Times* claimed that Guthridge "was guilty of forgery, and all manner of lying and swindling."[15] Wilder offered a reward of thirty dollars to anyone who would arrest him. Wilder added: "None but those that have deserted or been compelled to leave the regiment speak disparagingly of him [Hascall]."[16]

After organizing an Elkhart County regiment following Governor Oliver P. Morton's spring 1861 call for troops, Milo Hascall and the Seventeenth Indiana Volunteers traveled from Goshen to Camp Hascall, which was located in Parkersburgh, Virginia (today, West Virginia). The Seventeenth was encamped in Virginia about the time of First Bull Run, after which then-Colonel Hascall moved the regiment to Oakland, Maryland, to protect Pennsylvania from invasion by the Confederate Army. *(Photo from the Indiana Historical Society)*

Milo Hascall's brother, Melvin B. Hascall, resigned from the army in June 1862, apparently because he needed to attend to personal matters back in Goshen.[17] Melvin Hascall's men praised him in a letter to the Goshen *Times*: "We desire in this public manner to testify our appreciation of his high qualities as a gallant officer and courteous gentleman."[18] Two months later, CSA General Braxton Bragg invaded Kentucky, and southern Indiana prepared hastily for a possible invasion. Indiana sent several regiments to Kentucky to try to slow down the Confederates and give the federal military time to prepare a defense of Cincinnati. Hoosiers fought battles at Richmond and Munfordville, Kentucky, and produced just enough action for Buell to arrive in time to repell the Rebels from Perryville.[19]

The Seventeenth Regiment I.V. began to publish a paper, the *Union Comet*, occasionally in the fall of 1862. Readers were charged a small fee, which could be paid in cocks, whiskey, applejack, or toothbrushes. Providing news of Milo Hascall's brigade, it apparently was aimed at both the soldiers and their families.[20] Meanwhile, the Whitley County, Indiana, *Republican* reported that Hascall was sick and convalescing in Bardstown, Kentucky. The Whitley County *Republican* commented, "His extensive knowledge of military science and his great coolness in the hour of danger render him a very efficient officer."[21]

Joseph Ketchum Edgerton, a Democratic U.S. congressman from Indiana's Tenth District, defended freedom of the press against Hascall's General Order No. 9 in the spring of 1863. Shown here is his gravestone at Lindenwood Cemetery in Fort Wayne. *(Photo by David W. Bulla)*

After the Northern disaster at Fredericksburg, Virginia, with four Indiana regiments taking part in the battle, the behind-the-scenes machinations against Burnside as leader of the Army of the Potomac, and the major Democratic gains in Indiana, Illinois, and Ohio in the fall of 1862, the Union Army needed renewed confidence and energy.[22] Things were not much better for the Army of the Ohio. Hascall took part in the Stones River, Tennessee, battle of December 31, 1862, to January 2, 1863, fighting in the "Red Forest" under General Thomas J. Wood as a division commander. The battle is termed a draw, with casualties reaching 12,906 for the Union and 11,739 for the CSA.[23] Hascall reported his division had 211 men killed, 915 wounded, and 167 missing. When the battle started, his division had 4,887 men. Hascall added that "it rained very hard all day January 3rd and during the night, so that our men and officers suffered severely."[24] Hascall was in ill health during the battle.[25]

Hascall commanded the First Division of the Twenty-First Corps of the Army of the Cumberland from January 9 to February 19. He returned to Goshen and gave a patriotic speech in early March at Hascall's Hall. He told the crowd that the peace movement did more harm than good to the Union cause, and if all deserters would be returned to their regiments, then the draft would not have to be implemented.[26]

Indiana in the 1850s and 1860s was an agricultural state. More than half of the state's workers had occupations on farms. The overwhelming majority of farmers lived on small farms. Corn was the main crop, with wheat second, and hogs were the chief livestock. Indiana had the nation's seventh largest population in 1850 and the sixth largest in 1860, with population growth in the 1850s being 36.6 percent and 24.4 percent in the 1860s.[27] In 1850, only 4.5 percent of the population lived in cities, and the largest chunk of the population lived along the Ohio River, but the population in the center of the state was growing rapidly because of the superior topsoil in that part of the state. During the 1860s, the central part of the state became more populated than the southern part of the state.[28] Many of the settlers who migrated to the northern two-thirds of the state from western New York, Pennsylvania, and Ohio were attracted to the potential high crop yield in the Hoosier State. Leaving the farm to fight was a big sacrifice.

COMMANDER OF THE DISTRICT OF INDIANA

When Hascall gained command of the District of Indiana, the negative war news and the Emancipation Proclamation had helped the Democrats gain control of both houses of the state legislature and the majority in the congressional delegation. Resistance to the draft was intense in many counties, and counties on the Ohio were suffering economically because the Mississippi was closed to New Orleans. Governor Morton and his closest allies feared a guerilla invasion of the state by Confederate renegades.

Burnside brought in Hascall to relieve Carrington.[29] Hascall said he was ordered from Murfreesboro to Indianapolis "about the 1st of March" in 1863.[30] He was mentioned as being in Indianapolis a month before he issued General Order No. 9. The Goshen *Times* reported on March 5 that Hascall had established headquarters in Indianapolis, where Hascall recollected that General William S. Rosecrans had ordered him to Indianapolis to help with returning deserters from the Army of the Cumberland in Illinois, Indiana, and Ohio.[31] Rosecrans "charged [Hascall] with the duty of superintending the work of returning to their regiments all deserters and others absent without authority from the States of Ohio, Indiana, and Illinois."[32]

Hascall claimed there were more than 30,000 deserters in the three states.[33] The *Times* also reported the number of absent soldiers was "astonishingly large" and requested that both military and civilians assist in rounding up deserters.[34] Hascall estimated the number of deserters from the Army of Cumberland to be about one-third of Rosecrans' "entire army," and the Goshen officer believed that Copperhead influences had caused them to desert.[35]

Hascall wrote that he was transferred from the Army of the Cumberland to the Department of the Ohio by order of Secretary of War Edwin M. Stanton.[36] Brigadier General Henry B. Carrington was still the commander of the District of Indiana in April. As late as April 14, Carrington promulgated General Order No. 5, outlawing the carrying of concealed weapons and intimidating citizens into leaving their homes.[37] On April 19, he published General Order No. 6, charging the covert Knights of the Golden Circle with treason by agitating the public in the state with anti-Union, antiwar sentiment. Carrington also condemned the wearing of concealed weapons and subversive emblems, copperheads, and butternuts, and he pleaded with the press and public men to refrain from agitating the public.[38] Carrington's proclamations already had Democrats on edge when Hascall officially took power in April.

The brigadier general wrote that he took over for Carrington on April 15, 1863, although he actually took command on April 22.[39] The Indianapolis *Daily Journal*, the main Republican paper in the capital city, printed General Order No. 8 on April 23, stating Hascall's temporary assumption of command for the District of Indiana, with the rest of his commanding officers being long-time aide Captain Edmund Kerstetter, First Lieutenant James R. Hume, and First Lieutenant A. R. Franklin.[40] This order came just three days after the Indianapolis *Daily Journal* printed Carrington's General Order No. 6. Hascall's General Order No. 8 is dated April 22, 1863.

In describing the situation in Indiana as being a "quasi rebellion against the General government," Hascall added that "large number of copperheads & traitors being armed, and in camp drilling in Brown Co. and various other locations in the state. To meet this state of things I issued my order 'No. 9.'"[41] On April 29, the Indianapolis *Weekly Indiana State Sentinel* printed General Order No. 9, dated April 25, 1863, which stated that Hascall intended to enforce Major General Burnside's General Order No. 38, which outlawed treasonous words in the press and by politicians.[42] Hascall explicitly targeted those papers or speakers that encouraged resistance to the Conscription Act "or any other law of Congress passed as a war measure, or that endeavor to bring the war policy of the Government into disrepute."[43] The Goshen *Times* noted that Hascall had replaced Carrington, stating that the paper did not know the cause of the latter's removal, but Carrington had been a bit too active for Burnside's taste. The *Times* also remarked that "Gen. Hascall will undoubtedly fill the position with credit to himself and to the satisfaction of all loyal men" and recommended the careful reading of General Order No. 9 by all Copperheads.[44] Some Democratic editors thought Hascall would be easier or less effective on dissidents, but the *Times* said there were no grounds "for hoping that Gen. Hascall will be any more lenient with them than Gen. Carrington has been."[45]

General Order No. 9 stated that Hascall "had no partisan feelings or interests." Hascall asked men of both parties to cooperate with all measures that would keep the peace in Indiana. He said he did not intend to interfere with the civil matters. The order also stated that Hascall intended to carry

Milo Hascall took part at the very end of the battle at Shiloh in Middle Tennessee just north of Corinth, Mississippi, in April 1862. Shown is the Indiana Monument at Shiloh. *(Photo by David W. Bulla)*

out Burnside's General Order No. 38.[46] Hascall declared: "Unmistakable evidence has reached him [Hascall] that the provisions of this Order have been, and are being, violated in various parts of the State. This is unfortunately, in many instances, by well meaning men, who are led astray by newspapers and public speakers."[47] Thus, it is clear Hascall had a keen eye on the state's Democratic editors, and many of them decided to tone down their language.

General Order No. 9 also stated that Hascall would hold such editors and public speakers accountable for their words. Hascall added: "There is no use in trying to dry the stream while its fountains are allowed to flow."[48] He then mandated that newspapers and orators who advised or encouraged resistance to the draft, any measure Congress had passed for the prosecution of the war, or the Lincoln administration's war policy would be treated as having committed treason. To justify his proclamation, Hascall said: "The country will have to be saved or lost during the time that this Administration remains in power, and therefore he who is factiously and actively opposed to the war policy of the Administration, is as much opposed to this Government."[49] In effect, Hascall viewed dissent against the Lincoln administration as opposition to the government. The commander of the District of Indiana was, in effect, reiterating his April 1861 broadside against the Goshen *Democrat*.

The *Indiana State Sentinel* took Hascall to task for limiting civil liberties. The newspaper observed that candid discussion of unwise policy would be legitimate political speech, spoken or written. The editors of the *Sentinel* asked, "Does this mean that the war policy of the Administration is not to be discussed at all except to praise it?"[50] What if the policy of the administra-

The Shiloh Log Church gave the battleground its name. Hascall commanded a division of the Army of the Cumberland at this Tennessee battle and wrote an official report, observing that there was strong Union sentiment in that part of the Volunteer State, which was the last state to secede from the Union.
(Photo by David W. Bulla)

tion or the actions of the military was unnecessarily killing Union soldiers or unnecessarily prolonging the war? The *Sentinel* presumed that Hascall was acting alone and did not have the blessings of his superiors in striking down "fair and free discussion of public measures."[51] On May 1, Hascall announced General Order No. 10, in which he castigated those persons working for the government to collect deserters and other official business who "not unfrequently [sic] transcend the limits of their duties in an arrogant, overbearing manner."[52] Hascall said the confidence and respect of the community was being eroded by the actions of such men.

The Cannelton *Reporter*, a Democratic paper, wondered why Hoosier Democrats were being singled out. The editor there asked why Democrats in other states and all Republicans "who enjoy the right of denouncing what they think is wrong, and who exercise that right" did not have to watch what they printed.[53] The *Reporter* called for a special session of the Indiana legislature to overturn General Order No. 9.[54] The paper, which was prowar but antiabolition, mocked Hascall and the order, saying: "What is Order No. 9 like its author? Because it is a cipher [0] with a tail to it."[55] Later, the paper printed an attempt by Englebart Zimmerman, the editor of the suspended pro-Democratic Columbia City *News*, to call on Hascall in Indianapolis to ascertain why his paper was being singled out. The report of the talk between Zimmerman and Hascall made the brigadier general look weak and ineffective because he admitted fair criticism of the federal government was allowable.[56]

Hascall suppressed newspapers in the state, all Democratic, all in the northern half of the state. (See map of cities where suppression occurred in 1863 on page 164.) In addition to VanValkenburgh's Plymouth *Democrat*, Hascall suppressed or threatened to suppress the Bluffton *Banner*, Columbia City *News*, Franklin *Democratic Herald*, Hartford City *Blackford Democrat*, Huntington *Democrat*, Knox *Stark County Press*, Rushville *Jacksonian*, South Bend *Forum*, Warsaw *Union*, and the Winamac *Pulaski Press*. Hascall either had the editors arrested or threatened to arrest them. E. Van Long, the editor of the Warsaw *Union*, was also assaulted by a county marshal.

The brigadier general would also oversee a near disastrous security detail at a Democratic mass meeting in Indianapolis on May 20, in which he had received intelligence beforehand suggesting that some of the attendees would attempt the seize the government arsenal.[57] During his reign, a near riot would occur at a Union League mass meeting in heavily Democratic Fort Wayne, a draft riot took place in Blackford County, and protestors hampered the draft process in Fountain County.[58] To say the least, in the spring of 1863, Indiana was in a state of political instability that it had not seen since before statehood in 1816.

GENERALS' ORDERS

Yet Hascall was not acting alone. The brigadier general was carrying out the internal war policy of his commanding officer, Burnside, who in turn was doing what he thought Lincoln wanted him to do at a time when desertions were high and public opinion of the war effort was low. Burnside's General Order No. 38 had been promulgated on April 16, nine days before Hascall's General Order No. 9 was released by his aide, Captain Edmund R. Kerstetter. Burnside had ordered Hascall to act because of intelligence the major general had received from Hascall's predecessor Carrington. Governor Morton formed the latter's picture of what was happening in Indiana. Based on intelligence he was receiving from around the state, Carrington was convinced a rebellion was about to occur and planned a military buildup to put it down. Morton hoped to establish a strong military presence in the state. Morton defined resistance to the draft as treasonous and echoed Lincoln's words that dissidence was "fraught with great danger to the public peace."[59] Morton did, though, differentiate between those who criticized the war effort and those who advocated secession or rebellion. Yet he also upheld Burnside and the Lincoln administration's doctrine of temporary suspension of civil liberties—and his own prerogative to stymie the Indiana legislature by sending Republican representatives to Madison, Indiana, to prevent a quorum. Morton declared: "It must be borne in mind that the exercise of the plainest rights and privileges may be greatly modified by circumstances; that what may be proper or innocent and harmless at other times may be dangerous and criminal at another."[60]

Historian William Marvel observed that Burnside wanted "to discourage Southern sympathizers with the fear of brute force rather than the use of it."[61] Carrington, who seems to have been more willing to use force, said in General Order No. 6 that anyone in Indiana expressing sympathy with the Rebels would be forwarded beyond the Northern lines. Those who plotted for the benefit of the South would be tried. If convicted, they would face the death penalty.[62] Carrington also outlawed the wearing of butternut and copperhead emblems.[63] Of course, Morton, too, was worried. The governor believed secret societies had formed all over the state and was concerned about activities in Noble, Wayne, Fountain, Warren, Johnson, Blackford, Jay, and Knox counties.[64] Yet Morton did not like Hascall, even if the Goshen attorney's aggressiveness was much more in keeping with the governor's own personal ideas about how the war ought to be prosecuted. General Order No. 9 was not the wrong law. Rather, it was the wrong man making martial law.

What was happening under Hascall in Indiana was part of a larger effort by which Burnside hoped to control the political rhetoric in the Department of the Ohio. In the middle of Hascall's reign in Indiana, an editors' war occurred in Dayton, Ohio, after Clement Laird Vallandigham had been squirreled away to Cincinnati by Burnside's subordinates early on May 5 in a fashion similar to that of VanValkenburgh. The main characters in Dayton were editors William T. Logan of the pro-Democracy *Daily Empire* and Lewis Marot and William Rouzer of the pro-Republican *Daily Journal*. Vallandigham had been editor of the *Empire* from 1847 until 1849, and his prounion, propeace, and antiabolition ideas continued to color the paper's editorials through the Civil War.[65] Vallandigham was still writing some of the paper's editorials in 1863.[66]

In his May 5 commentary on the Vallandigham arrest, Logan pointed the finger at Provost Marshal Edward Parrott and the Republican leadership in town. He also told his readers to save their freedoms through "blood and carnage" if necessary and the day after Vallandigham's 3 a.m. arrest by 150 members of the 115th Ohio Regiment, Democrats burned the *Journal* office and six other adjacent businesses.[67] Logan was arrested and sent to Cincinnati, and martial law was declared in Dayton. The *Daily Empire* was closed, and Marot and Rouzer printed their paper on the press of the United Brethren House in Dayton.[68] Meanwhile, they offered an advertisement in the *Journal*

THE CRISIS.

COLUMBUS, OHIO, WEDNESDAY, MARCH 18, 1863.

I have not been able to find out the individuals who brought them there, and whilst there is no doubt of the fact that quite a number of the soldiers of this Regiment were concerned in the attack on your office on the night of the 5th inst. the difficulty is to fasten the act upon individuals, all my efforts to do so have, as yet, failed. No doubt if I or any one else were to play the police officer and lay the trape to catch the perpetrators, they would be caught; the however can scarcely be considered my duty. A civil and a military force is stationed in the city for the express purpose of protecting and punishing offences committed there; with them I am willing to co-operate with all the authority invested in me. All the officers of my Regiment present have signed a paper which has been communicated to the Colonel, a copy of which I herewith enclose, ignoring the act, and I truly believe that they are innocent of any complicity with the affair, whatever may be their private sympathies and prejudices.

No one regrets the matter more than I do, and on no one are the consequences likely to fall heavier than on myself. An officer of the old army, I have no sympathy with any particular party, and my duty is obedience to the laws and the General Government, whatever party may be in power. My own interest and those of the Regiment demand that this act should be punished, but how to do it is a question yet unanswered.— Whilst I might be morally certain as to the actors, to get testimony to convict them seems impossible. As to the cause of the outrage and why the 2d O. V. C. should deem it their peculiar duty to commit it, is entirely beyond my comprehension, for I had not the slightest warning that there was any special animosity against The Crisis in the Regiment. The duties of this—not failing upon me here, since I have been here, to a certain extent separated me from the Regiment, and deprives me of that control that I otherwise would have had over this matter.

Any evidence or testimony which you can furnish will be used by me to ferret the matter out and bring the perpetrators to justice. I would caution you, however, that there is no reliance to be placed upon the great mass of street rumors.

Very respectfully, your ob't serv't,
     AUGUST V. KAUTZ,
Colonel 2d O. V. C., Com'g Camp Chase.
S. MEDARY, Esq., Columbus, Ohio.

We, the undersigned officers of the 2d Ohio Vol Cavalry, learning that members of this Regiment are charged with having participated in the destruction of the "Crisis office" last Thursday evening, take this method of making known to all whom it may concern, that we had no knowledge of, or connection with, the occurrence whatever, that we are all entirely and utterly opposed to all such demonstrations, that we have ever used our best endeavors to prevent any breach of the civil law and that we will make every effort in our power to bring to punishment any member of this Regiment connected with said unlawful transaction.

Henry L. Burnett, Major 2d Ohio Vol. Cavalry.
Joseph T. Smith, Assistant Surgeon
Benj. C. Stanhope, Captain Co. B, 2d O. V. C.
M. F. Weeks,   "   "   A,   "
D. E. Welch,   "   "   G,   "
Albert Barnitz,   "   "   C,   "
G. W. Stewart,   "   "   E,   "
F. S. Case,   1st Lt "   H, Com'g Co.
W. F. Pedrick,   1st Lt. " 2 1 O. V. C.
B. J. Chamberlain, 1st Lt. and Q. M. "
John J. Jake,   Adjutant
F. E. Welborne,   2d Lt. Co. F, Com'g Co.
A. E. Millard,   2d Lt. " G, 2d O. V. C.
T. P. Hamlin,   "   "   H,   "
Warner Pearson,   "   "   E,   "
Warner Newton,   "   "   E,   "
Henry G. Woolcot,   "   "   C,   "
S A. Maner,   "   "   G,   "
Chas. H. Bill,   "   "   K,   "
Richard Parder,   "   "   M,   "
Henry O. Sampson,   "   "   A,   "
F. R. Dentap,   1st Lt. "   B,   "
A true copy of the original.
     AUGUST V. KAUTZ,
      Colonel 2d O V. C.

LETTERS FROM THE PEOPLE!

From Ohio.

ASHLAND, OHIO, March 6, 1863.

COL. S. MEDARY—Dear Sir :—Enclosed please find $2 00 subscription price for The Crisis for the present year.

The Democracy of this county are alive ...

"Union as it was," and for the constitutional freedom of all, for as well as Stand up manfully, as you ever have done for the blood bought privilege of free discussion, free speech and a free press, with out which liberty can exist only in name. Abolitionism may rant and foam and "gnaw the file" in vain, its doom is sealed as certain as the People ever speak again through the ballot boxes. If not, farewell to American liberty for the white race. I hope the cowardly villains who destroyed your office may be ferreted out and made to feel that "the way of the transgressor is hard." If the guilty ones are not brought to punishment, and that speedily, the long eared gentry at the Capital might be dispensed with, and let Old Abe manage things alone, or by some of his Provost Marshals which will soon swarm forth to devour and afflict the land.

We should all thank God that the Abolition Congress has at last terminated its labors and gone to its reward. May the good Lord deliver this nation from being afflicted by its like again. So mote it be.

Yours Democratically,
     W. W. V. BUCHANAN.

PROSPECT, MARION CO., O., }
     March 9, 1863. }

GOV. MEDARY—Dear Sir—We have just heard of the outrage committed upon you and The Crisis by the cowardly mob. We have not heard the details, nor do we know the extent of your loss, but we know you and we therefore feel fully assured that it will not be long until The Crisis will be again in circulation and battling as of old for the Constitution and the Union. Whatever you need let us know we are ever ready and willing up here. Do you want any money? If so let us know it and I will insure you that we will respond our share in that or any other thing that is necessary for the preservation of the rights of a free people. Hoping to hear from you soon. I subscribe myself your
     OLD FRIEND.

BRYAN, WILLIAMS COUNTY, OHIO, }
     March 12th, 1863. }

SAMUEL MEDARY, ESQ — Dear Sir : Enclosed you will please find two dollars for The Crisis one year. Address Christopher Welker, Bryan, Williams County, Ohio. He subscribed for your paper the day we heard of your misfortune at the hands of a cowardly mob of revolutionists and disorganizers of society. I presume their backbone was larger than they had nerve to bear up under. We did not get last week's issue of The Crisis—presume it was thrown out of the mails, as others got theirs at Edgerton and Farmer Center. If you have numbers you can spare from last week, send us some to this office; as some of your subscribers are filing them they want that number, (6). I hope for better times in future, when devils reign no longer in human form. If we live it through, I think the leading men of the Democratic party ought to make a stubborn stand against arbitrary power, and trampling on the rights of the Constitution, and the sooner and bolder the better, as Seymour of Connecticut says. They have the people with them, if they would make the move before our hands are tied like Missouri. Your friend, F. M. C.

FRAZEYSBURGH, MUSKINGUM CO., OHIO. }
     March 13th, 1863. }

DEAR COLONEL : — You have the well wishes of all the Democrats, and I hope you success, for you are on the right track. If this country is saved from the wreck, it will have to be done by the Democrats. That's so.

NEW DOVER, UNION CO., OHIO, }
     March 14, 1863. }

COL. MEDARY—Dear Sir—I wish to renew my subscription for your valuable paper.

Important Letter from One who Voted for Lincoln.

NEWARK, OHIO, March 14, 1863.

COL. MEDARY—Dear Sir : Enclosed you wil find two dollars for The Crisis one year. I must apologize some to you, I voted for Lincoln and hated your paper, and would not read it, and thought you to be a traitor to your country. I now take that all back, and firmly believe if the Union is saved it must be through your paper. I will just say that for all time to come, I denounce the Republican party as destructive to the Constitution and the Government.

No more but remain your friend.

If this is any advantage to you, use it any way you please.

Send the paper to Newark. Ohio.
     J. C. TOMPSON.

From Cleveland, Ohio.

SAMUEL MEDARY, Esq., Columbus, Ohio—

My Dear Sir: Please accept the enclosed check as my part of your indemnification against the lawless outrage which the abolition revolutionists recently perpetrated upon your office, and as an evidence of my appreciation of your manly and patriotic efforts in behalf of civil liberty. Prospectively these outrages may be hopefully regarded as beacons to guide the people in selecting their servants for the future and to avoid the folly they committed in 1860. God grant that our country may outlive the incubus of the present ruthless administration at Washington, as it will certainly require divine aid in addition to greatest wisdom of every patriot in the land to save anything worth preserving. Yours truly,

From Kentucky.

COOL SPRING, OHIO COUNTY, KENTUCKY, }
     January 25th, 1863. }

HON. S. MEDARY Dear Sir :—Enclosed I send $2, for which you will please send The Crisis to the above office.

It is a great blessing to have, (the truth,) and to be able to tell it in the cogent and irresistable manner your columns exhibit.

It is to be hoped that the cause of liberty has yet friends enough to save our noble institutions from the unhallowed conspiracies of either North or South ; that there are those who feel that the Union can be preserved, not by the assistance of armed negroes, nor by a process of negro equality, but by a satisfactory adjustment of the difficulties which now distract and divide this nation. At present our condition is deparable. We have an army in the field that, in point of warlike proficiency, has never been surpassed,—fighting under unconstitutional plans and proclamations to consummate which, they need only be successful ; and when the work is done we shall see what? That we have saved this government ! Nay, verily! We shall see that we have turned some 4,000,000 of negroes to corrupt, to burden, and ruin society. We shall have destroyed our great commercial interests in the Mississippi valley, by destroying those interests and institutions that have given it bone and sinew, force and vitality ; we shall have given rein to party ambition until we are involved in national bankruptcy ; and that, while fighting to subjugate a free people, we shall have lost our own liberties by bowing to the unhallowed despotism of a party who have wantonly violated and trampled under foot the very principles they have pretendingly sent us to defend.

Kentuckians have been blind to this, but they are beginning to see. The Lord increase their vision.

Yours truly,

From Illinois.

PITTSFIELD, PIKE COUNTY, ILLINOIS.

MR. EDITOR CRISIS—Sir :—Please find enclosed seven dollars and twenty-five cents, to pay for the above ; and we would bid you God speed in your fearless course and manly efforts in rebuking higher law doctrine, for which, we have no doubt, you have suffered many things almost intolerable. But should we not, as some of old, rejoice that we are counted worthy to suffer for the sake of those inestimable rights that nature's God has guaranteed to us, and the Constitution and laws of a common country preserved, until mad fanaticism, assumed to hold all laws and even the Constitution subservient to his will, even ...

Samuel Medary's thought-provoking and well-written Columbus *Crisis* in Ohio was attacked by Union soldiers in March 1863, a month before Milo Hascall went to work for Burnside in Indiana. These letters appeared in the newspaper the week after the attack. Medary, Clement L. Vallandigham, and Wilbur F. Storey were major leaders of the Peace Democrats. The attack on the *Crisis* set the tone for the antipress sentiment in Burnside's jurisdiction. *(From the Ohio Historical Society, the Columbus Crisis on microfilm)*

for the sale of a "Valuable Democratic Newspaper Establishment."[69] Logan restarted publication of the *Daily Empire* in August.

Although he had suspended the writ of habeas corpus the previous September, President Lincoln was embarrassed by the situation in the Midwest. He did not want his military agents to treat civilians with a heavy hand. He was also upset that he had learned about the matter in the newspapers, which would indicate he had not known beforehand about General Order No. 38 or Hascall's antipress order in Indiana.[70] Instead of letting Vallandigham sit in jail for the remainder of the war, the president exiled the ex-congressman to the South, but the Davis government did not want him either. Although Valiant Val, as he was called, hoped for reunion with the Southern states, he learned the Confederates wanted independence. He said he might be in favor of recognizing independence.[71] A man without a country, Vallandigham sailed for Bermuda and then Canada. Eventually, in absentia, he lost the 1863 Ohio gubernatorial race to former newspaperman John Brough in a landslide that ended Vallandigham's political career as an office seeker, though he still worked diligently behind the scenes.[72]

Just as Vallandigham was being arrested, tried, and convicted by a military tribunal, the attention of the state's Democratic editors had another cause to defend—the First Amendment rights of Indiana's newspaper editors. After Plymouth's Daniel E. VanValkenburgh was arrested on May 5, several papers received letters of intimidation from Hascall on May 8. The *St. Joseph County Forum* in South Bend received a letter from Hascall stating the general had copies of the May 3rd edition of the *Forum*.[73] Editor William Drapier, who opposed the war, apparently had stated his intention to violate General Order No. 9.[74] Drapier told Hascall to "get over" Order No. 9, writing: "We make no retraction of principle. We compromise no right of an American citizen."[75] Drapier closed the *Forum* after Hascall arrested him on May 23, and the paper returned to operation on June 16, 1866, Drapier sold the *Forum* that August to Edward Molloy.[76] A Union Army veteran, Molloy bought the paper and changed its title to the *National Union*.[77]

Daniel E. VanValkenburgh's *Plymouth Democrat* faithfully recorded acts of violence on and constraints against newspapers in Indiana. Shown is a story on the mobbing of the *Richmond Jeffersonian*. (*From the Indiana State Library,* Plymouth Democrat *on microfilm*)

On May 8, Engelbart Zimmerman, the editor of the Columbia City *News*, received a letter similar to Drapier's. It said: "You can now take your choice—publishing an article taking back your threats of resistance to that order [No. 9] and your comments designed to destroy its usefulness and hereafter publish a loyal paper or you can discontinue the publication of your paper until further orders," Hascall wrote.[78] Zimmerman, who had seen his paper mobbed by Republicans back in March, did not change his tone. Accordingly, Hascall, an attorney in Goshen before the war, had the editor arrested, but released him after listening to Zimmerman's side in the case.[79] Another paper receiving a letter from Hascall on May 8 was the Bluffton *Banner*. In a letter printed in *Dawson's Daily Times & Union* in nearby Fort Wayne, the editor of the *Banner* boldly said he would ignore Hascall's tyranny and continue business as usual.[80]

Hascall sent an intimidating letter to Warsaw *Union* editor Long on May 11.[81] In the letter, Hascall said he had seen the *Union* from three days before and that it contained Long's intention to violate General Order No. 9.[82] The brigadier general asked the editor to retract his statement. Hascall said, "A failure to attend promptly to this admonition will not be overlooked."[83] Long countered in an open letter that he could not retract anything because the brigadier general was not specific in what he found objectionable. Long went on to write that there was no rebellion in Indiana and therefore General Order No. 9 had no legitimacy in the state. "The civil law is ample for a redress of grievances. . . . If the force that has been placed at the disposal of Gen. Hascall to enforce this order were placed in the field to operate against the enemies of this country, it would be more in accordance with good sense," Long observed.[84] Hascall also shut down the Pulaski County *Democrat* in May of 1863.[85] The Pulaski *Democrat* was suspended for two weeks, but what words it printed that offended Hascall are not precisely known.[86]

Editor Daniel E. VanValkenburgh printed his Plymouth *Democrat* as a half-sized sheet after being arrested by Hascall and taking a loyalty oath. *(From the Indiana State Library,* Plymouth Democrat *on microfilm)*

Other Democratic papers that faced suppression by Hascall included the Huntington *Democrat*, the Rushville *Jacksonian*, the Franklin *Weekly Democratic Herald*, and the Hartford City Blackford County *Democrat*. Union Army soldiers attempted to arrest Huntington *Democrat* editor Samuel Winters, but a crowd sympathetic to the newspaper prevented the arrest. The Rushville editor was threatened with arrest not for words he wrote, but for a speech he made at a political rally. It is not clear whether the Franklin or Hartford City papers were merely threatened or actually suppressed.

More in keeping with the announced reason for his command in Indianapolis, Hascall had General Order No. 11 published on May 11.[87] It reported that all enemy prisoners in the state captured before April 1 had been exchanged. Ten days later, the Goshen *Times* reported that Hascall had "notified several Copperhead newspapers in this State, that they must apologize for recent articles in their papers and improve their loyalty, or their paper will be suppressed and the editors arrested."[88]

HASCALL AND A NEW YORK EDITOR

While all of this was happening, Hascall had an exchange with New York *Express* editor James Brooks. Democratic papers throughout Indiana published the Brooks and Hascall letters. Brooks' paper had already been suppressed from the mails in the Middle Department, roughly the mid-Atlantic states. In response to an *Express* editorial about his proclamation, Hascall called Brooks "witty and smart" and said Order No. 9 "was issued after mature deliberation and consultation."[89] Hascall added, "It is fortunate your publication is not published in my District."[90]

Brooks countered that even if Hascall was the commander of New York, the Democratic governor of the state, Horatio Seymour, would "find a place in the Tombs" for Hascall. Brooks continued, "You labor, I see, under the not uncommon delusion with men of your military caliber, that the Administration is the Government, and that the 'war policy' of the Administration is 'The Supreme Law of the Land,' not the Constitution of the United States. Or, in other words, that 'No. 38' or 'No. 39,' is the Government of the United States."[91] Eventually, Burnside himself would get irritated with Brooks and would stop the mailing of the *Express* to the Midwest.

While Hascall and Brooks took aim at one another, a flurry of activity occurred during the first week of June. Secretary of War Edwin M. Stanton sent a letter to Burnside on June 1 suggesting the Commander of the Department of the Ohio ask for Hascall's resignation. Stanton was alarmed that the press suspensions were irritating Hoosiers unnecessarily and might be hampering Morton's efforts to run the state. "The proper limit of military power in such cases," Stanton wrote, "is at the request to aid and not supersede the State authority."[92] The Secretary of War worried that "indiscreet commanders" would only irritate loyal governors and other state officials who were aiding the Union war effort.[93] Stanton concluded that Lincoln agreed with this point of view and encouraged the general to find a more circumspect military leader for Indiana.

Morton had wanted a large military force in the state, mainly to protect the capital in case of a thrust by Confederates from Kentucky. However, Hascall had sent every available man south to fight—exactly what Burnside wanted. Morton also thought Hascall knew less about the state than the governor did—and in a sense this was true because Hascall was from northern Indiana, and the state government had been dominated by the bottom two-thirds for most of its existence.[94] Plus, Hascall had been away. Most importantly, though, Carrington was closer to Morton and would do as he was told. On the other hand, Hascall worked for Burnside, not the governor.

On June 1, the Chicago *Times* printed a letter from a writer claiming to be a resident of Goshen, Indiana. In it, the writer claimed that Hascall had no common sense and "was always considered the family fool."[95] It is not clear if Burnside saw this broadside at his officer, but nonetheless he drew up orders to quiet the *Times* that very same day. Thus, weighing his options with Hascall, Burnside sent word to Chicago to shut down the *Times*, whose editor, Wilbur F. Storey, constantly criticized the Republicans and the Lincoln administration.[96] On June 3, Burnside had the *Times* suspended, in part because Storey's paper printed racist material and made fun of Lincoln, whom the editor called a despot.[97] After Burnside said the *Times* was disloyal and incendiary, the Republican-majority Illinois House of Representatives passed a resolution denouncing Burnside's action, saying it violated state and federal law. New York papers roasted the major general. Even the *New York Times*, generally supportive of Lincoln and Burnside, criticized his use of force. "Any person who knows anything of the character of our institutions, will readily see that such proceedings as the suppression of the Chicago *Times* by military force, will create far more formidable evils than they correct," the New York *Times* stated.[98]

Lincoln revoked the suspension, though he actually sent a second telegraph revoking the first order. However, Burnside received it too late.[99] The Columbia City *News* in Indiana then announced in its June 6 edition that Hascall had written the Starke County *Press* and ordered editor Joseph A. Berry to change his tone to one more loyal to the Lincoln government.[100] Hascall's letter to Berry must have been written before June 5. The signals from the government remained, at best, confusing for Democratic editors.

Both Republicans and Democrats were suspicious of one another in Indiana. Republican editors thought some Democratic editors were sending veiled messages to party members to lukewarmly support the war or not participate in the draft. Democrats feared Republicans were spying on them and telling Hascall about their political activities. For example, Plymouth *Weekly*

1863 press suppression
The map shows cities where government-sponsored
suppression occured in Indiana.

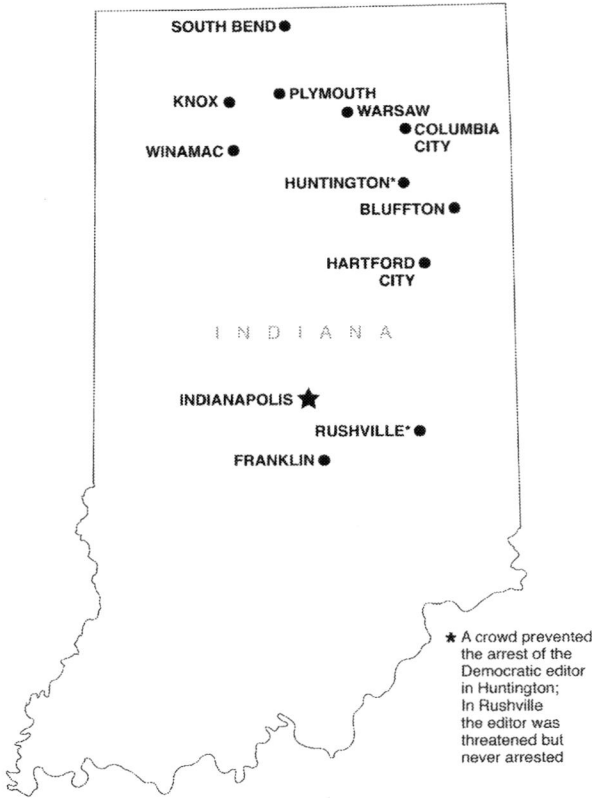

SOUTH BEND ●

KNOX ●   ● PLYMOUTH
            ● WARSAW
WINAMAC ●   ● COLUMBIA
                  CITY

HUNTINGTON* ●
        BLUFFTON ●

HARTFORD ●
CITY

I N D I A N A

INDIANAPOLIS ★

RUSHVILLE* ●

FRANKLIN ●

★ A crowd prevented
the arrest of the
Democratic editor
in Huntington;
In Rushville
the editor was
threatened but
never arrested

The cities where Milo Hascall suppressed newspapers in Indiana under
Order No. 9. *(Graphic by Kalpana Ramgopal)*

Democrat editor Ed VanValkenburgh, who missed publishing one issue of his
paper after he was arrested and shipped to Cincinnati, was sure that Republicans in Plymouth were feeding Hascall with a steady list of disloyal Democrats.
The editor wrote: "There have probably been one hundred names reported
from our county to Gen. Hascall, as fit subjects for arrest as disloyalists. . . . Of
all the contemptible, disreputable, groveling, low, mean, unmanly, despicable
occupations any human being can engage in, this reporting is the meanest
and lowest."[101] VanValkenburgh received a rumor about Hascall being fired
and published the report on May 28.[102]

Meanwhile, the Goshen *Times* tried to quell rumors that Hascall had
been relieved of his command. Reporting that Hascall was in Goshen, it

declared: "He was appointed to his present command by General Burnside without any solicitation on his part or that of his friends, and is sustained by the Commander-in-chief, Abraham Lincoln."[103] Goshen's Republican newspaper continued to support General Order No. 9 and provided an argument for suppression that was ambiguous in its definition of "aid" and "comfort" for the enemy. It proclaimed: "Open sympathy with treason and every thing that tends to give the rebels aid and comfort must be put down at any sacrifice!"[104] Based on the wording of Hascall's order, this meant that legitimate criticism of the Lincoln administration, the war policy, or the war effort would be seen as treasonous.

∞ CHAPTER EIGHT ∞

The Response to Press Suppression
in Civil War Indiana

The response to Brigadier General Hascall's General Order No. 9 in the press of Indiana was divided along party lines. Generally, Democratic editors defied the order, counseled defiance, or criticized Hascall for allowing only Republican newspapers to be critical of policy or performance. On the other hand, Republican editors hailed it as a necessary measure during a rebellion, and some forwarded the names of dissident Democratic editors to Hascall.

The arguments against Hascall's order centered on the free-expression tradition guaranteed by the U.S. Constitution. The Democrats did not make explicit appeals to the First Amendment, while the arguments for suppression sustained Lincoln's public safety argument for the suspension of the writ of habeas corpus during a rebellion or invasion. Oddly, the Republican editors did not cite the Indiana Constitution's bill of rights and its responsibility-for-abuse clause in the free-press section, although historically that clause referred to the responsibility the individual journalist had for libel after publication. Neither did Democratic journalists challenge responsibility-for-abuse, since this might have been a good time to question whether this phrase should even be in the state constitution, or to show that it had to do only with libel and not political expression or commentary. It seems as if the state constitution did not matter in the debate—in a sense, a sign that on this issue, the federal government was sovereign, even if Democrats did not admit it publicly. Yet Democrats acted as if the federal Constitution were the law of the land.

The arguments both sides would use in Indiana were reprises of those that were made in Ohio after Major General Ambrose Burnside had Clement Vallandigham arrested in Dayton on May 5, 1863, and tried the next day by the military commission in Cincinnati. Burnside charged Vallandigham with publicly "declaring disloyal sentiments and opinions, with the object and purpose of weakening the power of the Government in its effort to suppress an unlawful rebellion."[1] Although no copy exists of the Mount Vernon, Ohio, speech of May 1, Vallandigham allegedly said Lincoln had a plan to end the war the day before Fredericksburg and that Lincoln was about to set up district governments all over the country. The spies who took notes during the Mount Vernon speech also reported that Vallandigham said he would spit on General Order No. 38.[2]

VALLANDIGHAM TRIAL

At the trial, Vallandigham introduced a letter from a Confederate in Richmond proposing that Southern senators return to Congress. This was supposed to be evidence that some Southerners were ready to go to the peace table. The two plainclothes spies who were among the crowd at Mount Vernon testified against Vallandigham, while Congressman S. S. Cox of Ohio was the only witness called by the defense. After three hours of deliberations, the military commission found the ex-congressman guilty.

During the trial, Vallandigham applied for a writ of habeas corpus, but Judge Humphrey H. Leavitt, a Democrat, denied it.[3] Democratic editors were not charitable with Judge Leavitt's decision. Wilbur F. Storey, editor of the Chicago *Times*, found the decision to be "discouraging."[4] Storey reminded his readers that the power to suspend the writ of habeas corpus lay in the hands of Congress, not the president or any representative of the executive branch. Storey also was dismayed that Leavitt had made "support of the war policies of the administration the standard for loyalty."[5]

Meanwhile, an editor in Fort Wayne, Indiana, wondered why Democratic editors in Ohio and Indiana were being singled out for press suppression. "The Abolition citizens in the eastern states are permitted to exercise this privilege, without restraint, of questioning, opposing or condemning, the acts of the present administration," observed John Dawson.[6] New York editors could write what they pleased, but editors in Burnside's department had to choose their words carefully or face punishment.

Clement L. Vallandigham, an attorney, was the political leader of the Peace Democrats and had been the editor of the *Dayton Western Empire*. He was a skilled political rhetorician, though painfully long-winded. *(Photo from the Library of Congress)*

Some Republican editors denounced the proceedings, including Leavitt's legal decision and Vallandigham's conviction.[7] Yet most Indiana Republican editors supported Leavitt and the conviction. They rejoiced to have both Vallandigham and dissident Democratic editors put in their place. Likewise, they cheered Hascall's general order for being just as aggressive against dissidence as Burnside's order was. The editor of the *St. Joseph Valley Register* cheered Hascall's suppression of his Democratic competitor and concluded that the South Bend *Forum* editor's decision to stop publication proved how disloyal it was.[8] The editor of the Logansport *Journal* equated agitating against the draft with allowing a person to come into town to "incite our young men to commit robberies."[9] The *Journal* editor asked his readers if they would excuse such behavior on the principle of free speech.

While Democratic editors fashioned a consensus opposing General Order No. 9, they were too scattered to hold a meeting about the general orders and failed to lodge a formal collective protest. In New York, editors did not face that same problem of being so spread out.[10] They assembled to discuss federal suppression in the Midwest and its potential effect on the whole nation, but especially in New York City, where the majority of the newspapers were Democratic. Brothers Fernando and Benjamin Wood sponsored the protest meeting in New York, and most newspapers in the city encouraged citizens to attend.[11] "Everywhere public opinion, without distinction of party, is pronouncing against Burnside's course," observed James Gordon Bennett's New York *Herald*.[12] The New York *Evening Post* added, "The Government can not punish men for treason because their talk tends to give aid and comfort to the enemy."[13]

Nationally, a few Republicans looked at the general order in practical political terms. They worried that Burnside's actions were unnecessary and had gone too far. For example, Indiana Republican politician Orville Hickman Browning thought Vallandigham's arrest was arbitrary and did more harm than good.[14] Secretary of the Navy Gideon Welles declared the arrest and military conviction of Vallandigham to be unconstitutional.[15] Joel Parker, a law professor who provided the president's arguments for the suspension of the writ of habeas corpus in *Ex Parte Merryman*—in which Chief Justice Roger B. Taney declared only Congress could suspend the writ—opposed the Vallandigham arrest. *Harper's Weekly* editor George William Curtis also voiced his opposition.[16] Even Horace Greeley of the New York *Tribune* was lukewarm about the arrest, stating that Vallandigham was more a moral traitor than a legal one.[17] Later, when Vallandigham returned—illegally—from exile, Greeley counseled the president to leave the Ohioan alone.

One exception was Henry R. Raymond, editor of the New York *Times*, who ran both sides of the story in its news columns, while continually praising Burnside in his editorials throughout the spring and summer of 1863. The New York newspaper defended the trial of Vallandigham, claiming that the former congressman had hurt the military with his remarks. Therefore, in the *Times*' view, the military had jurisdiction since it was the offended party, and a department of the military did exist in Ohio.[18]

In explaining General Order No. 38, the New York *Times* proclaimed: "The military necessity for such a procedure is obvious to any intelligent man. No truly loyal man would think of complaining of it. None but a disloyal man would attempt to influence a crowd by denouncing it as usurpation, and declaring his intention to disregard it."[19] The *Times* editor added that self-preservation was the first necessity of war, implying that the rights guaranteed in the Constitution took on a secondary status in wartime.[20] Later, the *Times* celebrated the nomination of Vallandigham for the Democracy's gubernatorial slot in Ohio because it further established the differences between loyal and disloyal men in the North.[21]

The Southern press was gleeful that Vallandigham labeled Lincoln a despot. They also rejoiced that the ex-congressman's arrest was another example of the end of civil liberties under the radical Republicans. The arrest fed the Confederate propaganda machine. However, many Southern journalists saw Vallandigham's proposal for a confederacy of regional nations or a return to the status quo ante bellum as ridiculous by 1863. John M. Daniel of the Richmond, Virginia, *Examiner* thought Vallandigham's ideas would lead to the extinction of the independent Confederacy.[22]

Back in Washington, the Lincoln administration and the military effectively worked together to suspend the press while Republican editors explained why suspension had to be undertaken. Although they were being good team players during a time of the party press, Republican editors were rationalizing suppression of disloyal newspapers while applauding the benefits of a free press.[23] In effect, because the party press remained dominant during the Civil War, many newspapermen thought the First Amendment applied only to editors who supported the majority party.

Freedom of the press, in this view, was contingent upon the current standing of the political parties. Such a view potentially could give majority editors an upper hand that would have an economic impact on their enterprises. It opposed Madison's understanding that the press clause in the First Amendment was in place to protect the tyranny of the majority over the minority and to guarantee a plurality of political ideas that could be sorted out by citizens in the so-called market place of ideas.[24]

There is nothing that Madison wrote to suggest freedom of the press could be temporarily suspended or that majority opinions would be protected and minority opinions would not be protected. Indeed, Madison held to the opinion that the good that comes with the freedom of the press is "inseparable" from the evil of those who abuse the right. Madison declared: "However desirable those measures might be which might correct without enslaving the press, they have never yet been devised in America."[25] Little or no press legislation or judicial decisions occurred in the first six decades of the nineteenth century. Thus, no corrective measures were in place when the Civil War began.

HOOSIER REPUBLICAN EDITORS DEFEND HASCALL

When Brigadier General Hascall issued General Order No. 9 on April 25, 1863, the Republican editors of Indiana offered many of the same arguments Raymond did in their support of suppression. George D. Copeland, editor of the pro-Republican Goshen *Times*, said: "Hascall is on the right track and we hope he will not falter in his efforts to crush out home treason. . . . Open sympathy with treason and every thing that tends to give the rebels aid and comfort must be put down at any sacrifice!"[26]

Even before Hascall came to power in Indianapolis, Thomas H. Bringhurst and Joseph Dague, editors of the pro-Republican Logansport *Journal*, railed that free speech that aided the Confederacy was a "perversion."[27] The editors added: "The injury done the Government in its great struggle against rebellion, under this plea [for free speech] can never be estimated."[28] This, too, was a key distinction because it made it seem as if the extent of Northern collaboration with the Confederacy was sufficiently large enough to cause substantial problems for the prosecution of the war and the political stability of the states that remained in the Union. Thus, words that did not directly contribute to the war effort could be construed as being harmful to it. This indeed was a broad interpretation of press loyalty.

Later, the Logansport editors expanded this argument, stating that opposing the Lincoln administration was the same as opposing the Constitution—a broadside on the Democrats, who thought of themselves as having the upper hand along constitutional lines. Bringhurst and Dague wrote: "That instrument strictly requires the government it provides for, to suppress domestic insurrections, and maintain it as the supreme law of the land."[29] In other words, saving the U.S. government was the best way to save the U.S. Constitution.

This argument also moved the framing of the political argument away from the right of states to secede in the same way that the Americans had seceded from the British monarchy. The implication was that the U.S. Constitution was agreed upon by the majority of the representatives of the thirteen original colonies and that any state or states that seceded violated the spirit of democracy, where the majority's will—not the monarch's will—rules.

The prevailing line of reasoning emboldened Republican editors in Indiana and allowed them to focus on Democratic loyalty in a democratic nation and on the will of the majority—in the North—to fight and win the war. James Scott, editor of the Republican newspaper in Delphi, called the Democrats "vampires" because of their dissident words and said calls for a six-month truce would enable the Confederates to recruit more men.[30]

The Marshall County *Republican*, direct rival of the Plymouth *Democrat*, applauded Hascall and said the Democrats "may as well submit or travel, first as last."[31] To let *Democrat* editor VanValkenburgh's invective pass would have set a "precedent of mischievous effect."[32] Editors Ignatius Mattingly and John D. Devor reasoned that once Hascall made the order, he had to enforce it, or it would lose its efficacy. When Lincoln flip-flopped and reversed Burnside's June 3 suppression of Wilbur F. Storey's Chicago *Times*, Mattingly and Devor expressed disdain, saying: "We can not see [with] what consistency the President sends troops South to put down the rebellion, and leave those behind who are doing all they can to foster it."[33]

Alfred Wheeler, editor of the Republican paper in South Bend, stated that the definition of being Democratic was being disloyal, and it was "an impossibility to publish a paper that was both loyal and Democratic."[34] Wheeler implied that Democratic papers ought to shut down for the duration of the war. The Warsaw *Northern Indianian* proclaimed: "Eternal vigilance is the price of liberty. . . . They [Democrats] want their rights and they should receive them in the shape of a rope around their necks."[35]

The Indianapolis *Daily Journal* was far less emotional than the Warsaw paper, but it agreed that free expression had its limitations and conditions. Its editors argued there was no absolute free expression in the British common law tradition and liberty might be restrained in certain circumstances. The *Daily Journal* said: "A press reeking with licentiousness, or labouring in the interest of treason is not less dangerous than when muzzled by tyranny. No man has a right to publish what is pernicious to peace and good order and government and religion without incurring the penalty which the law has affixed to the crime of libel."[36]

RULINGS ON LIBEL

Few libel suits against newspapers were brought to Indiana's highest court before the Civil War, so there is little evidence to ascertain accurately the legal status of freedom of the press in the Hoosier State in the 1860s. In *Clarkson v. McCarty*, an 1841 decision, the Indiana Supreme Court ruled in favor of a plaintiff who sued a newspaper for printing a libelous statement by a third party.[37] The court held that allowing a paper to print a third-party libel threatened "the peace of society."[38]

In *Johnson v. Stebbins*, reviewed in 1854, the state supreme court said a defendant must prove the actions of which a plaintiff is alleged to be guilty before the justices could determine if a newspaper was justified in printing an article about the plaintiff.[39] In this case, Christopher C. Stebbins, publisher of *The Spirit of the West* in Columbus, printed an article that alleged the town postmaster lived and worked in a building that was of "low character." Stebbins said he received this intelligence from a writer in Taylorsville, and, if true, the publisher wished the post office were in the hands of others.[40] Stebbins believed the statements made in the letter to be true and said he had no malice against the plaintiff, Benajah Johnson, who sought $5,000 in damages because he claimed that the editor defamed his reputation. Stebbins said Johnson kept a grocery in the post office where liquor was stored, and those who purchased the liquor also stayed in the house and were said to disturb the peace.

The Bartholomew Circuit Court ruled in favor of Stebbins, but the Indiana Supreme Court overturned the ruling on a technicality. However, the court maintained that the plaintiff could not "have much reason to complain if the character of the house should be called low" because Johnson was selling liquor to "drunken men."[41] In effect, if the allegation was true and the actions in the house were infractions under the recently established temperance laws of Indiana, then libel did not occur. Neither case had much of a bearing on what Hascall did, but each showed that the courts in Indiana held newspaper editors responsible for the words they printed—that the words must be true and not malicious.

The Indiana Supreme Court, for most of the war, had a Democratic majority, led by Judge Samuel E. Perkins, a strict constructionist who emphasized personal liberty and opposed restraints on private property. A Perkins interpretation overturned the state's prohibition law in the 1850s. Perkins, who at one time had been the editor of the Richmond *Jeffersonian*, supported the war as long as it was prosecuted "constitutionally and for a constitutional object."[42] He feared the building of a "great consolidated military and enormously costly government."[43] After resolutions were passed in the Indiana legislature in 1863 condemning military arrests of civilians in the state, Perkins and the court took on several cases involving the suspension of the writ of habeas corpus, though none involved newspapers.

Generally, across the nation, journalists upheld libertarian notions of a free press in 1863. Horace Greeley, editor of the New York *Tribune* and a leading abolitionist, assembled a meeting of editors in New York after Burnside suppressed the Chicago *Times* in June of 1863. Greeley and a bipartisan group of editors struck a compromise. These editors inveighed against suppression of the press. While they also censured any inciting of treasonous actions, the editors still upheld the right of the "press to criticize freely and fearlessly the acts of those charged with the administration of the Government, and their civil and military subordinates, and that any limitations of this right, created by necessities of war, should be confined to the localities where hostilities exist, or are immediately threatened."[44]

Indiana was not such a place, although Confederate renegade John Morgan would invade briefly in July and Governor Oliver P. Morton constantly worried about Kentucky being overrun by the Southern army and what effect that would have on Indiana. The Greeley group upheld the freedom of the press in all cases except where battles were taking place—only there would restrictions apply.

In many ways this represented Lincoln's view in the case of the Chicago *Times*, except for the fact that the president had a change of heart at the last minute. The president telegraphed Burnside to forget his initial revocation of the suspension. However, this second communication arrived at the Burnside's office in Cincinnati too late, and the *Times* reopened.[45]

One Democratic newspaper in Indiana gave a measure of support to Hascall in the spring of 1863. The Goshen *Democrat* tried to be more circumspect than other Democratic papers. It backed the president "in all his lawful efforts to suppress the rebellion," though the newspaper did oppose the Emancipation Proclamation, mainly because the editors believed it overextended the chief executive's power.[46] Often more neutral in tone than its peers, the *Democrat* told its readers that it needed to support Hascall's order. It also told the brigadier general in his eagerness to suppress the Hoosier press to be careful because many of the reports of treason he was receiving were sent out of political spite. When a report that Hascall had been sacked reached its office in the middle of May, the *Democrat* responded: "We are inclined to doubt the truth of this report. This loss would be irreparable."[47] It also told the brigadier general to be careful in his eagerness.

THE HASCALL-EDGERTON DIALOGUE

The man making the strongest argument for unfettered communication that spring in Indiana was not an editor. He was a Democratic politician, and his defense of freedom of the press was played out in the newspapers across the state. Tenth District Congressman Joseph Ketchum Edgerton, a Fort Wayne attorney and businessman who had made much of his money on the railroads, argued that the Constitution was not suspended by war because Indiana was not a seceding state or a place where the war was taking place, and that the necessary civilian governments were in place to keep the peace and run the municipal governments of the state.

A Jeffersonian who believed in limited government, Edgerton said the Bill of Rights was the law of the land and that no military leader had the right to squelch free expression. Edgerton had written a letter to E. Van Long, editor of the pro-Democratic Warsaw *Union*. In the letter, which appeared in many northeast Indiana newspapers in early May of 1863, Edgerton denounced the Conscription Act. He also said that Hascall's order would backfire and mobilize Democrats.

Hascall countered that the security of the public and the need of the federal government to survive the war superseded free speech and press. This debate extended back to the days of Madison and Hamilton. The personal freedoms in the federal Bill of Rights were aligned with states' rights and against the power of the central government. Boiled down, this was a classic confrontation between the rights of the individual and the necessity for a viable government in a democracy. At a time of severe political instability, the tension between individual rights and state needs intensified—just as Fredrick Siebert's hypothesis would have predicted.

The debate began one week after Hascall's April 25 order was made public with Edgerton asking Hascall in a private letter to clarify a few items in

General Order No. 9. Somehow, the letter was leaked, and it was published in dozens of newspapers in the state. A prominent resident of Allen County, Edgerton expressed a civil tone, noting that Hascall's intentions in enacting the order seemed to be patriotic. "It seems to recognize the fact that opposing political parties may still be permitted to exist," Edgerton wrote, "and yet co-operate to restore harmony and good feeling in the State."[48] However, the congressman from Fort Wayne had questions about the specifics of the brigadier general's new policy regarding civil rights. Edgerton, as a politician, wanted Hascall to clarify exactly what he meant when he wrote that all newspaper editors and public orators who "endeavor to bring the war policy government into disrepute" and were "actively opposed to the war policy of the administration" would be subject to incarceration and trial by a military commission.[49] Was Hascall saying that Hoosiers could not publicly list grievances against the government and criticize government actions and policies—rights that are part and parcel of the democratic process in a society that has a free-expression clause in its constitution?

Hascall responded to Edgerton on May 5 in a letter sent to newspapers in the state and made public by Edgerton's brother, Alfred P. Edgerton.[50] In the document, the Union military leader defined allegiance as practical loyalty, not in legal or theoretical terms. Hascall wrote: "You know as well as I, that practically, during the next two years, there is no difference between the Administration and the [federal] Government. You cannot destroy or impair the one without effecting the other similarly."[51]

The Union administrator was at least technically right. Because of the federal election schedule and the war powers of the president granted by the Constitution, the Lincoln administration, with a Republican majority in both houses of Congress, was in fact the federal government for the next two years, until the 1864 elections. Lincoln had a mandate until March of 1865. This was a constitutional issue that the Democrats could do nothing about.[52]

Yet, in another sense, Hascall was off the mark. While the Democrats were effectively out of power and had, at best, minimum input on war policy, they certainly had the right to criticize the government and to use their criticisms to build a base of power that would oppose Lincoln and the Republicans in 1864. Nothing in the Constitution prohibits any opposition party from campaigning and devising political strategy during war, though sometimes there is a gentleman's agreement to moderate the partisan bickering during war.

The nature of the criticism was another matter. The Republicans' great leap was to make criticism synonymous with treason, which the Constitution defines as giving aid and comfort to the enemy. By the spring of 1863, the Republicans had come to see any criticism of the war and anything that was not directly aiding the war effort as treason. It is debatable whether some Democrats telling citizens not to join the military was actually giving the Confederates aid and comfort. After all, there had not been a draft before. Moreover, just because the Republicans had the upper hand in the federal government, especially with control of Congress and the executive branch, they did not dominate all state and local political institutions in the North. In many locales, Democrats held the majority. If they supported different war policies and objectives, including peace, Lincoln and the Republicans had no constitutional authority to stop it.

The first half of 1863 was a perilous time for the administration. The war effort generally was not going well, and the conflict had gone on far too long. Desertions from the Union Army were staggering. Burnside's failure at Fredericksburg and the opinion of so many soldiers about his competence after that defeat and the awful Mud March in January of 1863 had morale at an all-time low. Behind the scenes in the winter of 1863, Major General Joseph Hooker worked successfully to have Burnside demoted.[53] General McClellan had his allies working against Burnside too. When Hooker took charge of the Army of the Potomac on January 25, 1863, more than 85,000 men were absent without leave, and an average of 200 deserted each day.[54] The antipathy of the troops led to a prodigious amount of drinking of spirits, making many soldiers useless for combat.

Most Democratic organs in the state, led by the Indianapolis *Indiana State Sentinel*, commented on the exchange between Hascall and Edgerton. Most were caustic in their commentary on Hascall's dialogue with Edgerton. Even the Goshen *Democrat* commented that in its analysis "Free speech is no longer to be permitted" in Indiana.[55] Republican editors either backed Hascall without reservation or encouraged him to enforce No. 9 even more vigorously.

A CHANGE IN PUBLIC OPINION

Meanwhile, Northern political leaders feared that the elections of 1862 marked a major change in public opinion. The messy Civil War had sapped the popular will; hearts and minds had to be won. The spring of 1863 would be a key juncture in the war. Men with the background and knowledge of Hascall and Burnside knew this well. As West Point graduates, they believed that organization and planning would win the war. Now they found themselves in the position of having to apply their organizing and planning skills to political problems in the Midwest, not at the front.

While Hooker was busy refurbishing the Army of the Potomac, Burnside tried to make amends for Fredericksburg by building a model federal district government in Cincinnati, and he chose Hascall to carry out his policies in Indiana.[56] Burnside was called to the Queen City when Horatio Wright decided to step down from his command of the Department of the Ohio because the U.S. Senate had failed to confirm his promotion to major general.[57] Wright was convinced that a second invasion of Kentucky was about to take place. He called for 10,000 more men for his department—and Burnside would bring two divisions with him to Cincinnati.

Burnside and Hascall sought to devise and carry out practical political solutions in an environment that was still politically hot, in part, because the U.S. has two-year congressional terms. Practical politics had not been suspended, and the Democrats were not about to sit back and let the Republicans maintain power without a fight. Lincoln needed Congress to pass laws that were not covered under the war powers in areas such as internal revenue, confiscation, conscription, and emancipation.

The House of Representatives had changed dramatically in March of 1863 after Democrats made large gains in the previous fall. Illinois, Ohio, and Indiana's delegations to Washington all became majority Democratic, which helped to narrow the Republican lead in the House of Representatives. On the state and local levels, Democrats made gains as well. For example, both the Indiana and Illinois legislatures took on Democratic majorities, resulting in their governors literally shutting down the state houses for the remainder of the war.[58]

Hascall's view was that people were for the Republicans or against the government of the U.S. and therefore in favor of the government of the Confederacy. A citizen who might be against the war based on conscience, as a few Quakers were, or a citizen for the war but opposed, say, to conscription, would in Hascall's reasoning be a traitor. This was a perilous form of reasoning for a military governor to be making, particularly in a state not under attack. It irritated Governor Morton, who had not been enthusiastic about Hascall's command in Indianapolis from the start and worked to have him removed from the district command.[59]

Hascall also wrote that it was appropriate to carp about government policy and action during peacetime, but that such inveighing was inappropriate during wartime. The laws that Lincoln and Congress passed were the laws of the land until a new Congress and/or president were elected. "Possibly, they are not the wisest and best that could have been enacted," Hascall continued. "That, however, is a matter which does not concern either of us here.

Enough for us to know that they have been agreed upon by the only rightful and proper authorities known to our government."[60] Hascall could not see that an opposition policy might actually improve the war effort and decrease the number of men sacrificed. In his mind, the Lincoln administration offered the best approach to fighting the war.

The brigadier general also said that Democratic resolutions finding fault with the Republicans were "evil," and he implied that they were intended to wreck havoc on the Union war effort. In Hascall's calculations, criticism did not mean conscientious objection to the war or offering a better way to fight it. "The only practical effect, then, of allowing newspapers and public speakers to inveigh against these measures is to divide and distract our own people, and thus give material 'aid and comfort' to our enemies," Hascall wrote.[61]

Republican editors, politicians, and Union military officials frequently cited this argument. The war, they maintained, created a special circumstance, and harmony was essential to fighting it effectively. It would be awful, in their opinion, if the North lost the war because its citizens were fragmented and the out-manned South was less divided. Likewise, always in the back of the minds of the Republicans was the belief that the nation's history was in the balance. They feared that such a relatively young nation could be torn apart permanently by secessionism, and that the British or some other foreign power might use the conflict to further the divide. That the South courted the British and French for official recognition throughout the war was not lost on the Republicans or the Northern military leaders.

EDGERTON'S ARGUMENT

Hascall also claimed the Irish and "secessionist" element in Congressman Edgerton's district were delusional. He lumped Edgerton with Terre Haute Congressman Daniel W. Voorhees, a leading Hoosier Democrat and an ally of Vallandigham. Hascall said that he would hold Edgerton responsible for any violence or mob activity that took place in Fort Wayne as a result of antiwar rhetoric. "I take deep interests in you for more reasons than one," Hascall concluded.[62]

Thus, Hascall was setting up his governance as a sort of police state, keeping political intelligence on Democrats, something that Governor Morton was doing on his own but lacked the resources to do as effectively as the federal district commander. Morton, it must be noted, was so short of cash for the state government during the war that he had to use creative financing to keep the government in Indianapolis running.[63] Morton envied the sort of power and intelligence Hascall had at his disposal.

Brigadier General Hascall made it clear he wanted to go after political leaders, including newspaper editors, because they were the ones inflaming ordinary citizens, who were potential soldiers. He used two figures of speech to drive home this point. First, he compared the situation to a smallpox epidemic. Was it right to condemn his patients for the progress of the disease? Likewise, was it right to incarcerate citizens for what they say when newspaper editors and public speakers are spewing forth the ideas that contaminated them? Then he added memorably: "To kill the serpent speedily it must be hit on the head."[64]

Patently, Hascall believed he must initially stop the political leadership of the opposition, and then negative public opinion would die down. The district commander did not want to wait for litigation to figure out what was right. He preferred to silence the "disloyal" expeditiously, and given the perils that the Union faced in the spring of 1863, he had justification for precisely carrying out Burnside's wishes.

On his way to England after a congressional recess, Edgerton replied to Hascall on May 12, having read Hascall's May 6 Indianapolis *Daily Journal* letter in the New York *Evening Express* that had responded to the congressman's initial private letter asking for a clarification on the meaning of General Order No. 9. Edgerton wrote that any intelligent Hoosier construed the order to mean that free speech and free press were suppressed under Hascall's military administration in the state. Edgerton questioned whether General Order No. 9 would promote Hascall's intent to "restore harmony and good feeling in the State."[65] Edgerton said that Hascall should "recede as soon, and as gracefully as you can from the arbitrary purpose you have indicated." Edgerton, who had studied law under William Swetland in Plattsburg, New York, when the congressman was sixteen, said there would be no disturbance of the peace in Indiana as long as Hascall did not constrain the constitutional rights of the citizens of the nineteenth state.[66]

Edgerton claimed Indiana's citizens would ignore General Order No. 9. The congressman believed that Hoosiers had a legal government seated in Indianapolis and did not need a federal military presence in the state to supersede the civilian government. He noted: "It is not in rebellion, nor in a state of war, nor 'disloyal.' It has a constitution and laws of its own, all accordant with the constitution of the United States. . . . Among the civil rights of the people of Indiana are the rights of free speech, free press, and free courts. The people of Indiana have done nothing to forfeit these rights. They cannot forfeit them, for they are inherent and inalienable."[67] Forfeiture could occur only by amending the Indiana Constitution, in Edgerton's view.

This was where Edgerton had the rhetorical advantage on Hascall. The U.S. and Indiana constitutions guarantee freedom of the press, and the national founders believed it to be a natural right. No legal interpretation existed in Indiana or in Washington to indicate the suspension of the writ of habeas corpus superseded these rights. Thus, in a free state, freedom of the press was seen as unqualified. Edgerton said General Order No. 9 would not survive the ordeals of judicial review and popular defiance, though it is important to note that a U.S. Supreme Court decision about the suspension of the writ would not come until 1866. Thus, Hascall's order could stand, given this legal vacuum.

Edgerton launched into rhetoric that was popular with his largely Democratic constituents in Fort Wayne. He wrote: "The people of Indiana are not slaves—they are freemen. They will read and think; they will assemble and make and hear speeches; they will freely discuss public affairs, and freely resolve and vote upon them, and they organize political parties, some opposed to, some favoring the Administration, and you cannot prevent it."[68] He went on to say that the citizens of Indiana would form political parties and vote for and against the government in power. He compared the citizens' exercising these rights to the nature of the sea with its inevitable rolling of the tide on the beach—with Hascall vainly trying to tell the tide not to roll to the shore. Hascall might as well try to beat the air, Edgerton wrote.[69]

The congressman had no reason to mention the responsibility-for-abuse clause in the Indiana Constitution. If he had, then he would have had to admit that Hascall had justification to constrain some of the Democratic editors. Ironically, the states' rights argument along these lines would have hurt the Democrats and helped the Republicans. Perhaps that's why neither side referred to Indiana's press clause.

Neither the federal government nor the Republicans had the power to stop freedom of expression, Edgerton reasoned. "You may attack it and temporarily abridge or trammel it, but you can not subvert it," he wrote.[70] Rather, attempts at suppression would lead only to Republican losses at the polls, Edgerton held. The congressman found Hascall's threat to hold Democratic leaders responsible for the actions of others as unworthy of serious discussion.

Edgerton supported peace, prosperity, and the restoration of the Union, although he preferred to suppress the rebellion by nonmilitary means. The Fort Wayne congressman also said he opposed such federal laws as emancipation and confiscation. "I believe the administration has justly forfeited the confidence of a large majority of the people, even in the States faithful to the Union," he contended.[71] He continued that a change in the administration must come at the ballot box, and that such a change would only occur if politicians could freely express themselves as is guaranteed by the Constitution.

Edgerton added that his criticisms of Lincoln resonated with a majority of the Tenth District who voted Edgerton into office the previous fall. He said he would support Lincoln when he thought he ought to and oppose him when thought it necessary. Edgerton stated, "I will never, as long as life and intelligence remain, surrender my constitutional right to freely discuss, approve or condemn, in a constitutional way, and as I think the public good may demand, any policy or measure, be it for peace or war, of any administration, State or national."[72]

Likewise, the Evansville *Weekly Gazette*, a Democratic newspaper, made the case that political speech in particular was protected by the Constitution. That Evansville editor observed: "The real security . . . of the American constitution and government is the sentiment and opinion of the people, and it is consequently their duty to observe the conduct of the government, and it is the privilege of every man to give them full and just information on that important subject."[73] The editor concluded that freedom of the press was inseparable from the other freedoms guaranteed to the nation's citizens, and newspapers served as a "great public monitor."[74]

Edgerton asked why Governor Morton was silent as Hascall was making a mockery of the federal and state right to free speech and press. Morton ignored the pleas of Edgerton and failed to issue even the slightest rebuke to Hascall. The Fort Wayne congressman felt Hascall's federal administration was making Morton into "a mere cipher and pageant."[75]

In fact, Morton was upset with what the Union brigadier general was doing. Behind the scenes he was expressing his displeasure to his political allies.[76] Morton was afraid that Burnside and Hascall were doing more harm than good—that their edicts were only fanning the flames of Democratic defiance and indirectly decreasing Morton's power. Furthermore, the governor was infuriated with Burnside for removing Brigadier General Henry B. Carrington, who preceded Hascall as commander of the Indiana District. Carrington was Morton's close ally who had served as his military intelligence officer in the state. General Carrington was not as ostentatious as Hascall, preferring to work quietly in the background.

Morton wanted both Burnside and Hascall reassigned and sought to influence Henry W. Halleck, the chief of the military in Washington, in hopes Halleck would persuade Lincoln to fire both. He also enlisted the help of David Davis, a U.S. Supreme Court Justice, to lobby the Lincoln administration to have Hascall removed.[77] Morton sent a letter to Secretary of War Edwin M. Stanton asking that Hascall be reassigned.[78] Stanton then sent a letter to Burnside asking the general if it would be propitious to remove Hascall from command in Indiana.[79] In late May, the Delphi *Times* reported that Morton opposed "any further arrests in Indiana by the military authorities."[80]

The two problems with Hascall's General Order No. 9 were: (1) connecting loyalty to the U.S. government with loyalty to the Republican Party and (2) failing to make reference to the abuse clause in the Indiana Constitution's free-press provision. He made an argument for shutting down civil liberties, saying it was conditional based on loyalty to the Republican administration in Washington. Hascall made it an offense to endeavor to "bring the war policy of the government into disrepute." That is, even if a citizen made legitimate criticisms of the government's prosecution of the war, he was subject to military arrest and imprisonment. In effect, any opposition to the Lincoln administration amounted to treason. This would make it impossible to have democratic dialogue.

While many aspects of the war effort probably did not need exhaustive debate, major issues like conscription and funding did. Democratic speakers and writers justly felt they had the constitutionally protected right to express themselves freely and fearlessly. In essence, Hascall was saying that the Lincoln administration could act like a dictatorship and demand loyalty from all citizens. He gave no room for a loyal opposition or minority rights. Hascall could not conceive of the Union in any other terms than the successful prosecution of the war by Lincoln and the Republicans.

The Republican newspapers in Indiana supplied the arguments in favor of the criticism-is-treason approach. A Republican paper in Indianapolis wrote: "[Hascall's] determination to crush the budding disloyalty which, in the name of Democracy, has so nearly ripened into treason, is so manifest from his order, that no one can mistake his meaning. In this work he has the hearty cooperation and confidence of all loyal men."[81] Republicans deluged Hascall with intelligence about "disloyal" Democratic editors.[82]

Military leaders like Burnside and Hascall argued that silencing Lincoln's critics would stymie any signals the South might be getting that the Northern states were in political disharmony. Meanwhile, soldiers as well as civilians who favored the Republicans tended to take their general orders to mean that intimidation of Democratic free expression was acceptable. In fact, a strong case could be made that Lincoln and his generals acted more egregiously not by systematically suppressing free speech, but by looking the other way or not vigorously prosecuting mob intimidation of Democratic newspaper editors and Democratic public speakers. Such an example had occurred only a month before office when Union troops returning from the South ransacked the office of the Richmond *Jeffersonian* and tried the same against the *Indiana State Sentinel*.[83]

The military personnel of the Civil War operated under a different system from civilians, and it did not tend to promote freedom in a manner consistent with the Bill of Rights. It was a hierarchical rather than a democratic system, and in the case of Hascall, who had been educated at West Point, this hierarchy was imbedded in his thinking. Orders came from the top down, so Union soldiers themselves gave up freedoms and privileges when they entered the military. Officers and soldiers accustomed to fighting in a long and bloody war were more concerned with survival than peacetime rights. Information that might directly lead to one's death was certainly treasonous, and information that might indirectly help the enemy was noxious in the eyes of officers, soldiers, and their families. The personal was more important than the political to these men and women.

PROTECTING SOLDIERS V. SUPPRESSION OF THE PRESS

Hascall had on his mind the wives, children, parents, and siblings of the soldiers. This was by far the bloodiest conflict in U.S. history. Hascall did not want Indiana to contribute any more to the suffering than was necessary. It was a humanitarian argument, and perhaps his best. Hascall wrote: "As I value the lives of our hundreds of thousands of gallant soldiers in the field, as I regard the feelings, bereavements, and sufferings of their anxious families and friends at home, and as I regard the true interests of our State and nation, I am going to see to it that in Indiana, at least, such [disloyal] men have no abiding place."[84] In essence, Hascall thought giving up a few rights, privileges, and comforts during wartime was the least civilians could do as the body count rose every day.

Yet Hascall did not answer Edgerton's key charge: Why should the military government supersede the civilian government in the state? Governor Morton, the legislature, and state courts were in place and were they not sovereign? If Indiana's citizens felt that words spoken or written ought to be regulated, they could petition their representatives to vote for such regulations. Of course, the civilian government was operating, and Lincoln had not worked out this messy issue of jurisdiction when he suspended the writ of habeas corpus. Thus, the District of Indiana faced a legal conundrum that would not be settled until after the war, when the U.S. Supreme Court would decide the suspension of habeas corpus had been illegal.

James Elder, the editor of the pro-Democratic Richmond *Jeffersonian*, had provided an argument similar to Edgerton's in a late April editorial, claiming the U.S. Constitution was the supreme law of the land. "There can be no other just test of loyalty but fidelity to the Constitution," he wrote.[85] Elder said Democrats were obeying the law, and that such obedience was a Democrat's duty. "A man is no longer a Democrat when he fails this duty," Elder wrote. Likewise, Elder found a hole in Hascall's argument that the Lincoln administration was the government. He wondered what would happen if Lincoln lost in November 1864. Would that not suggest another political leader and his party could use different policies and measures to prosecute the war and save the Union? In Elder's understanding of government, the Constitution was sovereign, not the chief executive. Furthermore, Congress had no authority to abridge press freedom, and the role of the press was outside the executive's reach. The Constitution did not give the president the power to regulate the press, and the Supreme Court had made no ruling conceding such a prerogative.

Yet there was no all-encompassing conspiracy to suppress the Democratic press of Indiana. Lincoln had no master plan, but he did not stop the piecemeal assertions by the military against Democratic journalists, whether it was the loyal slave states of Missouri and Maryland early in the war or the Midwestern states in 1862 and 1863. Some military officers—Burnside, Hascall, John C. Fremont in Missouri, George Wright in Oregon, and Robert C. Schenck in Pennsylvania—were simply more zealous than other officers in cracking down on dissident editors.[86]

In the long run, Hascall and his ilk failed to permanently quell free expression. However, they showed that it could be done on a limited basis for a relatively short period of time. Furthermore, they had plenty of support from both Republican and War Democrat newspaper editors.

The partisan nature of Civil War era press ensured that there would be no consensus on the meaning of free expression during the war. Perhaps the most important thing to remember is that Lincoln, who had Burnside installed as head of the Department of the Ohio and who did not oppose the Vallandigham conviction, did not end the press suppression in Indiana himself. Lincoln tended to give the military leaders in the field broad powers to police the press. The policy of the federal government depended largely on the commanders in the field.

Edgerton, a one-term congressman, had the best argument against the military and government officials who wanted to establish a chilling effect on free expression: "You may attack it," he wrote, "and temporarily abridge

or trammel it, but you cannot subvert it. On the contrary, if you and the Administration and the party you serve persist in your attacks upon them, free
speech and free press will certainly in the end subvert you."[87] In Edgerton's
view, tyranny would impel a greater desire for liberty.

Lincoln had no hard-and-fast rule, except perhaps to try to measure
public opinion—that is, to evaluate matters on the pragmatic level of political
expediency.[88] If public opinion spiraled against suppression, Lincoln would
get involved and order his generals to stop. Otherwise, he stayed neutral, at
least publicly, and let matters play out.

Hascall's offensive against the Democratic editors did not come to an
end because either side won the war of ideas and words. Rather, Governor
Morton felt uncomfortable with Hascall in power. Morton covertly worked
to have both Hascall and Burnside removed from power in the Midwest. He
made several trips to Washington, D.C., to plead his case. Stanton wrote on
June 1 that he would give Morton half of his wishes:

> No one can understand better than yourself what harm may be done by
> an indiscreet or foolish military officer, who is constantly issuing military
> proclamations and engaging in newspaper controversies upon questions
> that agitate the public mind. For this reason it is thought by the President
> that General Hascall is not adapted to the service in which he is engaged
> in the State of Indiana.[89]

Hascall figured that Morton was miffed because the governor apparently had not been consulted when the decision was made to relieve Brigadier
General Carrington.[90] General Henry W. Halleck had warned Burnside not to
incite Democrats too much—that so doing would only make matters tougher
for the Republicans politically.[91] In a sense, though, it was because Burnside
irked and irritated Morton that the major general lost Hascall's services in
Indianapolis.

CHAPTER NINE

Aftermath of Hascall's Attempt to Constrain the Democratic Press in Civil War Indiana

Governor Oliver P. Morton said nothing publicly about his dissatisfaction with Hascall, even though he was working to have Hascall sacked through his political network. Burnside, who admired Hascall's loyalty and attempt to enforce the principles of General Order No. 38, decided to go along with Lincoln and Stanton. Burnside asked Hascall to resign, although Hascall claimed it was his idea to resign. The brigadier general did not challenge his removal from the District of Indiana. In fact, he seems in part to have wanted it, since so many Republicans had sent him letters about acts of disloyalty that it had become difficult to weed out the legitimate concerns of disloyalty from petty partisan payback.

On June 6, Hascall issued General Order No. 14 announcing his resignation.[1] Along with Hascall's resignation, the announcement included a paragraph from Burnside stating that the District of Indiana and the District of Michigan were being combined into one district under General Orlando B. Willcox.[2] Burnside, writing from Lexington, Kentucky, thanked Hascall for his "hearty co-operation and very efficient service and aid in carrying out the policy adopted by this department."[3] Hascall used the occasion to rescind General Order No. 9, saying he did it "without instructions from any source in order to leave his successor free to adopt such course as in his judgment will best subserve the public interest in the States of Indiana and Michigan."[4]

Hascall later admitted that General Order No. 9 had gained a "notorious" reputation "through the loyal states."[5] He said he was about to have the "traitorous papers and rabid copperheads in various parts of the state" dealt with the same way the federal government would with Lambdin P. Milligan, Joseph J. Bingham, Horace Heffren, William A. Bowlers, and the other alleged secret society members arrested for treason in 1864.[6] However, Hascall stated that "the president having revoked General Burnside's order for the suppression of the Chicago Times and not receiving the cooperation from the General government and state authorities which I deemed essential in carrying out my programme I informed General Burnside that I thought my usefulness was at an end in Indiana."[7] Hascall said that Willcox relieved him of his command of the District of Indiana on June 5.[8]

The intimidation of Democratic editors continued after June 5. On average, there were 17.5 acts of violence and intimidation carried out against Hoosier newspapers during the war. After Hascall's reign ended, five more cases of violence or intimidation occurred in the Hoosier State in 1863.[9] There would be twenty cases in 1864 and one in 1865.[10] Republican papers witnessed twenty-two cases of violence or threatened violence during the war.[11] Of the sixth-nine cases of violence or intimidation against Indiana papers during the war, twelve were clear cases of official suppression, and, of course, eleven of those twelve involved Hascall.

The twelfth instance occurred on November 28, 1862, when the Union Army arrested Lucienne G. Matthews, the editor of the pro-Democratic, pro-war New Albany *Ledger*, for publishing the identity of Indiana brigades and divisions and their locations and movements.[12] Matthews was arrested under the 57th Article of War and shipped to Cincinnati, where he claimed reprinting the information from another newspaper. Matthews was warned not to publish such information again.[13]

It is important to note than no incidences of press suppression occurred in Ohio, Michigan, or Illinois during the time Hascall was in charge in Indiana. Hascall ran two Democratic newspapers out of business with his bullying. Republican Congressman Godlove Orth of Indiana declared in 1864, "A man is free to speak as long as he speaks for the nation" and added that no member of the House should be allowed to speak against the nation.[14] Orth's feeling was a typical sentiment among Republicans and many War Democrats.

Burnside granted Hascall thirty days' leave after the brigadier general resigned from his Indiana command. Hascall went home to rest before

Orlando B. Willcox, seated, replaced Milo Hascall as commander of the District of Indiana. Here he is shown with his staff. *(Photo from the Library of Congress)*

rejoining the Army of the Cumberland later in the summer.[15] Except in the eyes of the editor of the Goshen *Times* and a few other Republican editors, Hascall had not been a popular leader in the state. According to Marvel, key Republicans in Indiana and Illinois wanted Hascall's removal. Along the way, Burnside learned that nobody in the cabinet approved of General Order 38 and its enforcement.[16] Plymouth's VanValkenburgh said Hascall "was a burning disgrace to our State, and has laid up for himself a treasure of infamy."[17] The New Albany *Ledger*, which had been prowar most of the first two years of the conflict, said Hascall "won more honorable fame in the field with his sword, than he has done as commander of this department by his 'orders' and arbitrary acts."[18] The Buffalo, New York, *Commercial Advertiser* called Hascall's actions in Indiana "unofficer-like."[19]

CESSATION OF NORMAL POLITICS

Despite the response to the Chicago *Times* suppression, Burnside believed that restrictions should be even tighter. On June 3, he made a public statement that best explained his rationale for suppressing civil liberties. In General Order No. 90, the major general stated that the rebellion required a cessation of normal politics and the need of citizens to suspend their civil liberties. He noted that the citizen-soldier had to give up his freedom of expression, so it was not too much to ask citizens to make similar sacrifices. Burnside observed: "The citizen would be unjust to the soldier, as well as unfaithful to his country, if, while enjoying the comforts of home, he would be unwilling to give a portion of a privilege which the soldier resigns altogether. That freedom of discussion and criticism which is proper in the politician and journalist in time of peace, becomes rank treason when it tends to weaken the confidence of the soldier in his officers and in his Government."[20] Burnside, of course, emphasized that the loss of civil liberties was a temporary state of affairs for both the citizen-soldier and the citizen.

Just before he demoted Hascall, Burnside read the open exchange between Hascall and Brooks. The major general was miffed with Hascall. In Cincinnati, Burnside asked for an explanation from the brigadier general in Indianapolis. Hascall explained that his letter was not meant to be published in any newspaper, but that Brooks and other Democratic editors chose to make it public. Hascall wrote: "If you had seen the article in their paper that called forth my letter I think you would say that I was justified in writing them the private letter I did."[21] Burnside then warned Hascall to be careful not to agitate the Democrats during an upcoming mass meeting in Indianapolis.[22]

After Hascall suppressed the St. Joseph County, Indiana, *Forum*, Storey's *Times* defended *Forum* editor William H. Drapier: "The publisher of the *Forum* prefers to suffer the destruction of his business rather than surrender the freedom of the press. The head and front of his offending is that he disapproves the partisan war policies of the administration and denies the legal power of Brig. Gen. Hascall to override the authority of the Constitution and laws."[23] Drapier chose to close his newspaper rather than to swear allegiance to Hascall and take the loyalty oath. The *Forum* remained closed until June of 1866.[24] The *Forum* would change titles to the South Bend *National Union* that year.[25]

Storey Raises a Little Hell

Storey, who held that it's "a newspaper's duty to print the news and raise hell," also ran a story about the suppression of the Columbia City, Indiana, *News*.[26] Outraged at the assault on the Democratic press in Indiana, Storey, who started his journalistic career in northern Indiana, went on the offensive. On May 19, the Chicago *Times* editor ran a rumor from the Philadelphia *Bulletin* alleging that Washington had relieved Hascall of his command in Indianapolis.

Storey commented: "As strong a stomach as the administration has, it could not swallow the proceedings [in Indiana]."[27] Another article in the *Times* reinforced the Hascall demotion rumor on May 22. The *Times'* correspondent in Indianapolis wrote: "A man better acquainted with the feeling and temper of the people is needed in Indiana if we need any military commander at all."[28] Storey printed further speculation the next day from his Cincinnati reporter, who claimed Burnside had called Hascall down for a meeting and relieved his fellow West Point alumnus.[29] This report was false. In a May 27 editorial, Storey claimed that both Burnside and Hascall would be removed from their current commands.[30] Storey was wrong about Burnside, but, as it would turn out, guessed right about Hascall.

On the same day, U.S. Supreme Court Justice David Davis, who just happened to be in Indiana for a few weeks, seconded Morton's assessment in a correspondence to Stanton: "I have been for several weeks, and am, perfectly satisfied that the immediate removal of General Hascall is demanded by the honor and interests of the government."[31] Davis, a personal friend of Lincoln's, apparently had been dispatched to Indianapolis by the president to ascertain what was really happening in the nineteenth state.[32] Morton also pressured Burnside to release A. J. Douglass, the detained state senator in Indiana. Burnside alleged Douglass had uttered treasonous words and had him arrested under General Order No. 38. Morton, who earlier had been a proponent of aggressive and rigorous suppression, sent a messenger to Cincinnati to tell Burnside to ease up.[33] On May 30, Morton sent a telegram to Lincoln expressing his concern with the political expediency of General Order No. 38.[34] Morton also said that governors, not district commanders, should handle internal problems. At the same time, Burnside sent Lincoln a telegram offering his resignation for his handling of the Vallandigham incident earlier in the month. Lincoln replied: "When I shall wish to supersede you I will let you know."[35]

Lincoln and Stanton conferred, and then the Secretary of War wrote a letter to Burnside telling him that the president was counseling the removal of Brigadier General Hascall from command of the District of Indiana. Stanton, too, suggested that Hascall be removed.[36] Basically, the president and his war secretary did not want to upset a Republican governor of a key Midwest state who zealously supported the war effort.[37] In essence, the governor was sovereign in Indiana and would determine what course to take to counter dissent. Stanton wrote: "The natural aversion of our people to the exercise of military powers without necessity will be greatly stimulated by any feeling the State Executives that the General Government is disposed to interfere in matters of administration which properly belong to them or which they are able to manage."[38] The results of the previous fall's elections were speaking volumes. Ironically, in a war that would decide the supremacy of the central government over states' rights, a governor of a Midwest state was successfully championing his right to run his state as he pleased, and the president of the United States concurred with the Indiana governor.

Lincoln believed a man of "discretion and prudence" should replace Hascall. Stanton added in his letter to Burnside: "It is not expected that with the arduous and responsible duties of your office you will be able under any circumstances to satisfy everyone. The utmost that can be expected is to avoid unnecessary irritation."[39] In some ways, this was the same thing that had happened to Burnside when he was the commander of the Army of the Potomac. Lincoln ordered him to prosecute the war vigorously. Burnside, ever dutiful, actively went after Robert E. Lee and the Army of Northern Virginia, but the offensive went poorly. Complicating the Hascall matter was the fact that Burnside had no great affection for Stanton. Burnside had written a letter on January 1, 1863, requesting that Lincoln fire the secretary for undercutting the general's leadership of the Army of the Potomac.[40]

The main problem with this Stanton-Burnside communication of June 1, 1863, was not its message but the fact that the secretary sent it by mail, not telegraph. It did not reach Cincinnati until June 12, ten days after Burnside's General Order No. 84. Because the order reached Ohio so late, Burnside likely felt he had a mandate from the president to continue his onslaught against the press since Lincoln did not accept the major general's resignation. Burnside's General Order had four parts: (1) it suppressed the publishing of the Chicago *Times*; (2) ordered Brigadier General Jacob Ammen to execute the suspension of the *Times*; (3) prohibited circulation of the New York *World* in the Department of the Ohio; and (4) ordered postmasters and newspaper sellers to comply with the suppression of both publications.[41] On June 2, Ammen dispatched Captain James S. Putnam of Camp Douglas in Chicago to see Storey and announce the order.[42] Once they received it, at approximately 11 a.m., Storey and his partner, Ananias Worden, ignored Burnside's order.[43]

Storey countered by applying for an injunction from Judge Thomas Drummond of the U.S. circuit court to prevent Putnam from suspending operations at the *Times*. The writ went through at midnight, though it was only a temporary injunction. Drummond would make a permanent ruling on June 3.[44] The *Times* staff, which was armed, continued to work into the night. Burnside, though, sent another order to Putnam: "You will see that no more publications of it [the *Times*] are made; and, if necessary, you will take military possession of the office."[45] Early in the morning of June 3, several members of the *Times'* staff stood guard and reported to the office that Union troops were on their way. Approximately 8,000 copies of the paper had been printed, and some were already circulating on the street. The soldiers took control of the office, and later that day the editor went to court.[46] However, Drummond, with Supreme Court Justice Davis at his side, refused to hold a hearing because Putnam had not been notified that it was taking place.[47]

RESPONSE TO THE SUPPRESSION OF THE CHICAGO *TIMES*

The reaction of a bipartisan group of politicians and editors to Burnside's squelching of the *Times* was as intense as the reaction to Vallandigham's arrest and Hascall's suppression of the Hoosier Democratic newspapers. The Democratic-majority Illinois House of Representatives passed a resolution by a forty-seven to thirteen vote denouncing Burnside's action, saying it violated state and federal law.[48] New York papers roasted the general. Even the New York *Times* criticized Burnside's use of force: "Any person who knows anything of the character of our institutions, will readily see that such proceedings as the suppression of the Chicago *Times* by military force, will create far more formidable evils than they correct."[49] The newspaper also noted: "Whether the powers which he claims to exercise over freedom of speech and of the press do actually belong to his office or not, it is very clear that they should never be instructed to any man whose zeal outruns his judgment."[50]

In Chicago, a group of Republicans met to sign a petition to Lincoln to revoke the order. Among the signees were Chicago Mayor Francis C. Sherman, Senator Lyman Trumbull, and Congressman Isaac N. Arnold, a friend of the president.[51] The petition was sent to Lincoln by telegraph. That night a crowd estimated by the *Times* to be 20,000 attended a mass meeting in the courthouse square in Chicago in which speakers from both parties condemned Burnside's order. Resolutions were passed, including recognition that the "military power is and must remain subordinate to the civil power."[52] Some Democrats in the crowd wanted to visit the office of the Republican Chicago *Tribune* to do harm to it, but cooler heads prevailed.[53]

Upset and embarrassed, Lincoln revoked the suspension, though he actually sent a second telegraph revoking the first order because further intelligence revealed that many Republicans in Indiana agreed with the suppression of the *Times*. However, Burnside received this rescinding of the president's revocation too late, and the major general dutifully revoked his suspension of the Chicago *Times* and his order to stop the circulation of the New York *World* in the Department of the Ohio.[54] Lincoln apparently put a great deal of weight on the telegraphic message he received from Trumbull and Arnold. Meanwhile, Stanton sent Burnside a message telling him that the secretary must be informed on all future newspaper questions.[55] Thus, on June 5, Storey's paper opened with the headline "REVIVED" and printed Burnside's revocation of General Order No. 84.[56] Storey wrote free expression was above even the Constitution. He added, "The safeguards thrown around them by our constitution are but a solemn and august recognition of their awful sanctity."[57]

Joseph Medill, editor of the Chicago *Tribune*, was aghast at the revocation of the order. Medill said the order should have been sustained and the president should not have buckled.[58] The *Tribune* editor even went so far as to call the lifting of the order "a triumph of treason."[59] Meanwhile, the New York *World* said the Chicago *Tribune* was fortunate Lincoln ordered the revocation because a Democratic mob was threatening to attack Medill's office. The *World* even said the *Tribune* wanted Storey's paper free to print so it would avoid violence. The *Tribune* countered that it could handle any mob action from "Copperheads that might attempt its destruction."[60] The truth of the matter is that both papers were so well fortified with arms that violence against either was unlikely.

On June 5, Hascall sent a telegram to Burnside saying that he would rescind General Order No. 9 because he thought Lincoln's decision to overturn the suppression of the Chicago *Times* indicated policy.[61] It is not known if Burnside responded to the telegram. Of course, that same day, Burnside placed Orlando B. Willcox in charge of the District of Indiana, and Hascall stepped down the next day. All along, the brigadier general had assumed his services in Indianapolis would only be temporary. On June 6, he rescinded General Order No. 9 and announced his leaving the District of Indiana. Burnside then instructed Hascall to take thirty days leave before going to Cincinnati for reassignment.[62] The news of his demotion traveled slowly in some places. For example, the Columbia City *News* in Indiana then announced in its June 6 edition that Hascall had written the Starke County *Press* and ordered editor Joseph A. Berry to change his tone to one more loyal to the Lincoln government.[63]

DAYTON, OHIO, PRESS WAR

In Ohio, events in Dayton had been deteriorating since the fall murder *of Daily Empire* editor J. Frederick Bollmeyer. The *Dayton Journal* had started a club called the Union League, and sons of Union Leaguers and sons of Copperheads, as the antiwar Democrats were known, clashed in the county's public schools. Union League students wore eagle buttons to school, while Copperhead students wore butternut charms. Unionist students tried to get the butternuts removed from school grounds, and eventually a fight took place. The Union League students were arrested and charged with assault.[64] Then the *Dayton Journal* reported on April 17 that two female students wearing red-white-and-blue rosettes on their blouses had been asked to remove them by Southeastern School principal John Hall.[65] *Journal* editor Lewis Marot called this a treasonous act, especially since no principal had taken action against those students wearing butternuts. Marot thought wearing the butternut was worthy of federal attention, knowing full well that little likely would be done on the local level since the majority of the Montgomery County Ohio School Board was Democrats. He wrote that General Order No. 38 had a direct application and that Burnside should punish the school's principal.[66]

In April, the *Daily Empire*, which Vallandigham had once edited and still heavily influenced, printed a short editorial noting that Horace Greeley, editor of the *New York Tribune* and a Lincoln confidant, had written during the winter that "if by the first of May the Administration had made no visible progress towards putting down the rebellion, it was their duty to make the 'the best attainable peace and end the war.' "[67] Upon hearing the contents of Hascall's General Order No. 9 in Indiana, Vallandigham sent a letter to former President Franklin Pierce expressing his indignation at this suppression of civil liberties.

On May 1, Vallandigham made a speech on the porch of the Curtis Hotel in Mount Vernon. The Columbus *Crisis* reported that Vallandigham "showed and established conclusively which was the true Union, and which the disunion party."[68] The ex-congressman also said that he did not have to ask Lincoln, Burnside, or the governor of Ohio for the right to speak.[69] He said that right came from the Constitution. He closed by saying that remedy for all evils is the ballot box and that citizens should use it to hurl "King Lincoln" from his throne.[70] Burnside had dispatched two plainclothesmen to the speech, and they took copious notes of the speech. Vallandigham knew the men were in the crowd. A magazine report said that the orator declared "the present war is an injurious, cruel and unnecessary war—a war not being waged for the preservation of the Union, but for the purpose of crushing out liberty and establishing a despotism—a war for the freedom of the blacks and the enslaving of the whites." It also reported Vallandigham characterized Order No. 38 as a "base usurpation of arbitrary authority, and that the sooner the people informed the minions of usurped power that they will not submit to such restrictions the better."[71]

On May 4, a visitor from Dayton was in Cincinnati and told Burnside he would send him a telegraph at 8 p.m. that night if Vallandigham were at his home on 323 First Street in Dayton.[72] That night, the telegraph sputtered its message and Burnside sent a detail of sixty-seven men of the 115th Ohio Regiment led by Captain Charles G. Hutton on the midnight train to Dayton. They arrested Vallandigham at 2:30 a.m. and conveyed the ex-congressman by train back to the Queen City, where he was placed in a military prison.

The headline in the *Daily Empire* on the day of the arrest read, "Vallandigham Kidnapped. A Dastardly Outrage!! Will Freemen Submit? The Hour For Action Has Arrived. Your Liberties Are Endangered!!! Does the Spirit of Freedom Still Live?"[73] With his paper selling for a vastly inflated 50 cents on the street that day, editor Logan wrote of the incident, "The frantic cries of a wife . . . the piteous tears of a little child for the safety of its father were all disregarded, as a savage would disregard the cries of a helpless infant he was about to brain."[74] Logan complained that no formal charges were made: "He was not told what crime he was charged with, and was dragged, in the dead hour of the night, from his family and friends."[75] Logan added that it was against the background of such illegal arrests that the people voted overwhelmingly for Democrats in the previous November's elections.

A group of Dayton citizens led by Mayor William H. Gillespie took the train to Cincinnati and demanded a chance to speak with the prisoner. Burnside had already moved Vallandigham from the military prison to the luxurious Burnet House. The general allowed the Dayton contingent to visit the prisoner and told them Vallandigham would have trial by a military commission. Vallandigham said the military commission had no jurisdiction to try him, but Gillespie said he would ask Cincinnati attorney Edward A. Ferguson and two Dayton politicians to defend the former congressman.[76]

That night a mob of agitated Democrats torched the Dayton *Journal* and six surrounding businesses.[77] The damage by the fire amounted to $40,000.[78] By 10 p.m., troops from Cincinnati had arrived and martial law was declared. Logan was arrested and sent to Cincinnati, and the *Daily Empire* was suspended by Burnside and put up for sale. The *Journal* missed a single day of publication before using a press offered by the United Brethern Printing House to resume work with a four-page paper printed on paper that was eight inches by twelve inches.[79]

The *Journal* blamed the *Empire* and Dayton's leading Democrats for the riot. Marot said that the whole thing began back in the fall when an *Empire* editorial inspired the mob to seek Brown's lynching. Logan's fall 1862 and May 1863 editorials sent a signal to Democrats that it was appropriate to shed blood in the streets, and the Columbus *Crisis* advocated violent retaliation after it had been ransacked by a mob in March of 1863.[80] By May 14, the *Journal* was printing a classified ad announcing the sale of "A Valuable Democratic Newspaper Establishment." Two days later, the *Journal* quoted the Toledo, Ohio, *Commercial* as saying that Vallandigham had given a speech in February 1861 saying the country should be divided into four or five independent districts. Each district would have representation in Congress, and each would have an absolute veto over any legislation.[81] In its May 18 edition, the Republican paper published a letter from a soldier named S. C. Mercer in the Thirty-third Indiana Volunteers stationed in Nashville, Tennessee. Mercer praised Burnside for the arrest of Vallandigham, saying it was encouraging the soldiers in the field.[82] In the military prison in Cincinnati, Vallandigham wrote to Greeley, asking the New York *Tribune* editor to write an editorial that would help earn Vallandigham his freedom from his military imprisonment. Burnside lifted martial law in Dayton on May 21, 1863, and offered his resignation to Lincoln on May 29.[83] Marot would continue his journalism career at the Chicago *InterOcean*, and Thomas and William Hubbard bought the *Empire*, which would be destroyed by Union soldiers a year later.[84]

Suppression was not confined to the Department of the Ohio that spring. In Tennessee, all of the newspapers in the state were suppressed on April 12, 1863.[85] On May 2, the Easton, Maryland, newspaper was suspended and the editor arrested.[86] In June, New York *Express* editor James Brooks saw his paper barred from the Middle Department by Major General Robert C. Schenck.[87] In the winter and spring of 1863, Brigadier General George Wright issued an order barring six Democratic papers in Oregon from circulation in the Department of Oregon.[88] Furthermore, press intimidation was rampant. In Indiana, after Hascall left office, four cases of press intimidation would occur: the publisher of the Warsaw *Union* was assaulted by a county provost Marshal; editor James Elder of the Richmond *Jeffersonian* was assaulted by a civilian; the Franklin *Weekly Democratic Herald* was ransacked by troops six months before its office burned; and the Rochester *Sentinel* faced civilians who attempted to incite an Indiana regiment to demolish the paper.[89] In Pennsylvania, the Philadelphia *Age* faced mob violence the day it published the Northern loss at Chancellorsville, which just happened to be the same day that it reported Vallandigham's arrest by Burnside in Dayton.[90]

KNOCKING ON FREEDOM'S DOOR: NEW YORK JOURNALISTS' RESOLUTIONS

One aspect of Civil War journalism that clearly left it operating under the party-press model was the fact that there were few unified calls for freedom of the press. Freedom of the press for the majority was the rule, not the exception. However, there was one bipartisan response to suppression in the North, and that came at the Astor House in New York on June 8, 1863.[91] Those attending the journalists' meeting included James Brooks of the *Express*, Horace Greeley of the *Tribune*, John Clancy of the *Leader*, Anson Herrick of the *Atlas*, Theodore Tilton of the *Independent*, William C. Prime of the *Journal of Commerce*, Oswald Ottendorfer of the *Staats Zeitung*, J. B. Beach of the *Sun*, Elon Comstock of the *Argus*, M. S. Isaacs of the *Jewish Messenger*, P. J. Meehan of the *Irish American*, Robert McFarlane of the *Scientific American*, C. Mathews of the *New Yorker*, and William Cauldwell and Horace P. Whitney of the *Sunday Mercury*. The editors chose Greeley to be president and Comstock to be secretary.[92] R. G. Horton of the New York *Caucasian* attended, but he abstained from voting for the resolutions. Not attending were James Gordon Bennett of the *Herald*, William Cullen Bryant of the *Post*, Manton Marble of the *World*, and Henry J. Raymond of the *Times*.[93] The majority of the attending editors were Democrats.

The journalists met in response to what the New York *Herald* called the "threatened cancer of . . . restrictions" on the press.[94] In addition to the constraints placed on the Indiana press by Hascall, the New York editors were concerned with Burnside's activities, including the banning of Marble's *World* from the Department of Ohio, and with telegraphic censorship throughout the North. An 1861 telegraphic pact that journalists had made with General Winfield Scott, which allowed them to report on battles as they happened, ended after First Bull Run. In the fall of 1861, the House Judiciary Committee investigated the telegraphic censorship of newspapers. During that investigation Congress voted to allow Lincoln the power to take control of the telegraph and the railroads. Nonetheless, the Judiciary Committee's report did chastise the executive branch for suppressing political and personal commentary, not just information about the military. In early 1862, Schuyler Colfax, a Republican from Indiana and the head of the Committee on the Post Office and Post Roads in the U.S. House of Representatives, introduced legislation barring the circulation of newspapers by railroad, express companies, or steamboats.[95] Indeed, Edwin M. Stanton's War Department actually took control of the Post Office in early 1862, and commanders in the field and the military districts of the North often had recalcitrant newspapers confiscated from the mails, although the U.S. Senate demanded to know on whose authority commanders in the field were using to seize the mail. Postmaster General Montgomery Blair defended the constraints on the mail by saying it was a matter of public safety.[96] In February 1862, Lincoln extended Stanton's heavy hand, giving him the power to censor all stories sent by telegraph.[97] In the next three years, Stanton, like William Seward before him, had more than a few journalists

Schuyler Colfax, speaker of the U.S. House of Representatives during the Civil War, also published the *St. Joseph County Register*. Colfax was friends with Horace Greeley but did not defend Indiana's editors from Hascall and Ambrose E. Burnside. *(Photo from the Indiana Historical Society)*

jailed, locked up their printing property, and asked them to swear loyalty oaths.

The group of New York journalists opened the gates to the era of professionalism in U.S. journalism because they agreed to a free-press philosophy that went beyond politics. They resolved that the press should criticize "freely and fearlessly the acts of those charged with the administration of the Government, also those of all their civil and military subordinates, whether with intent directly to secure greater energy, efficiency, and fidelity to public service, or in order to achieve the same ends more remotely through the substitution of other persons for those in power."[98] The editors also said that journalists had no privilege to "invite, advocate, abet, uphold, or justify treason or rebellion."[99] (See table 9.1 below.)

For Greeley, fair comment meant anything political that did not directly give aid and comfort to the Confederacy. Where the war was not actually going on and elections were still being held, freedom of the press was the law of the land. An editor could tell his readers not to vote for Lincoln's reelection if he thought the president was not prosecuting the war vigorously and expeditiously enough. Greeley knew that he could not argue for his right to criticize Lincoln for not going fast enough to eliminate slavery unless others had the same right to criticize on other issues and from different political perspectives. Multiple perspectives had to be tolerated. With this in mind, Greeley biographer Robert C. Williams observed: "Freedom of the press meant that Greeley got as good as he gave throughout the war."[100] In this model of freedom of the press, politicians and editors alike had to have thick skins.

However, the *Tribune* editor did want the president to have the power to deal with treasonous journals—which he compared to bad whiskey, meaning those papers that supported violent rebellion or overthrowing the federal government, or those that applauded Union battle defeats—though he did not want Lincoln or any other president to have the ability to censor legitimate and honest political discourse.[101] For Greeley, legitimate criticism was anything that would impel a public servant to perform his duties more efficiently, and if he did not, editors could encourage citizens to vote for his opponent in the next election. Greeley, whose paper provided the fullest account of the Astor House meeting, believed the president alone should be able to shut down a journal that exulted in a federal defeat or supported the enemy. Greeley said the president would later have to face public opinion or impeachment. The *Tribune* editor did not want military officers to have to face the task of acting in the civil realm

Relief of Horace Greeley at Columbia University School of Journalism in New York. Greeley, editor of the New York *Tribune*, set the tone for freedom of the press in wartime when he led an editors' conference at the Astor House on June 8, 1863. The editors passed resolutions saying in effect that the First Amendment applied at all times. *(Photo by David W. Bulla)*

and thought the president alone could be trusted to discreetly choose what was treasonous and what was not. Greeley also mentioned in passing that he had no problem when General George McClellan had excluded the *Tribune* from his camp.[102]

Greeley's proposal had a serious flaw. If an element of the Constitution was deemed repugnant by one segment of society but not by another—such as slavery—and the president went about jailing those editors with whom he disagreed on this issue, then a dictatorship would exist. Greeley did not want political opinion or performance to be subject to suppression. However, a president could make the argument that in wartime the sitting chief executive is in effect the government and therefore has the obligation to squelch journals that disagree with his policies and condemn his performance. It also meant the president could jail anyone who opposed some measure or policy in the Constitution or the laws of the land. For example, if a president before Lincoln had Greeley's executive power over the press, then he could have

Table 9.1   New York editors' resolutions on freedom of the press

Editors' Resolutions
8 June 1863, Astor House Hotel, New York, New York

Whereas, The liberty and rights of the press, as affected by the existence and necessities of a state of war, and especially of civil war, are topics of the highest public concerns; and

Whereas, Recent events indicate the existence of grave misapprehensions and lamentable confusion of ideas with regard to this vital question; therefore,

Resolved, That our conceptions of the rights and duties of the press, in a season of convulsion and public peril like the present, are briefly summed up in the following propositions:

1. We recognize and affirm the duty of fidelity to the Constitution, government, and laws of our country, as a high moral as well as political obligation resting on every citizen, and neither claim for ourselves nor concede to others an exemption from its requirements or privileges to evade their sacred and binding force.

2. That treason and rebellion are crimes by the fundamental law of this as of every other country; and nowhere else so culpable, so abhorrent, as in a republic, where each man has an equal voice and vote in the peaceful and legal direction of public affairs.

3. While we thus emphatically disclaim and deny any right as inhering in journalists or others to incite, advocate, abet, uphold, or justify treason or rebellion, we respectfully but firmly assert and maintain the right of the press to criticize freely and fearlessly the acts of those charged with the administration of the government, also those of their civil and military insubordinates, whether with the intent directly to secure greater energy, efficiency, and fidelity in the public service, or in order to achieve the same ends more remotely through the substitution of other persons for those now in power.

4. That any limitations on this right created by the necessities of war should be confined to localities wherein hostilities actually exist or are imminently threatened, and we deny the right of any military officer to suppress the issues or forbid the general circulation of journals printed hundreds of miles from the seat of the war.

Editors Attending

John Clancy	New York *Leader*
James Brooks	New York *Express*
Anson Herrick	New York *Atlas*
Theodore Tilton	New York *Independent*
William C. Prime	New York *Journal of Commerce*
Horace Greeley	New York *Tribune*
Oswald Ottendorfer	New York *Staats Zeitung*
J. B. Beach	New York *Sun*
William Cauldwell	New York *Sunday Mercury*
Horace P. Whitney	New York *Sunday Mercury*
Elon Comstock	Albany *Argus*
M. S. Isaacs	New York *Jewish Messenger*
P. J. Meehan	New York *Irish American*
Robert McFarlane	New York *Scientific American*
C. Mathews	New York *New Yorker*
*-R.G. Horton	New York *Caucasian*

*-Attended meeting, asked his name not be including in the resolutions

tossed abolitionist editors in jail at whim. Andrew Jackson certainly had such a sentiment.

As it turned out, the majority of the editors at Astor House disagreed with Greeley on the executive power to suppress journals, and the final endorsement of the resolutions included no clause giving the president that prerogative. The New York *World* called Greeley's proposal "self-denying."[103] The *World* was satisfied it did not pass and claimed that the true victory of the press resolutions was that the assembled editors were celebrating Burnside's lifting of the suppression of the Chicago *Times* and the general's revoking of General Order No. 84, which directly impacted Marble's paper. At the same time, the *World* took Greeley to task for even considering the delegation of any censorship power to the president. So while the editors condemned treason, they insisted that freedom of the press was inviolate. They resolved that the security argument that Lincoln used to defend the suspension of the writ of habeas corpus could only be used against journalists in "localities where hostilities exist or are immediately threatened."[104] This foreshadowed the conditions that Oliver Wendell Holmes would allow for the squelching of free expression—that is, his clear-and-present-danger test.

The New York resolutions were significant because they represented the bipartisan sentiments of a group of journalists from the nation's most fertile newspaper environment. However, Greeley and his associates did not make the committee into a permanent organization concerned with freedom of the press and other journalistic issues. Such organizations would not come into existence for another fifty years. Furthermore, no follow-up meeting was held to ascertain the impact of the initial resolutions.[105] The resolutions failed to make the strict constructionist's argument that the First Amendment contained no language that allowed for its violation. They did not discuss how much access their reporters needed to cover the war comprehensively and accurately, or the nature of the relationship between the military and the press during wartime. Thus, while a door had been constructed to the concept of the modern professional press with the beginnings of an openly libertarian philosophy, the entire house around that door would not be constructed until the twentieth century. Most importantly, though, as Greeley biographer Williams suggests, the resolutions during the middle of a civil war "reflected the ongoing tension between government policy and press freedom in wartime."[106]

What, then, to make of Hascall's general order and the suppression of newspapers in Civil War Indiana? First, the official suppression of Indiana's Democratic newspapers ended on June 6, 1863. This is important because no other official orders of suppression were handed down during the war. Editors were arrested, but that was for draft evasion or conspiracy, not for what amounted to, in the cases of the Hascall editors, seditious libel. What General Order No. 9 did, though, was help stimulate a climate of intimidation and violence that was uniquely intense in U.S. journalism history. Through Hascall's reign as commander of the District of Indiana, fifty-three cases of intimidation and violence had occurred in the state in twenty-six months, forty-eight against Democratic newspapers. After Hascall, in the last twenty-two months of the war, thirty-eight instances of violence and intimidation would occur, twenty-six against Democratic newspapers. Most of the violence would come from Union soldiers, who managed to burn or destroy two newspapers in the state—the Petersburg *Reporter* and the Franklin *Weekly Herald Democrat*, which would also be sacked by civilians in a separate incident.[107] Hascall served to fan the flames in a society that was already prone to violence against the press. What makes Hascall's place in the journalism of Indiana during the Civil War was that his actions were based on official policy that came from up the chain of command. He did what Burnside had ordered for the entire Department of the Ohio, and Burnside was doing what he thought Lincoln wanted based on the suspension of the writ of habeas corpus by the president and Congress in order to make arrests against those citizens who might be working directly or indirectly to aid the Confederates' cause. Indeed, Lincoln wrote Burnside on May 29, 1863, that once the Vallandigham arrest had been made, the whole cabinet was "for seeing you through with it."[108] In other words, the president neither stopped Burnside's enforcement of General Order No. 38 nor did he ask the general to rescind the order.

A month after the suppression of the *Times*, Chicago experienced riots over the draft. Five counties in Indiana and several in Ohio and Michigan also saw draft resistance, and in New York the draft riots turned into urban warfare with a decidedly racial overtone. General civil chaos was upon the North even as the victories at Vicksburg and Gettysburg brought the best military news of the war. In Indiana, the weeks after Hascall's removal were replete with acts of dissidence and violence. W. H. H. Terrell's 1869 report after the war lists seven of these, including the assassination of the draft officers in Sullivan and Decatur counties.[109] Morton issued his own proclamation about these acts of violence against draft officers, and it warned citizens not to resist any war measure. Morton said citizens could meet peaceably to criticize the government but could not urge or participate in armed resistance against any government officer "in the performance of his duties."[110] These post-Hascall incidents demonstrate Carrington, Hascall, Burnside, and Willcox's contention that Indiana, like several other Northern states, faced a very serious internal political crisis.

GENERAL MEREDITH AND THE REPUBLICAN PRESS

After Hascall faded away in early June 1863, arrests of editors by military authorities in Indiana were for draft evasion. This happened to Democratic editors in Lafayette, Decatur, and Hartford City.[111] However, these were not cases of official suppression abridging the free-press rights of the editor because they were arrested for violating the conscription act. However, two newspapers were threatened by a brigadier general in 1864, but in these cases the Union Army officer, Solomon Meredith, was not the commander of the District of Indiana.

Solomon, a native of Greensboro, North Carolina, who had been wounded at Gettysburg, was serving as the commander of the garrison at Cairo, Illinois. A friend of Indiana Governor Oliver P. Morton and now a permanent resident of Wayne County, Indiana, Meredith had agreed to run for Congress against George W. Julian, one of the governor's long-time political rivals. The Indianapolis *Journal* supported the six-foot-seven Meredith, portraying him as a military hero because of wounds he received at Second Manassas and Gettysburg as well as his contributions to the battles of Antietam, Fredericksburg, and Chancellorsville. Meredith, a former U.S. Marshal who had served four terms in the Indiana House of Representatives before the war, accused Julian of being an enemy of Lincoln. Julian's friends branded Meredith a Copperhead because he had opposed emancipation and the use of armed black troops.[112] Julian supporters also condemned Meredith for being a backer of George B. McClellan, whom Lincoln had fired as the commander of the Army of the Potomac in 1862.[113] Democrats in the district overwhelmingly favored Meredith to Julian, who was an abolitionist.

During the 1864 congressional race, the Delaware County, Indiana, *Free Press* claimed that Meredith had embezzled money from the U.S. government while he served as marshal. Based on information given by an anonymous source in Wayne County, the *Free Press* said the brigadier general owed the federal government $600 to $700.[114] Solomon threatened the *Free Press* and the Winchester *Journal*, both Republican papers supporting Julian.[115] The *Free Press* countered that anything it had written about Meredith could be proven.[116] Julian defeated Meredith in the election, but later the brigadier general assaulted the congressman with a rawhide whip. However, Meredith used his political connections to have the assault charges dropped.

By contrast, Hascall never engaged in such outlandish behavior. He was not temperamental or boorish. The brigadier general was a man who believed in reason, had a sense of fairness, and thought the law should be applied with a sense of consistency. Like Burnside, he seemed to want to make a name for himself by doing what he thought was wanted by Washington—that is, by being an effective military leader. His biggest military experience before he took over in Indianapolis in April of 1863 was at bloody Stones River, Tennessee.

Why did he pick on the Democratic newspaper editors only in the northern half of the state, mainly in the towns surrounding Goshen? (See map on page 164.) One reason is that he was a cautious man. If he was going to uphold the spirit of Burnside's General Order No. 38, Hascall wanted to take action only where he had intelligence. The best information he received came from friends and Republican editors in the northern third of Indiana. Furthermore, the Democrats were not as powerful in those counties as they were in the southern part of the state, and Hascall knew the politics and the people of northern Indiana better. This is a key finding in the study: in times of crisis, government is more likely to suppress a minority than a majority. It is easier to quell a mouthy minority than to suspend the civil rights of the majority, who may also criticize the government's actions and policies. It is also significant that what happened in Indiana deals with the layering of government. In the localities where suppression took place, the local authorities did not take action against the Democratic newspapers. Action was taken by Hascall, a representative of the federal government. The central body is more likely to take action against vituperative political utterances than the local because the local leaders have to deal with consequences at the local level. If a county judge or marshal had put, say, VanValkenburgh in jail for his words, then he would have had to worry about the political fallout during the next elections. In other words, his job would have been on the line. Hascall had no such worries. His job was controlled by Burnside, who had his own headaches with the civil peace and enrollments in Kentucky and even had several anonymous threats on his life in May of 1863.[117]

Furthermore, the Hascall suppression episode in Indiana showed that censorship is more likely to occur in times of crises against the minority. Likewise, as John Stevens' hypothesis predicts, heterogeneous conditions had an effect on press suppression in Indiana. Hascall's suppression was only somewhat effective in Indiana, precisely because the political and social conditions in the northern part of the state were less homogeneous during the Civil War than they were in the first few years of statehood and after the war. Comparatively, though, Indiana was far more homogeneous than, say, New York City. Suppression was rare in New York precisely because there was greater heterogeneity there—and because the Democrats had the majority in that city. Hascall was following what he thought Burnside wanted him to do in Indiana, and Burnside was doing what he thought Lincoln wanted him to do in the Midwest. Yet because of Lincoln's rescinding of the Chicago *Times* suppression order, many historians have portrayed the president as treating the press in an even-handed fashion—that, in effect, even if he abhorred the words of certain Democratic editors, he was not going to abridge their rights to publish freely.

As historian Gilbert R. Tredway has observed, Lincoln tends to get a whitewashing when it comes to suppression in the Midwest. Yet the president allowed Hascall and Burnside to suppress from April 13 until June 4. Tredway noted that on May 8 Lincoln sent a telegram to Burnside initially approving of the arrest and trial of Vallandigham, and that "six weeks afterwards Lincoln defended the treatment of Vallandigham by equating opposition to his administration with subversion, precisely the same reasoning Burnside had used."[118] In other words, the president was not the ultimate champion of unfettered expression, written or oral, and his

Solomon Meredith, a Union brigadier general who served at every key battle in which the Army of the Potomac fought. Meredith was wounded at Gettysburg. He threatened two newspapers during a rancorous 1864 congressional campaign against George W. Julian. Meredith had been a four-term member of the Indiana legislature before the Civil War and was a moderate Republican. *(Photo from the Indiana Historical Society)*

leadership in this regard certainly had some effect on Burnside and Hascall. Both the president and Governor Morton wanted a vigorous prosecution of the war, perhaps the governor even more so than the national leader of his party.[119] Morton said that the Union needed military leaders who were "men of strong intellect whose head is inspired by his heart, who believes our cause is sacred and that he is fighting for all that is dear to him and his country."[120] Hascall and Burnside, both West Point graduates, were such men, but Morton was concerned that enforcement of the two general orders would increase the growing Democratic opposition to the war. It would not be accurate to say that Lincoln and Morton were waffling on domestic dissidence. Rather,

Morton wanted a man he could control in Hascall's office, and the president
did not want to upset loyal governors, especially those who had written openly
that he should more vigorously prosecute the war.

LINCOLN AND SUPPRESSION

The best argument that Lincoln used to counter the chorus against the assault
on civil liberties came in his reply to a letter written by a group of pro-Union
Democrats in Albany, New York, on May 16, 1863. These Democrats held that
they had made considerable political sacrifices to support the war and now
were being asked to give up their constitutionally guaranteed civil liberties.
In what has become known as the "Corning Letter," the president replied that
the civil courts were "utterly incompetent" to handle the criminal problems
arising from the rebellion, simply because the sheer number of traitors involved—all the citizens of the seceding states and anybody in the North aiding or abetting the rebels.[121] He said the Constitution's provision that allowed
the writ of habeas corpus to be suspended in times of invasion or rebellion
showed that the founding fathers understood the necessity of suspension. He
added that suspension of the writ was primarily preventive, not reactive. Lincoln admitted that Vallandigham was arrested for his opposition to the war
effort. The president did not admit that a peace solution was even an option
in a theoretic sense. Then he uttered his most cogent words in the exchange:
"Must I shoot a simple-minded soldier boy who deserts, while I must not
touch a hair of a wily agitator who induces him to desert?"[122]

Burnside made much the same argument in March of 1864 when he
was speaking before a group in Chicago about his suppression of the Chicago
Times: "I am as much of an advocate for the liberty of speech and of the press
as any man on the face of the globe can be, but when I am sent into a department to command soldiers who are to fight the enemies of my country, and
who should be strengthened in all possible ways by giving them encouragement, and by giving them clothes to wear, and food to eat, and recruits to fill
their ranks; when I find men in that department opposing all these means of
strengthening the soldiers in the army, I will strike these men in precisely the
same way that I would strike an enemy in arms against them. It is my duty to
my country and my duty to God, to strengthen these men, who have daily for
years endangered their lives in the presence of the enemy. I would fail in my
duty if I did not risk all I have in this world in the way of reputation and position or even of life itself to defend and strengthen these poor soldiers who are
in the field, risking their lives in defense of their country."[123]

After the furor over the suppression of the *Times,* Lincoln was careful with the press. When Major General John M. Schofield arrested a Democratic editor in Missouri for printing a presidential letter, Lincoln replied: "Please spare me the trouble this is likely to bring," and only arrest editors when "they may be working palpable injury to the Military."[124]

Lincoln's situation was not constitutionally different from the one President James Madison faced in the War of 1812. Madison faced a British invasion, and when General Andrew Jackson suppressed the press in New Orleans, Madison chastised his military officer, saying that he had violated the Constitution and would have to answer for his conduct.[125] Jackson learned little about freedom of the press from Madison, for when serving as the seventh president Jackson denounced the abolitionist press and called for severe penalties against them.[126]

If Hascall and Burnside had an accurate understanding of the state of society in Indiana, their solutions to the problems they faced deserve serious deliberation. The level of treasonous activity in Indiana in the Civil War is hard to measure. Both parties had secret orders, the Democrats the Sons of Liberty and Knights of the Golden Circle, and the Republicans the Union League. Each side worked covertly to further its political aims, and all three societies were influential. Henry B. Carrington, Hascall's predecessor, issued an order restricting the sale of arms in an attempt to slow down the Sons and Knights. Carrington, who said the Knights of the Golden Circle had almost 100,000 armed members in the state, believed it to be serious enough that he thought Indiana was about to face its own internal civil war.[127] Yet Carrington, who wanted a political job and did not want to fight in the field, was entirely partisan and did nothing when Union troops destroyed the Richmond *Jeffersonian.* While secret societies existed in the Hoosier State during the war, Carrington overestimated their strength. However, the aggressive, cunning Morton believed Carrington and countered with a propaganda war against the covert societies.

When Orlando B. Willcox replaced Hascall on June 5, 1863, Willcox immediately sent a message to these secret cliques on both sides: "The common safety now demands that all such associations should be discontinued, no matter to what political party they belong." Willcox said their existence expose "the country to martial law, and discourage the people from enlisting in the defense of the nation."[128] Matters did not seem to improve in Indiana because the aggressive brigadier general had been removed. A month after Hascall's removal from Indianapolis, Burnside wrote to Stanton letting him know that the civilian authorities could not handle the discord there, especially as it related to enforcing the draft in Sullivan, Rush, Monroe, and Greene counties.[129]

The Goshen *Times* reported that Hascall and Kerstetter were in Goshen at the time of Gettysburg and Vicksburg, the two battles that did more for the Union and Republican cause nationally and in Indiana than anything that Burnside or Hascall could do with their internal war on dissent and treason. The *Times* reported that Hascall was on his way to Cincinnati and would "most likely be assigned a command in Burnside's Department immediately upon his arrival" there.[130] Before that, he helped in the pursuit of Confederate renegade John Hunt Morgan in Indiana in mid-July. Hascall replaced Carrington as leader of the Indiana soldiers attempting to track down Morgan. Carrington was either slow to respond to orders from Governor Morton, or, as Hascall alleged, he was too drunk and "utterly unfit to trust with that or any other duty."[131] After the failed pursuit of Morgan, Hascall reported to Major General George Lucas Hartsuff in the Twenty-third Corps of the Department of the Ohio and was stationed in Lexington, Kentucky.[132] By the fall, Hascall was in Knoxville, Tennessee, commanding a division under Burnside. Hascall helped defend the city from CSA Major General James Longstreet's attack.

In the next year, he would take part in the Union's attempt to reconquer East Tennessee and northern Georgia. He fought at Kennesaw Mountain, Georgia, in June of 1864—a late Southern victory over William T. Sherman's army—and in Atlanta in July. He did not receive the promotion to major general recommended by Major General Schofield and resigned from the Union Army on October 27, 1864.[133] By October of that year, he would retire for good from the Union Army. When he wrote his report about his wartime activities after the war, Hascall included very little detail about his suppression of the Democratic press in the state. Much more detail was given to the events of May 20 in Indianapolis and the pursuit of John Morgan. It was as if press suppression did not merit such specificity, but it also was a painful memory for the man from Goshen because public sentiment against General Order No. 9 was so strong. Hascall's loyalty to Lincoln, the Republicans, and the Union Army left him with a blind spot, and he was unable to foresee the predictable reaction of Indiana society of the 1860s to press suppression. Hoosiers were far too independent to let a military man dictate to them about freedom of the press.

After the war, Hascall returned to Goshen and, with John Irwin, became owner of Salem Bank and a manufacturer of lumber. Franklin A. Hascall, Milo's step-brother, also was part of Salem Bank management.[134] Milo also established the Hotel Hascall in Goshen in 1881. The last ten years of his life, he lived in Oak Park, Illinois, and worked in real estate. He died on August 30, 1904.

The Goshen *Democrat* remained in the Hascall family into the twentieth century. Melvin B. Hascall, who relied on his brother Milo for financial help in tough times, owned the newspaper in the 1870s, and Frank L. Hascall owned it from 1954 until the late 1980s.[135]

Hascall was a citizen-soldier. Before the war, he had worked as a prosecutor in Elkhart County, an elected position. He had responded as soon as Lincoln called for volunteers because he was a West Point graduate who might have made a career in the military. He did not think what Burnside asked him to do in Indiana was extraordinary. Hascall believed the situation merited drastic measures, and thus he implemented General Order No. 9.

In response to the negative public perception of General Orders No. 38 and No. 9, Burnside offered the president his resignation as commander of the Department of the Ohio in the summer of 1863—just as he offered his resignation as commander of the Army of the Potomac after Fredericksburg. Lincoln again did not accept it. He would go on to help with the Union Army's defense of East Tennessee in the fall of 1863. By December of 1863, Burnside headed home to Rhode Island for a rest and then was asked to run the army in the Northeastern states.[136]

For his part, Ed VanValkenburgh left journalism in the fall of 1863 to go to California. He left the Plymouth *Democrat* on October 22, 1863, but he returned to own the paper from 1868 until 1874. It continued until the start of another war—World War II.[137] VanValkenburgh, of course, took the oath of allegiance—which begs the question: did he miss an opportunity at political martyrdom? That is, did he miss a stage, created by General Order No. 9, that would have allowed him to take on not only Hascall but also the temporary suspension of freedom of the press that Republicans—and even some Democrats—championed during the war? Ignatius Mattingly, the editor of the *Marshall County Republican*, certainly thought so, and he reveled in it. Mattingly said that VanValkenburgh had "been brave as a lion" when the Plymouth *Democrat* editor was denouncing Hascall and his order, but when he had a chance to stand up for press freedom at any price, he took the oath "without a moment's hesitation." Mattingly, in an editorial headline "Personalities," said this demonstrated "to the world the difference between profession and practice, and to his friends that he was not the material out of which martyrs are made."[138] Spending a large amount of time in jail as Iowa's Dennis A. Mahony had done would have made a strong statement, but the personal-political press of Civil War Indiana was more about trading barbs with the opposition editors in one's town and region, and less about the kind of unified professional statement of press freedom that Horace Greeley and the other New York editors made at the Astor House on June 8. Thus, Van-Valkenburgh added little to the functional expansion of press freedom in wartime, especially since the owners of the *Democrat* paid a $5,000 bond in case VanValkenburgh violated General Order No. 9.[139] Indeed, the editor—whose newspaper had the poetic phrase "Here Let the Press the People's Rights Maintain" under its nameplate—advanced press freedom no more so than Hascall effectively hindered it since the majority of Indiana's suppressed editors faced few permanent constraints.

∞ CHAPTER TEN ∞

Conclusion

This study has shown how a Union officer briefly suppressed eleven news-papers in Indiana in May of 1863. What Brigadier General Milo S. Hascall did to the Democratic press of Indiana was implemented within the spirit of the responsibility-for-abuse clause in the press section of the Indiana Constitu-tion. Yet the state's courts had not interpreted the clause by the Civil War, at least not in terms of seditious libel, and neither the military nor journalists had any guidance from the judiciary as to what was acceptable and what was not. Meanwhile, public opinion generally favored letting newspaper editors publish what they pleased, although many Republican editors strongly sup-ported the power to suppress, especially when the words of the Democrats were deemed treasonous.

The suppressed Democratic editors and their allies claimed that they could not be restrained by a man serving under the federal chief executive. They held that the Constitution referred to no government power for press restraint and specifically said that Congress could not abridge the freedom of the press. Therefore, Hascall had no jurisdiction over the press and ought to leave editors alone. If legal complaints against the press needed action, then the civilian authorities had jurisdiction, not a military officer. Hascall, on the other hand, believed the North had a war to win and that civil rights could be abridged temporarily to prevent intentional or unintentional aiding of the

South. In that respect, the general was merely echoing the views of the Lincoln administration.

THE SPIRIT OF FREE PRESS

The general governing document that framed the debate on freedom of the press in Civil War Indiana was the U.S. Bill of Rights. However, each political camp had its interpretation of the federal press clause. In part, this is because the First Amendment of the U.S. Constitution is broad and vague. Similarly, the press section of the Indiana Constitution is confusing. It states: "The free communication of thoughts, and opinions, is one of the invaluable rights of man." It then says every citizen may speak and print freely, but is "responsible for the abuse of that liberty."[1] No cases of legal interpretation of this section of the state constitution had occurred by the start of the Civil War. General Order No. 9 offered an opportunity for such a judicial test. However, Democratic editors failed to challenge the abuse clause. On the other hand, Hascall could have argued that the Democratic editors were abusing their freedom of the press, but he did not choose to make the case that some editors were going beyond fair criticism and in effect hurting the Union war cause and, indirectly and perhaps intentionally, helping the Confederacy. Neither did Republican editors speak of the responsibility of the Democratic press for the abuse of its freedom to print what it pleased. Thus, neither side tested the wording in court, and without a legal test Hascall could have argued that he was responding to editors who were abusing their right to freedom of the press because they were potentially helping put Union soldiers in harm's way with words that were unsupportive of the war effort.

Likewise, Democratic editors did not choose to sue Hascall on grounds that he was violating their federal civil rights. Such litigation would not become standard until the twentieth century, and there was no precedent from Indiana's courts to give counsel on the issue. The Indiana Supreme Court had heard only a handful of libel cases, but none involved seditious libel. No such interpretation of the responsibility-for-abuse clause existed, although some states with similar declarations of responsibility for the printed word in their constitutions had seen litigation in that area on libel, not sedition. Subsequent federal judicial interpretation in the twentieth century would render the wording of state press clauses less binding than the interpretations of the First Amendment, but that had no effect on General Order No. 9. Similarly, Congress failed to take action against the executive branch when the commanders of the military districts took action against the civilian press.

The Goshen Elks Lodge (BPOE 798), located at 220 North Main Street in downtown Goshen, is on the lot where once stood Milo Hascall's home. Like the other major structures in Hascall's world, the home was near the stately Elkhart County Courthouse, located between Clinton and Lincoln Avenues. *(Photo by Jeff Arbogast, the* Goshen News*)*

The First Amendment advises Congress not to abridge the freedom of the press. The assumption is that this is a congressional area of concern and that the president has no power over the press. However, the green light that Congress gave to the president and his military leaders, with the passage of the Habeas Corpus Act of March 3, 1863, provided a level of confidence that any extralegal proceedings against newspaper editors might be tolerated by the legislature. There was a congressional investigation of telegraph censorship, but none of military suppression of the press.[2]

Thus, we are left with an abolition-suppression paradox in the Civil War North. That is, although President Abraham Lincoln had taken the high moral ground in freeing the slaves with the Emancipation Proclamation, his administration took the low ground in allowing the suppression of the rights of editors. However, it must be said that the permanent freeing of the slaves outweighed the temporary abridgement of freedom of the press. Legal historian Michael Curtis noted that Democrats' calls for unfettered free expression "would be more inspiring if so many Americans of African descent had not been omitted from their political calculus."[3] Hascall consistently held he was protecting Union soldiers by suppressing editors whose words might harm the war effort. The necessities of war required the temporary suspension of certain liberties to ensure all the liberties in the Bill of Rights would be restored for both white and black men after the war. Thomas Paine had maintained at the time of the American and French revolutions that freedom's limit was in "the power of doing whatever does not injure another." However, Paine also said those "limits are determinable only by the law," not by military leaders or commissions.[4] Hascall and the Republicans certainly went beyond the traditional understanding of the rule of law during the Civil War, although since it was the first sectional conflict in the nation's history that became full-scale war, no one had a precedent to work with to negotiate the legal minefield.

Hascall, with the approval of Major General Ambrose E. Burnside, his superior officer, and no interference from the president, suspended the free press guarantee of the First Amendment in a state that was not being attacked by the Confederate Army. Indiana was far from the front, although there were several raids on the state by renegade Confederates and the status of its southern neighbor, Kentucky, was up in the air for much of the war. If the First Amendment is subject to arbitrary wartime abeyance, the Constitution is clear that Congress cannot abridge the right. Thus, at times of war, presidents, including Lincoln, have assumed the power to suspend the writ of habeas corpus, and some have expanded that power to include temporary suspension of other civil liberties. Such a power for the president is fraught with the possibility of abuse, and this is what Thomas Jefferson had worried about at the beginning of the Republic: "I have sworn upon the altar of God, eternal hostility against every form of tyranny over the mind of man."[5]

The Lincoln administration's suspension of free expression pitted two contradictory needs in a democratic republic—the one for survival against the one for a free exchange of information and ideas so that the citizenry might make rational political choices when elections were still being held. In the long view, the clash between men like Hascall and the Democratic editors of Indiana served to strengthen the free press tradition in the United States. Yet it was a steep price to pay for both. Hascall lost his command of the federal district and returned to the front, while Plymouth *Democrat* editor D. E. VanValkenburgh and other Democratic editors of Indiana lost their clout. Furthermore, Hascall's actions further destabilized an already chaotic situation in that state and encouraged violence against and intimidation of the Democratic press. Not surprisingly, some Democratic editors began to make the counterargument that Democrats should take revenge on Republican journalists.

Lincoln and the majority in his cabinet thought they had the prerogative to see the First Amendment as elastic. They believed government self-preservation superseded individual rights in a rebellion. Lincoln also knew that he lived in a democratic society and had to win reelection and try to maintain Republican control of Congress. He also wanted the nation to still resemble what the founding fathers had in mind, except without slavery. Intimidating or arresting editors and suspending their newspapers had a chilling effect. Several newspapers, like the Democratic paper in South Bend, went out of business after they were suppressed. After the Hascall suppression episode, the suppressed Democratic newspapers in Indiana faced less stability in change of ownership than Republican papers in the same cities. Thus, the unconstitutional soft wall of support from the suspension of habeas corpus helped the sixteenth president win the internal political fight in Indiana and the North as a whole.

General Order No. 38 and General Order No. 9 acted as weather balloons about how far Lincoln and his military leaders could advance suppression. The waffling on the suppression of the Chicago *Times* showed that the president did not want to agitate potential Democratic voters, and yet he also knew a sizable number of Republicans and some War Democrats favored silencing recalcitrant editors. As long as these edicts produced politically expedient results, Lincoln was apt not to countermand them. However, if public opinion went too far against the president, he would overturn or modify a particular order. Yet Lincoln never requested the rescinding of either general order. He also never sent a general directive of his own outlawing the suppression orders.

Several antecedents existed for suppression. One precedent came from the American Revolution. At that time, Patriots routinely intimidated Loyalist speakers and editors, many of whom were thrown in jail without a writ of habeas corpus. Furthermore, Union military leaders rationalized that the war effort was supreme to other considerations, including civil rights. Many generals and other officers felt the free exercise of civil liberties was inappropriate when it either directly or indirectly led to aiding and abetting the enemy. Thus, it is not inaccurate to say that freedom of the press for the majority was not an unusual concept in the eighteenth and nineteenth centuries in the United States.

Yet it is important to remember that Lincoln needed the Democrats of Indiana. He knew full well that the fragile coalition in Indiana—and Ohio and Illinois—was essential to success in the war and for a second Lincoln term in the White House. The political situation required an appeal to the continued

Today the Lake City Bank, 102 North Main Street, has replaced the Salem Bank, which Milo Hascall co-owned after the Civil War. This lot was called the Hascall Block or Hascall Corner in the general's day, and one block north was one of the city's largest buildings, the Hascall Hotel. The original Salem Bank was a two-story wooden structure. *(Photo by Jeff Arbogast, the* Goshen News*)*

loyalty of the Indiana Democratic press. At the same time, if the war had ended in 1862 or 1863, the national Democratic Party would have remained in a position to determine the outcome of the 1864 election, precisely because it would have picked up a bloc of Southern voters. Of course, the war did not end in either of those years, and the Republican Party became more powerful after Gettysburg and Vicksburg.[6] Generally, the Democratic critique of the war lost momentum.

General Order No. 9 helped Republican newspapers in several Indiana cities to improve their competitive status against weakened Democratic counterparts. Democratic papers lost readers, and subscriptions were critical to their economic well-being. The implementation of the order was immediately followed by two major Union victories in July of 1863, giving Republicans the news they needed to turn the public agenda away from civil rights abuse. Suppression also helped destabilize the competition in these cities just as Republicans made advances in the fall 1863 elections and continued those gains the next fall. On the other hand, General Order No. 9 worked outside the framework of the federal constitution, and it often had the opposite effect that it was intended to have: rather than quiet the Democrats, it agitated them to shout against civil rights abuse and turned public opinion against the Republicans. Furthermore, Hascall's order and Burnside's suppression of the Chicago *Times* encouraged New York journalists to make resolutions about the nature of press freedom in wartime. The resolutions were not binding, but they represented the beginnings of a more unified press, one that went beyond party lines to advance a more libertarian view of the First Amendment at a time when an absolute right to free expression was not part of the legal landscape. That would not come until after World War I. Legal historian Charles Fairman has observed that anything more than Blackstone's definition of freedom of the press—that is, no prior restraint—would have been conjectural through the Civil War.[7]

This book has also shown that Democratic editors resisted suppression and Republican editors applauded it. Democrats held that political speech was sacred, while the Republicans agreed—as long as those political words were loyal to the majority. The suppressed newspapers faced difficult times in the years immediately after Hascall constrained them, but in the long run nine of eleven were back in business by 1875, with only one of those nine converting to the Republicans. Thus, in the long run freedom of the press in Indiana survived Hascall's official suppression. Moreover, Hascall's suppression policy confirmed Siebert's hypothesis about press-government relations in times when the stability of a government is in jeopardy. As forces threatened Indiana during 1863, Hascall tightened the reins.

HASCALL THE GOOD SOLDIER

It would be a mistake to vilify Hascall as a man who hated the press and acted upon that hatred. When the war began and just before he joined the army, he made a bitter verbal attack against the Goshen, Indiana, *Democrat*.[8] While he accused the *Democrat* of treason, he only asked that his subscription be canceled. He did not agitate rioters to destroy it, and he benefited from the support of the Democratic newspaper in his hometown. Later, in the spring of 1863, he may have acted imperiously and excessively. He would have been wise at that time to be more politic. Still, Hascall's understanding of the necessity of suppression was not that different from that of Lincoln, Burnside, and many Republican newspaper editors in the Hoosier State and elsewhere, and it certainly was not outside the spirit of the Indiana Constitution's responsibility-for-abuse clause. It would be more accurate to say that Hascall hated the press that did not throw its support behind the soldier in the field.

Hascall had been educated at West Point, and he understood, respected, and upheld the military culture well. Part of that culture included the sense of brotherhood, of watching the back of one's fellow soldiers. It also included the hierarchical structure of communication and command. The need to have information flow in the same way was not lost on the brigadier general from Goshen. Burnside wanted conformity in the Midwest, and Hascall set out to achieve that goal in Indiana. Burnside's handling of Vallandigham set a precedent, and Hascall did his job the way he thought Burnside wanted him to do it. Hascall was the good soldier. Good soldiers are not necessarily free communicators, and war and press freedom are often strange bedfellows.

Furthermore, Hascall was civic-minded and did not maintain an anti-press attitude throughout his life. After all, his brother, Melvin B. Hascall, owned the Goshen *Democrat* in the 1840s and again in the 1870s. Indeed, Milo S. Hascall helped his brother through some tough financial times and indirectly subsidized that Democratic paper.[9] Hascall did not see freedom of the press as a relic of the past as William Tecumseh Sherman did. Like his boss Burnside, Hascall thought that the freedom could be constrained in wartime if the war aims required it.

It is risky to infer Hascall's intentions in the spring of 1863. Because his tenure as the commander of the District of Indiana was so short—and he expected it would be quite temporary—it is impossible to know how far he would have taken suppression. He certainly thought a problem existed and acted accordingly. Yet no editor was thrown in jail for more than a few days. None was sent to a distant prison for six months like Iowan Dennis A. Mahony. Did Hascall just want to calm things down, or did he plan to shut down as many Democratic editors as he could investigate? The documentary evidence is scant, but his correspondence to and from Burnside suggests that Hascall would have maintained General Order No. 9 as long as he was the commander of the District of Indiana. If Morton had not sought his removal, suppression of the Democratic press in Indiana likely would have continued. The only other government-sponsored constraints on the Democratic press of Indiana for the remainder of the war came for draft evasion and the arrest of *Indiana State Sentinel* editor Joseph J. Bingham in a plot against the federal government, although Bingham never faced a trial.[10]

A year before the suppression spring in the Department of the Ohio, Burnside established a pro-Union newspaper in eastern North Carolina while the Union Army under his command occupied the coastal section of that state.[11] Burnside would have been wise to shape public opinion in the Midwest by building similar papers instead of suppressing Democratic orators and editors. The major general could have pushed his political and military objectives in the Department of the Ohio in a proactive instead of a reactive way. He and

Hascall had at their disposal thousands of men to run the department, and Hascall's troops had run a publication in the South after capturing a press.[12] Of course, the taking of a Democratic press in a rebel state was one thing. Doing it in a loyal state was another. The larger picture, though, is that the Lincoln administration and the military controlled the press in an ad hoc, haphazard manner during the Civil War. Lincoln did want to control the press to the extent that it could be done without hurting the Republicans' political fortunes, but his administration seemed ill equipped to do it in a systematic way, especially on the enforcement level since most able-bodied men were off fighting the war. When it worked, fine. Lincoln did not send off any reactive telegrams to his generals telling them to stop suppressing. When it did not, Lincoln preferred to close down restrictive policies and let editors print what they please. There is also the issue of the neces-

The front of the Goshen *News* (News Printing Company), 114 South Main Street. Frank L. "Budd" Hascall, whose grandfather Franklin A. Hascall was Milo Hascall's half brother, was one of its publishers in the twentieth century. The newspaper opened in 1837. *(Photo by Jeff Arbogast, the* Goshen News*)*

sity and legality of district commanders. Henry Halleck, the General-in-Chief of the U.S. Army, thought they were unnecessary and suggested that Burnside send his district commanders in the Department of the Ohio to the front.[13]

While Hascall was the only district commander in Burnside's department to issue a broad policy against printed words that opposed the president and the war, other district leaders in the Department of the Ohio suppressed newspapers. Brigadier General Jeremiah Tilford Boyle suppressed the Louisville, Kentucky, *Express* for its "general tone."[14] Brigadier General Henry B. Carrington, who preceded Hascall as the commander of the District of Indiana, censored the pro-Democratic *Indiana State Sentinel* of Indianapolis after he disputed its report on a row between Union troops and civilians over the arrest of a deserter.[15] Yet Carrington and Brigadier General Jacob Ammen in Illinois actually helped Democratic editors. Carrington paid back a paperboy for the Cincinnati *Enquirer* after Union soldiers threw copies of the paper into an Indianapolis creek.[16] Ammen stopped Union cavalrymen who were throwing the type of the Olney, Illinois, *Herald* into the street. Ammen made the men pay for the destroyed type.[17]

While General Order No. 9 did have an effect on eleven Democratic newspapers in Indiana, its enforcement was so-so at best. Many more papers than those printed anti-Lincoln or antiwar vituperation. In the end, Hascall mainly just scared Democratic editors of the Hoosiers State rather than shutting them down for the duration of the war. While there was a chilling effect, some Democratic editors were emboldened to increase the vituperation or resort to indirection and sarcasm, including VanValkenburgh, especially after Hascall was removed on June 6, 1863. Indeed, Hascall's attempt to tame the Democratic press of Indiana was less effective than other suppression efforts in the North during the Civil War. As has been discussed in these pages, H. M. Hoxie, the U.S. Marshal in Iowa, arrested and transported Dubuque *Herald* editor and former member of the Iowa legislature Dennis A. Mahony and Fairfield *Constitution and Union* editor David Sheward to Washington, D.C. There the pair stayed in jail for three months, effectively blocking Mahony's attempt to win a congressional seat. Keeping a popular conservative Democrat from earning a seat in Congress is a far more repressive act than detaining an editor for a day or two and asking him to swear an oath of allegiance to the Union. Thus, Hascall's rampage against the Democratic press of Indiana produced a relatively tepid chilling effect.

But divining what motivated Burnside and Hascall to take aim at the recalcitrant Democratic press in the Midwest is central to any understanding of press suppression in wartime. Perhaps Burnside, out of spite, wanted to embarrass the president for demoting him after Fredericksburg and the Mud March. However, that seems unlikely since Burnside felt from the beginning that he was not up to being the head of the Army of the Potomac and was generally viewed as a good-natured fellow. It is more likely that Burnside wanted to redeem himself, and he thought that Lincoln and Stanton expected him to perform political operations in a noncombat zone, which the Department of the Ohio was. Stanton, as well as his predecessor William Seward, was a champion of civil rights suppression during the war. This, of course, is difficult to reconcile: the Lincoln administration had given the war a civil rights objective—abolition—and yet one freedom, freedom of expression, was being temporarily sacrificed for the universal application of another, the freeing of the slaves. This abolition-suppression paradox, to borrow Lorman Ratner and Dwight Teeter's formulation, leaves the most knowledgeable experts on Lincoln and his presidency to conclude, as David Herbert Donald does, that civil rights "throughout the North were drastically curbed."[18]

Burnside intended to carry out these political operations with zeal and efficiency, demonstrating to Washington that he was a capable leader. As for Hascall, the man from Goshen had his eyes on making major general and wanted to satisfy his superior officer in Cincinnati in hopes of attaining what had become his military career goal. After all, he was educated at West Point and was witnessing how other graduates of the Academy were rising to the top of the army's hierarchy.

In the long run, what happened to Lincoln's Indiana censor in the spring of 1863 as he tried to perform what he thought were his duties in the nineteenth state represents the extremely haphazard and inefficient nature of Civil War press suppression. It was far more severe than the majority of historians have indicated. Stephen Towne's research opens the door to the likelihood that Shelby Foote's undocumented guess of at least 300 Democratic newspapers facing suppression is too low. The numbers, though, matter less than the efficiency of the attempt to silence the opposition press. It clearly was not done with the same bureaucratic efficiency of World War I after the federal government learned plenty from the experiences of the severely shackled American reporters covering the Russo-Japanese War of 1904. Press suppression in the Civil War was an ad hoc phenomenon, and its efficiency depended on a variety of factors. What can be said for sure is that in most cases it paid few dividends and only caused Democratic editors to be more critical.

At best, Civil War press suppression caused newspapers on shaky financial grounds to cease publication, but more typically it had only a temporary chilling effect. Hascall's attempt to cool down the Democratic editors in Indiana fit into the latter category, and since he actually provided financial help for his brother's Democratic newspaper back in Goshen from time to time, it is clear Milo Hascall was no permanent opponent of a free press. He was following what he thought Burnside wanted him to do in Indiana, and he believed the state of affairs in the Hoosier State warranted drastic measures. After all, it was the president—and not Burnside or Hascall—who had opened the martial law Pandora's box by suspending the writ of habeas corpus.

TRANSITION FROM PARTY-PERSONAL TO INDEPENDENT-COMMERCIAL PRESS

What happened in Civil War Indiana began the movement of the U.S. press away from partisanship toward professionalism, commercialism, and political independence. Ten of the eleven Democratic newspapers that Hascall intimidated faced multiple instances of threats of violence, intimidation, or suppression. (See Table 10.1 below.) Four of the eleven faced at least four attempts at suppression or intimidation, including five incidents against the Blackford *Democrat*. That kind of treatment obliged an increasing number of journalists to consider being less extreme in their views and less vituperative in their pronouncement of those views.

This movement away from the political press corresponded to an expansion of federalism and the expansion of presidential powers. The federally backed suppression of the Democratic editors in Indiana worked in a small, immeasurable way and was a minor setback for press freedom. This is not to say that state governments did not try to retard press freedom. Southern state governments did try to restrict freedom before the war with their antiabolitionist laws and attempts to extradite northern abolitionist editors. Furthermore, states like Indiana with its responsibility-for-abuse clause in the free press section of its constitution could have interpreted this responsibility in a way that narrowed the area of press freedom. However, with no test in the courts, interpreting the abuse of that freedom was up in the air. States also limited press freedom in other ways, by passing laws that were less protective of reporters or more protective of government secrecy.

After the Democratic editors' episode in Indiana, a less partisan press gradually became the norm in the state. The postwar press in Indiana became less interpretive and more informative. It became hard for newspapers that were on the losing side of a major political battle to stay afloat. By becoming politically independent, newspapers became more sustainable during times of extreme political conflict, and editors chose to be less vituperative than they had been in the war years. Readers bought newspapers for information, not for political vituperation.

In the long run, the emancipation effort put a greater emphasis on civil rights and increased freedom overall in the United States, but the irony is that Lincoln and the military trampled on the free-press rights of Democratic newspaper editors in Indiana, not just those editors who were pro-South, but also Democratic editors who had legitimate criticisms of the war, the conduct of the war, and the war policy. It made sense to Northern editors to suppress newspapers in the conquered lands of the South, but it was a hard sell to convince the majority of them to support suppression in the loyal states. So just as Lincoln and Burnside do not get absolved of their sins against the press, Hascall does not get a free pass on this.

What Hascall, as well as other Union generals, did to the First Amendment in the Civil War represented a significant moment in the history of freedom of the press in the United States. Thus, the general enhancement of

freedom had a bumpy road during the Civil War. Free labor, as
opposed to slave labor, won the
day, but all freedoms did not come
through the war unscathed, and
that, as Fredrick S. Siebert's hypotheses predict, is to be expected
in wartime when it comes to the
relationship between communication and power. The powerful tend
to contract the area of freedom of
expression. A number of communicators react to this contraction
with obedience and fear, while
others react with disobedience and
courage. In a time of a party press,
still others react with support of
such contraction in defense of
political allies making contractive
policies. However, the chilling effect rendered by Hascall was temporary. He made no permanent
dent in freedom of the press in In-

Frank L. "Budd" Hascall, who ran the
Goshen *News* in Indiana after World War
II, kept journalism in the family; he ran
the *News* for more than three decades.
His grandfather was Franklin A. Hascall.
(Photo from the Goshen News*)*

diana. Violence against the press in Indiana was intense in the war years, and
Hascall's six-week offensive helped stimulate that violence. However, Indiana,
like much of the United States, was still a frontier society. Violence was often
seen as a logical and honorable way to solve disputes.

The Democrats of Indiana were part of a national political party that
if it had managed to stay together in 1860 would have remained the majority party in the United States. The Republicans (Whigs) had been the minority party for decades, and the fragmentation of the Democrats allowed a
minority party to seize power in Washington. Yet what must be remembered
is that the balance of power was fragile. Despite a substantial margin of victory in 1860, the Republicans faced a much narrower lead over Democrats in
Congress after the mid-term 1862 elections. Furthermore, the command on
power that the Republicans had at the state level waned too, as Democrats
became the majority in Illinois, Indiana, and Ohio.

Republican newspaper editors supported the suppression of "disloyal"
editors, and their arguments for suppression were based on two premises: (1)
Not supporting the war fully hurt the war effort—discouraging enlistments

Table 10.1   Suppression, intimidation, arrests of Democratic editors

City	County	Newspaper	No. of Times Suppressed, Intimidated
Bluffton	Wells	Banner	2
Columbia City	Whitley	News	3
Franklin	Johnson	Democrat	4
Hartford City	Blackford	Blackford Democrat	5
Huntington	Huntington	Democrat	4
Knox	Starke	Starke County Press	2
Plymouth	Marshall	Democrat	2
Rushville	Rush	Jacksonian	2
South Bend	St. Joseph	Forum	1
Warsaw	Kosciusko	Union	4
Winamac	Pulaski	Pulaski Democrat	2
			Total: 31
			Average: 2.8

Frequency of Suppression, Intimidation

meant fewer men to fight the war and therefore lengthened it, and (2) not backing the Lincoln war policies lowered morale because it showed the South a less-than-united front, and therefore also gave a psychological boost to the Confederate Army. The truth is that any criticism of a government at war can be construed as giving aid to the enemy. When reduced to an either-or proposition, that is the inevitable conclusion.

A younger Abraham Lincoln did not see the war powers of the president the way the Abraham Lincoln who was the sixteenth president of the United States did. In 1848, Congressman Abraham Lincoln, a Whig of Illinois, voted for a resolution that said President James K. Polk did not have the power to wage war on Mexico. Ironically, Lincoln's law partner, William H. Herndon, thought the president had the war powers. Lincoln said that power solely rested with Congress: "Kings had always been involving and impoverishing their people in wars, pretending generally, if not always, that the good of the people was the object." Lincoln wrote that no one single man "should hold the power of bringing this oppression" on the people.[19] Yet Lincoln had a change of heart by the spring of 1863. Conditions had changed, and in the "Corning Letter" he gave his clearest defense for squelching dissident editors: How could he shoot a soldier who deserts but could not stop the pen of an editor who encourages him to desert? It was unjust, inconsistent, and undemocratic for him to enforce discipline in the army and yet not be able to prevent agitators against enrolling. In war, a journalist who publishes information that indirectly and even unintentionally helps put soldiers in harm's way is not necessarily immune from government restraints, but the problem in the Civil War is that Congress did not take up the issue. Of course, the federal government was trying to preserve itself, and freedom of expression was not a first priority for most legislators or for the president.

LONG-TERM EFFECT OF SUPPRESSION

So, by 1875, almost all of the Democratic newspapers suppressed by Hascall had returned to operate, although about half under new names and one had switched its affiliation to the Republicans. The resiliency of the Democratic press in Indiana demonstrated the strength of the newspaper tradition in the United States—that it could withstand temporary restraints on press freedom. Nonetheless, Hascall, Burnside, and Lincoln continued the tradition of Adams, Jackson, and Polk of the executive branch's itch to control the press during wartime—which would be repeated again in World War I, by a progressive president and a Democrat, in Woodrow Wilson. The Sedition Act of 1918 outlawed written contempt for the government, the Constitution, or the armed forces and gave the postmaster general the power to suppress the mail of violators.[20] Wilson also had the Censorship Board established to control information in and out of the government—and the nation.[21]

Ultimately, the suppression of Indiana Democratic newspapers in the Civil War comes down to two issues, the quality of life and the survival of the nation. For Lincoln and his military leaders, the maintenance of the Bill of Rights came into conflict with the war aims of the nation. Upton Sinclair once wrote President Wilson asking: "What good does it do us to fight for freedom abroad if, in the mean time, we are losing it at home?"[22] The same thing could have been asked of Hascall, Burnside, and Lincoln. Why fight for the freedom of black men in the South while asking white men in the North to relinquish some of their civil rights? They might have answered that the temporary suppression of free expression was a necessary compromise that had to be made until the war's outcome was no longer in doubt. Yet even members of Lincoln's cabinet tended to think that letting the press go was the best policy.

In the long run, the party press that exacerbated and condoned suppression gradually disappeared. There were still signs of it in Indiana in the late nineteenth century, and a few party-affiliated papers existed in the state in the twentieth century. However, political and financial independence, the informative function, and professionalism would become the hallmarks of the Indiana press by the end of the nineteenth century. Two generations after

Milo Smith Hascall, one of his descendants, Frank L. Hascall, the publisher of the Goshen *News*, would express these changes when he was interviewed near the end of his newspaper career: "I am 73 years old and I still get much satisfaction in knowing that the goal of our newspaper is to serve the community the best we can, and to give the readers a quality product every day."[23]

SUPPRESSION IN IRAQ

Yet suppression is a nasty subject that rears its ugly head each time the nation becomes involved in a war. In the war in Iraq, the United States suppressed two newspapers in that country, *Al Mustaqaillah* and *Al Hawza,* as well as two television networks. Under the direction of Paul Bremer, the Coalition Provisional Authority that led Iraq in the transition between Saddam Hussein and the new democratic government, cracked down on several media operations after it had established a law that made freedom of the press conditional. The CPA put in place Order Number Fourteen on June 10, 2003. This regulation prohibited publication of incendiary words in the Iraqi media.[24] Order Fourteen also banned the Iraqi media from advocating the return to power of Hussein's Ba'ath Party or changing the nation's borders. The CPA also gave Bremer the sole authority to suspend any media operations. The directive did provide an appeals process that required effected media to deliver a written appeal to Bremer.[25] The justification for the order was that it would promote civil stability.[26] The incitement condition was reasonable: words that incited might put troops in harm's way. The CPA leadership thought the publication of such an order to be routine. Bremer needed a legal way to clamp down on the most violent elements in the Iraqi press.

Accordingly, in July of 2003, Bremer closed *Al Mustaqaillah,* a newspaper, for publicizing clerics' calls for Iraqis to kill anyone cooperating with the United States because it was religious duty to assassinate such spies.[27] This repeated messages issued by insurgents.[28] CPA forces detained Abdul Sattar Shalan, editor of *Al Mustaqaillah.* Four months later, Bremer had the office of al-Arabiya, a television network, shut down for allegedly inciting violence. After seizing critical equipment, Iraqi police officers told the al-Arabiya journalists they would face a year in prison and a $1,000 fine if they violated the order.[29]

The following spring, the CPA closed the Baghdad-based *Al Hawza* for sixty days. The order, which came on March 28, 2004, proclaimed that anyone caught attempting to publish the newspaper in that two-month period faced up to a year in jail and a $1,000 (USD) fine. "They [U.S. troops] told us they would arrest us if we did not leave," said Ali Yasseri, an editor at *Al Hawza.* "They said our articles incite people against America."[30]

The CPA claimed the newspaper printed articles that incited violence against coalition troops. One article compared Bremer, the CPA chief, to Hussein.[31] Another article claimed Bremer was trying to starve Iraqis, and yet another said U.S. soldiers were firing rockets at mosques.[32] Bremer's order stated that *Al Hawza* had published articles that contained false information and that the newspaper was trying to "disturb public order and incite violence against the coalition forces and the employees of the CPA."[33] Bremer said *Al Hawza* had printed the names of Iraqi collaborators and told its readers to take action against those persons.[34] Bremer wrote: "These false articles not only mislead readers but constitute a real threat of violence against coalition forces and Iraqi citizens who cooperate with the coalition in the reconstruction of Iraq."[35] The CPA chief feared that if he did not close down Muqtada al Sadr's mouthpiece, Bremer would be seen as playing diplomatic favorites because *Al Hawza* was so blatantly and violently anti-American, and less vituperative papers had faced intimidation and harassment by the coalition.[36] In his book on running the CPA, Bremer wrote that Scott Castle, the coalition's general counsel, suggested that Bremer arrest Sadr. Bremer was not sure Washington would support such a move.[37] Thus, the move to close *Al Hawza* was a compromise, a way of trying to control Sadr.

The coalition government specifically cited an *Al Hawza* article on February 26, 2004, that claimed a U.S. Apache helicopter had fired a rocket that killed fifty Iraqi police recruits two weeks earlier in a Shiite city south of Baghdad. The CPA maintained that the destruction was the result of a suicide truck bombing by insurgents.[38] Another article in that same edition of the newspaper claimed Bremer was trying to starve Shiites the same way that Hussein had: "We are still under the rule of Saddam but with an American face."[39]

The newspaper castigated the CPA for bringing decadent Western values to Iraq, such as pornographic movies, liquor, and hashish.[40] One editorial termed the CPA-sponsored television network as the "Hebrew media network."[41] *Al Hawza* also criticized U.S.-led forces' attacks on mosques in Karbala and Baghdad on March 2, 2004, that resulted in the deaths of one hundred and seventy Iraqis.[42] Typical headlines in the paper were "America kills then apologizes," "Kurdistan always belonged to Iraq," and "America releases prisoners after al Hawza threatens them."[43]

Two days earlier, *Al Hawza* had published an article that criticized Iraqi participation in the CPA-sponsored elections. That same day, the newspaper called for Iraq to be Islamic, not secular. Only an Islamic government "can lead Iraq to liberation, sovereignty, and prosperity."[44] The paper also published Sadr's words that he would not be a part of any Iraqi government that the United States had a veto in.[45]

Al Hawza's criticisms of the CPA were not the only negative words aimed at the occupational government. Other political organs in Iraq made similar criticisms on a routine basis. For example, the newspaper Al Zawra carried an article that criticized U.S. forces for their random arrests of Iraqi civilians, including the arrest of 1,300 women without specific charges.[46] "Other papers published what might be called stronger editorials than Al Hawza did," said Basim al-Sheikh, editor of the Baghdad-based Al Dustur.[47] But Bremer saw the Iran-backed Sadr as a major threat to stability, especially after a Sadr mob had murdered Ayatollah Abdul-Majid al-Khoei on April 10, 2003.[48]

The chilling effect of Order Fourteen could be seen when Al-Sheikh warned other editors to be careful and behave responsibly.[49] Al Dustur criticized the United States for labeling it a journal that opposed occupation. Columnist Ibrahim Zaydan went on to ask if Iraq occupied the United States, would the American people accept the occupation.[50] Al-Basa'ir denounced the CPA and interim government as illegitimate and said the permanent constitution would therefore also be illegitimate. The paper also said that the United States lost the war in Iraq, that the CPA planned to divide the nation into three confederations after the war, and that Israeli troops took part in the battle of Fallujah.[51] Al-Mu'tamar disparaged Bremer for dissolving the Iraqi Army and thus undercutting the nation's security. The paper called on the CPA to strengthen Iraq's security forces to overcome terrorism in the country.[52]

The closing of Al Hawza also elicited immediate protests in the streets of Sadr City, a section of Baghdad named in the honor of Sadr's murdered father, Muhammad Baqr al Sadr. Thousands of Iraqis denounced the closing of Al Hawza on March 31, 2004, and the repression of journalists in general. Members of the crowd also burned U.S. flags.[53] Another report said that a sit-in occurred in front of the newspaper office and that the demonstrators indicated they would not leave until the CPA reopened the paper.[54] The protestors held signs that read "Let Journalists Work With No Terror" and "Let Journalists Do Their Work."[55] Others said, "Long live Sadr! America and the Interim Governing Council are infidels!"[56] The Washington Post claimed that the closing of Al Hawza led directly to the uprising in Fallujah that would turn into a major battle between Shiites and CPA forces.[57] Author Thomas Ricks says the Shiite reaction in Baghdad to the suppression of Al Hawza was an insurrection that lasted for two months, and at the end of that period "much of what the occupation had been trying to achieve in Iraq lay in ruins."[58]

The reaction to Bremer invoking Order Number Fourteen and shutting down Al Hawza was pronounced in much of the world, including in the United States. Free expression advocates took the side of Sadr's newspaper, not knowing the complex context on the ground in Iraq. First Amendment attorney Floyd Abrams, who represents the New York *Times*, said: "Of all the messages the United States could send to the people of Iraq, the sorriest is this: If you say things we disapprove of, we'll shut you down."[59] The San Diego *Union-Tribune* observed:

> The Bush administration wants to create democracy in Iraq. Democracies include newspapers of all stripes, good and bad, those that support governments and those that don't. . . . Does censorship ever do anything but create more interest in what has been censored and more anger in those who, denied the pen, are left with the sword?[60]

The Miami *Herald* noted: "In America, the best way to defeat irrational opinions isn't through suppression, but by allowing the truth to speak for itself."[61] The *Herald* said that the way to combat lies was by allowing competing papers to publish the truth.

The American Society of Newspaper Editors sent a letter to Donald Rumsfeld, the Secretary of Defense, saying: "Suppression of dissent, even dissent that is wrong-headed in the view of the occupying government, will lead only to deeper mistrust." The ASNE letter, signed by its president, Peter K. Bhatia, said the CPA should "stand for the same First Amendment-inspired freedom of speech bedrock principles that are relied on in our own society."[62]

The San Francisco *Chronicle* said the newspaper's "main offense seems to have been disseminating rumors that were in circulation anyhow" and that the suppression would only serve to spike *Al Hawza*'s circulation when it reopened.[63] Jonathan Steele, reporting from Baghdad for the Manchester, England, *Guardian*, wrote that the "closure seemed intended to reduce Mr Sadr's influence."[64] The New York *Times* later would observe that the action "became a catalyst for some of the worst anti-U.S. mayhem of the occupation."[65] In Lebanon, Al-Manar Television ran a statement from Al-Sayyid Abd-al-Aziz al-Hakim demanding accountability from the suppressors.[66] Meanwhile, the CPA-sponsored *Al-Sabah* daily newspaper stated that "freedom of expression in speeches and writings will not be restricted."[67]

Once again, the principles of democracy stood in opposition to war necessity. Instead of an abolition-suppression paradox, there now existed a development-suppression paradox. The U.S. military wanted to protect the coalition soldiers. Yet at the same time the United States was trying to develop democratic habits and structures in Iraq. Squelching press freedom countered the attempt to build the democracy there. The military, though, used the same arguments Hascall, Burnside, and Lincoln used: temporary suppression was

necessary in such an extreme political crisis. In other words, developing countries sometimes experience emergency periods when freedom of the press has
to be temporarily suspended.

The military itch to suppress and a minority's desire to openly and freely
communicate words that might stimulate resistance or counter the war effort
collide. Perhaps in both cases, the military would have been better off coun-
tering the strident vituperation of the minority press by either getting its side
out clearly and effectively through the majority press or by building its own
newspapers to counter the untruths and agitations of the minority press. Of
course, as noted above, Burnside had experimented in newspaper building in
eastern North Carolina in 1863, and Hascall's regiment had published a paper
at the front. Furthermore, more than a century later, the United States published a newspaper in Iraq and planted stories in that nation's media.

Still, a government-sponsored news operation cannot be expected to be
strong enough always to counter the harmful words of those who use the media to serve violent and destabilizing ends. People do use the news media to
transmit messages that incite violence. These words put many in harm's way.
Thus, journalists of good intentions face the dilemma of supporting unlimited
freedom of the press when there are those who take advantage of this bulwark
democratic principle toward the end of advancing antidemocratic objectives.
Indeed, theocratic or authoritarian political factions come to power with the
aid of freedom of speech, press, and religion, and proceed to squash such
freedoms. Furthermore, in some stages in a nation's development, a level playing field does not exist, and at such times the marketplace of ideas seems
ridiculous.

John M. Daniel of the Richmond, Virginia, *Examiner* knew that criticism and other harmful words caused his government grief. Nonetheless,
Daniel asked the eternal question: "Is the press, that faithful sentinel on the
watch-tower of liberty, to be gagged and manacled at a time when all power
is in the army and all authority in the Government?"[68] In Daniel's estimation,
the watchdog role of the press was necessary when the prosecution of war
policy was unproductive. Like Horace Greeley and the New York editors who
made their resolutions for wartime press freedom, Daniel saw the need for a
robust journalism at precisely the moment of the greatest social instability.
Daniel and the New York editors upheld the rights of journalists to "freely
and fearlessly" criticize government policy and performance, including the
actions and orders of military officers.[69] These journalists agreed that martial
suppression should be tolerated in the area of hostilities. Although the ma-
rauding Confederate John H. Morgan briefly entered Indiana in the summer

of 1863, he was nowhere near the northern third of the state where Hascall constrained the dissident press. Daniel and the New York editors showed that a united front by professional journalists trumped freedom of the press for the majority, the principle of the party press. Thus, out of the nation's most partisan and bloody period came a transcendent journalistic principle.

FURTHER STUDY ON PRESS SUPPRESSION IN THE CIVIL WAR

In the years after the Civil War, it is not entirely clear how well the Democratic editors of Indiana—and the North—learned the journalistic lessons that Milo Hascall's descendant, Goshen *News* editor Frank L. Hascall, would absorb in the twentieth century—namely, that the best newspapers serve the civic needs of their readers first. Future study needs to explore exactly what happened to the nature of Indiana journalism from 1865 to 1880 and to the end of the nineteenth century. Indiana journalism modernized and became less political and personal. Yet the majority of newspapers continued to be affiliated with political parties, as had been the pattern throughout the nineteenth century, though political affiliation gradually vanished.

Journalism historians also need to further develop the portrait of suppression and intimidation that occurred in the North during the Civil War, particularly in Lincoln's Midwest. The picture of press suppression and intimidation in Indiana is fairly focused, but the depiction of what happened in Ohio, Illinois, Iowa, Michigan, and Wisconsin requires further study.

For example, Dennis A. Mahony, the editor of the Dubuque *Herald* in Iowa, was jailed in August of 1862 and imprisoned in Washington, D.C., until mid-November. In the meantime, his supporters in Iowa put his name up to run for Congress, but he lost. The Democratic editor was sent home after the election.

Of course, Mahony was one of thousands of political prisoners in the war. Yet the evidence does not suggest that there was an orchestrated effort to quell the press. Rather, it was random, though more widespread than historians have suggested. Thus, Hascall's actions in Indiana represent a microcosm of constraints on civil liberties during the war. The policies of the Lincoln administration were enforced indiscriminately and arbitrarily. His military censors were often ineffective, and in the worst cases the policies were employed for political purposes. Such cases are unacceptable in both times of peace and war. Lincoln knew this and advised one general to only arrest editors whose words exacted palpable injury on the military.[70]

Robert S. Harper, in a study that is now more than a half century old, had only two instances of official press suppression by Hascall in Indiana in

1863. Jon Dilts did not specifically list the 1863 incidents in his 1986 study. He gave only a cumulative figure of 13 for the entire year. Stephen E. Towne's 2005 and 2006 studies show a more extensive pattern of violence and intimidation against the Democratic press in Indiana. Thus, the historical record remains incomplete, but the picture is becoming clearer. The conditions that the Democratic press in Indiana faced in the Civil War were fraught with peril. A more thorough study is needed to develop a more complete picture of Democratic press suppression in the North during the war, especially in the Midwest where the political tide was beginning to turn against Lincoln in 1862 and 1863.

Furthermore, too many studies of Civil War journalism have come from the perspective that the press was an instrument of advancing freedom and unity—and this was true of the Republican press, but not of all of the Democratic press in the North. It was a time of a partisan press. Eighty percent of the press was affiliated with a political party at the start of the war. Much of the historical literature fails to capture the ever-changing political conditions in which a large number of newspapers operated. Both the North and South were witness to editors who dissented from the national administrations.

The Union Army suppressed newspapers throughout the South, especially in coastal cities like Norfolk, Virginia, and Key West, Florida. What connections, if any, can be made between the effort to suppress Southern papers and those in the Midwest? The final piece of the puzzle would be to look at how the Confederate government handled its dissident press, which has been characterized as nonexistent, but was fairly widespread, especially among Quakers, former Whigs, and folks who were tired of the carnage. Thus, a comprehensive study is also needed for Southern press suppression.

CHAPTER ELEVEN

Bibliographic Essay

The literature that informed this study was produced primarily in the last fifty-odd years, a time when scholarly activity on this issue has been most vigorous. The period starts with the 1951 publication of Robert S. Harper's *Lincoln and the Press*, which attempted to document press suppression throughout the North. Harper's book, though, underestimated the degree of suppression and intimidation in Indiana in particular. It is also likely that Harper underestimated suppression and intimidation throughout the North.

The suppression of Democratic newspapers in Indiana has been dealt with in several studies. The first significant study came from Craig D. Tenney, whose 1977 Indiana University dissertation titled "Major General A. E. Burnside and the First Amendment" focuses on Burnside and the press of the Midwest. Tenney says Burnside was working in the political realm, "subduing Copperhead influence."[1] This is important for the full understanding of the Hascall affair because he was working as Burnside's surrogate in Indiana. Tenney's study focuses on Burnside's suppression of Storey's Chicago *Times*. Tenney provides some detail of Hascall as commander of the District of Indiana in 1863. This study is the first to show that Harper's 1951 study was not rigorous enough.

The first focused study of press suppression in Indiana was Jon Dilts' 1986 attempt to test Fredrick Siebert's hypothesis about press freedom and government stability. Siebert's hypothesis claims that the area of freedom of expression decreases during times of political crises. Dilts' study focused on the variables of Union military losses and the pressure of political opposition and whether press restraints increased as a consequence of these factors. The Indiana University professor assumed that the state government would be the institution that would constrain the press. While the stability of the state government in Indiana was a key issue in 1863, the larger issue was the stability of the federal government. Hascall and Burnside were agents of the federal government, and indeed they were doing primarily political actions as members of the military a long way from the battle zone. There is a distinction between state and federal action, but Siebert's hypothesis does not take into account such an arrangement. The officers and soldiers who suppressed and intimidated newspapers in Indiana in effect did the handiwork of the Lincoln administration, which benefited politically from the vigilantism. Dilts admitted that "we would have expected 1863, the most critical year for Indiana, to be the year with the greatest number of incidents [of suppression], as it was."[2] Thus, he supported Siebert's proposition. The strong arm of Hascall only came to bear on Indiana's newspaper editors because the political fortunes of the state were changing, because the war news since December of 1862 was anything but good for the Lincoln administration, and because Democrats were disenchanted with conscription, the income tax, civil rights violations, and emancipation.

Three recent studies have shown the depth of press suppression and intimidation in the state. Towne's "Killing the Serpent Speedily" looks at the behind-the-scenes politics during Hascall's tenure as Commander of the District of Indiana. His "Works of Indiscretion" counts the number of acts of violence against editors in Indiana during the war. Towne includes suppression as an act of violence or intimidation against the press, mainly by Union soldiers. Towne concludes that Hascall's policy had a chilling effect on Democratic editors: "Outspoken editors backed away from their usually acidic attacks on the Lincoln administration and its policies and trod carefully with some counseling their readers to measure their words before speaking."[3] Furthermore, Towne's study suggests that the Union military conducted a more intense "war" against the Democratic press, not just in Indiana but also in the Midwest as a whole, than previous studies had found.[4] Towne suggests a more thorough analysis of press intimidation and suppression needs to be conducted in other Northern states, especially in Indiana's neighbors, Illinois and Ohio, where the Democrats had a majority in both the state legislatures and the national congressional delegation after the 1862 elections, to "reevaluate our understanding of the phenomenon of violent attack on political speech in United States history."[5] This will help show if Indiana was an anomalous or typical. Towne and Bruce Bigelow studied some of the sociological factors of suppression in "Democratic Opposition to the Lincoln Administration: The Polls and the Press."[6] They found that the Democratic editors were relatively young—the average age was 30—and that they were from diverse backgrounds.

Towne's "West Point Letters of Cadet Milo S. Hascall, 1848–1850"[7] in the *Indiana Magazine of History* examined letters Hascall wrote while he was at the U.S. Military Academy. These letters provide a snapshot into Hascall's state of mind during his formative years at the academy. W. H. H. Terrell's *Indiana in the War of the Rebellion* was the Morton administration's official report.[8] The version used for this study was a reprint of the first volume published in 1960. It includes basic statistical data about the number of men from Indiana who participated in the war and the development of the state militia as well as reports on internal discontent about the prosecution of the war. Charles E. Canup's "Conscription and Draft in Indiana" found that despite some resistance to the draft, the conscription system in the state worked and that only 10,822 Hoosiers were forced into the war out of a total of 173,178 who were eligible to be drafted in the fall of 1862.[9]

Another Civil War study of Indiana is John D. Barnhart's "The Impact of the Civil War on Indiana."[10] Barnhart's cultural study emphasizes the effect of the war on the institutions of Hoosier society, such as family, churches, and political parties. Barnhart points out that the war severely challenged democracy in Indiana, embarrassed the Democratic Party at the outset, and later divided Hoosier families and political parties. Barnhart's study touches on the importance of the press in Indiana society and notes that major political players like Caleb B. Smith, Schuyler Colfax, and Samuel E. Perkins owned or edited newspapers. Barnhart also discussed the ease that the state had in filling its military quota in the first two years of the war, but that changed after emancipation and the fall elections of 1862. It was much more difficult to raise volunteers after that.

Kenneth M. Stampp's *Indiana Politics During the Civil War* detailed the overall political background to Hascall's suppression of the Democratic press.[11] Emma Lou Thornbrough's *Indiana in the Civil War Era: 1850–80* provided much of the context for what was happening in Indiana in the war period.[12] Thornbrough's study showed that Indiana was a fast-growing state that had almost a religious reverence for union, yet much of the state was settled by Southerners who wanted no part of a war to beat down the South. Gilbert R. Tredway's *Democratic Opposition to the Lincoln Administration* showed that Hoosiers Democrats were not a homogeneous group and the "Copperhead" label was inaccurate.[13] Some wanted peace for economic and cultural reasons, and others supported Lincoln and the war, and still others sided with the Confederacy.

Extending these studies to the Midwest in general is Edward C. Smith's *The Borderland in the Civil War*, which looked at the economic, political, and social dimensions of life in the Ohio River Valley during the Civil War.[14] It put the war into a context, observing that the country was not evenly split between North and South, that the Midwest was another powerful region that was pro-Union but not antislavery.

John W. Miller's *Indiana Newspaper Bibliography* is a compendium of information about newspapers in the state.[15] Miller put together a history of every newspaper in every country of the nineteenth state from 1804 until 1982. Some of the anecdotal evidence in Miller's study conflict with information in the county histories. William Wesley Woollen's "The Indiana Press of the Olden Time" provided sketchy information about several of the suppressed papers and their Republican counterparts.[16] For example, Ignatius Mattingly, editor of Marshall County *Republican*, became the postmaster in Bourbon, Indiana, and editor of the Bourbon *Mirror* after the war. His loyalty to the Republicans earned him a federal position. Donald F. Carmony's "Highlights in Indiana Newspaper History" provided a history of daily newspapers in the nineteenth century.[17] Carmony said that daily papers only began to thrive when telegraph lines were established throughout the state.

Norma Jean Thiele's master's thesis titled "A History of the Fort Wayne News-Sentinel" analyzed the conditions the paper faced in nineteenth-century Fort Wayne, including labor disputes, health concerns, and immigration.[18] Thiele also unearthed the fact that the Goshen *Democrat* was a benefactor of the *Sentinel*. James Hannam Butler's "Journalism in Indiana" dealt with the political nature of the state's early newspapers.[19] Butler pointed out that a boom in newspaper startups took place during closely contested state and political contests.

An abundance of information about the Hascall family is available at the Center for Archival Collections in the Jerome Library at Bowling Green State University in Ohio. Box number six of the Bentley Family Papers includes twelve folders devoted to the Hascalls, including "The Hascall Family in America," whose author is unknown.[20] It details the migration of the Hascalls from Somerset, England, to Salem, Massachusetts, and eventually to Le Roy, New York, and then to Goshen, Indiana. The family history focuses on Milo Smith Hascall's father, Amasa Hascall. The Bentley Family Papers also include some of the papers of Ebenezer Mattoon Chamberlain, Hascall's law partner and a relative of Gettysburg hero Joshua Lawrence Chamberlain. Milo Hascall's postwar financial endeavor is described in Wilber L. Stonex's "Salem Bank of Goshen, Indiana."[21]

Frank Smith Bogardus' "Daniel W. Voorhees" showed a prominent pro-union Democrat who wanted to avoid war at all costs eventually coming around.[22] Voorhees, who had a profound influence on Indiana's Democratic editors, was a stalwart opponent of Lincoln. Yet he did not let that get in the way of his support for ordinary soldiers. Bogardus said Voorhees could keep abstract argument separate from the needs of the men who fought the war. Emma Lou Thornbrough's "Judge Perkins, the Indiana Supreme Court, and the Civil War" discussed Jeffersonian-Jacksonian ideology and the explication of that ideology by Indiana Supreme Court Justice Samuel E. Perkins.[23] Bruce Bigelow's "The Clash of Cultures: Border Southerners and Yankees in Antebellum Indiana" scrutinized the understanding of social life in Civil War Indiana, observing that it was the most "Southern" of the Midwestern states in that at least a quarter of its citizens had come from the South and wanted to be left alone to live a simple agrarian lifestyle without federal government interference.[24]

During the war, federal oversight of civil rights was a major area of interest for Indiana's Democrats. Because Lincoln either encouraged or tacitly approved of many cases of federal suppression, his understanding of the First Amendment requires description in this study. Lincoln valued the civil liberties enumerated in the Bill of Rights, but he thought the rebellion to be a special case that required certain rights to be suppressed for security reasons. David Herbert Donald's *Lincoln* included a narration of the events leading up to the May 5, 1863, arrest of Clement L. Vallandigham, the ex-congressman from Ohio whom Burnside silenced, and the White House view of Democratic criticism of the war.[25] A Consensus historian, Donald showed how Burnside had been defrocked and moved to the Department of the Ohio, and that the general wanted to show how loyal and competent he was to the president. Donald also demonstrated how there was plenty of pressure on Lincoln to do something about the Peace Democrats. The abolitionists not only wanted to win the war, but also wanted to end slavery. They complained that some the Union generals were going slowly in the first two years of the war because of their ties to the Democratic Party. This was perhaps true of George McClellan, who would run against Lincoln as a Democrat in 1864. Furthermore, Donald noted that Lincoln had to deal with calls for the resignation of Seward, was seen as too moderate by radicals, and the embarrassment of losing three major battles in Virginia between August of 1862 and May of 1863, Second Manassas, Fredericksburg, and Chancellorsville.

James G. Randall's *Lincoln the President: Midstream* defended Lincoln's abuse of civil rights because they were temporary and because the author contends that Lincoln always knew there were boundaries.[26] Randall failed to report that Lincoln waffled on the suppression of the Chicago *Times* and paints the president as almost a civil libertarian who was sensitive to the sovereignty of Morton as governor of Indiana. He failed to mention Morton's fervid support of suppression of the *Times*, the Indianapolis *Indiana State Sentinel*, and Dayton, Ohio, *Empire*.

William Marvel's *Burnside* provided a study of what the major general was going through in the second half of 1862 and first half of 1863.[27] Marvel's portrait helped establish Burnside's motives for establishing General Order No. 38. This consensus study showed that while Burnside was not a champion on the battlefield, he was a competent soldier who was generally admired by his men. His command of the Department of the Ohio gave him the opportunity to redeem himself for the disaster at Fredericksburg on December 13, 1862. The study showed a man who often had to deal with a critical press.

Stephen W. Sears' *Chancellorsville* provided insight into the behind-the-scenes politics that led to Burnside's dismissal as commander of the Army of the Potomac in January of 1863.[28] Sears shows how two brigadier generals, John Newton and John Cochrane, fooled the president into reassigning Burnside in a misguided attempt to restore George B. McClellan to the head of the Union's largest army.[29] Joseph E. Stevens' *1863: The Rebirth of a Nation* looked at the social revolution that took place in the North during the war and complements Marvel and Sears.[30] However, Stevens underplayed the complexity of the political turmoil in the Midwest. Stevens claimed that Democrats in the Midwest who thought the South would enter into a Confederation that excluded New England were mistaken, since Jefferson Davis wanted an independent nation, not a South-Midwest confederacy.[31]

James L. Vallandigham's *A Life of Clement L. Vallandigham* supplied information such as speeches, letters, and editorials the Ohio congressman wrote.[32] It also included a chapter on his years as editor of the *Dayton Empire*. William V. McPherson's "Clement Laird Vallandigham: The Forgotten Radical" argued that Vallandigham was too rational in his rhetoric and that he failed to meet the emotional needs of his audience.[33] It is an interesting take on Vallandigham as a failed orator as opposed to a political martyr. Robert C. Cheeks' "Clement Laird Vallandigham: American Constitutionalist" noted that Vallandigham introduced legislation in Congress that would make it a crime for Lincoln to suppress antiwar editors.[34] The proposed bill did not survive in the Republican-controlled House of Representatives.

Carl M. Becker's "Newspapers in Battle: The *Dayton Empire* and the *Dayton Journal* During the Civil War" gave the background of Vallandigham's arrest by Burnside.[35] The man who replaced Vallandigham as editor of the Democratic *Empire* was murdered just before Vallandigham's Mount Vernon speech, the basis for Burnside's arrest of the former congressman. Mount Vernon is where Vallandigham called Lincoln a despot, but he also told his audience that political change should be made at the ballot box. The day after the Ohio Democrat was arrested, the Republican Dayton *Journal* was burned to the ground by readers of the *Empire*.

Frank L. Klement's *The Limits of Dissent* had the most in-depth look at Vallandigham's arrest, trial, exile, and return.[36] It examined Democratic opposition to the war, and Klement paid particular attention to public opinion and its role in the elections of 1862 and 1864. Klement wrote critically of the Democrats but is much more concerned with publicizing Lincoln's civil rights abuses. Although it is not exactly a defense of Vallandigham, the book serves to legitimize his politics and dissent. Klement's *Lincoln's Critics* stated that it is an exaggeration to suggest only political opponents of the Lincoln administration were suppressed, "but too many Democratic newspapers were suppressed."[37] The author also explored mob rule and the political activity of secret societies at this time. This revisionist study emphasized Lincoln's abuse of civil rights, including freedom of the press, and portrayed Vallandigham as a martyr for free expression. Klement's *The Copperheads in the Middle West* was the first work in his trilogy on Democratic dissent, and it holds that Republican editors and politicians overestimated the strength of the secret societies.[38] It also showed that the term "Copperhead" came to mean just about all Democrats. Klement's work is significant; however, it may go too far in underestimating the potential harm some Democrats intended for the Lincoln administration.

The War of the Rebellion: A Compilation of the Official Records of the Union and Confederate Armies offered evidence from official government documents of the war, including orders by and correspondence between Hascall and Burnside.[39] It also contained correspondence from Indiana Governor Oliver P. Morton to Secretary of War Edwin Stanton about Hascall, as well as Chief of Staff Henry W. Halleck's opinion of the situation in Indiana in the spring of 1863. However, it did not include enough of the record to show what motivated Hascall and Burnside in the spring of 1863. Little of their official correspondence with subordinates and each other is included here. Gil

Hinshaw's "From 10,500 Battles: A Handbook of Civil War Engagements" is a resource for obtaining battle statistics and key dates in the war.[40]

The general background of the Civil War is provided in a trio of works by Princeton historian James M. McPherson, who sees the war in revolutionary terms and thus legitimizes the perspective that sees the Northern Democrats as being resistors to national progress. McPherson's *Antietam: The Battle That Changed the Course of the Civil War* maintains that Antietam was the key battle of the war, not Gettysburg, because it gave Lincoln the opportunity to announce the Emancipation Proclamation as a war measure.[41] *Battle Cry of Freedom: The Civil War Era* shows Lincoln's response to the Democratic opposition to his administration.[42] This chapter looks at Vallandigham, New York's Horatio Seymour, and Ohio's Samuel S. Cox, as well as the political background to the suppression movement. At 862 pages, McPherson's book is a modestly brief overview of the Civil War period. *Ordeal by Fire: The Civil War and Reconstruction, Third Edition* puts the war into context and is critical for understanding what went before and what went after.[43] Another Consensus study of war comes from David Herbert Donald and James G. Randall's *The Civil War and Reconstruction*.[44] This interweaves the military aspects of the war with its political and legal components.

Christopher Dell's *Lincoln and the War Democrats* demonstrated the fragile prowar coalition that existed in the North.[45] Dell showed how the coalition of Republicans and War Democrats worked together to overturn Peace Democratic gains made in the elections of 1862. Mildred C. Stoler detailed the influence of Democrats on the Republican Party in her 1938 Indiana University dissertation.[46] Indiana Democrats who became Republicans over Kansas-Nebraska in the 1850s were conservative and did not want a radical as their president. Thus, they settled on Lincoln as the moderate choice for president, and Lincoln did well in the northern two-thirds of the state in 1860—especially in Indianapolis and Lafayette—in large part because of former and current Democrats who saw him as the best middle-ground candidate.

The McPherson and Donald-Randall studies attempted to respond to Progressive interpretations of the war that put greater emphasis on economic inequality. The Progressives tended to see the press as being agents working in a holistic framework in which journalists worked toward the ultimate reuniting of the nation. This may have been the case of the overwhelming majority of Republican editors, but the majority of Democratic editors did not have the same notions of reunion as their counterparts and did not work for the same kind of reunion. The political unity that these historians ascribe to journalism did not exist since the majority of the papers in the North were partisan in nature.

Kevin Phillips' *The Cousins' War: Religion, Politics, and the Triumph of Anglo-America* examines religious, political, and economic variables.[47] Phillips explained the migration patterns of East Coast Americans into the Midwest. He explained that the lower Midwest—along the Ohio River—had people of very different stock from those of the upper Midwest. Editors in places such as Cincinnati, Dayton, Columbus, Louisville, and New Albany were from Virginia, Kentucky, Tennessee, and the mountains of North Carolina. The editors in Detroit, Chicago, Cleveland, and Fort Wayne were from New England or were descendants of German and Dutch settlers from New York, New Jersey, and Pennsylvania. Thus, the author claimed in this book that the lower North was basically conservative and much more likely to be sympathetic to the Confederacy, while the upper North had fewer cultural ties to the South and was less sympathetic. Phillips pointed out that there were no gubernatorial elections in the key states of Illinois, Indiana, and Ohio in 1862, a year when those three states gained Democratic majorities in their delegations to the U.S. House of Representatives, though Republicans maintained overall control of the House. Phillips said that Lincoln was fortunate that those states did not have statewide elections in 1862. If they had, the Peace movement would have likely reached a critical mass.

Harper's *Lincoln and the Press* discussed how the Lincoln administration wanted censorship but could not find a department that could best handle press relationships.[48] As a result, Treasury, War, and State all took turns at it. Harper's study also looked at how Democratic newspapers barred from the mail by several military officers. David B. Sachsman, S. Kittrell Rushing, and Debra Reddin van Tuyll's *The Civil War and the Press* is a series of essays coming out of the annual Symposium on the Nineteenth Century Press, the Civil War, and Free Expression at the University of Tennessee at Chattanooga.[49] The most useful essays for the present study include Janice L. Bukovac's look at the Michigan Democratic Party and the Fifteenth Amendment, John Glen's look at Sherman and the press, and Reed W. Smith's examination of Samuel Medary. Another key journalism study is Justin E. Walsh's *To Print the News and Raise Hell!*, a biography of Chicago *Times* editor Wilbur F. Storey.[50] Walsh's revisionist work sees the Democrats of the Midwest as having many factions, but that Storey's anti-Lincoln voice was the party's loudest. Walsh's study provided a developmental study of Storey, chronicling the editor's professional career from its start in Indiana to its end in Chicago. It has less depth on the suppression of the Chicago *Times* than Tenney's study, but it places Storey's career into context without minimizing his contributions to journalism because of his verbal attacks on Lincoln and the war.

Historians have developed the literature of press suppression in the South during the Civil War to a lesser degree than they have that of the North, but some contributions merit mention here. Debra Reddin van Tuyll has dealt with the topic in several articles, including one about Jefferson Davis' attempt to remove the draft exemption for journalists and about the conflict between North Carolina Governor Zebulon Vance and William H. Holden, the editor of the Raleigh *Standard* and by midwar a peace advocate. Van Tuyll also notes that there was a censorship resolution in the North Carolina General Assembly. Richard Roper and Richard Reid have both tackled the enigmatic Holden. Carl Osthaus wrote about the attempt to silence John M. Daniel, editor of the Richmond *Examiner*. Daniel, who opposed the removal of the draft exemption for printers, believed the constraints on press freedom would not help the Confederate win the war. He also thought that a free press benefited society in wartime. Patricia Towery and Richard B. Kielbowicz have written about Southern censorship.[51]

Hazel Dicken-Garcia's *Journalistic Standards in Nineteenth Century America* helped establish the journalistic culture of the time.[52] Dicken-Garcia's study correctly depicts the partisan nature of the Northern press at the time. Edwin and Michael Emery's *The Press and America, Seventh Edition: An Interpretive History of the Mass Media* gave an overview of press-government relations during the Civil War.[53] Frederic Hudson's *Journalism in the United States* is a developmental study that looks at the journalism of the antebellum and war period.[54] Hudson saw the major development of the period as being the movement toward reporting and away from opinion-making. Hudson thought the party press was a dark period in the development of U.S. journalism.

J. Cutler Andrews in *The North Reports the Civil War* developed Burnside's motivation for issuing Order No. 38.[55] Burnside and Hooker hardly got along at Fredericksburg, another major Union loss, and Burnside was subjected to fierce criticism in the New York press.[56] In *Reporting the Wars*, Joseph J. Mathews showed that so thorough was the degree of conflict in the Civil War that major battles were fought without reporters on hand.[57] In effect, American journalism of the 1860s did not have enough resources to adequately cover all facets of the war. This was a major handicap for Indiana's press. No paper in the state routinely had a reporter at the front line, so Hoosiers were mainly reading accounts of corresponding papers or from the

Associated Press. Frank Luther Mott's *American Journalism, A History* saw the party press as "the Dark ages of American Journalism."[58] Mott is critical of military censorship. He said the coverage of the war was more direct than in previous wars, but that journalism standards, particularly in terms of writing, were low. Mott's flaw is that he saw twentieth-century journalism as being superior and measures the practices of the 1860s against that bar.

John F. Marszalek's *Sherman's Other War* teased out much of the history of media-government relations during times of American war.[59] If Lincoln offered some sort of middle ground in government-press relations, General William Tecumseh Sherman offers the extreme. Any student of this subject needs to start his or her study with the first chapter of this book. It looks at telegraphic and mail censorship, official and unofficial guidelines, General Burnside silencing Vallandigham, and General Dix closing down two anti-war New York papers. "During the course of the war," Marszalek observed, "some ninety-two newspapers were subjected to some form of restriction, while forty-seven others were attacked by mobs, often times soldiers on leave." Sherman had a standing order that anybody who wrote anything for publication would be arrested and treated as a spy.

In *Bohemian Brigade*, Louis Starr noted: "The Lincoln administration had stumbled onto controlling the news almost inadvertently."[60] A riot had occurred in Baltimore involving those who favored Southern secession. Reporters in Washington were comparing notes on the riot and preparing to telegraph their reports north. An order came down at the telegraph office not to send any transmissions. As it turned out, the blackout was ordered by a colonel who was trying to seize conspirators in Washington who had loaded several ships with flour and other provisions for the Southern army. From there the censorship efforts of the Lincoln administration were arbitrary and haphazard.

Press suppression involved legal considerations, and *War and Press Freedom: The Problem of Prerogative Power* by Jeffery A. Smith concludes that media and military must work together because neither has ultimate legal authority over the other.[61] The chapter titled "The Rise of Presidential Prerogatives" looks closely at how Lincoln suppressed free speech and press during the war. A neolibertarian, Smith pointed out that there was never any action from Congress that specifically gave Lincoln the power to suppress the press. This is mainly a constitutional study that relies on primary sources.

Other key studies on the relationship between the press and the government included David M. Rabban's *Free Speech in the Forgotten Years*; Geoffrey R. Stone's *Perilous Times: Free Speech In Wartime*; and Michael S.

Sweeney's *The Military and the Press*. Rabban examined the Comstock Act of 1878 and the libertarian tradition between the Civil War and World War I; Stone's book looked at the full range of free expression history in the United States; and Sweeney inspected press-government relations from the time of the Spanish-American War to the present.[62]

In his book *Free Speech "The People's Darling Privilege,"* Michael Kent Curtis retreats to Blackstone's definition of a free press—no prior restraint—as his starting point for studying sedition and freedom of expression.[63] It pointed to the odd twists and turns in this story as Southern legislatures suppressed abolitionist speech and writings before the war and then the Republican administration of Lincoln suppressed critics of his political and military policies during the war. This study placed suppression in the context of Lincoln's need to keep Maryland, Missouri, and Kentucky in the Union. It provides an in-depth look at Burnside's General Order No. 38 and the subsequent arrest and exile of Vallandigham. It also looks at Burnside's suppression of the *Chicago Times* and Democrats' pleas to Lincoln to not further damage the Bill of Rights. Curtis makes a connection between press freedom and constitutional democracy. In "Democratic Ideals and Media Realities," Curtis showed how freedom of the press has both functional and formal protections, commenting: "A strong public commitment to free speech values can itself protect free speech, though judicial doctrine would allow (but not require) suppression."[64] Functional protections are those practices, standards, and values journalists construct themselves to expand the area of press freedom. On the other hand, government officials often work to constrain when legal protections are absent or ambiguous. Thus, a tension exists between functional practices of both journalists and government officials.

Fredrick S. Siebert's *Freedom of the Press in England 1476–1776: The Rise and Decline of Government Controls* cautioned, "Freedom of the press is not and never can be absolute."[65] Furthermore, his four major propositions offer a framework for studying the issue of press freedom during wartime: (1) "the extent of government control of the press depends on the nature of the relationship of the government to those subject to the government"; (2) "the area of freedom contracts and the enforcement of restraints increases as the stresses on the stability of the government and of the structure of society increases"; (3) "the more heterogeneous a society, the more freedom of expression it will tolerate; and (4) "the more developed a society, the more subtle will be the controls it exerts on expression." The second proposition comes into play in the present study, but the other three are relevant also.

Thomas Carleton Hanson's "Press Freedom and War Restraints: Siebert's Proposition II and Stevens' Proposition III in the Case of the *Los Angeles Star*" discussed the suppression of the *Los Angeles Star* by Lincoln during the Civil War.[66] Henry Hamilton, the *Star* editor, criticized the management of the war at a time when the Union was losing. Hanson makes the argument that society in Los Angeles shared Hamilton's views, and that the editor was simply giving his readers what they wanted.

In *The Fate of Liberty: Abraham Lincoln and Civil Liberties*, Mark E. Neely focused on the suspension of the writ of habeas corpus and looked at the suspension of free speech and free press in Maryland, Missouri, Kentucky, Indiana, and Ohio.[67] It also shows how Lincoln rarely suppressed political dissent in the press in New York because the Democrats were in power there and controlled the majority of the city's newspapers.

Harold L. Nelson's *Freedom of the Press from Hamilton to the Warren Court* examined primary documents from the Civil War, many from Secretary of War Edwin M. Stanton, and helps develop the mindset of the Union's military leaders.[68] Stanton did not oppose suppression in theory because he wanted to get a hold on dissent in the Midwest. Yet Stanton, like Lincoln, was a pragmatist and preferred subtle forms of control. He told a major general to allow the suppressed *Chicago Times* to resume publication: "The irritation produced by such acts is in his [Lincoln's] opinion likely to do more harm than the publication would." Stanton would later produce a Republican victory in the New Hampshire gubernatorial campaign of 1863 by having a War Democrat run as a third-party candidate and producing a draw in the election, which sent the choice to the majority-Republican legislature.[69] Randall's *Constitutional Problems Under Lincoln* attempted to soften Lincoln's record on civil rights.[70] Randall showed the regrets Lincoln and his cabinet had for Burnside's arresting and trying of Vallandigham. William H. Rehnquist's *All the Laws But One: Civil Liberties in Wartime* offered a narrative of Lincoln's suspension of habeas corpus and its ramifications for civil rights.[71] The title comes from this statement Lincoln made to Congress on July 4, 1861: "Are all the laws, but one, to go unexecuted, and the government itself go to pieces, lest that one be violated." Rehnquist deals with Vallandigham, Burnside, and Lambdin P. Milligan, an Indiana Democrat closely associated with the Huntington *Democrat* and a former friend of Stanton's who was jailed for treason near the end of the war for his alleged role in a secret society. The Supreme Court Justice said martial law in the Civil War was largely ad hoc, depending almost entirely on the officer in charge in a particular part of the country.

Rehnquist recounted the Indianapolis Treason Trials, and he says the *Milligan* decision of 1866 "is justly celebrated for its rejection of the government's position that the Bill of Rights has no application in wartime."[72]

Margaret A. Blanchard's essay "Free Expression and Wartime: Lessons from the Past, Hopes for the Future" narrated how John Merryman of Maryland recruited men to form a squad that would join the Confederate Army, and Lincoln had Merryman thrown in jail without cause.[73] The case blew up on the president when Supreme Court Justice Roger B. Taney, working as a federal district judge, issued a writ of habeas corpus. It was ignored, and Taney wrote an opinion challenging Lincoln's right to suspend the writ. Blanchard showed that the case never went to the Supreme Court, and the issue was not resolved until 1866 in *Ex Parte Milligan*, which said that if civil courts are open, then military commissions do not have jurisdiction.

A series of articles dealt with legal education in nineteenth-century Indiana. These included William Watson Woollen's "Marion County Bar" and Leander J. Monks' "Legal Education in Indiana."[74] Both provided information about what lawyers had to read to prepare for their careers. Charles W. Taylor's *Biographical Sketches and Review of the Bench and Bar of Indiana* provided portraits of nineteenth-century Indiana attorneys, including their education.[75]

Notes

CHAPTER ONE

1. Plymouth, Indiana, *Weekly Democrat*, 14 May 1863.
2. Daniel McDonald, *History of Marshall County, Indiana* (Mount Vernon, IN: Windmill Publications, 1908), 394–395.
3. "History" of Plymouth, Indiana, Chamber of Commerce. URL: http://www. plychamber.org/pages/cityhistory.html. Accessed July 16, 2004.
4. Richmond, Indiana, *Jeffersonian*, 30 April 1863.
5. Plymouth, Indiana, *Weekly Democrat*, 30 April 1863.
6. McDonald, 394–395.
7. Plymouth, Indiana, *Weekly Democrat*, 14 May 1863.
8. Robert N. Scott et al. ed., *The War of the Rebellion: A Compilation of the Official Records of the Union and Confederate Armies* (Washington, DC: Government Printing Office, 1899), Series II, Vol. V, 480.
9. William Marvel, *Burnside* (Chapel Hill, NC: University of North Carolina Press, 1991), 222.
10. Detroit, Michigan, *Free Press*, 5 June 1863.
11. Stephen E. Towne, "Works of Indiscretion: Violence against the Press in Indiana during the Civil War," *Journalism History*, Vol. 31, No. 4 (Fall 2005), 142–143.
12. Robert S. Harper, *Lincoln and the Press* (New York, NY: McGraw-Hill, 1951), 231–232.
13. Columbia City, Indiana, *News*, 5 May 1863. The *News* charged either $2 a year if a customer paid in advance or $2.50 if paid within the year.
14. Indianapolis, Indiana, *Weekly Indiana State Sentinel*, 18 May 1863. Richmond, Indiana, *Jeffersonian*, 28 May 1863. Fort Wayne, Indiana, *Dawson's Daily Times & Union*, 18 May 1863.
15. S.N.D. North, "The Newspaper and Periodical Press," Tenth Census (Washington, DC: Government Printing Office, 1884), 186–187.
16. Hazel Dicken Garcia, *Journalistic Standards in Nineteenth-Century America* (Madison, WI: University of Wisconsin Press, 1989), 54.
17. Fort Wayne, Indiana, *Dawson's Daily Times & Union*, 11 May 1863. New Albany, Indiana, *Daily Ledger*, 16 May 1863.
18. Phillip J. Tichenor, "Copperheadism and Community Conflict in Two Rivertowns: Civil War Press Battles in Prairie du Chien and La Crosse, Wisconsin, 1861–65," presented to the Symposium on the 19th Century Press, the Civil

War, and Free Expression, University of Tennessee at Chattanooga, October 2002, 8. Also see the Richmond, Indiana, *Jeffersonian*, "Extra," 20 March 1863.

19. Gilbert R. Tredway, *Democratic Opposition to the Lincoln Administration* (Indianapolis, IN: Indiana Historical Bureau, 1973), 28–29.

20. Joseph J. Mathews, *Reporting the War* (Minneapolis, MN: University of Minnesota Press, 1957), 81. Mathews notes that not only was there no legal context for censorship or suppression, there was no major war experience for U.S. journalism to put to use when the conflict began. The Mexican War had taken place far from most of the newspapers in the country.

21. Harper, 154. Harper discusses Charles C. Fulton, editor of the Baltimore *American*, who was arrested on orders from Secretary of War Edwin M. Stanton for reporting he did at the Peninsula in Virginia. See 141–153 for press suppression in Missouri.

22. Carl M. Becker, "Newspapers in Battle: The Dayton Empire and the Dayton Journal During the Civil War," *Ohio History: The Scholarly Journal of the Ohio Historical Society*, vol. 99, 1990, 44.

23. John W. Miller, *Indiana Newspaper Bibliography* (Indianapolis, IN: Indiana Historical Society, 1982), 205.

24. Harper, 231–233. Lincoln barred California papers from the mails, and Brigadier General George Wright ordered the suspension of mail delivery of several Democratic papers in Oregon.

25. See Wendy E. Swanburg, "Ex Parte McCardle and the First Amendment during Reconstruction," presented to the Symposium on 19th Century Journalism, the Civil War, and Freedom of Expression, University of Tennessee at Chattanooga, November 2006. Also see "1898 Wilmington (N.C.) Race Riot Report: Final Report, 31 May 2006," http://www.ah.dcr.state.nc.us/1898%2Dwrrc/report/report.htm. Accessed: 27 November 2006.

26. Michael S. Sweeney, *The Military and the Press: An Uneasy Truce* (Evanston, IL: Northwestern University Press, 2006), 3–4.

27. Jeffery A. Smith, *War and Press Freedom: The Problem of Prerogative Power* (Cary, NC: Oxford University Press, 1999), 56–66.

28. Towne, 2005, 138.

29. Jon Dilts, "Testing Siebert's Proposition in Civil War Indiana," *Journalism Quarterly*, Vol. 63, No. 1, Spring 1986, 367. Dilts' study was admittedly limited. He looked at only 37 newspapers when there were 186 in Indiana in 1860 and, by 1870, there were 293.

30. Towne, 2005, 142–143. Throw out two of the incidents against Republican newspapers that Towne discovered in his study because those were cases were tornadoes destroyed newspaper offices.

31. Norma Jean Theiel, "A History of the Fort Wayne Sentinel," master's thesis (Bloomington, IN: Indiana University, 1958), 23.

32. Harry J. Maihafer, *War of Words: Abraham Lincoln and the Civil War Press* (Washington, DC, Brassey's, 2001), 1.
33. Maihafer, 1. Also see S.N.D. North, *The Newspaper and Periodical Press*, U.S. Census Office (Washington, DC: Government Printing Office, 1884), 186–187.
34. William David Sloan, *The Media in America, A History* (Northport, AL: Vision Press, 2002), 200.
35. Gerald J. Baldasty, "The Press and Politics in the Age of Jackson," *Journalism Monographs*, No. 89, August 1984, 1–28. Baldasty's study shows how the press of the 1820s and 1830s, Indiana's formative years, was intricately related to political parties. Parties cultivated newspapers, and editors often were major political figures. Parties subsidized newspapers through patronage and start-up money. Little of this had changed by 1861, at least in the nation's interior, including Indiana. This is a key understanding because newspapers were defined by their structural limitations—that is, those who funded them, who made them, and who read them. With mid-nineteenth-century newspapers so close to political parties and so politically oriented, an understanding of press suppression at that time starts with this basic structural framework.
36. William P. McLauchlan, *The Indiana State Constitution: A Reference Guide* (Westport, CT: Greenwood Press, 1996), 40.
37 William David Sloan and James D. Startt, *Historical Methods in Mass Communication* (Hillsdale, NJ: Erlbaum, 1989), 117.
38. Thomas P. Lowry, *Don't Shoot That Boy! Abraham Lincoln and Military Justice* (Mason City, IA: Savas, 1999), 129. Hascall recommended to Burnside that William Aughenbaugh, who had deserted the 44th Ohio, not be shot since five other deserters tried by the same military court had not received a death sentence. Burnside pardoned Aughenbaugh and had him returned to duty. President Lincoln signed Burnside's pardon order.
39. Adams, Jackson, and Polk all participated in the suppression of newspapers and gave Lincoln precedents to justify a heavy-handed approach to government-press relations. Adams forced the Alien and Sedition acts on the country. Jackson used military censorship during the Battle of New Orleans in the War of 1812. Polk allowed military officers to suppress five U.S. and five Mexican newspapers during the Mexican War. Adams and Polk's actions against the press came while they were president. Jackson's came while he was an army general.

CHAPTER TWO

1. Stephen E. Towne, "West Point Letters of Cadet Milo S. Hascall, 1848–1850," *Indiana Magazine of History*, Vol. 90, No. 3, September 1994, 278.
2. "The Hascall Family in America," Bentley Family Papers, Center for Archives Collection, Jerome Library, Bowling Green State University, Bowling Green, Ohio, MS-720, Box 6, Folder 2, 7.

3. Ibid., 7.
4. Ibid., 9.
5. Ibid., 18.
6. Towne, 1994, 289.
7. Ibid., 290.
8. Ibid., 286–287.
9. Ibid., 293. See footnote 38.
10. "Hascall Family in America," 19.
11. Ebenezer Mattoon Chamberlain, "Journal of Chamberlain of a Trip from Maine to Indiana in 1832," *Indiana Magazine of History*, Vol. 15, No. 3, September 1919. Chamberlain calls the prairie of northern Indiana "the glory of the west." He adds, "There is something new and wild and romantic in the country of this region, which notwithstanding the absence of the long friends, and that social intercourse in the jarring elements of society here to which I have been accustomed, in the land I remembered with fond regret, has tolerably reconciled me to this place." Chamberlain said the farmers of the region were "pleasant," and he enjoyed spear-fishing for pike and sturgeon in the little lakes of Elkhart County.
12. Ibid.
13. "Hascall Family in American," 19. Ebenezer Mattoon Chamberlain said that one of the reasons he migrated to Indiana was because the standards for obtaining the bar were lower in Indiana. Chamberlain had read for three years under Elisha H. Allen in Bangor from 1829 to 1832. He said he would have to "read law three years longer" in Maine, but "I could save one of two years' practice in the profession" by moving to Indiana. See "Journal of Ebenezer Mattoon Chamberlain, 1832–1935," in Bentley Family Papers, Center for Archives Collection, Jerome Library, Bowling Green State University, Bowling Green, Ohio, MS-720.
14. Charles W. Taylor, *Biographical Sketches and Review of the Bench and Bar of Indiana* (Indianapolis, IN: Bench and Bar Publishing, 1895), 165. Also see Leander J. Monks, ed., *Courts and Lawyers of Indiana, Volume II* (Indianapolis, IN: Federal Publishing Company, 1916) 474.
15. See *Benjamin Hoover v. George Hoover, William A. Shafer, and R.M. Randall* as an example, Elkhart County, Indiana, *Times*, 25 November 1858. Benjamin Hoover sought foreclosure against George Hoover, Shafer, and Randall in Common Pleas Court.
16. Goshen, Indiana, *Democrat*, 5 November 1846.
17. Ibid.
18. Ibid.
19. John W. Miller, *Indiana Newspaper Bibliography* (Indianapolis, IN: Indiana Historical Society, 1982), 98–99. Melvin B. Hascall owned the Goshen *Demo-*

crat in 1873. Frank L. Hascall owned the Goshen *News* from 1954 until the 1980s.

20. Goshen, Indiana, *Democrat*, 14 January 1847.
21. Ibid., 26 June 1858.
22. Ibid., 6 April 1853.
23. Elkhart County, Indiana, *Times*, 6 May 1858.
24. Towne, 1994, 281.
25. "Hascall Family in America," 20.
26. Ibid., 21.
27. Elkhart County, Indiana, *Times*, 24 June 1858.
28. Ibid., 8 July 1858.
29. Goshen, Indiana, *Times*, 6 October 1859.
30. Ibid., 3 November 1859.
31. Ibid., 28 June 1860.
32. Goshen, Indiana, *Democrat*, 15 October 1858.
33. Ibid., 16 July 1856.
34. Ibid., 16 July 1856.
35. Phillip J. Tichenor, "Copperheadism and Community Conflict in Two River-towns: Civil War Press Battles in Prairie du Chien and La Crosse, Wisconsin, 1861–1865," presented at the Symposium on the 19th Century press, the Civil War, and Free Expression, Chattanooga, Tennessee, October 2002, 8.
36. Stephen E. Towne, "Works of Indiscretion: Violence against the Press in Indiana during the Civil War" *Journalism History*, Vol. 31, No. 4 (Fall 2005), 135.
37. Kenneth M. Stampp, *Indiana Politics During the Civil War* (Indianapolis, IN: Indiana Historical Bureau, 1949), 1.
38. Ibid.
39. James G. Randall and David Herbert Donald, *The Civil War and Reconstruction, Second Edition* (Lexington, MA: D.C. Heath and Company, 1969), 8.
40. William H.H. Terrell, *Indiana in the War of the Rebellion: Report of Adjutant General of Indiana* (Indianapolis, IN: 1859), Vol. 1, 396. Republished in 1960 by the Indiana Historical Bureau (one volume, 603 pages).
41. Emma Lou Thornbrough, *Indiana in the Civil War, 1850–1880* (Indianapolis, IN: Indiana Historical Society, 1995), 363.
42. Randall and Donald, 5–6.
43. United States Bureau of the Census, *10th Census*, I, 431.
44. Thornbrough, 547–549. Many Germans who came to Indiana were escaping the failing potato crop back home. Others came for political reasons after the uprisings in 1848. While the first generation of Germans belonged to the bottom half of the socioeconomic spectrum, they would rise quickly in Indiana. By 1880, many were businessmen, especially in the brewery business.

Others owned theaters. Germans were also represented well as attorneys and physicians.

45. Ibid., 553.
46. Ibid., 549.
47. Indiana State Board of Agriculture, *Annual Report* (Indianapolis, IN: 1851), 255.
48. Stampp, 2.
49. Thornbrough, 540.
50. Ibid.
51. Ibid., 541.
52. Ibid., 545.
53. United States Bureau of the Census, *Tenth Census*, I, 431–432.
54. Thornbrough, 547.
55. Ibid., 541.
56. Joseph A. Wright, *An Address Delivered at the Installation of Rev. L. W. Berry, D.D., as President of Indiana Asbury University, July 16, 1850* (Indianapolis, IN: 1850), 15.
57. Stampp, 3.
58. Ibid., 191.
59. Thornbrough, 3.
60. William W. Woollen, *Richard W. Thompson Papers* (Indianapolis, IN: Indiana Division, Indiana State Library, 8 June 1847 manuscript), 355.
61. United States Bureau of the Census, *Tenth Census* (1880), XV, 646–647.
62. Ibid., 928–931.
63. Ibid.
64. Stampp, 79.
65. Thornbrough, 13.
66. Ibid., 13–14.
67. Ibid., 14.
68. Ibid., 14–15.
69. Ibid., 16.
70. Ibid.
71. Ibid., 17.
72. Ibid., 21.
73. Ibid., 22.
74. Ibid., 24.
75. Charles Kettleborough, editor, 1851 Indiana Constitution, *Manuscript Constitution* (Indianapolis, IN: Indiana Historical Bureau, Indiana State Library).
76. Thornbrough, 599.
77. Ibid., 618.
78. Baseball was still mainly an urban and Eastern sport in the 1860s, but it was played in Indiana, especially in the larger cities—Indianapolis, Fort Wayne,

Evansville, Lafayette. Before the war, it was more likely to be played by children. After the war and interaction with men from the East Coast, interest in baseball increased among adults. Before that happened, Hoosiers were more likely to hunt and fish in their spare time. They also bet on horse racing or boxing, but the latter was looked down upon by society's elites. Cricket was also played. See Thornbrough, 702. Many Hoosiers had come from the South, where baseball did not become popular until after the war. Southerners thought hunting to be a more appropriate recreation, one that helped test one's manhood—in particular, the ability not to flinch at the key moment of confronting, say, a bear. See Kenneth S. Greenberg, *Honor and Slavery: Lies, Duels, Noses, Masks, Dressing as a Woman, Gifts, Strangers, Humanitarianism, Death, Slave Rebellions, the Proslavery Argument, Baseball, Hunting, and Gambling in the Old South* (Princeton, NJ: Princeton University Press, 1996), 125.

79. Ibid., 622–623.
80. Estel Neace, "Methodism in Indiana during the Civil War," Unpublished Master's Thesis (Indianapolis, IN: Butler University, 1961), 21–22.
81. Thornbrough, 462.
82. Charles W. Moores, "Caleb Mills and the Indiana School System" (Indianapolis, IN: Indiana Historical Society Publications, III, No. 6, 1905), 414.
83. Indiana State Constitution of 1851, Article VIII, Section 1.
84. Thornbrough, 469, 476.
85. Ibid., 470.
86. See Charles Blanchard, *History of the Catholic Church in Indiana* (Logansport, IN: two volumes, 1898).
87. Ibid., 25.
88. What these Northern Democrats coveted was free land for poor settlers. See Jonathan H. Earle, *Jacksonian Antislavery & the Politics of Free Soil, 1824–1854* (Chapel Hill, NC: University of North Carolina Press, 2004), 5. These disaffected Democrats who would start the Free Soil Party also preferred hard money.
89. Eric Foner, "The Wilmot Proviso Revisited," *Journal of American History*, 61 (September 1969), 270.
90. Thornbrough, 28.
91. Holman Hamilton, *Prologue to Conflict: The Crisis and Compromise of 1850* (Lexington, KY: University of Kentucky Press, 1964), 174–176. The 1860 census showed only twenty-nine slaves in Utah, which would not become a state until 1896. In 1859, the New Mexico legislature passed a law that protected slave ownership in the territory. This included Native American slavery, which was far more significant in that territory than African American slavery. New Mexicans, though, generally sided with the Union in the Civil War. New Mexico did not become a state until 1912.

92. James McPherson, *Ordeal By Fire: The Civil War and Reconstruction, Third Edition* (New York: McGraw-Hill, 2001), 90.

93. Thornbrough, 32.

94. Ibid., 33.

95. Ibid., 37. See the Indianapolis *Indiana State Sentinel,* 15 June 1851.

96. Kettleborough, 1851 Indiana Constitution.

97. McPherson, *Ordeal By Fire,* 101.

98. Thornbrough, 55.

99. For more information about the rise of the Republicans in Indiana, see Roger H. Van Bolt, "Indiana in Political Transition, 1851–1853," *Indiana Magazine of History,* Vol. 49, 1953, 131–160.

100. *Indiana Free Democrat,* 16 February 1854.

101. Thornbrough, 56.

102. Ibid., 57.

103. United States Bureau of the Census, *Tenth Census* (1880), I, 431.

104. Thornbrough, 61.

105. Ibid. The Know Nothing movement in the 1840s and 1850s was a coalition of secret societies and minority political parties that joined forces with the Whigs in 1854. Their main purpose was to serve as a political and cultural blocking force against immigrants, especially Irish and German Roman Catholics. The Free Soil Party opposed slavery's expansion into the territories and advocated the federal government's giving away land in the West. Free Soilers were attempting to move away from some of the labor issues that arose in the East as immigration engulfed the coastal cities. Their slogan was "free soil, free speech, free labor, and free men."

106. Indianapolis, Indiana, *Indiana State Sentinel,* 8 September 1854.

107. Thornbrough, 64.

108. Ibid., 67. The Indiana prohibition law made it illegal to manufacture and sell alcohol, except for medicinal purposes.

109. Ibid., 68.

110. Ibid., 69.

111. Ibid., 51.

112. In Indiana, the party that would become the Republican Party still called itself the People's Party in 1856. At that time, Whigs were gaining greater control of this fusion party.

113. Thornbrough, 76.

114. Ibid., 75.

115. Ibid., 76.

116. Ibid., 40.

117. Mark W. Summers, *The Plundering Generation: Corruption and the Crisis of the Union, 1849–1861* (New York: Oxford University Press, 1987), 63.

118. Thornbrough, 40.

119. Ibid., 41.

120. Ibid., 77.

121. Ibid., 79.

122. Ibid., 80.

123. Ibid., 85.

124. Ibid., 87.

125. Ibid., 89.

126. Thornbrough, 101. Also see fn. 30 in William Dudley Foulke, *Life of Oliver P. Morton, Including His Important Speeches*, Bowen-Merrrill, Indianapolis, 1898, Volume I, 93.

127. Stampp, 78.

128. Thornbrough, 106.

129. Ibid., 107.

130. Terrell, 8.

131. Thornbrough, 108.

132. Stampp, 85.

133. The Crittenden resolutions went through several incarnations, and the group that rejected them the most was the Republicans. Congressional debate on the resolutions started as early as December 1960, about the same time that South Carolina seceded. The Republican leadership opposed the compromise because they did not want to hamstring the president-elect. In February, at the Virginia Peace Conference in Washington, resolutions passed in favor of the Missouri Compromise line for existing U.S. territories. The federal government could only set up new territories with dual majorities of Southern and Northern senators. The Senate rejected the Virginia Peace Conference version on early 4 March 1861, the same day Abraham Lincoln was inaugurated as president. The Senate also rejected Crittenden's original compromise of the 1820 line permanently extended to the Pacific, with the North and South sharing equally in the development of the continent. In effect, the Republicans' opposition to Crittenden left it in Lincoln's hands alone whether to accept or reject secession. Thus, the antislavery wing of the Republican Party won at this critical juncture in the march toward war, and in their minds the reason to resist Crittenden was because they feared the expansion of slavery into the Caribbean, especially Cuba. See Robert E. May, *The Southern Dream of a Caribbean Empire*, 1854–1861 (Baton Rouge, LA: Louisiana State University Press, 1973), 212–215.

134. Frank L. Klement, *Limits of Dissent: Clement L. Vallandigham and the Civil War* (Lexington, KY: University of Kentucky Press, 1970), 1. While Vallandigham was best known for saying the "Union as it was" line, it is not clear who originated it. Indiana Congressman Daniel W. Voorhees frequently said it in his speeches, and many Democratic editors in Indiana adopted it as a political slogan.

135. Thornbrough, 114.

136. Ibid., 124. Terrell, 5. Since the militia was a state entity, it had to be offered over to the federal government to fight the war. It was as if Lincoln and the War Department were renting out the troops from the various states in the North.

137. *Pictorial and Biographical Memoirs of Elkhart and St. Joseph Counties, Indiana* (Chicago, IL: Goodspeed Brothers, 1893), 721.

138. Stampp, 88.

139. Thornbrough, 130.

140. Ibid., 131.

141. Ibid., 125. Also see Catharine Merrill, *The Soldier of Indiana in the War for the Union*, two volumes (Indianapolis, IN: Merrill and Company, 1866–1869).

142. Ibid., 126.

143. Ibid., 131.

144. Ibid.

CHAPTER THREE

1. Goshen, Indiana, *Times*, 18 April 1861.

2. *Gitlow v. New York* nationalized the First Amendment. That is, state constitutions could not trump the federal Constitution's free-expression guarantee. Justice Edward T. Stanford, writing for the 7–2 majority, said: "We may and do assume that freedom of speech and of the press—which are protected by the First Amendment from abridgement by Congress—are among the fundamental rights and 'liberties' protected by the due process clause of the Fourteenth Amendment from impairment by the States." See 268 U.S. 652, 45 Supreme Court 625, 630, 1925. It is also worth noting here that the Court stated in *Gitlow*: "It is a fundamental principle, long established, that the freedom of the speech and of the press which is secured by the Constitution, does not confer an absolute right to speak or publish, without responsibility, whatever one may choose, or an unrestricted and unbridled license that gives immunity for every possible use of language and prevents the punishment of those who abuse this freedom." Ibid., 666. In *Near v. Minnesota*, the Supreme Court struck down a state's prior-restraint regulation. See *Near v. Minnesota* ex rel. Olson, 283 U.S. 697, 51 Supreme Court 625, 1931. *New York Times v. Sullivan* established that public figures would have to accept the criticisms that come with life in the political arena. It established the test of "actual malice," knowledge that a statement about a public official was false or "with reckless disregard of whether it was false or not." See *New York Times v. Sullivan*, 376 U.S. 254, 84 Supreme Court 710, 1964. A publisher would not have to prove the truth of statements made in his/her publication. Rather, the plaintiff would have to prove the falsity of the statements. In other words, the

Supreme Court ruled criticism of the government was protected by the First Amendment, and combined with *Gitlow* this was universal.

3. John D. Zelezny, *Communications Law: Liberties, Restraints, and the Modern Media* (Belmont, CA: Wadsworth, 1997), 36.

4. Ibid.

5. Robert J. Wagman, *The First Amendment Book* (New York, NY: Pharos Books, 1991), 34–36. Wagman points out that the Virginia Declaration of Rights convention draft said: "Liberty of the press cannot be canceled, abridged, restrained or modified by any authority of the United States." For the national document, James Madison toned it down to: "The people shall not be deprived of their right to speak, to write, or to publish their sentiments, and the freedom of the press, as one of the great bulwarks of liberty, shall be inviolable." In 1789, a Madison-led select committee of the U.S. House of Representatives edited this down to: "The freedom of speech and of the press, and the right of the people peaceably to assemble and consult for their common good, and to apply to the government for a redress of grievances, shall not be infringed." This was the basis for the final draft of the First Amendment, which was ratified along with the other nine amendments in the Bill of Rights in 1791.

6. Zelezny, 31. Milton wrote: "Give me liberty to know, to utter, and to argue freely according to conscience, above all other liberties." The Puritan poet, who was arguing for the right to advocate divorce, felt government should not restrain communication, that truth and falsehood grappled in debate, and that ultimately truth would win.

7. Don R. Pember, *Mass Media Law* (Madison, WI: Brown & Benchmark Publishers, 1997), 34.

8. Thomas M. Cooley, *A Treatise on the Constitutional Limitations Which Rest Upon the Legislative Power of the States of the American Union, Eighth Edition* (Boston, MA: Little, Brown, and Company, 1927), 901–902.

9. Alexander Hamilton, "Federalist Number Eighty-Four," in *The Federalist Papers*, Clinton Rossiter, ed. (New York, NY: Mentor Book, Penguin Putnam, Inc., 1999), 481–482. Hamilton asked: "Why . . . should it be said that the liberty of the press shall not be restrained, when no power is given by which restrictions may be imposed?" Hamilton thought it better to leave out the Bill of Rights because the exactness of the definitions would tempt those men with tyrannical tendencies to exercise regulatory powers that would limit the very freedoms the Americans had fought for in their revolution. He did not want the federal government to have the power to regulate the press. Hamilton also thought a bill of rights was necessitated by the existence of a monarch—that is, it was a compact between the regal governor and the governed. Since the United States would have no monarch, it did not need a bill of

rights. Indeed, in Hamilton's view, the Constitution itself was a declaration of a bill of rights—a formal declaration of independence from the monarchial form of government. In a sense, Hamilton was a minimalist and wanted to keep the Constitution as tight as possible and not open to interpretation that would increase rather than decrease the government's regulatory powers.

10. Marc A. Franklin, David A. Anderson, and Fred H. Cate, *Mass Media Law: Cases and Materials, Sixth Edition* (New York, NY: Foundation Press, 2000), 3.

11. Pember, 37.

12. Ibid., 3.

13. Leonard W. Levy, *Emergence of a Free Press* (New York, NY: Oxford University Press, 1985), 38.

14. Pember, 34, 37.

15. Zelezny, 32–34.

16. Dwight L. Teeter Jr. and Don R. Le Duc, *Law of Mass Communications: Freedom and Control of Print and Broadcast Media* (Westbury, NY: The Foundation Press, 1995), 10.

17. Wagman, 37.

18. Garry Wills, *James Madison* (New York, NY: Times Books, 2002), 39. Madison had thought the Constitution perfect. Then he ran for Congress on a proamendment platform to counter Virginia political foe Patrick Henry's strongly antifederalist platform that called for amendments. Madison would oversee the call for 19 amendments to the U.S. Constitution, 10 of which were ratified.

19. Jeffery A. Smith, *War and Press Freedom: The Problems of Prerogative Power* (New York, NY: Oxford University Press, 1999), 29.

20. Wagman, 40.

21. Franklin, Anderson, and Cate, 3.

22. Wagman, 45.

23. James Morton Smith, *Freedom's Fetters: The Alien and Sedition Laws and American Civil Liberties* (Ithaca, NY: Cornell University Press, 1956), 136.

24. J. A. Smith, 85.

25. Herbert A. Johnson, ed., *The Papers of John Marshall* (Chapel Hill, NC: University of North Carolina Press, 1974), John Marshall to St. George Tucker, 18 November 1800, 6: 14–15.

26. C. G. Remmo, "Freedom of the Press," *Notre Dame Lawyer*, Vol. 20, No. 3, 1944–1945, 316, 318. Jefferson said of the Sedition Act: "I considered and now consider that law to be a nullity, as absolute and as palpable as if Congress had ordered us to fall down and worship a golden image."

27. Franklin, Anderson, and Cate, 3. Also see "An Act in Addition to the Act, Entitled 'An Act for the Punishment of Certain Crimes against the United

States," The Avalon Project [online], New Haven, CT: Yale University Law School, accessed: 12 April 2004; available at: http://www.yale.edu/lawweb/avalon/statutes/sedact.htm.

28. Teeter and Le Duc, 29.

29. Leonard W. Levy, *Emergence of a Free Press* (New York, NY: Oxford University Press, 1985), 309.

30. Levy, 281. Levy writes: "James Madison, the most influential of all the Framers, is possibly the one person of outstanding distinction whose record is clean and consistent [as a libertarian on free expression]."

31. Margaret A. Blanchard, in her essay "Filling in the Void, Speech and Press in State Courts Prior to Gitlow," in Bill Chamberlin and Charlene J. Brown's *The First Amendment Reconsidered* (New York, NY: Longman, 1982), 14–59, shows that states interpreted freedom of the press in the nineteenth century, but she offers no citations from Indiana.

32. Wagman, 46.

33. J. A. Smith, 92–93.

34. Ibid., 92.

35. Ibid.

36. Ibid., 95.

37. Ibid.

38. Ibid., 94.

39. Ibid., 95.

40. Washington, DC, *National Daily Intelligencer*, 25 May 1847.

41. Zachary Taylor to William L. March, 3 March 1847, in 30th Congress, First Session, House Executive Documents, Vol. 7, No. 60, 8–9–810.

42. J. A. Smith, 95.

43. Ibid., 46.

44. Ibid., 93.

45. John W. Burgess, *The Civil War and the Constitution 1859–1865, Volume II* (New York, NY: Charles Scribner's Sons, 1910), 222–223. Postmaster General Montgomery Blair defended the suppression of the New York *Daily News* from entering Philadelphia via the mail in August of 1861 because of the emergency of the rebellion. Blair said no such power existed in peacetime, and he said that only the postmaster general, not any local postmaster, could determine what publications should not be delivered. The House Judiciary Committee investigated Blair and upheld his power, even though that contradicted the wording of the First Amendment.

46. Wendy E. Swanberg, "*Ex Parte McCardle* and the First Amendment during Reconstruction," presented to the Symposium on the 19th Century Press, the Civil War, and Free Expression, University of Tennessee at Chattanooga, November 2006, 3, 29.

47. Timothy B. Tyson, "Time for Truth, 100 Years Later. The Wilmington Riots: How They Shaped North Carolina History," Greensboro, North Carolina, *News & Record*, 19 November 2006, 1, 12.

48. J. A. Smith, 45.

49. Fort Wayne, Indiana, *Dawson's Daily Times & Union*, 26 May 1863.

50. Plymouth, Indiana, *Democrat*, 4 June 1863. See also Article 1, Section 7 from the Declaration of Rights of the Constitution of the Commonwealth of Pennsylvania (http://sites.state.pa.us/PA_Constitution.html), and Article XII of the Constitution of Pennsylvania, 1776 (http://www.yale.edu/lawweb/avalon /states/pa08.htm).

51. J. A. Smith, 115.

52. Mark E. Neely, *The Fate of Liberty: Abraham Lincoln and Civil Liberties* (New York, NY: Oxford University Press, 1991), 68.

53. James Garfield Randall, *Constitutional Problems Under Lincoln* (Urbana, IL: University of Illinois Press, 1964), 178.

54. Ibid., 174.

55. Ibid., 179.

56. Ibid., 180.

57. Ibid., 181.

58. *Ex Parte Milligan*, 71 U.S., 4 Wallace, 1–143, 1866.

59. Randall, 1964, 183.

60. Ibid., 184.

61. Neely, 1991, 223.

62. Paul Finkelman, "Civil Liberties and Civil War: The Great Emancipator as Civil Libertarian," *Michigan Law Review*, Vol. 91, No. 6, May 1993, 1361. Review of Mark E. Neely Jr., *The Fate of Liberty: Abraham Lincoln and Civil Liberties* (New York, NY: Oxford University Press, 1991).

63. Ibid., 1362.

64. Neely, 233.

65. Roy P. Basler, *The Collected Works of Abraham Lincoln* (Piscataway, NJ: Rutgers University Press, 1990), 269. In response to Vallandigham, Lincoln wrote Erastus Corning of New York that the "permanent right" of free expression "suffered no detriment whatever by that conduct of General Jackson or its subsequent approval by the American Congress." See Robert N. Scott, et al., *The War of the Rebellion: A Compilation of the Official Records of the Union and Confederate Armies* (Washington, DC: Government Printing Office, 1899), Series II, Vol. VI, 9.

66. Cincinnati, Ohio, *Commercial*, 23 April 1863.

67. United States Constitution, 1789.

68. Harold L. Nelson, editor, *Freedom of the Press from Hamilton to the Warren Court* (Indianapolis, IN: Bobbs-Merrill, 1967), xxvii.

69. Fredrick Seaton Siebert, *Freedom of the Press in England 1476–1776: The Rise and Decline of Government Controls* (Urbana, IL: University of Illinois Press, 1952), 10.

70. Ronald T. Farrar and John D. Stevens, *Mass Media and the National Experience: Essays in Communication History* (New York, NY: Harper & Row, 1971), 14. Stevens added a second proposition: "The more developed a society, the more subtle will be the controls it exerts on expression" (26). In World War II, the Roosevelt administration developed a highly sophisticated public relations campaign that included an Office of Censorship, led by Byron Price, who opposed prior restraint. A former reporter, columnist, and Associated Press news executive, Price insisted on voluntary self-censorship.

71. Bruce Bigelow and Stephen E. Towne, "Democratic Opposition to the Lincoln Administration in Indiana: The Polls and the Press," *Journal of the Indiana Academy of the Social Sciences*, Vol. 5, October 2001, 78–79. Bigelow and Towne found that violence against Democratic editors was lower in counties with high percentages of descendants from the South in them than in counties with high percentages of descendants from the Northeast. Thus, Democratic editors were more vituperative in counties where Hascall had fewer Republican connections. The presence of a Democratic majority in a county developed a sense of immunity from government constraints.

72. Wagman, 60–65.

73. J. A. Smith, 63. The writ of habeas corpus was effectively suspended during World War II when Japanese Americans were rounded up and placed in concentration camps in the western half of the country. During World War II, Congress passed the Smith Act with almost no resistance from Congress. The Smith Act made it illegal to say or write words that favored the violent overthrow of the U.S. government. Roosevelt quote, in Betty H. Winfield, *FDR and the News Media* (New York, NY: Columbia University Press, 1994), 155.

74. Scott, Series II, Vol. 5, 634.

75. Robert S. Harper, *Lincoln and the Press* (New York, NY: McGraw-Hill, 1951), 242.

76. Michael Kent Curtis, *Free Speech, "The People's Darling Privilege"* (Durham, NC: Duke University Press, 200), 311.

77. Indiana Manuscript Constitution, 1816, Article I, Section 9, Indiana State Library.

78. The New York Constitution says: "Every citizen may freely speak, write, and publish his sentiments on all subjects, being responsible for the abuse of that right; and no law shall be passed to restrain or abridge the liberty of speech, or of the press" (quoted in Blanchard, 18).

79. Blanchard, 18–19. Blanchard notes: "The movement toward this freedom-and-responsibility standard cannot be termed accidental. The same language

appeared in far too many state constitutions to be happenstance." Yet it is also worth noting that the defender of such a press guarantee, James of the New York Supreme Court, wrote his opinion in favor of responsibility in 1804, two years after Thomas Jefferson let the Alien and Sedition acts die out.

80. Alexander Meiklejohn, "The First Amendment Is an Absolute," *The Supreme Court Review*, Philip B. Kurland, ed. (Chicago, IL: University of Chicago Press, 1961), 257.

81. Ibid., 258. Meiklejohn says: "Every citizen . . . may be required to pledge loyalty, and to practice loyalty, to the nation. But his loyalty may never be tested on the grounds of adherence to, or rejection of, any belief. Loyalty does not imply conformity of opinion. Every citizen of the United States has Constitutional authority to approve or to condemn any laws enacted by the Legislature, any actions taken by the Executive, any judgments rendered by the judiciary, any principles established by the Constitution."

82. Siebert, 9.

83. Ibid.

84. Ibid., 10.

85. Ibid.

86. G. R. Tredway, *Democratic Opposition to the Lincoln Administration in Indiana* (Indianapolis, IN: Indiana Historical Bureau, 1973), 26.

87. Richmond, Indiana, *Jeffersonian*, 30 April 1863.

88. Tredway, 27.

89. Ibid., 29–30.

90. Jeffrey Manber and Neil Dahlstrom, *Lincoln's Wrath: Fierce Mobs, Brilliant Scoundrels and a President's Mission to Destroy the Press* (Naperville, IL: Sourcebooks, Inc., 2005), 282.

91. Tredway, 30.

92. Ibid., 29.

93. Ibid., 27.

94. Ibid., 29.

95. Jon Paul Dilts, "Testing Siebert's Proposition in Civil War Indiana," *Journalism Quarterly*, Spring 1986, Vol. 62, No. 12, 368.

96. Tredway, 31.

CHAPTER FOUR

1. Kathleen Enders, "The Press and the Civil War, 1861–1865," in *The Media in America: A History, Fifth Edition*, William David Sloan, ed. (Northport, AL: Vision Press, 2002), 159.

2. Ibid.

3. Richmond, Indiana, *Jeffersonian*, 20 March 1863.

4. Some of the Penny Press publishers became fabulously wealthy. James Gordon Bennett started the New York *Herald* in 1835 with only $1,000 in his pock-

ets, but he was worth $100,000 in the 1840s and was making approximately $80,000 a year in the 1850s. Arunah S. Abell of the Philadelphia *Public Ledger* and Baltimore *Sun* made so much money that he was able to purchase one of the most expensive mansions in Baltimore for just under a half million dollars. Hoosier editors did not become so wealthy. However, both the *Journal* and *State Sentinel* in Indianapolis grew into something other than one-man shops in the 1850s and 1860s, and were among several Indiana newspapers that turned to financial backers, instead of patronage, to develop their capital bases. See Susan Thompson, *The Penny Press: The Origins of the Modern News Media, 1833–1861* (Northport, AL: Vision Press, 2004), 184–185; Mitchell Stephens, *A History of News, Third Edition* (New York, NY: Oxford University Press, 2007), 188.

5. Lorman A. Ratner and Dwight L. Teeter Jr., *Fanatics and Fire-eaters: Newspapers and the Coming of the Civil War* (Urbana, IL: University of Illinois Press, 2003), 13.

6. John W. Miller, *Indiana Newspaper Bibliography* (Indianapolis, IN: Indiana Historical Society, 1982), 38.

7. Enders, 160. The writing was more concise but would still look stilted by 20th- and 21st-century standards. Some Civil War reporting was even poetic. Still, in general, Civil War reporters and editors tended to get to the main point far earlier in a story than had been the case before the war, when overblown prolixity permeated journalism.

8. Ibid. Abolitionist, women's, and other specialty newspapers had already moved to by-lines before the war.

9. Fort Wayne, Indiana, *Dawson's Daily Times & Union*, 13 May 1863.

10. William David Sloan, ed., *The Media in America: A History, Sixth Edition* (Northport, AL: Vision Press, 2005), 165–166.

11. Fort Wayne, Indiana, *Dawson's Daily Times & Union*, 23 May 1863.

12. Miller, 340.

13. Jeffrey Manber and Neil Dahlstrom, *Lincoln's Wrath: Fierce Mobs, Brilliant Scoundrels and a President's Mission to Destroy the Press* (Naperville, IL: Sourcebooks, Inc., 2005), 13. Although he did it surreptitiously, Lincoln financed the *Illinois Staats-Anzieger*. Lincoln bought the German paper in May of 1859, at a cost of four hundred dollars. The Springfield attorney wanted an organ that would deliver his speeches to German immigrants, a growing political bloc. The paper was moved from Alton to Springfield to be closer to its new owner. It was edited by Theodore Canisius, who only had to support the Republicans and print anything Lincoln said or did. Also see Robert S. Harper, *Lincoln and the Press* (New York, NY: McGraw-Hill, 1951), 76–77.

14. Emma Lou Thornbrough, *Indiana in the Civil War Era, 1850–1880* (Indianapolis, IN: Indiana Historical Society, 1995), 672, 679.

15. Ibid., 672.

16. For example, see the Richmond, Indiana, *Jeffersonian* on 7 May 1863.
17. Warsaw, Indiana, *Northern Indianian*, 7 May 1863.
18. Richmond, Indiana, *Jeffersonian*, 21 May 1863.
19. Fort Wayne, Indiana, *Dawson's Daily Times & Union*, 3 June 1863.
20. Ibid., 15 May 1863.
21. Fort Wayne, Indiana, *Daily Gazette*, 9 November 1864.
22. Fort Wayne, Indiana, *Weekly Sentinel*, 4 July 1863.
23. Indianapolis, Indiana, *Journal*, 6 June 1863.
24. Fort Wayne, Indiana, *Weekly Sentinel*, 30 May 1863.
25. Fort Wayne, Indiana, *Dawson's Daily Times & Union*, 6 June 1863.
26. South Bend, Indiana, *St. Joseph County Forum*, 16 May 1863.
27. Richmond, Indiana, *Jeffersonian*, 10 March 1864.
28. Ratner and Teeter, 12.
29. Richmond, Indiana, *Jeffersonian*, 14 May 1863.
30. Douglas, 62.
31. Paul F. Johnson, *A History of the American People* (New York, NY: Harper-Collins, 1997), 318.
32. Tichenor, 5.
33. Emma Lou Thornbrough, *Indiana in the Civil War Era: 1850–1880* (Indianapolis, IN: Indiana Historical Society, 1995), 14.
34. Ronald Lora and William Henry Longton, ed., *The Conservative Press in Eighteenth and Nineteenth Century America* (Westport, CT: Greenwood Press, 1999), 10.
35. Fort Wayne, Indiana, *Dawson's Daily Times & Union*, 4 May 1863.
36. Joyce Appleby and Terence Ball, *Thomas Jefferson, Political Writings* (Cambridge, UK: Cambridge University Press, 1999), 276–277. Letter to William Short, 6 September 1808.
37. Ibid., 273. Letter to Thomas Seymour, 11 September 1807.
38. South Bend, Indiana, *Forum*, 16 May 1863; Indianapolis, Indiana, *Indiana Daily Sentinel*, 9 June 1863.
39. Thomas Jefferson, *Writings* (New York, NY: The Library of America, 1984), 1344–1345.
40. Chicago, Illinois, *Times*, 5 June 1863.
41. Fort Wayne, Indiana, *Dawson's Daily Times & Union*, 2 June 1863.
42. Ibid., 26 May 1863.
43. Ibid., 16 May 1863.
44. Ibid.
45. Klement, 1999, 32.
46. Frank Luther Mott, *American Journalism: A History of Newspapers in the United States through 250 years, 1690 to 1940* (New York, NY: Macmillan, 1941), 180.
47. Jeffery A. Smith, *War and Press Freedom: The Problem of Prerogative Power* (New York, NY: Oxford University Press, 1991), 25.

48. Ibid., 26.

49. Leander J. Monks, *Legal Education in Indiana, Volume II* (Indianapolis, IN: Federal Publishing Company, 1916), 472.

50. Cowden, 214.

51. Dayton, Ohio, *Daily Empire*, 14 April 1863.

52. David R. Roediger, *The Wages of Whiteness, Revised Edition* (New York, NY: Verso, 1991), 43.

53. Klement, 1999, 54.

54. Ibid.

55. Ibid., 48.

56. Harry L. Watson, *Liberty and Power: The Politics of Jacksonian America* (New York, NY: Noonday Press, 1990), 121–122. At a Jefferson birthday dinner in Washington on April 13, 1830, Jackson had followed a speech by states' rights advocate Robert Y. Hayne with the toast, "Our Federal Union. It must be preserved." Vice President John C. Calhoun countered, "The Union, next to our liberties, the most dear."

57. Rushville, Indiana, *Indiana Jacksonian*, 28 October 1852.

58. Ibid.

59. Roediger, 44.

60. Ibid., 45.

61. Ibid., 47.

62. Cited in the Indianapolis, Indiana, *Indiana State Sentinel*, 14 February 1863.

63. Indianapolis, Indiana, *Indiana State Sentinel*, 10 February 1853.

64. Lora and Longton, 73.

65. Ibid., 74.

66. Ibid., 75.

67. Ibid.

68. Ibid., 76.

69. Ibid., 78.

70. Thornbrough, 675.

71. Miller, 211.

72. Thornbrough, 679.

73. Ibid., 683.

74. Ibid., 681. Their circulations did not generate enough revenue. Most papers were weeklies with between 500 and 5,000 readers. Also see the United States Bureau of Census, *Tenth Census*, 1880, VIII, Part 1, 170–171, 181–183.

75. Ratner and Teeter, 18.

76. Ford Risley, "The Confederate Press Association: Cooperative News Reporting of the War," *Civil War History* (Kent, OH: Kent State University Press), Vol. 47, No. 3, September 2001, 222.

77. Miller, 274.

78. Thornbrough, 686.

79. Ibid.

80. Miller, 268.

81. Thornbrough, 686–687.

82. Miller, 6.

83. Hazel Dicken-Garcia, in *The Age of Mass Communication*, William David Sloan, ed. (Northport, AL: Vision Press, 1998), 160.

84. Michael Buchholz, "The Penny Press," in *The Media in America: A History, Fifth Edition*, William David Sloan, ed. (Northport, AL: Vision Press, 2002), 138.

85. J. A. Smith, 100.

86. Ibid.

87. John F. Marszalek, *Sherman's Other War: The General and the Civil War Press* (Kent, OH: Kent State University Press, 1991), 141–163.

88. Smith, 103.

89. Until the Russo-Japanese War of 1904, American reporters faced a low degree of systematic constraints on their activities. The Japanese, though, developed a very structured pool approach that the U.S. federal government studied carefully and began incorporating into its wartime press policies in World War I. See Michael S. Sweeney, *The Military and Press: An Uneasy Truce* (Evanston, IL: Northwestern University Press, 2006), 3–4.

90. Miller, 22, 38, 98, 138, 197, 205, 225, 420, 446, 509.

91. Ibid., 128.

92. J. Cutler Andrews. *The North Reports the Civil War* (Pittsburgh, PA; University of Pittsburgh Press, 1955), 576–577.

93. Goshen, Indiana, *Times*, 2 October 1862.

94. Plymouth, Indiana, Marshall County *Republican*, 6 November 1862. *St. Joseph County Valley Register*, 21 May 1863.

95. Indianapolis, Indiana, *Indiana Daily State Sentinel*, 11 May 1863.

96. Plymouth, Indiana, *Democrat*, 11 June 1863.

97. Fort Wayne, Indiana, *Sentinel*, 14 April 1863.

98. Gilbert R. Tredway, *Democratic Opposition to the Lincoln Administration in Indiana* (Indianapolis, IN: Indiana Historical Bureau, 1973), 41.

99. Alfred Wheeler letter to Schuyler Colfax, Colfax MSS, Lilly Library, Indiana University, Bloomington, IN, 4 March 1860.

100. Thornbrough, 678.

101. Ibid., 676.

102. Ibid.

103. Stephen E. Towne. "Works of Indiscretion: Violence against the Press in Indiana during the Civil War," *Journalism History*, Vol. 31, No. 4 (Fall 2005), 142. Bingham was threatened for what was perceived to be a disloyal editorial on April 18, 1861, and a pro-Union crowd forced him to take the loyalty oath on August 31, 1863.

104. James Madison to N.P. Trist, Montpelier, Virginia, April 23, 1828; quoted in Hazel Dicken-Garcia, *Journalistic Standards in Nineteenth-Century America* (Madison,WI: University of Wisconsin Press, 1989), 102–103.

105. Richmond, Indiana, *Jeffersonian*, 12 March 1863.

106. Ibid., 28 May 1863.

107. Miller, 113.

108. Fort Wayne, Indiana, *Dawson's Daily Times & Union*, 5 May 1863

109. Tredway, 33–34.

110. Miller, 494.

111. Jon Paul Dilts, "Testing Siebert's Proposition in Civil War Indiana," *Journalism Quarterly*, Vol. 63, No. 1 (Spring 1986), 366.

112. Stephen E. Towne, "Killing the Serpent Speedily: Governor Morton, General Hascall, and the Suppression of the Democratic Press in Indiana, 1863," *Civil War History*, Vol. 52, No. 1, 2006, 50 and 56.

113. Towne, 2006, 57.

114. Dilts, 368.

CHAPTER FIVE

1. The figure of 135 comes from Joe Skidmore, "The Copperhead Press and the Civil War," *Journalism Quarterly*, Vol. 16, No. 1, 1939, 349. The figure of 300 comes from Shelby Foote, *The Civil War: A Narrative, Volume Two* (New York, NY: Random House, 1963), 635. Skidmore wrote that there were 360—or more—Peace Democratic papers in the North, though his article does not cite from where he obtained this number, and of those only 225 were "unmolested." Foote wrote: "From start to finish, despite Lincoln's instructions for department commanders to exercise 'great caution, calmness, and forbearance' in the matter, no less than 300 newspapers large and small, including such influential publications as the New York *World*, the Louisville *Courier*, the New Orleans *Crescent*, the Baltimore *Gazette*, and the Philadelphia *Evening Journal*—Democratic all—were suppressed or suspended for a variety of offenses, ranging from the usual 'extension of aid or comfort to the enemy' to the release of a bogus proclamation which had the President calling for '400,000 more.'" The latter refers to General John A. Dix suspending both the New York *World* and *Journal of Commerce* for printing a hoax perpetrated by Joseph Howard of the Brooklyn *Eagle*. See Mott, 351–352. The best overviews of suppression come from Harper, Skidmore, and Mott. The most comprehensive examination of violence and intimidation of the press in a single state comes from Stephen E. Towne, "Works of Indiscretion: Violence Against the Democratic Press in Indiana during the Civil War," *Journalism History*, Vol. 31, No. 13 (Fall 2005), 138–149. It is a published version of his paper delivered at the University of Tennessee at Chattanooga in 2003. His study also includes a list of Republican papers in the state that faced mob violence.

2. New York *Herald*, 28 August 1861.

3. Harold L. Nelson, ed., *Freedom of the Press from Hamilton to the Warren Court* (Indianapolis, IN: Bobbs-Merrill, 1967), 48–49.

4. Robert S. Harper, *Lincoln and the Press* (New York, NY: McGraw-Hill, 1951), 233–235.

5. Skidmore, 349.

6. Harper, 142.

7. *American Annual Cyclopedia and Register of Important Events* (New York, NY: Appleton & Company, 1862), Vol. 1, 328–329.

8. Harper, 143.

9. Ibid., 142.

10. Ibid., 232–233.

11. Miller, 275.

12. Ibid.

13. Tredway, 48.

14. Indianapolis, Indiana, *Daily Sentinel*, 5 January 1863.

15. Indianapolis, Indiana, *Daily Sentinel*, and Indianapolis, Indiana, *Daily Journal*, 2 September 1861.

16. Miller, 8.

17. Towne, 2005, 142.

18. Smith, 105.

19. Robert K. Thorp, "The Copperhead Days of Dennis Mahony," *Journalism Quarterly*, Vol. 43, No. 1, 1966, 680.

20. Ibid., 684.

21. Des Moines *Iowa Daily State Register*, 16 August 1862. Another account of the arrest, from the Davenport *Daily Democrat and News* of 15 August 1862, said the arrest took place at 3 a.m. It reported a "special warrant from the War Department" was issued to Mahony. Hoxie, it must be noted, had been a district court clerk in Des Moines, tavern keeper, Underground Railroad activist, and gold seeker. After the war, he would play a key role in the building of the Union Pacific Railroad across Iowa and was in Utah when the final spike was driven between the Union Pacific and Central Pacific in 1869.

22. Harper, 148–149.

23. Des Moines *Iowa Daily State Register*, 21 August 1862.

24. Edwin M. Stanton letter to H. M. Hoxie, July 26, 1862, cited in John A. Marshall, *American Bastille: A History of the Illegal Arrests and Imprisonment of American Citizens during the Late Civil War* (New York: De Capo Press, 1970), 719–720; also cited in Robert N. Scott et al., editors, *The War of the Rebellion: A Compilation of the Official Records of the Union and Confederate Armies* (Washington, DC: Government Printing Office, 1899), Series III, Vol. 2, 321–322. Stanton had told Hoxie to be vigilant about disloyal persons

in Iowa as early as October of 1861. Stanton was worried about guns and gunpowder being shipped across the southern border to Missouri and eventually to rebels. See Hubert H. Wubben, *Civil War Iowa and the Copperhead Movement* (Ames, IA: Iowa State University Press, 1980), 53. Hoxie arrested George Frane of Rochester in October of 1861. He opposed abolitionists' attempt to enroll a black child in school. Later, Hoxie arrested William Hill of Magnolia who had written to a newspaper in Virginia criticizing abolitionists and indicated that western Iowa would supply troops to the Union Army. Stanton believed Hill was a spy. He was eventually freed after taking the loyalty oath and agreeing not to sue Hoxie at a later date.

25. Edwin M. Stanton, "Executive Order in relation to State Prisoners, No. 1," 14 February 1862.

26. Harper, 149.

27. Mahony called his arrest a kidnapping in *The Prisoner of State* (New York, NY: Carleton, 1863), 117. Months after his August arrest, Mahony came to the conclusion that he should have resisted Hoxie. In his book *The Prisoner of State*, he remarks: "I blame myself as well as others for having submitted as I did to be taken from my home by Marshal Hoxie without making some effort, even though it should have been unsuccessful to preserve my personal rights as an American citizen. Had I shot him down, or any one of the party who accompanied him, I would have only performed my duty and exercised my inalienable and constitutional rights as an American." Mahony does not make reference to what constitutional right would allow a citizen to shoot an officer of the federal government.

28. Mahony, 129.

29. Ibid.

30. Dubuque *Herald*, 15 August 1862.

31. In his study of Mahony, Skidmore says, "No one editorial outburst brought the authorities to Mahony's door. . . . It was, rather, almost two years of editorial hammering, his leadership of the Dubuque and Iowa Democrats, and the order of Secretary Stanton" (681). There is no specific reference to Mahony's discouraging enlistments.

32. F. T. Oldt, editor, *History of Dubuque County, Iowa* (Chicago, IL: Goodspeed, 1911), 355.

33. Hubert H. Wubben, "Dennis Mahony and the Dubuque Herald, 1860–1863," *Iowa Journal of History*, Vol. 56, No. 4 (October 1958), 300. Later, Mahony would come to see the draft as unconstitutional. See Dubuque *Herald*, 25 April 1863.

34. Dubuque *Herald*, 7 May 1862.

35. Des Moines *Iowa Daily State Register*, 16 August 1862.

36. Des Moines *Iowa Daily State Register*, 16 August 1862.

37. Fairfield *Weekly Ledger*, 14 August 1862.
38. David L. Lendt, "Demise of the Democracy: The Copperhead Press in Iowa, 1856–1870) master's thesis, Iowa State University, 1971, 78. George W. Jones wrote the letters to Jefferson Davis in 1860 while the former served as a minister to Columbia. Jones expressed sympathy for Davis and the South but urged the preservation of the Union.
39. Lendt, 79. Also joining the Confederate Army was the son of Stephen Hemstead, Iowa's second governor.
40. Fairfield *Weekly Ledger*, 14 August 1862.
41. Burlington *Hawkeye* quoted in the *Iowa Daily State Register*, 2 September 1862.
42. Des Moines *Iowa Daily State Register*, 21 August 1862.
43. Burlington *Argus*, 16 September 1862.
44. Des Moines *Iowa Daily State Register*, 24 August 1862. The *Register* writer asked tongue in cheek, "What would have become of the country if MAHONY had forgotten to send that message?"
45. Dubuque *Herald*, 14 August 1862; Dennis A. Mahony, *The Prisoner of State* (New York: Carleton, 1863), 122.
46. Dubuque *Herald* quoted in the Des Moines *Iowa Daily State Register*, 21 August 1862.
47. Ibid.
48. Des Moines *Iowa Daily State Register*, 21 August 1862.
49. Dubuque *Herald* article quoted in Des Moines *Iowa Daily State Register*, 20 September 1862.
50. Mahony, 169–170.
51. Davenport *Daily Democrat and News*, 23 September 1862.
52. Russell L. Johnson, *Warriors into Workers: The Civil War and the Formation of Urban-Industrial Society in a Northern City* (New York, NY: Fordham University Press, 2003), 79.
53. Wubben, 1958, 303.
54. Des Moines *Iowa Daily State Register*, 26 August 1862.
55. Ibid.
56. Ibid. Also see Wubben, 1958. 303.
57. Fairfield *Weekly Ledger*, 4 September 1862.
58. Chicago *Tribune* paraphrased in Des Moines *Iowa Daily State Register*, 5 September 1862.
59. Chicago *Times* quoted in the Davenport *Daily Democrat and News*, 27 August 1863.
60. Dubuque *Herald*, 7 October 1862.
61. Allison served in the U.S. House of Representatives from 1863 to 1871, then served in the Senate from 1873 until 1908. He was a candidate for the Repub-

lican nomination for president twice. He also defeated Mahony for the Third District seat in 1864.

62. Des Moines *Iowa Daily State Register*, 18 November 1862.

63. Burlington *Hawkeye*, 18 October 1862.

64. Paul S. Pierce, "Congressional Districting in Iowa," *Iowa Journal of History and Politics*, Vol. 1 (July 1903), 341–343.

65. Dubuque *Herald*, 26 October 1862.

66. Martin Edward McGrane, "Dubuque—Editorial Battleground 1860–1862," master's thesis, Iowa State University, Ames, Iowa, 1972, 90.

67. Wubben, 1958, 307. Illinois Judges John H. Mulkey and Andrew D. Duff, also imprisoned in Washington, took the same oath as Mahony and Sheward, pledging not to file future suits against government officials over the arrest.

68. McGrane, 90–91. The estimated crowd for Mahony's return to Dubuque was in the thousands.

69. Wubben, 1958, 313.

70. New York *Caucasian*, 2 May 1863.

71. Dubuque *Times*, 18 July 1863. Mahony would file a libel suit against the *Times*, but a grand jury failed to indict the editor, G. T. Stewart.

72. Canton, Ohio, *Stark County Democrat*, quoted in the Goshen, Indiana, *Democrat*, 29 October 1862.

73. Paul Finkelman, "Civil Liberties and Civil War: The Great Emancipator as Civil Libertarian," *Michigan Law Review*, Vol. 91, No. 6, 1993, 1376; review of *The Fate of Liberty: Abraham Lincoln and Civil Liberties* by Mark E. Neely, Jr.

74. Ibid., 229.

75. Miller, 462.

76. Ibid. Cookerly's paper, destroyed by Union soldiers on October 21, 1861, was suspended for two months, and he sold it in 1862.

77. Ibid., 432.

78. Ibid.

79. Ibid.

80. Ibid.

81. Harper, 232–233.

82. Ibid., 232.

83. J. A. Smith, 99–100.

84. Chicago *Times*, 7 May 1863.

85. Ibid., 16 February 1863.

86. John D. Barnhart, "The Impact of the Civil War on Indiana," *Indiana Magazine of History*, Vol. 57, No. 3 (September 1961), 212.

87. Harper, 231–233. Lincoln barred California papers from the mails, and Brigadier General George Wright ordered the stoppage of mail delivery of Democratic newspapers in Oregon.

Chapter Six

1. Some Peace Democrats did prefer a divided country, and some wanted to let the Northeast go and to unite with the South to form a new confederation.

2. John D. Barnhart, "The Impact of Civil War on Indiana," *Indiana Magazine of History*, Vol. 57, No. 3 (September 1961), 187–188.

3. Ibid., 188.

4. Joseph E. Stevens, *1863: The Rebirth of a Nation* (New York, NY: Bantam Books, 1999), 73. Clement L. Vallandigham was best known for the phrase, but Daniel W. Voorhees, the Indiana Congressman, picked it up and it spread to the Democratic editors of the state.

5. Gilbert R. Tredway, *Democratic Opposition to the Lincoln Administration* (Indianapolis, IN: Indiana Historical Bureau, 1973), 60.

6. Indianapolis, Indiana, *Indiana Daily State Sentinel*, 10 May 1861.

7. Emma Lou Thornbrough, *Indiana in the Civil War Era, 1850–1880* (Indianapolis, IN: Indiana Historical Society, 1995), 3.

8. Indiana *Senate Journal*, 1849–1850, 15.

9. Thornbrough, 97.

10. Kenneth M. Stampp, *Indiana Politics During the Civil War* (Indianapolis, IN: Indiana Historical Bureau, 1949), 51.

11. Indianapolis, Indiana, *Indiana Journal*, 10 November 1860.

12. Israel George Blake, *The Holmans of Veraestau* (Oxford, OH: University of Miami Press, 1943), 94–96.

13. Tredway, 70–71.

14. Indianapolis, Indiana, *Indiana State Sentinel*, 24 June 1862.

15. Voorhees beat the anticompensation theme often. One such speech came in the U.S. House of Representatives on February 23, 1863. See Charles S. Voorhees, ed., *Speeches of Daniel W. Voorhees of Indiana, Embracing His Most Prominent Forensic, Political, Occasional, and Literary Addresses* (Cincinnati, OH: Robert Clarke & Co., Printers, 1875), 115–116.

16. James M. McPherson, *Ordeal by Fire: The Civil War and Reconstruction* (Boston, MA: McGraw Hill, 2001), 383. McPherson, in footnote 42 on 306, says that 2.1 million served in the Union Army and Navy. The 189,000 black soldiers and sailors made up 9 percent of the total—but that would have been 22 percent of the CSA military force.

17. Quoted in Doris Kearns Goodwin, *Team of Rivals: The Political Genius of Abraham Lincoln* (New York, NY: Simon & Schuster, 2005), 502. See Oliver P. Morton to Edwin M. Stanton, 9 February 1863, reel 3, Stanton Papers, DLC.

18. Infoplease.com, "Composition of Congress by Political Party" [online]: accessed: March 17, 2003; available at: http://www.infoplease.com/ipa/A0774721.html. Also see James G. Randall and Herbert David Donald, *The Civil War and Reconstruction, Second Edition* (Lexington, MA: D.C. Heath

and Company, 1969), 458. Randall and Donald say the Republican majority went from 64 to 27.

19. Frank L. Klement. *Lincoln's Critics: The Copperheads of the North* (Shippensburg, PA: White Mane Books, 1999), 95–96.

20. Technically, the Republican Party did not exist during the war. At the outset, Governor Morton appealed to Democrats to join him in a single political party for the duration of the war. This became Indiana's Union Party.

21. Barnhart, 198.

22. Thornbrough, 676.

23. Barnhart, 200.

24. Tredway, 27.

25. Ibid., 27–28.

26. Cannelton, Indiana, *Reporter*, 19 December 1862.

27. Stewart Sifakis, *Who Was Who in the Civil War* (New York, NY: Facts on File Publications, 1988), 290.

28. Gil Hinshaw, "From 10,500 Battles: A Handbook of Civil War Engagements" (Hobbs, NM: Superior Printing Company, 1996), 30.

29. Dell, 214.

30. W. H. H. Terrell, *Indiana in the War of the Rebellion: Report of the Adjutant General* (Indianapolis, IN: Indiana Historical Bureau, 1960), 50. By Terrell's computations, Indiana contributed 8,008 men more than was called for by the August 4, 1862, call from the president.

31. Fort Wayne, Indiana, *Sentinel*, 11 March 1863.

32. Christopher Dell, *Lincoln and the War Democrats: The Grand Erosion of Conservative Tradition* (Rutherford, NJ: Fairleigh Dickinson University Press, 1975), 214.

33. Tredway, 15.

34. Ibid., 16.

35. Ibid., 15.

36. Indianapolis, Indiana, *Indiana State Sentinel*, 24 September 1862.

37. Barnhart, 198.

38. Stampp, 99.

39. Barnhart, 204.

40. Ibid., 98. The federal government began to organize black troops in May of 1863. Indiana did not begin raising black troops until November 30, 1863, five months after Hascall's reign as federal commander of the District of Indiana.

41. Indianapolis, Indiana, *Daily Journal*, 28 February 1863.

42. Donna Lee Dickerson, *The Course of Tolerance: Freedom of the Press in Nineteenth-Century America* (Westport, CT: Greenwood, 1990), 166. Chris A. Paterson, "Transference of Frames in Global Television," in Stephen D. Reese *et al., Framing Public Life* (Mahwah, NJ: Elbaum, 2001), 341.

43. Ibid., 1990, 166.

44. Robert M. Entman, "Framing: Toward Clarification of a Fractured Paradigm," *Journal of Communication*, Vol. 43, No. 4, 1993, 52.

45. Ibid.

46. Ibid., 55.

47. Charlotte Ryan, *Prime Time Activism: Media Strategies for Grassroots Organizing* (Boston, MA: South End Press, 1991), 73.

48. Hinshaw, 26.

49. Frank L. Klement, "Catholics as Copperheads during the Civil War," *Catholic Historical Review*, Vol. 80, No. 1 (January 1994), 37.

50. Dell, 214. The Democrats conveniently forgot that state conscription had been employed in the War of 1812.

51. Fort Wayne, Indiana, *Sentinel*, 23 September 1862.

52. Goshen, Indiana, *Times,* 2 October 1862.

53. Ibid., 8 January 1863.

54. Ibid., 2 October 1862.

55. Ibid.

56. Marshall County, Indiana, *Republican*, 8 January 1863.

57. Plymouth, Indiana, *Republican*, 15 January 1863.

58. South Bend, Indiana, *St. Joseph Valley Register*, 8 January 1863.

59. Logansport, Indiana, *Journal*, 27 September 1862.

60. Ibid.

61. Ibid.

62. Ibid.

63. John W. Miller, *Indiana Newspaper Bibliography* (Indianapolis, IN: Indiana Historical Society, 1982), 276.

64. Ibid.

65. Indianapolis, Indiana, *Indiana Journal*, 5 January 1863.

66. Ibid.

67. Goshen, Indiana, *Times,* 8 January 1863.

68. Indianapolis, Indiana, *Daily Journal*, 10 October 1862.

69. Stampp, 147. Caleb B. Smith was Lincoln's Secretary of the Interior from 1861 to 1863. Joseph A. Wright was one of Indiana's two U.S. Senators in 1862–1863. Appointed by Governor Oliver P. Morton, Wright replaced long-time political rival Jesse D. Bright, expelled from the U.S. Senate for allegedly expressing sympathy for Jefferson Davis.

70. Indianapolis, Indiana, *Indiana State Sentinel*, 17 July 1862.

71. Evansville, Indiana, *Weekly Gazette*, 14 October 1862.

72. Jeffery A. Smith, *War and Press Freedom: The Problem of Prerogative Power* (Cary, NC: Oxford University Press, 1999), 115. Congress went along with Lincoln and passed the Habeas Corpus Act in March 1863.

73. Plymouth, Indiana, *Democrat*, 2 October 1862.

74. Plymouth, Indiana, *Democrat*, 2 October 1862. "Would my word free the slaves when I cannot even enforce the Constitution in the rebel States," Lincoln asked. Lincoln also worried about the fate of freed blacks in the South after the war.

75. Plymouth, Indiana, *Democrat*, 2 October 1862.

76. Goshen, Indiana, *Democrat*, 24 September 1862.

77. Ibid., 24 October 1862.

78. Ibid., 7 January 1863.

79. Plymouth, Indiana, *Democrat*, 30 October 1862.

80. Fort Wayne, Indiana, *Sentinel*, 23 September 1862.

81. Ibid.

82. Logansport, Indiana, *Democratic Pharos*, 7 January 1863.

83. Ibid.

84. Ibid., 8 October 1862.

85. Ibid.

86. Ibid., 16 January 1863.

87. The vote was 116 to 4.

88. Delphi, Indiana, *Weekly Times*, 4 October 1862.

89. Ibid.

90. Indianapolis, Indiana, *Indiana State Sentinel*, 24 September 1862.

91. Hazel Dicken-Garcia, Giovanna Dell'Orto, and Brian Gabrial, "'Grossly Assailed by a Maniacal Press': James Gordon Bennett, Emancipation, and Press Freedom," unpublished paper, 2005, 20.

92. McPherson, 2001, 493.

93. Ibid., 515.

94. William J. Small, *Political Power and the Press* (New York, NY: W. W. Norton & Company, 1972), 71.

CHAPTER SEVEN

1. W. H. H. Terrell, *Indiana in the War of the Rebellion: Report of the Adjutant General* (Indianapolis, IN: Indiana Historical Bureau, 1960), 6.

2. Milo Smith Hascall, "Report" to W. H. H. Terrell (Indianapolis, IN: Indiana State Archives, Commission on Public Records), 1.

3. Goshen, Indiana, *Times*, 25 April 1861.

4. Milo Smith Hascall, "Autobiography," Indiana State Archives, Indianapolis, Indiana, undated, 2.

5. Terrell, 12.

6. Goshen, Indiana, *Times*, 18 April 1861.

7. Ibid.

8. A history of the Goshen *Democrat* appears in the "News Printing Company, Incorporated," http://www.indianahistory.org/HBR/business_pdf/news_printing .pdf. Accessed: December 21, 2006. Also see John W. Miller, *Indiana*

Newspaper Bibliography (Indianapolis, IN: Indiana Historical Society, 1982), 97–98.

9. Goshen, Indiana, *Times*, 30 January 1862.

10. Ibid.

11. Ibid., 13 February 1862.

12. Ibid.

13. Ibid., 24 April 1862.

14. Ibid.

15. Ibid., 5 June 1862.

16. Ibid.

17. It is not clear why Melvin B. Hascall resigned from the army. His wife, Mary Euphemia Moore Hascall, had accompanied him to the front, but their 2-year-old daughter Kate Vesta Hascall was sickly. She would die on October 17, 1863, and nephew Jerome Hascall Chamberlain observed in a letter to his sister "Molly," Mary Henriette Chamberlain Grosh, that "Uncle Mell has gone to drinking again." See Jerome Hascall Chamberlain to Mary Henriette Chamberlain Grosh, Nov. 19, 1863, Bentley Family Papers, MS-720, Box 1, Folder 12, Center for Archival Collections, Jerome Library, Bowling Green State University, Bowling Green, Ohio.

18. Goshen, Indiana, *Times*, 3 July 1862.

19. John D. Barnhart, "The Impact of the Civil War on Indiana," *Indiana Magazine of History*, Vol. 57, No. 3 (September 1961), 197.

20. Goshen, Indiana, *Times*, 30 October 1862.

21. Reprinted in the Goshen, Indiana, *Times*, 30 October 1862.

22. Barnhart, 195.

23. Gil Hinshaw, "From 10,500 Battles: A Handbook of Civil War Engagements" (Hobbs, NM: Superior Printing Company, 1996), 30.

24. Goshen, Indiana, *Times*, 12 February 1863.

25. Robert S. Harper, *Lincoln and the Press* (New York, NY: McGraw-Hill, 1951), 252.

26. Goshen, Indiana, *Times*, 5 March 1863.

27. United States Bureau of the Census, *Tenth Census* (1880), I, 5.

28. Ibid., I, 388–389.

29. The District of Indiana included all the counties in the Hoosier State, and Hascall had his command in Indianapolis. It was part of the Department of the Ohio, which included Ohio, Indiana, Michigan, Kentucky, and Illinois. In June of 1863, Indiana and Michigan would be combined into one district. These districts gave the Union military a presence in the North. The army protected key cities, attempted to round up deserters and wayward Confederate prisoners, and maintain civic order.

30. Hascall, "Autobiography," 7.

31. Hascall, "Report," 3.

32. Goshen, Indiana, *Times*, 5 March 1863.

33. Hascall, "Autobiography," 7.

34. Goshen, Indiana, *Times*, 5 March 1863.

35. Hascall, "Report," 3.

36. Ibid.

37. Indianapolis, Indiana, *Daily Journal*, 14 April 1863.

38. Ibid., 20 April 1863.

39. Hascall, "Report," 3.

40. Indianapolis, Indiana, *Daily Journal*, 23 April 1863.

41. Hascall, "Report," 3.

42. Indianapolis, Indiana, *Weekly Indiana State Sentinel*, 29 April 1863.

43. Ibid.

44. Goshen, Indiana, *Times*, 30 April 1863.

45. Ibid.

46. Richmond *Jeffersonian*, 30 April 1863.

47. Ibid.

48. Ibid.

49. Ibid.

50. Indianapolis, Indiana, *Weekly Indiana State Sentinel*, 6 May 1863.

51. Ibid.

52. Plymouth, Indiana, *Democrat*, 14 May 1863.

53. Cannelton, Indiana, *Reporter*, 22 May 1863.

54. Ibid., 29 May 1863.

55. Ibid.

56. Ibid., 5 June 1863.

57. Hascall, "Report," 4.

58. Barnhart, 200.

59. Goshen, Indiana, *Times*, 18 June 1863, proclamation by Gov. Oliver P. Morton, dated 11 June 1863.

60. Ibid.

61. William Marvel, *Burnside* (Chapel Hill, NC: University of North Carolina Press, 1991), 232.

62. Plymouth *Weekly Democrat*, 16 April 1863.

63. Ibid., 23 April 1863.

64. Terrell, 353–359.

65. James L. Vallandigham, *A Life of Clement L. Vallandigham* (Baltimore, MD: Turnbull Brothers, 1872), 55–60.

66. Frank L. Klement, *The Limits of Dissent* (Lexington, KY: University Press of Kentucky, 1970), 151.

67. Robert S. Harper, *Lincoln and the Press* (New York, NY: McGraw-Hill, 1951), 241.

68. Carl M. Becker, "Newspapers in Battle: The *Dayton Empire* and the *Dayton Journal* During the Civil War," *Ohio History: The Scholarly Journal of the Ohio Historical Society*, Vol. 99 (Winter-Spring) 1990, 44.

69. Dayton, Ohio, *Daily Journal*, 19 May 1863.
70. James M. McPherson, *Battle Cry of Freedom: The Civil War Era* (New York, NY: Ballantine Books, 1988), 597.
71. Ibid., 598.
72. Harper, 251.
73. Ibid., 252.
74. Robert N. Scott, et al., eds., *The War of the Rebellion: A Compilation of the Official Records of the Union and Confederate Armies* (Washington, DC: Government Printing Office, 1891), Series II, Vol. V, 725.
75. Indianapolis, Indiana, *Daily State Sentinel*, 18 May 1863.
76. Miller, 402.
77. John B. Stoll, *History of Indiana From Its Exploration to 1922; Also an Account of St. Joseph County from Its Organization* (Dayton, OH: Dayton Historical Publishing, 1922), 151.
78. *The War of the Rebellion*, Series II, Vol. V, 725.
79. Vincennes, Indiana, *Western Star*, 16 May 1863.
80. Fort Wayne, Indiana, *Dawson's Daily Times & Union*, 13 May 1863.
81. *The War of the Rebellion*, Series II, Vol. V, 725–726.
82. Indianapolis, Indiana, *Daily State Sentinel*, 26 May 1863.
83. Ibid.
84. Ibid.
85. Miller, 373.
86. Stephen E. Towne, "Killing the Serpent Speedily: Governor Morton, General Hascall, and the Suppression of the Democratic Press in Indiana, 1863," *Civil War History*, Vol. 52, No. 1, 2006, 51. Towne says that VanValkenbugh's April 30 editorial probably produced the offending words, in that the Plymouth editor called the general a braying donkey who had no jurisdiction over the citizens of Indiana.
87. Goshen, Indiana, *Times*, 14 May 1863.
88. Ibid., 21 May 1863.
89. Indianapolis, Indiana, *Daily State Sentinel*, 19 May 1863.
90. Ibid.
91. Ibid.
92. *The War of the Rebellion*, Series II, Vol. V, 724.
93. Ibid., 723–726.
94. Towne, 2006, 49.
95. Chicago, Illinois, *Times*, 1 June 1863.
96. *The War of the Rebellion*, Series II, Vol. V, 726.
97. Jeffery A. Smith, *War and Press Freedom: The Problem of Prerogative Power* (New York: Oxford University Press, 1999), 115.
98. New York *Times*, 13 June 1863, 4.
99. Smith, 116.

100. Columbia City, Indiana, *News*, 6 June 1863.
101. Plymouth *Weekly Democrat*, 21 May 1863.
102. Ibid., 28 May 1863.
103. Goshen, Indiana, *Times*, 4 June 1863.
104. Ibid.

CHAPTER EIGHT

1. Robert N. Scott, et al., eds., *The War of the Rebellion: A Compilation of the Official Records of the Union and Confederate Armies* (Washington, DC: Government Printing Office, 1899), Series II, Vol. 5, 634.
2. Robert S. Harper, *Lincoln and the Press* (New York, NY: McGraw-Hill, 1951), 242.
3. Michael Kent Curtis, *Free Speech, "The People's Darling Privilege": Struggles for Freedom of Expression in American History* (Durham, NC: Duke University Press, 2000), 311.
4. Chicago, Illinois, *Times*, 20 May 1863.
5. Ibid.
6. Fort Wayne, Indiana, *Dawson's Daily Times & Union*, 27 May 1863.
7. Harper, 245.
8. South Bend, Indiana, *St. Joseph County Register*, 21 May 1863. The *Register* also reported that the South Bend *Forum* was on shaky financial grounds, although it offered no proof.
9. Logansport, Indiana, *Journal*, 28 February 1863.
10. No evidence exists to suggest that Democratic editors met May 20 in Indianapolis at the mass meeting in the state capital. Yet many Democratic editors attended the mass meeting and they almost certainly exchanged opinions about and strategies for dealing with Hascall and General Order No. 9.
11. Frank L. Klement, *The Limits of Dissent* (Lexington, KY: University Press of Kentucky, 1970), 180.
12. Indianapolis, Indiana, *Indiana Daily State Sentinel*, 20 May 1863.
13. Ibid., 25 May 1863.
14. David Herbert Donald, *Lincoln* (London: Jonathan Cape, 1995), 441.
15. Gideon Welles, *Diary of Gideon Welles* (New York: W. W. Norton, 1911), 321–322. Burnside's friend Rev. Augustus Woodbury also had some reservations about the arrest and conviction of Vallandigham along constitutional lines.
16. David Williams, *A People's History of the Civil War: Struggles for the Meaning of Freedom* (New York, NY: The New Press, 2005), 258. *Ex parte Merryman*, 17 F. Cas. 144 (1861).
17. Klement, 1970, 175; Williams, 258.
18. New York *Times*, 23 June 1863.
19. Ibid.
20. Ibid., 15 May 1863.

21. Ibid., 13 June 1863.

22. Jennifer L. Weber, *Copperheads: The Rise and Fall of Lincoln's Opponents in the North* (New York, NY: Oxford University Press, 2006), 99.

23. Mark E. Neely Jr., *The Union Divided: Party Conflict in the Civil War North* (Cambridge, MA: Harvard University Press, 2002), 93.

24. Robert Allen Rutland, *James Madison: The Founding Father* (Columbia, MO: University of Missouri Press, 1987), 162–163. Madison held that the press had an unlimited right to criticize officeholders of all ranks. It is assumed this would include military personnel, who represent the executive branch. The Democratic editors of Indiana also could have used Madison's separation-of-powers argument against Burnside and Hascall. Madison, in analyzing the Alien and Sedition acts, said they gave the president both legislative and judicial powers.

25. James Madison, "Address to the People," Jan. 23, 1799, quoted in Merrill D. Peterson, ed., *James Madison: A Biography in His Own Words* (New York, NY: Harper & Row, 1974), 225–226.

26. Goshen, Indiana, *Times*, 4 June 1863.

27. Logansport, Indiana, *Journal*, 28 February 1863.

28. Ibid.

29. Ibid., 16 May 1863.

30. Delphi, Indiana, *Journal*, 20 May 1863.

31. Marshall County, Indiana, *Republican*, 14 May 1863.

32. Ibid.

33. Ibid., 11 June 1863.

34. South Bend, Indiana, *St. Joseph Valley Register*, 21 May 1863.

35. Warsaw, Indiana, *Northern Indianian*, 21 May 1863.

36. Greencastle, Indiana, *Putnam Banner Republican*, 21 May 1863. The Greencastle newspaper reprinted an editorial by the Indianapolis *Journal*. Supreme Court Chief Justice William Rehnquist, who studied civil liberties cases during the Civil War in depth, said Lincoln could not by any manner or means be described as a supporter of civil rights. The goal of accomplishing military political objectives outweighed individual civil liberties in the Civil War. Rehnquist said courts may be better off not considering suppression-writ cases until a war had ended. See Rehnquist's remarks to the Indiana University School of Law, Bloomington, Indiana. October 28, 1996.

37. Isaac Blackford, *Report of Cases Argued and Determined in the Supreme Court of the Judicature of the State of Indiana* (Indianapolis, IN: Bowen-Merrill, 1890), 574–575.

38. Ibid., 575.

39. Albert G. Porter, *Indiana Reports of Cases Argued and Determined in the Supreme Court of the Judicature of the State of Indiana* (Indianapolis, IN: Bowen-Merrill, 1886), 376.

40. Ibid.
41. Ibid., 378.
42. Samuel E. Perkins, "Speech of Judge Perkins at Mass Meeting Held at Richmond, Indiana, 25 September 1860," pamphlet, no date, no printer.
43. Quoted in Emma Lou Thornbrough, "Judge Perkins, the Indiana Supreme Court, and the Civil War," *Indiana Magazine of History*, Vol. 60, No. 1 (March 1964), 82.
44. Fort Wayne, Indiana, *Sentinel*, 10 June 1863.
45. Stephen E. Towne, "Killing the Serpent Speedily: Governor Morton, General Hascall, and the Suppression of the Democratic Press in Indiana, 1863," *Civil War History*, Vol. 52, No. 1, 2006, 61.
46. Goshen, Indiana, *Democrat*, 24 July 1862; Goshen, Indiana, *Democrat*, 7 January 1863.
47. Goshen, Indiana, *Democrat*, 20 May 1863.
48. Columbia City, Indiana, *News*, 21 May 1863.
49. Ibid.
50. Indianapolis, Indiana, *Indiana Daily State Sentinel*, 6 May 1863
51. Ibid., 13 May 1863.
52. Neely, 118. Neely observed: "With the possible exception of the depth of Confederate resolve, nothing shaped the Civil War more than the United States Constitution. For the war effort, the most important provisions were Article II, section 1, establishing the four-year term for the president, and Article, section 2, making the president the commander-in-chief of the army and navy." The U.S. system calls for four-year terms for the president, who can only be recalled by an impeachment process that requires two-thirds of senators to vote for removal. There are no calls for election such as those that exist in parliamentary systems or no recalls as is the case for the chief executive of some states.
53. Stephen W. Sears, *Chancellorsville* (Boston, MA: Houghton Mifflin, 1996), 1–4. Desertions in general during the war were amazingly high, probably more than 200,000 for the four years. Low pay—$11 to $16 a month—and late pay combined with the high carnage rate, bureaucratic incompetence, lack of arms and other materials, excessive marching, weather-related illnesses, over-extended service, monotony in the camps, and panic on the eve of battle contributed to the desertion rate. See James G. Randall and David Herbert Donald, *The Civil War and Reconstruction, Second Edition* (Lexington, MA: D.C. Heath, 1969), 329–331. Also see Sears, 17. Sears shows that the Emancipation Proclamation ran off many Union soldiers in the winter of 1863.
54. Joseph E. Stevens, *1863: The Rebirth of a Nation* (New York, NY: Bantam, 1999), 173. General Joseph Hooker rejuvenated the Army of the Potomac by increasing discipline, granting furloughs, and instilling pride by giving each corps its own special insignia badge.

55. Goshen, Indiana, *Democrat*, 13 May 1863.

56. Stevens, 109. Stevens believes Burnside attempted "to rebuild his reputation" as the commander of the Department of the Ohio. It is reasonable to assert that Burnside's zealousness in pursuing dissidents in Ohio was a personal attempt to overcome his recent past and prove his worth to Lincoln and his fellows in the military.

57. William Marvel, *Burnside* (Chapel Hill, NC: University of North Carolina Press, 1991), 222.

58. James M. McPherson, *Battle Cry of Freedom: The Civil War Era* (New York, NY: Ballantine Books, 1988), 596. Faced with calls for peace and moves for the legislatures to take over the state militias, the governors of Indiana and Illinois closed down their capitols. Indiana's Oliver P. Morton told Republican legislators to take the rest of the war off, and the Democrats were left without a quorum to stay open. He ran the government on private funds for the duration of the war. Illinois' Richard Yates, with the tacit approval of the White House, closed the legislature in Springfield in June of 1863. Press suppression in such an atmosphere does not seem like such a major issue.

59. Towne, 2006, 57.

60. Columbia City, Indiana, *News*, 21 May, 1863.

61. Ibid.

62. Indianapolis, Indiana, *Indiana Daily State Sentinel*, 13 May 1863.

63. McPherson, 1988, 596. Not only did Morton create a private treasury to run the state government by borrowing from banks and businesses, he also drew on a special service fund in the U.S. War Department for approximately $250,000.

64. Columbia City, Indiana, *News*, 21 May 1863.

65. New York *Times*, 18 May 1863.

66. *Valley of the Upper Maumee River, with Historical Account of Allen county and the City of Fort Wayne, Indiana. The Story of its Progress From Savagery to Civilization, Volume II* (Madison, WI: Brant and Fuller, 1889), 63–66. Edgerton's law background was more impressive than Hascall's. Edgerton's father, Bela Edgerton, had been educated at Middlebury College and served as an attorney and magistrate in Clinton County, New York. Joseph K. Edgerton attended the public schools of Clinton County and then Plattsburg Academy. In addition to reading law with William Swetland in Plattsburg, he later became "a student in the law office of Dudley Selden and James Mowatt" in New York, New York, and was admitted to the New York bar in 1839. He practiced law in New York for five years before moving to Fort Wayne in 1844.

67. Indianapolis, Indiana, *Indiana Weekly State Sentinel*, 18 May 1863.

68. Fort Wayne, Indiana, *Dawson's Daily Times & Union*, 18 May 1863.

69. Ibid.

70. Ibid.

71. Ibid.
72. Ibid.
73. Evansville, Indiana, *Weekly Gazette*, 9 May 1863.
74. Ibid.
75. Fort Wayne, Indiana, *Dawson's Daily Times & Union*, 18 May 1863.
76. Towne, 2006, 57.
77. Ibid., 58.
78. Ibid.
79. Scott, *War of the Rebellion*, Series II, Vol. 5, 664–665.
80. Delphi, Indiana, *Times*, 30 May 1863, quoting the *Indiana State Sentinel*.
81. Indianapolis, Indiana, *Daily Journal*, 28 April 1863.
82. Gilbert R. Tredway, *Democratic Opposition to the Lincoln Administration in Indiana* (Indianapolis, IN: Indiana Historical Bureau, 1973), 27.
83. Harper, 230.
84. Columbia City, Indiana, *News*, 21 May 1863.
85. Richmond, Indiana, *Jeffersonian*, 30 April 1863.
86. Harper, 142; 232; 234.
87. Indianapolis, Indiana, *Daily State Sentinel*, 15 May 1863.
88. Lincoln was one of only four presidents in U.S. history to grant the military the power to suspend newspaper publication—the others were James K. Polk in the Mexican War, Franklin D. Roosevelt in World War II, and George W. Bush in the Iraq War, though none suspended U.S. newspapers. Under Polk, U.S. officers suspended Mexican and Texas newspapers, but Texas was not in the Union yet. Roosevelt allowed newspapers in Japanese-American concentration camps to be censored or suppressed, thus violating Blackstone's no prior restraint principle. Bush's underlings had two Iraqi newspapers and two Arab television networks suspended during the Iraq War.
89. Scott, *War of the Rebellion*, 1899, Series II, Vol. V, 724.
90. Craig D. Tenney, "Major General A.E. Burnside and the First Amendment: A Case Study of Civil War Freedom of Expression," Dissertation. Indiana University, Bloomington, IN, 1977, 173.
91. Scott, *War of the Rebellion*, 1899, Series II, Vol. V, 664–65.

CHAPTER NINE

1. Indianapolis, Indiana, *Daily State Sentinel*, 8 June 1863.
2. Indianapolis, Indiana, *Daily Journal*, 8 June 1863.
3. Ibid.
4. Ibid.
5. Milo S. Hascall, "Report" to Indiana Adjutant General W. H. H. Terrell, Indiana State Archives, Commission on Public Records, Indianapolis, IN, undated.
6. Ibid.
7. Ibid.

8. Ibid.

9. Stephen E. Towne, "Works of Indiscretion: Violence against the Press in Indiana during the Civil War," *Journalism History*, Vol. 31, No. 3, Fall 2005, 142.

10. Ibid., 13.

11. Ibid., 14.

12. Ibid.

13. Robert S. Harper, *Lincoln and the Press* (New York, NY: McGraw-Hill, 1951), 231–232.

14. *Congressional Globe*, Thirty-Eighth Congress, First Session, 1506, 1864.

15. *The War of Rebellion*, Series II, Volume V, 759.

16. Marvel, 238.

17. Plymouth *Democrat*, 28 May 1863.

18. Reprinted in the Indianapolis, Indiana, *Weekly Indiana State Sentinel*, 15 June 1863.

19. Ibid.

20. Indianapolis, Indiana, *Weekly Indiana State Sentinel*, 8 June 1863.

21. Milo S. Hascall to Ambrose E. Burnside, *Burnside Papers*, Record Group 94, Box 25, National Archives, Washington, DC.

22. Ambrose E. Burnside to Milo S. Hascall, Order Book, 86, Department of the Ohio, March through June 1863, Ambrose Everts Burnside Collection, Rhode Island State Historical Society, Manuscripts Division, Providence, Rhode Island.

23. Chicago, Illinois, *Times*, 19 May 1863.

24. John B. Stoll, *History of Indiana from Its Exploration to 1922; Also an Account of St. Joseph County from Its Organization* (Dayton, OH: Dayton Historical Publishing Company, 1922), 151. D. C. Rush purchased the St. Joseph County *Forum* in November of 1866 and installed Edward Molloy as editor.

25. John W. Miller, *Indiana Newspaper Bibliography* (Indianapolis, IN: Indiana Historical Society, 1982), 401–402. Molloy, who had been a Union soldier, began to edit the *Forum* in 1866 and bought it in 1867, when he changed the title to *The National Union*. The *Forum* operated in one of the hotbeds of Republicanism in the state in South Bend. Congressman Schuyler Colfax had owned the *St. Joseph County Register* before the war and continued to assert influence on editor Alfred Wheeler during the war. It must also be noted Storey began his journalism career in St. Joseph County, at the *Mishawaka Tocsin*.

26. Chicago, Illinois, *Times*, 19 May 1863.

27. Ibid.

28. Ibid., 21 May 1863.

29. Ibid., 22 May 1863.

30. Ibid., 27 May 1863.

31. *The War of the Rebellion*, Series I, Vol. 23, 369. The Davis-to-Stanton letter is dated May 27, 1863.

32. Gilbert R. Tredway, *Democratic Opposition to the Lincoln Administration in Indiana* (Indianapolis, IN: Indiana Historical Bureau, 1973), 273.

33. Craig D. Tenney, "Major General A.E. Burnside and the First Amendment: A Case Study of Civil War Freedom of Expression," Doctoral dissertation, Indiana University, Bloomington, Indiana, 1977, 189.

34. Roy Basler, ed., *The Collected Works of Abraham Lincoln* (New Brunswick, NJ: Rutgers University Press, 1953), Vol. 6, 237.

35. Scott, *The War of the Rebellion*, Series II, Vol. 5, 717. The letter is dated May 29, 1863.

36. Ibid., 723.

37. Journalist William H. Smith recounted that Morton wanted Stanton to allow incapacitated Indiana soldiers to be moved from the western front to hospitals back home. Stanton refused before Morton appealed to Lincoln, who overruled the Secretary of War. It is not clear when this occurred, but the incident shows how forceful Morton could be. See New York *Herald-Tribune*, 7 February 1932.

38. Ibid., 723–724. The letter is dated June 1, 1863.

39. Ibid., 723–724.

40. Robert G. Scott, ed., *Forgotten Valor: The Memoirs, Journals, and Civil War Letters of Orlando B. Willcox* (Kent, OH: Kent State University Press, 1999), 392.

41. Harper, 258.

42. Ibid., 259.

43. Tenney, 198.

44. Harper, 259.

45. Chicago, Illinois, *Tribune*, 4 June 1863.

46. Harper, 259.

47. Chicago, Illinois, *Tribune*, 4 June 1863.

48. Harper, 260.

49. New York *Times*, 13 June 1863.

50. Quoted in the Richmond, Indiana, *Jeffersonian*, 18 June 1863.

51. Harper, 260, and Chicago *Times*, 5 June 1863.

52. Chicago *Times*, 5 June 1863.

53. Ibid., 260.

54. Jeffery A. Smith, *War and Press Freedom: The Problem of Prerogative Power* (New York, NY: Oxford University Press, 1999), 116.

55. Harper, 261.

56. Chicago *Times*, 5 June 1863.

57. Ibid.

58. Chicago *Tribune*, 5 June 1863.

59. Ibid.

60. Philip Kinsley, *The Chicago Tribune*, Volume I (New York, NY: Knopf, 1943), 275.

61. Milo S. Hascall to Ambrose E. Burnside, Burnside Papers, Box 25.

62. Scott, *War of the Rebellion*, Series II, Vol. 5, 759.

63. Columbia City, Indiana, *News*, 6 June 1863.

64. Carl M. Becker, "Newspapers in Battle: The *Dayton Empire* and the *Dayton Journal* During the Civil War," *Ohio History: The Scholarly Journal of the Ohio Historical Society*, Vol. 99 (1990), 37.

65. Ibid., 41.

66. Dayton, Ohio, *Journal*, 17 April 1863.

67. Dayton, Ohio, *Daily Empire*, 23 April 1863.

68. Vallandigham, 252.

69. Frank L. Klement, *The Limits of Dissent: Clement L. Vallandigham and the Civil War* (Lexington, KY: University of Kentucky Press, 1970), 153.

70. Klement, 1970, 154.

71. *Frank Leslie's Illustrated Newspaper*, 23 May 1863, 130.

72. Klement, 1970, 154.

73. Dayton, Ohio, *Daily Empire*, 5 May 1863.

74. Ibid.

75. Ibid.

76. Klement, 1970, 160.

77. Harper, 241.

78. *Frank Leslie's Illustrated Newspaper*, 23 May 1863, 130.

79. Becker, 44. Also see Harper, 241.

80. Dayton, Ohio, *Journal*, 6 May 1863

81. Ibid., 16 May 1863.

82. Ibid., 18 May 1863.

83. Harper, 248.

84. Ibid., 249.

85. Scott, *War of the Rebellion*, Series II, Vol. 5, 476.

86. Tenney, 234.

87. Harper, 254–255.

88. Ibid., 232.

89. Towne, 2005, 142.

90. Jeffrey Manber and Neil Dahlstrom, *Lincoln's Wrath: Fierce Mobs, Brilliant Scoundrels and a President's Mission to Destroy the Press* (Naperville, IL: Sourcebooks Inc., 2005), 291–292.

91. New York *Times*, 9 June 1863.

92. Ibid.

93. Tenney, 236; New York *Times*, 9 June 1863. It is not clear who J. Beach of the New York *Sun* was. At the time, Moses S. Beach and Alfred E. Beach were editors of the *Sun*.

94. New York *Herald*, 9 June 1863.

95. Cincinnati, Ohio, *Enquirer*, 23 January 1862.

96. J. A. Smith, 101.
97. Ibid., 100.
98. Fort Wayne, Indiana, *Dawson's Daily Times & Union*, 9 June 1863.
99. New York *Times*, 9 June 1863.
100. Robert C. Williams, *Horace Greeley: Champion of American Freedom* (New York, NY: New York University Press, 2006), 230.
101. New York *Daily Tribune*, 9 June 1863.
102. New York *Times*, 9 June 1863.
103. New York *World*, 9 June 1863.
104. Fort Wayne, Indiana, *Dawson's Daily Times & Union*, 9 June 1863.
105. Mark E. Neely Jr., *The Union Divided: Party Conflict in the Civil War North* (Cambridge, MA: Harvard University Press, 2002), 101.
106. Williams, 229.
107. Towne, 2005, 142.
108. Abraham Lincoln to Ambrose E. Burnside, in Roy P. Basler, ed., *The Collected Works of Abraham Lincoln* (New Brunswick, NJ: Rutgers University Press, 1953), 237.
109. W. H. H. Terrell, *Indiana in the War of the Rebellion: Report of the Adjutant General, A Reprint of Volume One of the Eight-Volume Report Prepared by W.H.H. Terrell and Published in 1869* (Indianapolis, IN: Indiana Historical Bureau, 1960), 359–360. One of the murdered draft officers was State Senator J. Frank Stevens of Manilla, Indiana.
110. Ibid., 360–361.
111. Towne, 2005, 142.
112. Kenneth M. Stampp, *Indiana Politics during the Civil War* (Indianapolis, IN: Indiana Historical Bureau, 1949), 226.
113. Delaware County, Indiana, *Free Press*, 24 March 1864.
114. Ibid., 17 March 1864.
115. Towne, 2005, 143.
116. Delaware County, Indiana, *Free Press*, 31 March 1864.
117. William Marvel, *Burnside* (Chapel Hill, NC: University of North Carolina Press, 1991), 245.
118. Tredway, 274.
119. See Oliver P. Morton MSS, 1862–1863, Manuscript Division, Indiana State Library, Indianapolis, Indiana. Morton wrote an open letter to Lincoln on October 17, 1863, in a Washington, DC, newspaper saying: "In my opinion, if our arms do not make great progress within the next sixty days our cause will be almost lost."
120. Ibid.
121. Scott, *War of the Rebellion*, Series II, Vol. 6, 6. One of the attendees who signed the resolutions was Erastus Corning.
122. Ibid., 8.

123. Indianapolis, Indiana, *Daily Journal*, 24 March 1864.

124. Roy P. Basler, ed., *Works of Abraham Lincoln, Volume VI*, Abraham Lincoln to John M. Schofield, 1 October 1863.

125. Smith, 93.

126. Ibid.

127. Scott, *War of the Rebellion*, Series II, Vol. 5, 363–367. An Indianapolis grand jury investigating secret societies in the summer of 1862 put the number of Knights of the Golden Circle in the state at 15,000. See Tredway, 115. The grand jury indicted sixteen men, but not a single one was convicted.

128. New Albany, Indiana, *Ledger*, 8 July 1863.

129. Scott, *War of the Rebellion*, Series III, Vol. 3, 371.

130. Goshen, Indiana, *Times*, 2 July 1863.

131. Hascall, "Report," 6.

132. Ibid., 4.

133. Goshen, Indiana, *Times*, 24 November 1864.

134. After Milo S. Hascall's mother Phoebe died on October 17, 1852, Amasa Hascall remarried—to her cousin, Vesta G. Alderman. Franklin Hascall was born to Amasa and Vesta Hascall on August 12, 1846.

135. Goshen, Indiana, *News*, 8 March 1990. The *Democrat* became the Goshen *News-Times and Democrat* in 1933. Frank L. Hascall shortened the title to the Goshen *News* in 1954.

136. Marvel, 335–336.

137. Miller, 302.

138. Plymouth, Indiana, *Marshall County Republican*, 4 June 1863.

139. John D. Barnhart, "The Impact of the Civil War on Indiana," *Indiana Magazine of History*, Vol. 57, No. 3 (Sept. 1961), 210.

CHAPTER TEN

1.   Charles Kettleborough, *Constitution Making in Indiana, Volume I* (Indianapolis, IN: Indiana Historical Collections, Indiana Historical Society, 1916), 296.

2.   Robert S. Harper, *Lincoln and the Press* (New York, NY: McGraw-Hill, 1951), 130–132. The House Judiciary Committee investigated press complaints of censorship the winter of 1861–1862. The committee concluded that censorship of the telegraph occurred and resolved that "the government shall not interfere with free transmission of intelligence by telegraph, when the same will not aid the enemy in his military of naval operations, or give him information concerning such operations on the part of the government, except when it may become necessary for the government, under the authority of Congress, to assume exclusive control of the telegraph for its own legitimate purpose, or to assert the right of priority in the transmission of its own dispatches."

3. Michael Kent Curtis, *Free Speech, "The People's Darling Privilege": Struggles for Freedom of Expression in American History* (Durham, NC: Duke University Press, 2000), 356.

4. Thomas Paine, *Common Sense, Rights of Man, and other Essential Writings of Thomas Paine* (New York, NY: Signet Classic, 2003), 217–218.

5. Thomas Jefferson to Benjamin Rush, September 23, 1800, from Thomas Jefferson, *The Life and Selected Writings of Thomas Jefferson*, Adrienne Koch and William Harwood Peden, eds. (New York, NY: The Modern Library, Random House, 1944), 558.

6. As James G. Randall and David Herbert Donald observed about the political fortunes of the war: "Many who voted for Lincoln in 1864 were supporting with some reluctance a party which was being transformed contrary to their desires. This transformation of the Republican party and its attainment of dominating power was one of the major political developments of American history." See James G. Randall and David Henry Donald, *The Civil War and Reconstruction, Second Edition* (Lexington, MA: D.C. Heath and Company, 1969), 454.

7. Charles Fairman, *History of the Supreme Court of the United States, Volume VI, Reconstruction and Reunion, 1864–88, Part One* (New York, NY: Macmillan, 1971), 458–459.

8. Goshen, Indiana, *Times*, 18 April 1861.

9. A Republican like Milo Hascall helping a Democratic newspaper in times of financial need was not unique. Schuyler Colfax, the owner of the *St. Joseph Valley Register* and a Republican politician, had provided modest financial support to the *Indiana State Sentinel* in Indianapolis after that paper had been destroyed by fire in 1857. See Willard H. Smith, *Schuyler Colfax: The Changing Fortunes of a Political Idol* (Indianapolis, IN: Indiana Historical Bureau, 1952), 88.

10. Emma Lou Thornbrough, *Indiana in the Civil War Era, 1850–1880* (Indianapolis, IN: Indiana Historical Society, 1995), 677.

11. Richard H. Abbott, "Civil War Origins of the Southern Republican Press," *Civil War History*, Vol. 43, No. 1, 41–42. Burnside installed George Mills Joy, a sergeant in the Union Army from Massachusetts, to edit the New Bern *Daily Progress*. Previously, the paper had been a pro-secession paper. It supported Lincoln and North Carolina loyalist Edward Stanly, though for a time it opposed abolition. Joy was able to earn a federal government printing contract with the help of Lincoln's Secretary of State, William H. Seward. In the fall of 1863, Joy renamed the newspaper the *North Carolina Times* and became an advocate for emancipation.

12. For further information about soldiers' newspapers in the Civil War, see Wallace B. Eberhard's "Editors in Uniform: The Historiography of Civil War Soldier Newspapers," presented to the Symposium on the 19th Century Press,

the Civil War, and Free Expression, University of Tennessee at Chattanooga, November 11, 2006.

13. Robert N. Scott, et al., eds., *The War of the Rebellion: A Compilation of the Official Records of the Union and Confederate Armies* (Washington, DC: Government Printing Office, 1891), Series III, Vol. 3, 385.

14. Harper, 212.

15. Ibid., 327.

16. Cincinnati, Ohio, *Gazette*, 19 March 1863.

17. Harper, 226.

18. David Herbert Donald, *Lincoln Reconsidered: Essays on the Civil War, Third Edition* (New York, NY: Vintage Books, 2001), 134.

19. Abraham Lincoln to William Herndon, February 15, 1848. Cited in Jeffery A. Smith, *War and Press Freedom: The Problem of Prerogative Power* (New York, NY: Oxford University Press, 1999), 94.

20. Ibid., 132.

21. Ibid.

22. Upton Sinclair to Woodrow Wilson, October 22, 1917, in Arthur S. Link, ed., *The Papers of Woodrow Wilson* (Princeton, NJ: Princeton University Press, 1966–1994), Vol. 44, 467–472. Cited in J. A. Smith, 133.

23. Goshen, Indiana, *News*, 8 March 1990.

24. "CPJ Troubled by Closure of Newspaper," Committee to Protect Journalists, 29 March 2004.

25. Brian Katulis, "Freedom of the Press 2004: A Global Survey of Media Independence," Karin Deutsch Karlekar, editor, Freedom House, New York, 22.

26. Ibid.

27. "Protests as U.S. closes Iraqi paper," CNN.com, 28 March 2004. Accessed: June 15, 2005.

28. Katulis, 23.

29. Anthony Shadid, "Iraqi Council Halts Arab TV Network's News Broadcasts," Washington *Post*, 25 November 2003.

30. "U.S. Administration Bans Iraqi Shi'ite Newspaper," *Reuters*, 28 March 2004.

31. Naomi Klein, "You Can't Bomb Beliefs," *The Nation*, 18 October 2004.

32. George Packer, *The Assassins' Gate* (New York, NY: Farrar, Straus and Giroux, 2005), 322.

33. "CPJ Troubled by Closure of Newspaper," Committee to Protect Journalists, 29 March 2004.

34. L. Paul Bremer III, *My Year in Iraq: The Struggle to Build a Future of Hope* (New York, NY: Simon & Schuster, 2006), 313.

35. L. Paul Bremer III, letter to *Al Hawza*, reprinted March 28, 2004 by Reuters.

36. Packer, 322.

37. Bremer, 313.

38. Katulis, 23.

39. "CPJ Troubled by Closure of Newspaper," Committee to Protect Journalists, 29 March 2004. The Coalition Provisional Authority also cited on August 2003 article in *Al Hawza* that said the United States was waging a war on Islam and that the Western superpower was more interested in stealing Iraqi oil than deposing Saddam Hussein. Also see Nir Rosen, "U.S. newspaper ban plays into cleric's hands," *Asia Times*, 30 March 2004.

40. Nir Rosen, "U.S. newspaper ban plays into cleric's hands," *Asia Times*, 30 March 2004.

41. Ibid.

42. "American seen as imperial power in Iraq," *The Irish Times*, 30 December 2004.

43. Rosen.

44. Baghdad, Iraq, *Al Hawza*, 24 February 2004. The Sadr-backed paper was in particular incensed at the backing the CPA-sponsored elections received from religious authorities.

45. Rosen.

46. *Al Zawra*, BBC Monitoring, 29 March 2004.

47. Rohan Jayasekera, "A Parting Gift of a Poisoned Chalice in Iraq?" Media Conflict Prevention and Reconstruction, United Nations Educational, Scientific, and Cultural Organization, 2004, 84.

48. Packer, 312. A warrant was made for Sadr's arrest in the Khoei murder, but the CPA kept it sealed and never acted upon it. The U.S. military repeatedly had plans in place to arrest or murder Sadr, but the CPA would not allow them to be carried out. See Thomas E. Ricks, *Fiasco: The American Military Adventure in Iraq* (New York, NY: Penguin Press, 2006), 336.

49. "A Limitless Inferno," Worldpress.org, April 3, 2004. Online: http://www.worldpress.org/print_article.cfm?article_id=196&don't=yes. Accessed: September 10, 2005.

50. *Al Dustur*, 6 January 2005.

51. *Al Basa'ir*, 6 January 2005.

52. *Al-Mu'tamar*, 6 January 2005.

53. The exact number of protestors the day after closing is unclear. Jonathan Steele, writing for the *Guardian*, reported the number of protestors to be in the hundreds. CNN reported thousands of protestors, as did Nir Rosen writing in *Asia Times* and a report from the television network Aljazeera.

54. "Iraqi Cleric Al-Sadr's Supporters Protest Closure of Al-Hawzah Newspaper," Aljazeera, BBC Monitoring, 28 March 2004.

55. Klein.

56. Nermeen Al-Mufti, "Free to be like U.S.," Cairo, Egypt, *Al-Ahram*, 14 April 2004, No. 685.

57. Washington *Post* quoted in "Homefront Confidential: How the War on Terrorism Affects Access to Information and the Public's Right to Know," The Reporters' Committee for Freedom of the Press, September 2004, 17.

58. Packer, 295.

59. Floyd Abrams, *Newsday*, 30 March 2004. On the same day, the New York *Times* wrote: "Newspapers like *Al Hawza* do not create the hostility Americans face in Iraq—they reflect it. Shutting them down, however satisfying it may feel to the Bush administration, is not a promising way to dissolve that hostility."

60. "How to drive Iraqi dissent underground," San Diego *Union-Tribune*, 31 March 2004.

61. "Anti-American news silenced in Iraq," Miami *Herald*, 30 March 2004.

62. ASNE letter to Donald Rumsfeld about *Al Hawza*, 31 March 2004, www.asne. org/index.cfm?ID=5135. Accessed: September 11, 2005.

63. "A free press in Iraq," San Francisco *Chronicle*, 5 April 2004.

64. Jonathan Steele, "Pro-Sadr weekly newspaper reopens in Iraq," Manchester, England, *Guardian*, 19 July 2004.

65. Ian Fisher, "Newspaper reopens after U.S. shutdown," New York *Times*, 19 July 2004.

66. "Iraqi Shi'ii Leader Al-Hakim Criticizes Coalition Closure of Newspapers," Al-Manar Television, Beirut, Lebanon, BBC Monitoring, April 5, 2004. Al-Sayyid Abd-al-Aziz al-Hakim was head of the Supreme Council for Islamic Revolution in Iraq.

67. Al-Mufti.

68. Richmond, Virginia, *Examiner*, 3 February 1862.

69. New York *World*, 9 June 1863.

70. Quoted in Richard Carwardine, *Lincoln: A Life of Purpose and Power* (New York, NY: Alfred A. Knopf, 2003), 258.

CHAPTER ELEVEN

1. Craig D. Tenney, "Major General A.E. Burnside and the First Amendment: A Case Study of Civil War Freedom of Expression," Dissertation (Bloomington, IN: Indiana University School of Journalism, 1977), 228.

2. Jon Paul Dilts, "Testing Siebert's Proposition in Civil War Indiana," *Journalism Quarterly* 63, no. 1 (1986), 368.

3. Towne, "Works of Indiscretion: Violence Against the Democratic Press in Indiana during the Civil War," *Journalism History*, Vol. 31, No. 3, 2005, 144.

4. Harper. His 1951 study is the basis for this entire vein of historic research on Union press suppression in the Civil War. It is clear now that Harper's examination was a first foray into the subject and that the degree of press suppression in the North was more intense than his study reveals.

5. Towne, 2005, 147.

6. Bruce Bigelow and Stephen E. Towne, "Democratic Opposition to the Lincoln Administration in Indiana: The Polls and the Press," *Journal of the Indiana Academy of the Social Sciences*, Vol. 5 (October 2001), 71–81.

7. Stephen E. Towne, "West Point Letters of Milo S. Hascall, 1848–1850," *Indiana Magazine of History*, Vol. XC, No. 3 (September 1994), 278–294.

8. W. H. H. Terrell, *Indiana in the War of Rebellion: Report of the Adjutant General, A Reprint of Volume One of the Eight-Volume Report Prepared by W.H.H. Terrell and Published in 1869* (Indianapolis, IN: Indiana Historical Bureau, 1960). Terrell's report describes the development of the militia and the draft in the state. It is a one-sided, pro-Morton document that portrays dissidence and antiwar sentiment in broad terms.

9. Charles E. Canup, "Conscription and Draft in Indiana," *Indiana Magazine of History*, Vol. 10, No. 2 (June 1914), 70–83.

10. John D. Barnhart, "The Impact of the Civil War on Indiana," *Indiana Magazine of History*, Vol. 57, No. 3 (September 1961), 185–224.

11. Kenneth M. Stampp, *Indiana Politics During the Civil War* (Indianapolis, IN: Indiana Historical Bureau, 1949).

12. Emma Lou Thornbrough, *Indiana in the Civil War Era, 1850–80* (Indianapolis, IN: Indiana Historical Society, 1995).

13. Gilbert R. Tredway, *Democratic Opposition to the Lincoln Administration* (Indianapolis, IN: Indiana Historical Bureau, 1973).

14. Edward C. Smith, *The Borderland in the Civil War* (New York, NY: AMS Press, 1970).

15. John W. Miller, *Indiana Newspaper Bibliography* (Indianapolis, IN: Indiana Historical Society, 1982).

16. William Wesley Wollen, "The Indiana Press of the Olden Time," *Biographical and Historical Sketches of Early Indiana* (Indianapolis, IN: Hammond and Company, 1883), 538–559.

17. Donald V. Carmony, "Highlights in Indiana Newspaper History," *The Indiana Publisher*, Vol. 9, No. 1 (December 1944), 3, 6.

18. Norm Jean Thiele, "A History of the Fort Wayne News-Sentinel," M.A. thesis, Indiana University, Bloomington, Indiana, 1958.

19. James H. Butler, "Journalism in Indiana," *Indiana Magazine of History*, Vol. 22, No. 3 (September 1926), 297–333.

20. Bentley Family Papers, Center for Archives Collection, Jerome Library, Bowling Green State University, Bowling Green, Ohio, MS-720.

21. Wilber L. Stonex, "Salem Bank of Goshen, Indiana," *Indiana Magazine of History*, Vol. 23, No. 1, 1927, 83–91.

22. Frank Smith Bogardus, "Daniel W. Voorhees," *Indiana Magazine of History*, Vol. 27, 1931, 91–103.

23. Emma Lou Thornbrough, "Judge Perkins, the Indiana Supreme Court, and the Civil War," *Indiana Magazine of History*, Vol. 60, No. 1 (March 1964), 79–96.

24. Bruce Bigelow, "The Clash of Culture: Border Southerners and Yankees in Antebellum Indiana," *Journal of the Indiana Academy of the Social Sciences*, Vol. 2, 1998, 1–8.

25. David Herbert Donald, *Lincoln* (London: Jonathan Cape. London. 1995).

26. James G. Randall, *Lincoln the President: Midstream* (Binghamton, NY: Vail-Ballou Press, Inc., 1952).

27. William Marvel, *Burnside* (Chapel Hill, NC: University of North Carolina Press, 1991).

28. Stephen W. Sears, *Chancellorsville* (Boston, MA: Houghton Mifflin, 1996).

29. Ibid., 1–25. Brigadier generals John Newton and John Cochrane visited President Lincoln on December 30, 1862, on behalf of Major generals William Franklin and William Smith. Newton and Cochrane told Lincoln that Major General Ambrose E. Burnside, who had replaced General George B. McClellan as commander of the Army of the Potomac, could not possibly succeed leading the Union's most important army. Both feared that a repeat of Fredericksburg was not just possible but probable, and that it would be the destruction of the Northern army. Lincoln listened carefully and did nothing. He left Burnside in power, for the time being. A month later, after an unsuccessful attempt to reengage the Confederates, Burnside was relieved of his command and replaced, not by McClellan, but by Joseph Hooker. Before he stepped down, Burnside had both Newton and Cochrane dismissed from the Army of the Potomac. Newton was reassigned to the Florida Keys, and Newton, a Democratic politician from New York before the war, resigned and went home to resume his political career.

30. Joseph E. Stevens, *1863: The Rebirth of a Nation* (New York, NY: Bantam Books, 1999).

31. Ibid., 110.

32. James L. Vallandigham, *A Life of Clement L. Vallandigham* (Baltimore, MD: Turnbull Brothers, 1872).

33. William V. McPherson, "Clement Laird Vallandigham: The Forgotten Radical," M.A. thesis (Warrensburg, MO: Central Missouri State University, 1993).

34. Robert C. Cheeks, "Clement Laird Vallandigham: American Constitutionalist," *Southern Partisan*, Winter 2001.

35. Carl M. Becker, "Newspapers in Battle: The Dayton Empire and the Dayton Journal During the Civil War," *Ohio History: The Scholarly Journal of the Ohio Historical Society*, Vol. 99, Winter-Spring 1990, 29–50.

36. Frank L. Klement, *The Limits of Dissent* (Lexington, KY: University Press of Kentucky, 1970).

37. Frank L. Klement, *Lincoln's Critics* (Shippensburg, PA: White Mane Books, 1999).

38. Frank L. Klement, *The Copperheads of the Middle West* (Chicago, IL: University of Chicago Press, 1960). Klement's book opened a vein of revision-

ism about Civil War dissidence in the North. It showed that Democrats in Ohio, Indiana, and Illinois had policy differences with Republicans that were not treasonous but politics as usual—in wartime. For example, Hoosier antipathy for increased federalism, in the form of taxation, conscription, and emancipation, was not simply going to disappear because a war was under way. Klement also brought to light Burnside's intimidation of the electoral process in Kentucky, an even more serious offense than the suppression and intimidation of the press in Ohio, Indiana, and Illinois. In several Kentucky precincts, military officials literally prevented citizens who were unlikely to vote Republican from casting their ballots.

39. Robert N. Scott, et al., *The War of the Rebellion: A Compilation of the Official Records of the Union and Confederate Armies* (Washington, DC: Government Printing Office, 1899).

40. Gil Hinshaw, "From 10,500 Battles: A Handbook of Civil War Engagements" (Hobbs, NM: Superior Printing Company, 1996).

41. James M. McPherson, *Antietam: The Battle Changed That Course of the Civil War* (New York, NY: Oxford University Press, 2002).

42. James M. McPherson, *Battle Cry of Freedom: The Civil War Era* (New York, NY: Ballantine Books, 1988).

43. James M. McPherson, *Ordeal by Fire: The Civil War and Reconstruction, Third Edition* (New York, NY: McGraw-Hill, 2001).

44. David Herbert Donald and James G. Randall, *The Civil War and Reconstruction, Second Edition* (Lexington, MA: Heath, 1969).

45. Christopher Dell, *Lincoln and the War Democrats: The Grand Erosion of Conservative Tradition* (Rutherford, NJ: Fairleigh Dickinson University Press, 1975).

46. Mildred C. Stoler, "Influence of the Democratic Element in the Republican Party of Illinois and Indiana, 1854–1860," Doctoral dissertation, Indiana University, Bloomington, Indiana, 1938.

47. Kevin Phillips, *The Cousins' War: Religion, Politics, and the Triumph of Anglo-America* (New York, NY: Basic Books, 1999).

48. Robert S. Harper, *Lincoln and the Press* (New York, NY: McGraw-Hill, 1951).

49. David B. Sachsman, Kittrell Rushing, and Debra Reddin van Tuyll, *The Civil War and the Press* (New Brunswick, NJ: Transaction Publishers, 2000).

50. Justin E. Walsh, *To Print the News and Raise Hell! A Biography of Wilbur F. Storey* (Chapel Hill , NC: University of North Carolina Press, 1968). The story of Storey is his development as an editor in northwest Indiana and in Michigan. In 1839, the nineteen-year-old Storey criticized a La Porte, Indiana, judge, who countered with the threat of verbal chastisement. It was the first brush Storey had with a government official, and it was far from the last.

51. Patricia Towery, "Censorship of South Carolina Newspapers, 1861–1865," In James B. Meriweather, ed., *South Carolina Journals and Journalism* (Spartanburg, SC: The Reprint Co. Publishers, 1975), 147–160; Richard B. Kielbowicz,

"The Telegraph, Censorship and Politics at the Outset of the Civil War," *Civil War History*, Vol. 40, 1995, 95–118; Horace W. Raper, "William W. Holden and the Peace Movement in North Carolina," *North Carolina Historical Review*, Vol. 31, 1954, 493–516; Horace W. Raper, "William W. Holden: North Carolina's Political Enigma," James Spunt Studies in History and Political Science, Vol. 59 (Chapel Hill, NC: University of North Carolina Press, 1985); Richard Reid, "William W. Holden and Disloyalty in the Civil War," *Canadian Journal of History*, Vol. 20 (April 1985), 23–44; and Carl R. Osthaus, *Partisans of the Southern Press: Editorial Spokesmen of the Nineteenth Century* (Lexington, KY: University of Kentucky Press, 1994).

52. Hazel Dicken Garcia, *Journalistic Standards in Nineteenth Century America* (Madison, WI: University of Wisconsin Press, 1989).

53. Edwin Emery and Michael Emery, *The Press and America, Seventh Edition: An Interpretive History of the Mass Media* (Englewood Cliffs, NJ: Prentice Hall, 1992).

54. Frederic Hudson, *Journalism in the United States* (New York, NY: Harper's, 1873).

55. J. Cutler Andrews, *The North Reports the Civil War* (Pittsburgh, PA: University of Pittsburgh Press, 1955).

56. Marvel, 159–160. Burnside generally liked most people, but he did not like Joseph Hooker because the latter had a tendency to criticize openly those above him—a no-no in the world of the military. It was also personal between Burnside and Hooker, going back to the battle of South Mountain when one of Burnside's best men, Jesse Reno, had been killed in part because Hooker was slow to move when called upon by Burnside. Hooker also was reluctant to hold a position at Fredericksburg and rode back to tell Burnside his view of the situation. This was based in large part on the wholesale slaughter of Northern troops Hooker had witnessed at Marye's Heights. Hooker would decide the city could not be defended by the Army of the Potomac. Burnside agreed. Later, in late January of 1863, Burnside would hand Lincoln and ultimatum: either Hooker goes or Burnside goes. The president chose to remove Burnside and elevate Hooker to commander of the Army of the Potomac.

57. Joseph J. Mathews, *Reporting the Wars* (Minneapolis, MN: University of Minnesota Press, 1957).

58. Frank Luther Mott, *American Journalism, A History: 1690–1960, Third Edition* (New York, NY: Macmillan, 1962).

59. John F. Marszalek, *Sherman's Other War: The General and Civil War Press* (Memphis, TN: Memphis State University Press, 1981).

60. Louis M. Starr, *Bohemian Brigade: Civil War Newsmen in Action* (New York, NY: Alfred A. Knopf, 1954).

61. Jeffery A. Smith, *War and Press Freedom: The Problem of Prerogative Power* (Cary, NC: Oxford University Press, 1999).

62. David M. Rabban, *Free Speech in Its Forgotten Years* (New York, NY: Cambridge University Press, 1997); Geoffrey R. Stone, *Perilous Times: Free Speech in Wartime, From the Sedition Act of 1798 to the War on Terrorism* (New York, NY: W. W. Norton & Company, 2004); Michael S. Sweeney, *The Military and the Press: An Uneasy Truce* (Evanston, IL: Northwestern University Press, 2006).

63. Michael Kent Curtis, *Free Speech, "The People's Darling Privilege"* (Durham, NC: Duke University Press, 2000).

64. Michael Kent Curtis, "Democratic Ideals and Media Realities: A Puzzling Free Press Paradox," *Social Philosophy and Policy*, Vol. 21, No. 2 (July 2004), 287.

65. Fredrick Seaton Siebert, *Freedom of the Press in England 1476–1776: The Rise and Decline of Government Controls* (Champaign-Urbana, IL: University of Illinois Press, 1952).

66. Thomas Carleton Hanson, "Press Freedom and War Restraints: Siebert's Proposition II and Stevens' Proposition III in the Case of the Los Angeles Star," M.A. thesis (Fullerton, CA: California State University at Fullerton, 1995).

67. Mark E. Neely, *The Fate of Liberty: Abraham Lincoln and Civil Liberties* (New York, NY: Oxford University Press, 1991).

68. Harold L. Nelson, *Freedom of the Press from Hamilton to the Warren Court* (Indianapolis, IN: Bobb-Merrill Company, 1967).

69. Christopher Dell, *Lincoln and the War Democrats: The Grand Erosion of Conservative Tradition* (Rutherford, NJ: Fairleigh Dickinson University Press, 1975), 232–233.

70. James. G. Randall, *Constitutional Problems Under Lincoln* (Urbana, IL: University of Illinois Press, 1964).

71. William H. Rehnquist, *All the Laws But One: Civil Liberties in Wartime* (New York, NY: Alfred A. Knopf, 1998).

72. Ibid., 137.

73. Margaret A. Blanchard, "Free Expression and Wartime: Lessons from the Past, Hopes for the Future," *Journalism Quarterly*, Spring 1992, Vol. 69, No. 1, 5–17.

74. William Watson Woollen, "Reminiscences of the Early Marion County Bar," *Indiana Historical Society Publications, Volume VII* (Indianapolis, IN: C.E. Pauley & Company, 1923), 185–208; Leander J. Monks, ed., "Legal Education in Indiana," *Courts and Lawyers of Indiana, Volume II* (Indianapolis, IN: Federal Publishing Company, 1916), 470–479.

75. Charles W. Taylor, *Biographical Sketches and Review of the Bench and Bar of Indiana, Together with a History of the Judiciary of the State and Review of the Bar from the Earliest Times to the Present, with Anecdotes, Reminiscences, etc.* (Indianapolis, IN: Bench and Bar Publishing, 1895).

References

BOOKS AND SCHOLARLY ARTICLES

Abbott, Richard H. "Civil War Origins of the Southern Republican Press." *Civil War History*. Vol. 43, No. 1, March 1997, 38–50.

Abzug, Robert H. "The Copperheads: Historical Approaches to Civil War Dissent in the Midwest." *Indiana Magazine of History*. Vol. 66, No. 1, March 1970, 40–55.

Andrews, J. Cutler. *The North Reports the Civil War*. University of Pittsburgh Press, Pittsburgh, PA, 1955.

Andrews, J. Cutler. *The South Reports the Civil War*. Princeton University Press, Princeton, NJ, 1970.

Angelo, Frank. *On Guard: A History of the Detroit Free Press*. Detroit Free Press, Detroit, MI, 1981.

Appleby, Joyce and Terence Ball. *Thomas Jefferson, Political Writings*. Cambridge University Press. Cambridge, UK. 1999.

Ashley, Perry J., editor. *American Newspaper Journalists 1690–1872*. Gale Research Company, Detroit, MI, 1985.

Baldasty, Gerald J. "The Press and Politics in the Age of Jackson." *Journalism Monographs*. No. 89, August 1984, 1–28.

Banta, D. D. *History of Johnson County, Indiana*. Brant & Fuller, Chicago, 1888.

Barnhart, John D. *Valley of Democracy: The Frontier versus the Plantation in the Ohio Valley*. Indiana University Press, Bloomington, IN, 1953.

Barnhart, John D. "The Impact of the Civil War on Indiana." *Indiana Magazine of History*, Vol. 57, No. 3, September 1961, 185–224.

Bartholomew, Henry. *Pioneer History of Elkhart County, Indiana*. Goshen Printing, Goshen, IN, 1930.

Basler, Roy P. *The Collected Works of Abraham Lincoln*. Rutgers University Press, New Brunswick, NJ, 1990.

Becker, Carl M. "Newspapers in Battle: The *Dayton Empire* and the *Dayton Journal* During the Civil War." *Ohio History: The Scholarly Journal of the Ohio Historical Society* (Columbus, OH), Vol. 99, 1990, 29–50.

Beathard, Ronald. "Indiana Newspaper History: An Annotated Bibliography." Ball State University, Muncie, IN, 1974.

Bigelow, Bruce. "The Clash of Cultures: Border Southerners and Yankees in Antebellum Indiana." *Journal of the Indiana Academy of the Social Sciences* (Indianapolis, IN), Vol. 2, 1998, 1–8.

Bigelow, Bruce and Stephen E. Towne. "Democratic Opposition to the Lincoln Administration in Indiana: The Polls and the Press." *Journal of the Indiana Academy of the Social Sciences* (Rensselaer, IN), Vol. 5, 2001, 71–81.

Biographical and Historical Sketches of Kosciusko County, Indiana. Lewis Publishing County, Chicago, 1887. Merrill, Indianapolis, 1967.

Blackford, Isaac. *Report of Cases Argued and Determined in the Supreme Court of the Judicature of the State of Indiana*. Bowen-Merrill, Indianapolis, IN, 1890.

Banchard, Charles. *History of the Catholic Church in Indiana*. Logansport, IN, two volumes, 1898.

Blanchard, Margaret A. "Filling in the Void: Speech and Press in State Courts Prior to *Gitlow*." *The First Amendment Reconsidered*. Bill F. Chamberlin and Charlene J. Brown, eds. Longman, New York, 1982, 14–59.

Boatner, Mark Mayo. *The Civil War Dictionary*. David McKay Company, New York, 1959.

Bogardus, Frank Smith. "Daniel Wolsey Voorhees." *Mississippi Valley Historical Review*. Vol. 6, 1919–1920, 532–555.

Brown, Austin H. Papers. Indiana Division. Indiana State Library. Indianapolis, IN.

Buchholz, Michael. "The Penny Press," in *The Media in America: A History, Fifth Edition*. William David Sloan, ed. Vision Pres. Northport, AL, 2002.

Buley, R. Carlyle. *The Old Northwest: Pioneer Period, 1815–1840*. Vol. 2. Indiana University Press, Bloomington, IN, 1978.

Burgess, John W. *The Civil War and the Constitution 1859–1865, Volume Two*. Charles Scribner's Sons, New York, 1910.

Burke, Edmund. *The Portable Edmund Burke*. Isaac Kramnick, ed. Penguin, New York, 1999.

Burnside, Ambrose E. *Burnside Papers*, Record Group 94, National Archives, Washington, DC.

Butler, James Hannam. "Newspapers in Indiana." *Indiana Magazine of History*, Vol. 22, No. 3, September 1926, 297–333.

Calhoun, John C. *A Disquisition on Government*. C. Gordon Post, ed. Bobbs-Merrill Company, Indianapolis, IN, 1953.

Canup, Charles E. "Conscription and Draft in Indiana." *Indiana Magazine of History*, Vol. 10, No. 2, June 1914, 70–83.

Carmony, Donald F. "Highlights in Indiana Newspaper History." *The Indiana Publisher*, Vol. 9, No. 1, December 1944, 3, 6.

Catton, Bruce. *Civil War*. Fairfax Press, New York, 1984.

Chamberlain, Ebenezer Mattoon. "Journal of Chamberlain of a Trip from Maine to Indiana in 1832." *Indiana Magazine of History*, Vol. 15, No. 3, September 1919.

Cheek, H. Lee, Jr. *Calhoun and Popular Rule: The Political Theory of the* Disquisition *and* Discourse. University of Missouri Press, Columbia, 2001.

Collins, Lewis and Richard H. Collins, *History of Kentucky, Volume I*. John P. Morton Company, Louisville, KY, 1924.

Cooley, Thomas M. *A Treatise on the Constitutional Limitations Which Rest Upon the Legislative Power of the States of the American Union, Eighth Edition*. Little, Brown, and Company, Boston, MA, 1927.

Cowden, Joanna D. *"Heaven Will Frown on Such a Cause as This": Six Democrats Who Opposed Lincoln's War*. University Press of America, Inc., Lanham, MD, 2001.

Cravens, James A. Papers. Lilly Library. Indiana University. Bloomington, IN.

Crozier, Emmet. *Yankee Reporters 1861–65*. Oxford University Press, New York, 1956.

Curran, Thomas F. "Pacifists, Peace Democrats, and the politics of perfection in the Civil War era." *Journal of Church & State*, Vol. 38, No. 3, Summer 1996, 487–505.

Curtis, Michael Kent. *Free Speech, "The People's Darling Privilege."* Duke University Press, Durham, NC, 2000.

Curtis, Michael Kent. "Democratic Ideals and Media Realities: A Puzzling Free Press Paradox." *Social Philosophy and Policy*. Vol. 21, No. 2, July 2004, 385–427.

Dell, Christopher. *Lincoln and the War Democrats: The Grand Erosion of Conservative Tradition*. Fairleigh Dickinson University Press, Rutherford, NJ, 1975.

Dicken-Garcia, Hazel, Giovanna Dell'Orto, and Brian Gabrial. "'Grossly Assailed by a Maniacal Press': James Gordon Bennett, Emancipation, and Press Freedom." Unpublished paper. 2005.

Dicken-Garcia, Hazel. *Journalistic Standards in Nineteenth Century America*. University of Wisconsin Press, Madison, 1989.

Dickerson, Donna Lee. "Framing 'Political Correctness': The New York Times' Tale of Two Professors," in *Framing Public Life: Perspectives on Media and Our Understanding of the Social World*. Stephen D. Reese, Oscar H. Gandy Jr. and August E. Grant, ed. Lawrence Elbaum Associates, Mahwah, NJ, 2001, 163–174.

Dilts, Jon Paul. "Testing Siebert's Proposition in Civil War Indiana." *Journalism Quarterly*. Vol. 63, No. 1, Spring 1986, 365–368.

Donald, David Herbert. *Lincoln*. Jonathan Cape, London, 1995.

Donald, David Herbert. *Lincoln Reconsidered: Essays on the Civil War Era, Third Edition*. Vintage Books, New York, 2001.

Donald, David Herbert. *Why the North Won the Civil War*. Touchstone, New York, 1960 (1996).

Douglas, George H. *The Golden Age of the Newspaper*. Greenwood Press, Westport, CT, 1999.

Dowling, John. Papers. Indiana Historical Society Library. Indianapolis, IN.

Earle, Jonathan H. *Jacksonian Antislavery and the Politics of Free Soil, 1824–1854.* University of North Carolina Press. Chapel Hill, NC, 2005.

Ellis, L. E. "The Chicago Times During the Civil War." Illinois State Historical Society Transactions for the Years 1932. Illinois State Historical Library Publication No. 39.

Emery, Edwin and Michael Emery. *The Press and America, Seventh Edition: An Intepretive History of the Mass Media.* Prentice Hall, Englewood Cliffs, NJ, 1992.

Enders, Kathleen. In "The Press and the Civil War, 1861–1865," in *The Media in America: A History, Fifth Edition*, ed. by William David Sloan. Vision Press. Northport, AL. 2002.

Entman, Robert M. "Framing: Toward Clarification of a Fractured Paradigm." *Journal of Communication*, Vol. 43, No. 4, 1193, 51–58.

Ex Parte Milligan, 71 U.S. Supreme Court, 4 Wallace, 1–143, 1866.

Farber, Daniel. *Lincoln's Constitution.* University of Chicago Press. Chicago, IL. 2003.

Farrar, Ronald T. and John D. Stevens. *Mass Media and the National Experience: Essays in Communication History.* Harper & Row, New York, 1971.

Finkelman, Paul. "Civil Liberties and the Civil War: The Great Emancipator as Civil Libertarian." Review of Mark E. Neely Jr., *The Fate of Liberty: Abraham Lincoln and Civil Liberties,* in *Michigan Law Review.* Vol. 91, No. 6, May 1993, 1353–1381.

Fitzhugh, George. *Sociology For The South, Or The Failure of Free Society.* Ayer Company Publishers, Manchester, NH, 1998.

Foner, Eric. "The Wilmot Proviso Revisited," *Journal of American History.* 61, September 1969.

Foote, Shelby. *The Civil War, a Narrative: Fredericksburg to Meridian.* Random House, New York, 1963.

Foulke, William Dudley. *Life of Oliver P. Morton, Including His Important Speeches (Two Volumes).* Bowen-Merrrill, Indianapolis, 1898.

Franklin, Marc A., David A. Anderson, and Fred H. Cate. *Mass Media Law: Cases and Materials, Sixth Edition.* Foundation Press, New York, 2000.

French, William M., *Life, Speeches, State Papers and Public Services of Gov. Oliver P. Morton.* Cincinnati: Moore, Wilstach & Baldwin, 1866.

Gary, A. L. and E. B. Thomas. *Centennial History of Rush County, Indiana, Volume I.* Historical Publishing Company, Indianapolis, 1921.

Gienapp, William E. *Abraham Lincoln and Civil War America: A Biography.* Oxford University Press, New York, 2002.

Goodwin, Doris Kearns. *Team of Rivals: The Political Genius of Abraham Lincoln.* Simon & Schuster. New York, 2005.

Goshen: The First One Hundred Fifty Years, 1831–1981. News Printing Company, Goshen, IN, 1981.

Grant, Alfred. *The American Civil War and the British Press*. McFarland & Company, Inc., Jefferson, NC, 2000.

Grant, Ulysses S. *Personal Memoirs of U.S. Grant*. Charles L. Webster & Company, New York, 1885.

Gray, Ralph D. *Indiana History: A Book of Readings*. Indiana University Press, Bloomington, IN, 1994.

Gray, Wood. *The Hidden Civil War: The Story of the Copperheads*. Viking, New York, 1942.

Greenberg, Kenneth S. *Honor and Slavery: Lies, Duels, Noses, Masks, Dressing as a Woman, Gifts, Strangers, Humanitarianism, Death, Slave Rebellions, the Proslavery Argument, Baseball, Hunting, and Gambling in the Old South*. Princeton University Press, Princeton, NJ, 1996.

Hamilton, Holman. *Prologue to Conflict: The Crisis and Compromise of 1850*. University of Kentucky Press, Lexington, KY, 1964.

Hanson, Thomas Carleton. "Press Freedom and War Restraints: Seibert's Proposition II and Stevens Proposition III in the Case of the *Los Angeles Star*." Master's thesis. California State University at Fullerton, Fullerton, CA, 1995.

Harper, Robert S. *Lincoln and the Press*. McGraw-Hill Book Company, Inc., New York, 1951.

Harris, Brayton. *Blue & Gray in Black & White: Newspapers in the Civil War*. Brassey's, Washington, DC, 1999.

Hinshaw, Gil. "From 10,500 Battles: A Handbook of Civil War Engagements." Superior Printing Company, Hobbs, NM, 1996.

History of Elkhart County, Indiana. Charles Chapman & Company, Chicago, 1881.

History of Huntington County, Indiana. Brant & Fuller, Chicago, 1887.

History of Lawrence and Monroe Counties, Indiana. Indianapolis, 1914.

Jefferson, Thomas. *The Life and Selected Writings of Thomas Jefferson*. Adrienne Koch and William Harwood Peden, eds. The Modern Library, Random House, New York, 1944.

Jefferson, Thomas. *Writings*. The Library of America, New York, 1984.

Johnson, Herbert A., ed. *The Papers of John Marshall*. University of North Carolina Press, Chapel Hill, NC, 1974.

Johnson, Paul. *A History of the American People*. HarperCollins Publishers, Inc., New York, 1997.

Johnson, Russell L. *Warriors into Workers: The Civil War and the Formation of Urban-Industrial Society in a Northern City*. Fordham University Press, New York, 2003.

Kaler, S. P. and P. H. Maring. *History of Whitley County, Indiana*. Bowen, Chicago, 1907.

Kenworth, Leonard S. *The Tall Sycamore of the Wabash*. Bruce Humphries Publishers, Inc., Boston, 1936.

Kettleborough, Charles. *Constitution Making in Indiana, Volume I* (Reprint). Indiana Historical Collections, Indianapolis, 1971.

Kettleborough, Charles, ed. *Manuscript Constitution* (1851 Indiana Constitution). Indiana Historical Bureau, Indianapolis.

Kielbowicz, Richard B. "The Telegraph, Censorship and Politics at the Outset of the Civil War." *Civil War History.* Vol. 40, 1995, 95–118.

Kinsley, Philip. *The Chicago Tribune, Volume I.* Knopf, New York, 1943.

Klement, Frank L. "Carrington and the Golden Circle Legend in Indiana during the Civil War." *Indiana Magazine of History*, Vol. 61, No. 1, March 1965, 31–52.

Klement, Frank L. "Catholics As Copperheads During the Civil War." *Catholic Historical Review*, January 1994, Vol. 80, No. 1, 36–58.

Klement, Frank L. *The Copperheads in the Middle West.* University of Chicago Press, Chicago, 1960.

Klement, Frank L. *The Limits of Dissent.* University Press of Kentucky, Lexington, 1970.

Klement, Frank L. *Lincoln's Critics.* White Mane Books, Shippensburg, PA, 1999.

Kriegbaum, Patricia A. "Historical Background of Blackford County, Hartford City, Indiana." Undated.

Lendt, David L. "Demise of the Democracy: The Copperhead Press in Iowa, 1856–1870." Master's thesis. Iowa State University, 1971,

Levy, Leonard W. *Emergence of a Free Press.* Oxford University Press, New York, 1985.

Lofton, John. *The Press as Guardian of the First Amendment.* University of South Carolina Press, Columbia, 1980.

Long, E. B. *The Civil War Day by Day: An Almanac, 1861–1865.* Doubleday, New York, 1971.

Lora, Ronald and William Henry Longton, ed. *The Conservative Press in Eighteenth and Nineteenth Century America.* Greenwood Press, Westport, CT, 1999.

Lowry, Thomas P. *Don't Shoot That Boy! Abraham Lincoln and Military Justice.* Savas Publishing Company, Mason City, IA, 1999.

Manber, Jeffrey and Neil Dahlstrom. *Lincoln's Wrath: Fierce Mobs, Brilliant Scoundrels and a President's Mission to Destroy the Press.* Sourcebooks. Naperville, IL, 2005.

Maihafer, Harry J. *War of Words: Abraham Lincoln and the Civil War Press.* Brassey's, Washington, DC, 2001.

Manual of Goshen. Butler & Knox. Goshen, IN, 1889.

Marshall, John A. *An American Bastille: A History of the Illegal Arrests and Imprisonment of American Citizens during the Late Civil War.* Philadelphia, 1879.

Marszalek, John F. *Sherman's Other War: The General and Civil War Press.* Memphis State University Press, Memphis, 1981.

Marvel, William. *Burnside*. University of North Carolina Press, Chapel Hill, 1991.

Mathews, Joseph J. *Reporting the Wars*. University of Minnesota Press, Minneapolis, 1957.

Matthews, Lloyd J., ed. *Newsmen & National Defense: Is Conflict Inevitable?* Brassey's, Washington, DC, 1991.

May, Robert E. *The Southern Dream of a Caribbean Empire, 1854–1861*. Louisiana State University, Baton Rouge, LA, 1973.

McCormick, Joseph N. *A Standard History of Starke County, Indiana, Volume I*. Lewis Publishing Company, Chicago, 1915.

McDonald, Daniel. *A Twentieth History of Marshall County, Indiana, Volume I*. Lewis Publishing Company, Chicago, 1908.

McDonald, Joseph D. Papers. Lilly Library. Indiana University. Bloomington, IN.

McGrane, Martin E. "Dubuque—Editorial Battleground 1860–1862." Master's thesis, Iowa State University, Ames, IA, 1972.

McLuachlan, William P. *The Indiana State Constitution: A Reference Guide*. Greenwood Press, Westport, CT, 1996.

McPherson, James M. *Abraham Lincoln and the Second American Revolution*. Oxford University Press, New York, 1990.

McPherson, James M. *Antietam: The Battle That Changed the Course of the Civil War*. Oxford University Press, New York, 2002.

McPherson, James M. *Battle Cry of Freedom: The Civil War Era*. Ballantine Books, New York, 1988.

McPherson, James M. *Ordeal by Fire: The Civil War and Reconstruction, Third Edition*. McGraw-Hill, New York, 2001.

Media Law in Indiana. Indiana Continuing Legal Education Forum. Indianapolis, IN, 1987.

Meiklejohn, Alexander. "The First Amendment is an Absolute." *The Supreme Court Review*. Philip B. Kurland, ed. University of Chicago Press, Chicago, 1961, 245–264.

Merrill, Catharine. *The Soldier of Indiana in the War for the Union*, two volumes. Merrill and Company, Indianapolis, 1866–1869.

Miller, John W. *Indiana Newspaper Bibliography*. Indiana Historical Society, Indianapolis, 1982.

Monks, Leander J., ed., *Courts and Lawyers of Indiana, Volume II*. Federal Publishing Company, Indianapolis, 1916.

Moores, Charles W. "Caleb Mills and the Indiana School System." Indianapolis, IN: Indiana Historical Society Publications, III, No. 6, 1905.

Morton, Samuel George, J. C. Nott, and George R. Gliddon. *Types of Mankind: Or, Ethnological Researches, Based Upon the Ancient Monuments, Paintings, Sculptures, and Crania of Races and Upon Their Natural, Geographical, Philological, and Biblical History*. Lippincott, Grambo & Company, Philadelphia, 1854.

Mott, Frank Luther. *American Journalism: A History of Newspapers in the United States Through 250 Years, 1690 to 1940*. Macmillan, New York, 1941.

Neace, Estel. "Methodism in Indiana during the Civil War," Unpublished Master's Thesis. Butler University, Indianapolis, IN, 1961.

Neely, Mark E.: *The Fate of Liberty: Abraham Lincoln and Civil Liberties*. Oxford University Press, New York, 1991.

Neely, Mark E. *The Union Divided: Party Conflict in the Civil War North*. Harvard University Press, Cambridge, 2002.

Oldt, F. T. ed. *History of Dubuque County, Iowa*. Goodspeed, Chicago, IL, 1911.

Perkins, Samuel E. "Speech of Judge Perkins at Mass Meeting Held at Richmond, Indiana, 25 September 1860," pamphlet, no date, no printer.

Perman, Michael. *Major Problems in the Civil War and Reconstruction, Second Edition*. Houghton Mifflin, Boston, 1998.

Perry, James M. *A Bohemian Brigade: The Civil War Correspondents—Mostly Rough, Sometimes Ready*. Wiley & Sons, Inc., New York, 2000.

Peterson, Merrill D., ed. *James Madison: A Biography in His Own Words*. Harper & Row, New York, 1974.

Phillips, Kevin. *The Cousins' Wars: Religion, Politics, and the Triumph of Anglo-America*. Basic Books, New York, 1999.

A Pictorial History of Wells County: Towns and Townships. Donning Company, Virginia Beach, VA, 1999.

Pictorial and Biographical Memoirs of Elkhart and St. Joseph Counties, Indiana. Goodspeed Brothers, Chicago, 1893.

Porter, Albert G. *Indiana Reports of Cases Argued and Determined in the Supreme Court of the Judicature of the State of Indiana*. Bowen-Merrill, Indianapolis, IN, 1886.

Power, Richard L. *Planting Corn Belt Culture: The Impress of the Upland Southerner and Yankee in the Old Northwest*. Indiana Historical Society Publications, Vol. 17, Indianapolis, 1953.

Rabban, David M. *Free Speech in Its Forgotten Years*. Cambridge University Press. New York, 1997.

Randall, James G. *Constitutional Problems Under Lincoln*. University of Illinois Press, Urbana, 1964.

Randall, James G. *Lincoln the President: Midstream*. Vail-Ballou Press, Inc., Binghamton, NY, 1952.

Randall, James G. "The Newspaper Problem in Its Bearing upon Military Secrecy During the Civil War." *American History Review*, Vol. 23, January 1918, 303–324.

Randall, James G. and David Henry Donald. *The Civil War and Reconstruction, Second Edition*. D.C. Heath and Company, Lexington, MA, 1969.

Raper, Horace W. "William W. Holden and the Peace Movement in North Carolina." *North Carolina Historical Review*. Vol. 31, 1954, 493–516.

Ratner, Lorman A. and Dwight L. Teeter Jr. *Fanatics and Fire-eaters: Newspapers and the Coming of the Civil War*. University of Illinois Press, Urbana, IL, 2003.

Reese, Stephen C., Oscar H. Gandy, and August E. Grant, ed. *Framing Public Life: Perspectives on Media and Our Understanding of the Social World*. Lawrence Erlbaum Associates, Mahwah, NJ, 2001, 7–65.

Rehnquist, William H. *All the Laws But One: Civil Liberties in Wartime*. Alfred A. Knopf, New York, 1998.

Rehnquist, William H. "Civil Liberty and The Civil War: The Indianapolis Treason Trials." Law School, Indiana University, Bloomington, 1997.

Reidelbach, John G. "A Century of Achievement in Pulaski County, Indiana." Self-published, 1939.

Remmo, C.G. "Freedom of the Press." *Notre Dame Lawyer*, Vol. 20, No. 3, 1944–1945, 314–321.

Reynolds, Donald E. *Editors Make War*. Vanderbilt University Press, Nashville, 1966.

Risley, Ford. "The Confederate Press Association: Cooperative News Reporting of the War," *Civil War History*, Vol. 47, No. 3, September 2001, 222–239.

Roberts, Nancy L. "Ten Thousand Tongues Speaking for Peace: Purposes and Strategies of the Nineteenth-Century Peace Advocacy Press." *Journalism History*, Vol. 21, No. 1, Spring 1995, 13–28.

Rodgers, Thomas E. "Liberty, Will, and Violence: The Political Ideology of the Democrats of West-Central Indiana During the Civil War." *Indiana Magazine of History*, Vol. 92, No. 2, June 1996, 131–159.

Roediger, David R. *The Wages of Whiteness (Revised Edition)*. Verso, New York, 1991.

Rossiter, Clinton, ed. *The Federalist Papers*. Mentor Book, Penguin Putnam, Inc., New York, 1999.

Rusk, Ralph Leslie. *The Literature of the Middle Western Frontier, Volume I*. Frederick Ungar Publishing Company, New York, 1962.

Rutland, Robert Allen. *James Madison: The Founding Father*. University of Missouri Press, Columbia, MO, 1987.

Ryan, Charlotte. *Prime Time Activism: Media Strategies for Grassroots Organizing*. South End Press, Boston, MA, 1991.

Sachsman, David B., S. Kittrell Rushing, and Debra Reddin van Tuyll. *The Civil War and the Press*. Transaction Publishers, New Brunswick, NJ, 2000.

Scott, Robert Garth. *Forgotten Valor: The Memoirs, Journals, and Civil Wars Letters of Orlando B. Willcox*. Kent State University Press, Kent, OH, 1999.

Scott, Robert N. et al., eds. *The War of the Rebellion: A Compilation of the Official Records of the Union and Confederate Armies*. Government Printing Office, Washington, DC, 1891.

Sears, Stephen W. *Chancellorsville*. Houghton Mifflin, Boston, 1996.

Shinn, Benjamin G. *Biographical Memoirs of Blackford County, Indiana.* Bowen, Chicago, 1900.

Siebert, Fredrick S., Wilbur Schram, and Theodore Peters. *Four Theories of the Press.* University of Illinois Press, Urbana, IL, 1963.

Siebert, Fredrick S. *Freedom of the Press in England 1476–1776: The Rise and Decline of Government Controls.* University of Illinois Press, Urbana, IL, 1952.

Sifakis, Stewart. *Who Was Who in the Civil War.* Facts on File Publications, New York, 1988.

Skidmore, Joe. "The Copperhead Press and the Civil War." *Journalism Quarterly,* Vol. 16, No. 1, 1939, 345–355.

Sloan, William David. *The Age of Mass Communication, First Edition.* Vision Press, Northport, AL, 1998.

Sloan, William David. *The Media in America: A History, Fifth Edition.* Vision Press, Northport, AL, 2002.

Small, William J. *Political Power and the Press.* W. W. Norton & Company, New York, 1972.

Smith, Edward Conrad. *The Borderland in the Civil War.* AMS Press, New York, 1970.

Smith, Jeffery A. *War and Press Freedom: The Problem of Prerogative Power.* Oxford University Press, New York, 1999.

Smith, James Morton. *Freedom's Fetters: The Alien and Sedition Laws and American Civil Liberties.* Cornell University Press, Ithaca, 1956.

Smith, Reed W. *Samuel Medary & the Crisis: Testing the Limits of Press Freedom.* Ohio State University Press, Columbus, 1995.

Smith, Reed. W. "The Paradox of Samuel Medary, Cooperhead Newspaper Publisher." *The Civil War and the Press.* David B. Sachsman, S. Kittrell Rushing, and Debra Riddin van Tuyll, eds. Transactions Books, Piscataway, NJ, 2001, 291–306.

Smith, Willard. *Schuyler Colfax: The Changing Fortunes of a Political Idol.* Indiana Historical Bureau, Indianapolis, 1952.

Stampp, Kenneth M. *Indiana Politics During the Civil War.* Indiana Historical Bureau, Indianapolis, 1949.

Starr, Louis M. *Bohemian Brigade: Civil War Newsmen in Action.* Alfred A. Knopf, New York, 1954.

Stevens, Joseph E. *1863: The Rebirth of a Nation.* Bantam, New York, 1999.

Stephens, Mitchell. *A History of News, Third Edition.* Oxford University Press. New York, 2007.

Stoll, John B. *History of Indiana From Its Exploration to 1922; Also an Account of St. Joseph County from Its Organization.* Dayton Historical Publishing, Dayton, OH, 1922.

Stoler, Mildred C. "Influence of the Democratic Element in the Republican Party of Illinois and Indiana, 1854–1860." Doctoral dissertation. Indiana University, Bloomington, IN, 1938.

Stone, Geoffrey R. *Perilous Times: Free Speech in Wartime From the Sedition Act of 1798 to the War on Terrorism.* W. W. Norton & Company, New York, 2004.

Stonex, Wilber L. "Salem Bank of Goshen, Indiana." *Indiana Magazine of History.* Vol. 23, No. 1, 1927, 83–91.

Stowe, Harriett Beecher. *Uncle Tom's Cabin.* Bantam Books, New York, 1981. Originally published in 1851.

Sulgrove, Berry R. *History of Indianapolis and Marion County, Indiana.* Philadelphia, PA, 1884.

Summers, Mark W. *The Plundering Generation: Corruption and the Crisis of the Union, 1849–1861.* Oxford University Press, New York, 1987.

Swanberg, Wendy E. "*Ex Parte McCardle* and the First Amendment during Reconstruction." Presented to the Symposium on the 19th Century Press, the Civil War, and Free Expression, University of Tennessee at Chattanooga, November 2006.

Sweeney, Michael S. *The Military and the Press: An Uneasy Truce.* Northwestern University Press, Evanston, IL, 2006.

Tankard, J., L. Hendrickson, J. Silberman, K. Bliss, and S. Ghanem. "Media frames: Approaches to conceptualization and measurement." AEJMC, Boston, MA, August 1991.

Taylor, Charles W. *Biographical Sketches and Review of the Bench and Bar of Indiana, Together with a History of the Judiciary of the State and Review of the Bar from the Earliest Times to the Present, with Anecdotes, Reminiscences, etc.* Bench and Bar Publishing, Indianapolis, IN, 1895.

Teeter, Dwight L. and Don R. Le Duc. *Law of Mass Communications: Freedom and Control of Print and Broadcast Media.* The Foundation Press, Westbury, NY, 1995.

Tenney, Craig D. "Major General A.E. Burnside and the First Amendment: A Case Study of Civil War Freedom of Expression." Doctoral Dissertation. Indiana University, Bloomington, IN, 1977.

Terrell, W. H. H. Terrell. *Indiana in the War of the Rebellion: Report of the Adjutant General, A Reprint of Volume One of the Eight-Volume Report Prepared by W.H.H. Terrell and Published in 1869.* Indiana Historical Bureau, Indianapolis, IN, 1960.

Thiele, Norma Jean. "A History of the Fort Wayne News-Sentinel." Doctoral Dissertation. Indiana University, Bloomington, IN, 1958.

Thomas, Benjamin P. and Harld M. Hyman. *Stanton: The Life and Times of Lincoln's Secretary of War.* Greenwood Press, Westport, CT, 1962.

Thompson, Susan. *The Penny Press: The Origins of the Modern News Media, 1833–1861.* Vision Press, Northport, AL, 2004.

Thornbrough, Emma Lou. *Indiana in the Civil War Era, 1850–80.* Indiana Historical Society, Indianapolis, IN, 1995.

Thornbrough, Emma Lou. "Judge Perkins, the Indiana Supreme Court, and the Civil War." *Indiana Magazine of History.* Vol. 60, No. 1. March 1964, 79–96.

Thorp, Robert K. "The Copperhead Days of Dennis Mahoney." *Journalism Quarterly*. Vol. 43, 1966, 680–686, 696.

Tichenor, Phillip J. "Cooperheadism and Community Conflict in Two Rivertowns: Civil War Press Battles in Prairie du Chien and La Crosse, Wisconsin, 1861–65." Paper delivered at the Fall 2002 Symposium on the 19th Century Press, the Civil War, and Free Expression, held at University of Tennessee at Chattanooga, Chattanooga, TN, October 2002.

Towne, Stephen E. "Killing the Serpent Speedily: Governor Morton, General Hascall, and the Suppression of the Democratic Press in Indiana, 1863." Paper delivered at the Fall 2002 Symposium on the 19th Century Press, the Civil War, and Free Expression, held at University of Tennessee at Chattanooga, Chattanooga, TN, October 2002.

Towne, Stephen E. "West Point Letters of Cadet Milo S. Hascall, 1848–1850." *Indiana Magazine of History*. Vol. 90, No. 3, September 1994, 278–294.

Towne, Stephen E. "Works of Indiscretion: Violence against the Press in Indiana during the Civil War." Paper presented to the Symposium on the 19th Century Press, the Civil War, and Free Expression. Chattanooga, TN, October 31, 2003.

Towery, Patricia. "Censorship of South Carolina Newspapers, 1861–1865," in James B. Meriweather, ed., *South Carolina Journals and Journalism*. The Reprint Co. Publishers, Spartanburg, SC, 1975, 147–160.

Tredway, G. R. *Democratic Opposition to the Lincoln Administration*. Indiana Historical Bureau, Indianapolis, IN, 1973.

Tredway, Gilbert R. "Indiana against the Administration, 1861–1865." Doctoral dissertation. Indiana University, Bloomington, IN, 1962.

Vallandigham, James L. *A Life of Clement L. Vallandigham*. Turnbull Brothers, Baltimore, MD, 1872.

Valley of the Upper Maumee River, with Historical Account of Allen county and the City of Fort Wayne, Indiana. The Story of its Progress From Savagery to Civilization, Volume II. Brant and Fuller, Madison, WI, 1889.

Van Bolt, Roger H. "Indiana in Political Transition, 1851–1853," *Indiana Magazine of History*. Vol. 49, 1953, 131–160.

van Tuyll, Debra Reddin. "Necessity and the Invention of a Newspaper: A Case Study of the Press and Political Culture in Civil War North Carolina." Presented to the Symposium on the 19th Century Press, the Civil War, and Free Expression. University of Tennessee at Chattanooga, October 2002.

van Tuyll, Debra Reddin. "The Rebels Yell: Conscription and Freedom of Expression in the Civil War South." *American Journalism*. Vol. 17, No. 2, 2000, 15–29.

Voorhees, Charles S., ed. *Speeches of Daniel W. Voorhees of Indiana, Embracing His Most Prominent Forensic, Political, Occasional, and Literary Addresses*. Robert Clarke & Company, Printers, Cincinnati, OH, 1875.

Wagman, Robert J. *The First Amendment Book*. Pharos Books, New York, 1991.

Walsh, Justin. *To Print the News and Raise Hell! A Biography of Wilbur F. Storey*. University of North Carolina Press, Chapel Hill, NC, 1968.

Warner, Ezra J. *Generals in Blue: Lives of Union Commanders*. Louisiana State University Press, Baton Rouge, LA, 1964.

Watson, Harry L. *Liberty and Power: The Politics of Jacksonian America*. Noonday Press, New York, 1990.

Watts, Edward and David Rachels. *The First West: Writing from the American Frontier, 1776–1860*. Oxford University Press, New York, 2002.

Weaver, Abraham E. *A Standard History of Elkhart County, Indiana: An Authentic Narrative of the Past, with Particular Attention to the Modern Era in the Commercial, Industrial, Educational, Civic and Social Development*. Two Volumes. American Historical Society, Chicago, IL, 1916.

Webben, Hubert H. *Civil War Iowa and the Copperhead Movement*. Iowa State University, Ames, IA, 1980.

Weber, Jennifer L. *Copperheads: The Rise and Fall of Lincoln's Opponents in the North*. Oxford University Press, New York, 2006.

Welles, Gideon. *Diary of Gideon Welles*. Houghton Mifflin, Boston, MA, 1911.

Williams, David. *A People's History of the Civil War: Struggles for the Meaning of Freedom*. The New Press, New York, 2005.

Williams, Robert C. *Horace Greeley: Champion of American Freedom*. New York University Press, New York, 2006.

Willis, High E. "Freedom of Speech and of the Press," *Indiana Law Journal*, Vol. 4, No. 7, April 1929, 445–455.

Wills, Garry. *James Madison*. Times Books, New York, 2002.

Woollen, William Watson. *Biographical and Historical Sketches of Early Indiana*. C.E. Pauley & Company, Indianapolis, IN, 1883.

Woollen, William Watson. "Reminiscences of the Early Marion County Bar." *Indiana Historical Society Publications, Volume VII*. C.E. Pauley & Company, Indianapolis, IN, 1923, 185–208.

Woollen, William Watson. *Richard W. Thompson Papers*. Indianapolis, IN, Indiana Division, Indiana State Library, June 8, 1847, manuscript.

Woollen, William Wesley. "The Indiana Press of the Olden Time." *Biographical and Historical Sketches of Early Indiana*. Hammond & Company, Indianapolis, IN, 1883, 538–559.

Wright, Joseph A. *An Address Delivered at the Installation of Rev. L. W. Berry, D.D., as President of Indiana Asbury University, July 16, 1850*. Indianapolis, IN, 1850.

Wright, Joseph A. "Eulogy of Stephen A. Douglas." *Indiana State Sentinel* Print. Indianapolis, IN, 1862.

Wubben, Hubert H. *Civil War Iowa and the Copperhead Movement*. Iowa State University Press, Ames, IA, 1980.

Wubben, Hubert H. "Dennis Mahony and the Dubuque Herald, 1860–1863." *Iowa Journal of History*. Vol. 56, No. 4, October 1958.

Zelezny, John D. *Communications Law: Liberties, Restraints, and the Modern Media*. Wadsworth, Belmont, CA, 1997.

MANUSCRIPTS, PAPERS, AND REPORTS

Burnside, Ambrose. Burnside Papers. National Archives. Washington, DC.

Colfax, Schuyler. Papers. Lilly Library. Indiana University. Bloomington, Indiana.

Hanna, John. Papers. Lilly Library. Indiana University. Bloomington, Indiana.

Hascall, Milo Smith. "Autobiography." Indiana State Archives. Indianapolis, Undated.

"Hascall Family in America," Bentley Family Papers, Ms-720, Center for Archives Collection, Jerome Library, Bowling Green State University, Bowling Green, Ohio.

Hascall, Milo Smith. "Personal recollections & experiences: concerning the Battle of Stone River." Goshen, Indiana, *Times* Publishing Company, 1889, a paper read by request before the Illinois Commander of the Military Order of the Loyal Legion of the US, at Chicago, Feb. 14, 1889.

Hascall, Milo Smith. "Report" to Indiana Adjutant General W. H. H. Terrell. Indiana State Archives, Commission on Public Records. Indianapolis, Undated.

Holman, William S. Papers. Manuscript Division. Indiana State Library. Indianapolis, Indiana.

Hovey, Alvin P. Papers. Lilly Library. Indiana University. Bloomington, Indiana.

Indiana State Board of Agriculture, *Annual Report*. Indianapolis, IN,1851.

Lane, Henry S. Papers. Lilly Library. Indiana University. Bloomington, Indiana.

Letter Books, Department of the Ohio, "Letters Sent," No. 5, Record Group 94, National Archives Building, Washington, DC.

Morton, Oliver P. Papers. Manuscript Division. Indiana State Library. Indianapolis, Indiana.

"Order Books." Department of the Ohio, March through June 1863, Ambrose Everts Burnside Collection, Rhode Island State Historical Society, Manuscripts Division, Providence, RI.

NEWSPAPERS, MAGAZINES

Blackford County, Indiana, *Democrat*.

Bluffton, Indiana, *Banner*.

Burlington, Iowa, *Argus*.

Burlington, Iowa, *Hawkeye*.

Cannelton, Indiana, *Reporter*.

Chicago, Illinois, *Times*.

Chicago, Illinois, *Tribune*.

Cincinnati, Ohio, *Commercial*.

Cincinnati, Ohio, *Enquirer*.

Cincinnati, Ohio, *Gazette*.

Columbia City, Indiana, *News.*

Connersville, Indiana, *Fayette and Union Telegraph.*

Davenport, Iowa, *Daily Democrat.*

Dayton, Ohio, *Daily Empire.*

Dayton, Ohio, *Journal.*

Delaware County, Indiana, *Free Press.*

Delphi, Indiana, *Journal.*

Delphi, Indiana, *Weekly Times.*

Des Moines, Iowa, *Iowa Daily State Register.*

Detroit, Michigan, *Free Press.*

Dubuque, Iowa, *Herald.*

Evansville, Indiana, *Weekly Gazette.*

Fairfield, Iowa, *Weekly Ledger.*

Fort Wayne, Indiana, *Daily Gazette.*

Fort Wayne, Indiana, *Dawson's Daily Times & Union.*

Fort Wayne, Indiana, *Sentinel.*

Frank Leslie's Illustrated Newspaper.

Franklin, Indiana, *Weekly Democratic Herald.*

Goshen, Indiana, *Democrat.*

Goshen, Indiana, *News.*

Goshen, Indiana, *Times.*

Greensboro, North Carolina, *News & Record.*

Harper's Weekly.

Howard County, Indiana, *Tribune.*

Huntington, Indiana, *Democrat.*

Huntington, Indiana, *Herald.*

Indianapolis, Indiana, *Daily Journal.*

Indianapolis, Indiana, *Indiana State Sentinel.*

Lafayette, Indiana, *Journal.*

Lawrenceburg, Indiana, *Democratic Register.*

Logansport, Indiana, *Democratic Pharos.*

Logansport, Indiana, *Journal.*

Madison, Indiana, *Daily Courier.*

Marshall County, Indiana, *Republican.*

New Albany, Indiana, *Ledger.*

New York *Caucasian.*

New York *Daily News.*

New York *Express.*

New York *Herald.*

New York *Herald-Tribune.*

New York *Jewish Messenger.*

New York Journal of Commerce.

New York *Times.*
New York *Tribune.*
New York *World.*
Plymouth, Indiana, *Democrat.*
Pulaski County, Indiana, *Democrat.*
Richmond, Indiana, *Jeffersonian.*
Richmond, Indiana, *Palladium.*
Rockport, Indiana, *Weekly Democrat.*
Rushville, Indiana, *Jacksonian.*
Salem, Indiana, *Democratic Banner of Liberty.*
Salem, Indiana, *Union Advocate.*
Salem, Indiana, *Washington Democrat.*
South Bend, Indiana, *Forum.*
South Bend, Indiana, *St. Joseph Valley Register.*
Starke County, Indiana, *Press.*
Sullivan, Indiana, *Democrat.*
Terre Haute, Indiana, *Wabash Express.*
Vincennes, Indiana, *Weekly Gazette.*
Vincennes, Indiana, *Western Sun.*
Wabash, Indiana, *Intelligencer.*
Wabash, Indiana, *Plain Dealer.*
Warsaw, Indiana, *Northern Indianian.*
Warsaw, Indiana, *Union.*
Washington, DC, *National Daily Intelligencer.*

OTHER PUBLICATIONS

Congressional Globe, 38th Congress, First Session, 1506, 1864.
North, S.N.D. "The Newspaper and Periodical Press." U.S. Census Office, Government Printing Office, Washington, DC, 1884.
United States Bureau of the Census, *Tenth Census*, Washington, DC, 1880.

Index

Abell, Arunah S., 263n4

abolition-suppression paradox in Civil War, 213, 221, 229

abolitionist newspapers, 67–68

abolitionists, 17; antiabolitionist laws, 5, 67–68; and Quakers, 40

Abrams, Floyd, 229

Abrams v. U.S., 9, 75

Adams, John, 21, 36, 63, 225, 249n39

advertising in newspapers, 5, 10, 11, 84, 85, 117; primitive nature of, 127

African Americans, 9; antiblack codes, 38, 88; black population in Indiana in the 1860s, 35, 38; black troops in Civil War, 126, 273n40, 273n490; colonization solution, 39–40, 142; Emancipation Proclamation, 17, 101, 118, 120, 146, 213; freeing black men to fight, 143, 145–46; Fugitive Slave Law, 40, 44, 53; *herrenvolk*, 91; Indiana Yearly Meeting of Anti-Slavery Friends, 40; inferiority of, 92, 94; intermarriage, 38; interracial sex as rape, 68; and Jacksonianism, 91; and mob rule, 68; Negrophobis, 38; public school attendance, 38, 42; racial equality, 45; slavery and Indiana, 36, 38–40; suffrage of, 46, 53, 88; Underground Railroad, 39. *See also* slavery

aftermath of press suppression in Indiana, 22, 186–210; cessation of normal politics, 188–89; Dayton, Ohio, press war, 157, 193–96; end of suppression of Indiana's Democratic newspapers, 201; Lincoln and suppression, 206–210; Meredith and the Republican press, 203–206; New York editors' resolutions on freedom of the press, 196–202, 210, 217, 231–32; response to suppression of the Chicago

Times, 192–93; Storey raises a little hell, 189–192

Age, Philadelphia, 196

agriculture and farming in Indiana in the 1860s, 32, 34, 151

"aid and comfort for the enemy," 165, 175–76, 178, 206, 215

Ainsworth, F. C., 72

Al-Arabiya, 226

Al-Basa'ir, 228

Al Dustur, 228

Al-Hakim, Al-Sayyid Abd-al-Aziz, 229

Al Hawza, 226–29, 291n39, 292n59; protesting closing of, 228, 291n53

Al-Manar Television, Lebanon, 229

Al Mustaqailla, 226

Al-Mu'tamar, 228

Al-Sabah, 229

Al-Shiekh, Basim, 228

Al Zawra, 228

Alderman, Charles B., 29

Alien and Sedition Acts, 5, 100, 249n39, 280n24

Aljazeera, 291n53

All the Laws But One: Civil Liberties in Wartime (Rehnquist), 245–56

Allen, Elisha H., 250n13

Allison, William B., 110, 111, 270–71n61

American, Baltimore, 248n21

American Journalism, A History (Mott), 243

American Party. *See* Know Nothings

American Revolution, 60, 90, 137, 214; antecedent for press suppression, 215; and freedom of the press, 62

American Society of Newspaper Editors, 229

Ammen, Jacob, 191, 220

Andrews, J. Cutler, *North Reports the Civil War, The*, 98, 242

anti-Nebraska Democrats, 31

Sulgrove, Berry R., 96, 99, 124, 125, 138–39
Sullivan, Jeremiah, 46
Sumner, Charles, 51
Sun, Baltimore, 105
suppression of newspapers during Civil War, 7–8. *See also* legal and theoretical context of suppression; press suppression
Sweeney, Michael S., *Military and the Press, The*, 244
Swetland, William, 179, 282n66
Symposium on the Nineteenth Century Press, the Civil War, and Free Expression, University of Tennessee at Chattanooga, 241

Taney, Roger B., 90–91, 169, 246
Taylor, Charles W., *Biographical Sketches and Review of the Bench and Bar of Indiana*, 246
Taylor, Zachary, 43, 67
technology and newspapers, 83–84
Teeter, Dwight, 87–88, 221
Telegraph: and censorship, 213, 288n2; control of lines by Lincoln, 68, 97, 197; invention of, 5, 32; military takes over, 112; and newspapers, 83–84; one-page daily telegraph sheets, 127
telegraphic pact, 197
television, 16; networks suppressed in Iraq, 226
temperance, 31, 46, 48, 49
Temperance Advocate (Osborn), 46
Tenney, Craig, "Major General A. E. Burnside and the First Amendment," 233
Terre Haute *Journal*, 112
Terrell, W. H. H., 102; *Indiana in the War of the Rebellion*, 235
Thiele, Norma Jean, "History of the Fort Wayne News-Sentinel," 236
Thirteenth Amendment, 126
Thomas, Mary F., 46
Thompson, Richard W., 36, 45
Thornbrough, Emma Lou: on Civil War, 55, 56; *Indiana in the Civil War Era: 1850–80*, 235; "Judge Perkins, the Indiana Supreme Court, and the Civil War," 237; on peace movement, 46; on

prohibition, 49; on slavery in Indiana, 38, 39; on voting in Indiana, 51
Thrasher, John, 95
Tigar, Thomas, 10, 22, 106, 141
Tilford, Joseph M., 138
Tilton, Theodore, 197
Times, Chicago. *See* Chicago *Times*
Times, Delphi, Indiana, 182
Times, Goshen, Indiana, 29, 139, 147, 153, 165
Times, New York, 96, 163, 169, 192, 229
Times, Vicksburg, Mississippi, 68
To Print the News and Raise Hell! (Walsh), 241–42
Toledo *Commercial*, 196
Towery, Patricia, 242
Towne, Stephen E., 10, 221, 232; "Killing the Serpent Speedily," 234–35; "West Point Letters of Cadet Milo S. Hascall, 1848–1850," 235
Towne, Stephen E. and Bruce Bigelow, "Democratic Opposition to the Lincoln Administration: The Polls and the Press," 235
transitional phase of journalism in Civil War Indiana, 82, 221–25
treason, 72–73, 176, 211; Article III, Section 3 of the Constitution, 72–73; criticism-is-treason approach, 182; in Indiana in the Civil War, 207; Indianapolis Treason Trials, 246; and newspapers, 198–99; and opposition to Lincoln, 182
Treaty of Ghent, 65
Tredway, Gilbert R., 80, 81, 99, 205; *Democratic Opposition to the Lincoln Administration*, 235–36
Tribune, Chicago, 193
Tribune, New York, 83, 84, 98, 169, 173, 192
True Wesleyan, The (Methodist newspaper), 40
Trumbull, Lyman, 192
two-party political system, 4

Uncle Tom's Cabin (Stowe), 35, 49, 93
Underground Railroad, 39; and Quakers, 88–89

About the Author

David W. Bulla is a native of Greensboro, North Carolina, where he attended Grimsley Senior High School. His father, Joseph Redding Bulla, was an industrial engineer for Western Electric and a commander in the Naval Reserves. Father and son were amateur radio operators and avid readers of newspapers. Joseph Bulla died in 1986. David's mother, Rebecca Williams Bulla, is a retired administrative assistant for the Graduate School of the University of North Carolina at Greensboro. Bulla earned his B.A. in English from UNC at Greensboro, his M.A. in journalism from Indiana University in Bloomington, and his doctoral degree in mass communication at the University of Florida. He has an extensive background in journalism, having worked for the *Greensboro News & Record, Durham Sun, Winston-Salem Chronicle, Black College Sports Review,* and *Peegs.com.* Bulla won journalism awards from the National Newspaper Publishers Association and the North Carolina Press Association in 1986–87. He also taught high school journalism and English in North Carolina throughout the 1990s. He was the adviser of newspapers at Greensboro Smith and Dudley high schools and served as vice president for newspapers of the North Carolina Scholastic Media Association in 1999. Bulla focuses his research on the history of U.S. journalism, especially the history of freedom of the press and Civil War journalism. Other research interests include convergence, sports communication, scholastic journalism, and literary nonfiction. He won the Frances Wilhoit Award for research at Indiana University in 2001; had the outstanding student research paper in 2002 and the top faculty paper in 2006 for the Scholastic Journalism Division of the Association for Education in Journalism and Mass Communication; and was named

Author David W. Bulla.
(Photo by Kalpana Ramgopal)

the top teaching assistant for UF's College of Journalism and Communications and honored as a top teaching assistant for the university in 2002–03. He is an active member of AEJMC and the American Journalism Historians Association. Bulla teaches reporting and the history of the mass media at the Greenlee School of Journalism and Communication at Iowa State University in Ames, Iowa. He also teaches at the High School Journalism Institute at Indiana University. The ISU professor is married to journalist Kalpana Ramgopal, a newspaper designer. They have a son, Viraj Joseph Bulla, and two Shetland Sheepdogs, Cocoa and Iris. Bulla enjoys sports, nature, reading, music, and traveling. He is a former high school basketball and cross-country coach. He has had the good fortune to be associated with the following master teachers: Steve Hankins, Walter Beale, Richard Whitlock, Warren Ashby, Irwin Smallwood, Allen H. Johnson, Cleve Wilhoit, Jack Dvorak, Kay Phillips, Julie Dodd, and Bernell Tripp.